The Best Tax Book Nobody Buys

How Life Events Affect Your Taxes and What You Should Do About It
Kirk Taylor, EA

2023 Edition (2023.1)

Tax rules and advice for use on 2023 tax returns and living life in 2024 (until the IRS changes the rules in December).

Contains new and previously published information. Previously published information has been updated with tax year 2023 numbers and laws unless noted otherwise.

Table of Contents:

1. Read Me First

Welcome to the latest edition of The Best Tax Book Nobody Buys (formerly Everyday Taxes and Everyday Tax Advice). This book is designed to be significantly different from, and significantly more useful than, the rest of the tax books out there. For one, it will be written in English, not Taxese (made up word of the Day!). I will endeavor to use normal, everyday words to describe the tax rules, and will define any Taxese that I use, as I use it. This means that it will be very common for what I write to not look or sound anything like what your tax professional or the Internal Revenue Service (IRS) is saying. That's by design! The IRS and tax professionals seem like they ENJOY making things as complicated as possible!

I designed the book for the pen and paper crowd, the software crowd, and the pay a professional crowd, but it is not a substitute for the instructions and publications provided by the IRS, your software, or your tax professional. It is designed for everyday usefulness, not just tax time usefulness. It will be mostly organized by life topics, not Form 1040 topics. You can skip right to the chapters that apply to you, when they apply to you, and you don't have to read the whole damn thing (that's why I told you to read this first).

Getting a divorce? Look up the I'm Getting Divorced (or Already am) chapter.

Having a child? Look up the I'm Having a Child chapter.

I will attempt to cross-link and reference as much as possible so that you can find what you are looking for and not have to wade through a bunch of crap. If you haven't figured it out already, underlined text indicates links which will be functional for e-books. This also means that the book is deliberately repetitive. I focus on how the tax rules apply to the specific situations addressed in the chapter title. Relevant information is provided in each chapter to which it is applicable, as opposed to listing all the tax rules and making you figure out which ones apply.

This book will be an ongoing project. I am going to publish whatever chapters are done between May and September – depending on when Congress tosses new laws out and the status of massive projects in my life. Then I am going to keep expanding and revising it, publishing a new edition every year. This means that some information will be changed by

Congress or the IRS after I publish – 2020 and 2021 were INSANE for them doing this! For this reason, I will update changes on my blog. I will let people know there are changes on my Facebook page: STG Tax, so follow me there. It also means that I will not be instantly deleting outdated information. I will instead clearly identify what rules apply to what year, so you can go back and amend any returns that you find can be changed based on the information in this book.

Be aware that the first Biden Coronavirus relief bill had a few changes that applied to 2021 ONLY. These will be covered in the relevant chapters as well as a special 2021 Only Chapter.

2020 was also a year of big changes, so I am going to add an extra chapter on things to check on your 2020 tax return – I'll call it: Things to Check on your 2020 Tax Return (or something close to that). It will not cover things in excruciating detail but will give you a starting point to figure out if you need to revisit your 2020 tax return. April 15th 2024 will be your LAST chance to get a refund based on law changes affecting 2020!

You should read the 2020 and 2021 chapters in their entirety. These are the only years with specific chapters on them, since they are the only truly weird years.

2022 had mostly minor changes to energy efficient rules so I won't be including a separate chapter for 2022. Thank God! I really get tired of massive changes to tax laws as it only makes it harder for everyone to comply with them.

It may seem strange that a lot of information from 2018 is STILL included in this book, but there is a good reason, and something to be aware of. Many of the biggest tax law changes from the Trump/GOP tax law that started in 2018 will expire after 2025 if no action is taken by Congress. It is worth paying attention to these things since it will be ANOTHER dramatic change to how taxes work if they let them expire.

Here is a link to my website and blog:

http://STGtax.com

Some chapters will refer you to my other book series called The Short Cheap Tax Books. There is one for Everyone, which is cleverly titled The Short Cheap Tax Book for Everyone, one for Multi-Level Marketing (you can probably figure the title out yourself) one for the Military, one for Students and one on the Trump/GOP Tax Law. These books have short, sweet and to the point pieces of advice that make for an easy read and a much easier tax life. Unlike this book, they are meant to be read cover to cover, and should not take long to read. If you do not already own the one for everyone, you should buy it now. You can see what books I've finished on my Amazon Author Page.

Military Members: In 2015 I added a "Military" paragraph at the end of most chapters to highlight specific rules that are affected by being in the military. I have also added a very basic state by state breakdown of military rules: State by State Tax Guide for Military. In addition, I wrote The Short Cheap Tax Book for the Military in 2018 (periodically updated). It has a ton of simple pieces of advice specifically tailored to active-duty military, with some advice for reservists and retirees tossed in. It's a much easier read than this book.

How to use this book: After reading this chapter, read (or skim) chapters 3 through 7. After that, the best method is to look up a chapter based on what is happening in your life. It should link you around until you have everything you need, though I will try to include it all in each chapter. The forms chapter will tell you a bit about each form, and then reference the appropriate chapter. So, if you get a strange form, just look it up and you're off.

Once a new edition comes out for a new tax year, generally in June of the first title year, the previous editions will not be updated as court cases or law changes affect what is written. For example, in a previous edition, I changed the chapters on cancelled debt due to new information on how pensions should be handled. This information will not be changed in previous editions, even though it makes them no longer fully accurate. Speaking of which…

The Coronavirus and its Ongoing Tax Implications:

The last major bill passed before this edition was Joe Biden's Inflation Reduction Bill in August of 2022 (there was also a student loan forgiveness executive order which affected a few things and is still in litigation at this time). It and the previous COVID bills had a myriad of changes. I have sprinkled the information in most chapters as appropriate but also covered the majority of the COVID stuff in Disasters Chapter.

Stimulus payment information was removed from this edition since they should all have already been paid out.

A few notes about my conventions:

1. I tire of saying, "A bigger refund or lower balance due," so for the rest of the book, when I say, "A bigger refund," I mean a bigger refund or lower balance due.

2. As a general rule, your age for tax purposes is determined by your age on January 1st of the tax year. So, for 2023 tax returns, your age is how old you were on January 1, 2023. I will not specify this when referring to age, so you can assume that is the criteria unless I specify otherwise.

3. I will abbreviate Social Security Number as SSN. I will often abbreviate Filing Statuses: MFJ for Married Filing Jointly, MFS for Married Filing Separately, S for Single (though I use the whole word a lot), QSS for Qualifying Surviving Spouse and HH for Head of Household.

4. Despite saying I will not use Taxese, there are a few terms I must use:
    a. Adjusted Gross Income (AGI): This is so frequently used that I need to define it. AGI is your total income, minus a few specific deductions listed on the front page of your tax form. On the 2023 Form 1040 it is on Line 11. For other years it might be a different line but it will have (with the bold): "this is your **adjusted gross income**". Most of the times you use it, you are using it to determine some limitation or maximum income above which you don't get a deduction or credit. When this happens, they almost always use a "modified" AGI, where you add or subtract some other tax number from the AGI. These "modifications" almost never apply, so your AGI and modified AGI are almost always the same. For the most part, I am going to use AGI and modified AGI interchangeably. If you have Puerto Rico income, excluded savings bond interest, or have a Foreign Earned Income Exclusion, you will want to pay more attention to modified AGI. I will try to identify things that commonly affect modified AGI when talking about them, as opposed to defining modified AGI every time it comes up. When filing with software, it is going to ask you for your prior year's AGI, supposedly to help ensure you are not an ID Thief, so write it down and keep it handy. I will use the abbreviation AGI from now on.
    b. Deduction: This is something that reduces your taxable income.
    c. Credit: This is something that reduces the amount of tax you owe, which is obviously better than a deduction.

d. Refundable Credit: This is a credit that you get even after you have reduced your total taxes to zero, thus allowing you to get more money back than you paid in.

5. I am going to try to avoid using lists of tests for claiming something. Generally, I will list only the things you need to pay attention to in a given situation. For example, under "I'm Having a Child," I list the assumption that it is your own child and that you live in and are residents of the United States. I will not then list those requirements during the discussion. This means that my list of requirements will differ from what an IRS publication or tax professional will say, but that's because there are a lot of stupid tests that are obvious. A good example is when you are married but do not live with your spouse and are trying to file Head of Household, one of the tests is that you do not file Married Filing Jointly—duh!

6. I am not using any specific layout for all the chapters, though you will notice patterns in many of the chapters:
- An introduction with assumptions I'm making.
- A discussion of the most common scenarios.
- A discussion of more complicated situations.
- Lists of the nit-picky details.
- A section with my personal advice that most people can use.
- Military details if applicable.

Some chapters will be different. Many will be completely different. There are also a few chapters that aren't really about life events, especially early in the book (like this one). I want the chapters to be as easy to use as possible, so I am going to lay them out in whatever way I think meets that goal.

7. The unextended deadline for filing taxes is April 15th, or the next business day, if April 15th happens to be a holiday. This includes weird Washington, DC holidays, such as Emancipation Day. For example, the deadline for 2016 was 4/18/17 because of Emancipation Day. That said, I will use April 15th as the deadline throughout this book and will only talk about extensions in chapters where they are likely to apply. Most states have the same deadline, though some extend it for their own weird holidays (Patriot's Day in Massachusetts – the day they run the Boston Marathon). You can be very confident that if you meet the Federal deadline that you will meet the state deadline. Obviously 2019 turned out a little weird, since they extended the deadline for filing and paying taxes until July 15th and in 2020 the deadline was extended to May 17th, but the

general rule is April 15th. You probably noticed that major extensions to the deadline were enacted in the past few years. This book does not cover those since they are almost always last-minute changes in the middle of tax season. I will publicize extensions on my blog and Facebook page.

8. Unless otherwise specified, I am going to assume that your tax year is a calendar year: January 1st through December 31st. There are very few situations where the average taxpayer will have any other tax year. So, if I say tax year, I mean calendar year.

9. Many times in the book I am going to suggest getting professional help. This does not mean you have to use a professional to file your taxes (though many times it will); it means getting advice or assistance from a professional with expertise in the area we are talking about. Some tax issues are difficult to explain on paper in a way that assures there will not be confusion. You can research it yourself; just be aware that an experienced professional will be familiar with the rules and able to explain them as they apply to you. Be careful when doing your own research!

10. This one is for grammar and consistency psychos. I think State and Federal should be capitalized when referring to tax returns, but I am wildly inconsistent in doing this. In fact, I can be pretty inconsistent in this book with a lot of conventions. I suck at Title Case. My over-arching goal is to be as clear as possible with regard to the subject I am currently writing about. A lot of these chapters are written at significantly different times and that only adds to the inconsistency. Heck, I only just removed double spaces after periods two years ago! I am also my own editor. So please bear with me if the grammar, consistency, and spelling is not absolutely perfect. I'm trying my best, and tax accuracy and ease of understanding is the most important thing I am going for.

Which brings me to the disclaimer: I have attempted, to the best of my ability, to ensure that the information contained in this book is as accurate as possible. However, the IRS is constantly changing the rules, and I am, in fact, a human being. So, do your own due diligence and do not rely solely on this book for your tax information. It is designed to get you doing the right things, but I take no responsibility or liability for any issues that arise based on your utilizing this information. Sorry. I also must say that this book is my interpretation of the tax code only and does not necessarily represent the opinion of the IRS.

Nothing in this book is meant as a partisan political statement, though my disdain for policy writers, bureaucrats and Congress will probably slip through at times. If it feels like I am targeting a particular party, that is purely coincidental.

In addition, unless explicitly stated, nothing in this book should be seen as an endorsement of any product (other than my own books and blog).

All client anecdotes are semi-fictional. In order to protect client confidentiality, it is necessary for me to modify, aggregate and twist the stories sufficiently to prevent identification or embarrassment. While the underlying point of the anecdote will be based in fact, the actual story will be mostly made up.

If you are or were my client, and you think you recognize your story...it is not you.

2. Do I Have to File a Tax Return?

For most people, the determination of whether or not you have to file a tax return is fairly straightforward. The basic answer is determined with the following calculation:
- Take your standard deduction.
- Add any increases for being 65 or over.
- If your income is equal to or more than the number calculated above, then you have to file.

Of course, you have to know your filing status first, which is covered in another chapter: Filing Status. Once you know that, you can quickly figure out where you need to go.

That said, in the last few years there have been stimulus checks, Child Tax Credit advances and changes that have made filing a return, even when not required, something that should be strongly considered. There has also always been Earned Income Credit, Additional Child Tax Credit and other refundable credits that can get you a refund even when you aren't required to file. When in doubt, file is the new mantra.

Here are the details:

1. You need to know your Gross Income. Your gross income is everything you made, anywhere in the world, that is not exempt from tax. It includes gains on sales of investments or properties, but not losses. It includes income from a business, before you take expenses into account. It includes only the taxable portion of Social Security, which is a complicated situation and you pretty much need to prepare a tax return to figure it out. If you are filing MFJ, you include both you and your spouse's income.
2. You are considered 65 or older if you were 65 on December 31st of the tax year.
3. For Single Filing status, you have to file if your Gross Income is at least $13,850 ($15,700 if you are 65 or older).
4. For MFJ status, you have to file if your Gross Income is at least $27,700 ($29,200 if you or your spouse are 65 or older, $30,700 if both of you are 65 or older).
5. For Married Filing Separately (MFS) status, you have to file if your Gross Income is at least $5.
6. For HH status, you have to file if your Gross Income is at least $20,800 ($22,650 if you are 65 or older.)

7. For Qualifying Surviving Spouse (QSS) status, you have to file if your Gross Income is at least $27,700 ($29,200 if you are 65 or older.)

8. You must also file if any of the following apply to you, regardless of income:

   a. You owe Alternative Minimum Tax (there is a whole chapter on this later called What the Hell is the Alternative Minimum Tax?).

   b. You owe a penalty on early retirement plan withdrawals. (You'll get a Form 1099-R with a Code 1 for the distribution code.)

   c. You owe taxes on household employees, such as a maid or house cleaner.

   d. You owe taxes on tips you didn't report to your employer. I have a chapter on this, too.

   e. You have to pay back a First-Time Homebuyer Credit.

   f. You owe other recaptured taxes or penalties.

   g. You receive distributions from a Health Savings Account (reported on Form 1099-SA), Archer MSA, or Medicare Advantage MSA.

   h. Your NET profit from self-employment (your business) was at least $400, regardless of your gross income.

   i. You made at least $108.28 from a church that was exempt from Social Security and Medicare taxes.

   j. You received an Affordable Care Act Premium Tax Credit (you should get form 1095A if this happened).

   k. You need to receive additional stimulus payments or reconcile Advance Child Tax Credit payments (2020 and 2021 tax years).

   l. For 2021 ONLY: You have dependents under the age of 18, even if you have no income.

9. If you are claimed as a dependent by someone else, you have a more interesting problem. To determine if you need to file, you need to know your earned income, unearned income (investment income, unemployment, annuities, etc.) and the total. You have to file if one of the following applies:
   - Your unearned income was over $1,250.
   - Your earned income was over $13,850.
   - Your total income was larger than your earned income plus $400, or $1,250, whichever is larger (basically if you have earned income and more than $400 of unearned income, you have to file)

10. Even if not required to file, you should file if you have withholding or other credits that you can get back. You may also need to file in order to get stimulus payments due to Coronavirus (2020 and 2021 tax years) or Advance Child Tax Credit Payments (file 2020 to get advance payments and file 2021 to reconcile them.)

11. In a lot of cases, if you are not required to file a federal return, you do not have to file a state return, but you should check the website for your state.

12. In 2021, you can get Child Tax Credit even if you have no income. If you have children 17 or under living with you in 2021, you should ask a tax pro if it makes sense for you to file and claim them.

Bottom line is that unless you have a very simple tax life, you practically need to finish your tax return to know if you have to file, or if you should file to get money back. Also, in 2020 and 2021, filing a tax return ultimately ends up being the only way to get stimulus payments not received, or to ensure you get Advance Child Tax Credit Payments.

My Advice:

1. Run a tax return to see if you need to file. Most tax software will not charge you until you file your return.
2. If you are getting a refund, you have essentially 3 years from the due date to claim the refund. Do not wait – if they owe you money, file a tax return and claim it.
3. When in doubt, file a return. It is the easiest way to ensure stimulus checks and other goodies make it to you.
4. Update your address with the IRS every time you move between tax filing (filing a tax return will automatically update your address). Use form 8822 – available at the IRS website.
5. Sign up for an IRS account online at www.irs.gov.

Military: Combat zone time can reduce your income below your filing threshold causing you to not have to file, but you will almost always do better filing a tax return. Always check to see if you qualify for a refund.

3. How Should I Be Preparing my Taxes?

The tax preparer in me says use a professional, preferably me.

I know, we are expensive, inconvenient and can be a bit arrogant and prickly. Still, unless you have a very simple return, you should at least have it reviewed by a professional every couple of years. You can find many willing to check it for free, in the hopes that they can find a mistake and can offer to charge you for fixing it. If you do this, make sure you know up front that the review is free, and that there is no obligation to allow them to be the one to fix it if they find an error. Of course, one of the biggest mistakes I see is people thinking their tax return is simple when it could be more complicated and result in a bigger refund. That's why you need to get it checked. You can fix a return for a bigger refund for 3 years after it is filed or due (April 15th)—no extensions for the oldest tax return! If you have a tax return reviewed every 4 years and they find a mistake, you can have them check the prior three that weren't reviewed.

I have had two military clients in the last few years who have been paying State taxes that they were not required to. One for 10 years and the other for 18 years. The vast majority of that money (tens of thousands of dollars) is gone forever. Both of them were basic 1040EZ filers using software. The 1040EZ went away in 2018 with the new tax law, but the point is that these were very easy tax returns, and it is ridiculous that the software was unable to ensure their state taxes were correct – but that's the deficiency in do-it-yourself tax software: Easy isn't accurate!

So, what are your options for filing? You have a few: you can do it pen and paper, online, with store-bought software, or you can use a professional. The IRS is not a fan of pen and paper, and it is the slowest method of getting a refund, so keep that in mind. Anyway, let's go over the ins and outs of each option.

2021 Update: The changes to the Child Tax Credit and Child and dependent Care Credit that apply to 2021 ONLY, and the massive changes made in the various Coronavirus bills make not only tax preparations, but also tax planning extremely complicated. I HIGHLY recommend paying a professional to review your 2020 tax return and talk about actions to take for 2021. You should do this SOON! Tax planning is an aspect of paying for tax preparation that doesn't get enough attention. Do yourself a favor and make a point of doing it this year. It is probably too late to take advantage of this, but the basic advice of consulting a professional periodically still applies.

So, you want to do it yourself...

Pen and Paper. For pen and paper, make sure you download the current year's forms. The internet is the best way to get them—the post office and libraries generally do not carry them anymore. They are available at www.irs.gov, and there is a prominent link to forms and publications. Download the form you need and the instructions. I would also recommend downloading a copy of the Publication 17. It is the basic tax publication that covers the majority of individuals' tax situations.

So how do you know which form to use? Starting in 2018, it does not matter. There is only the 1040 (and 1040SR starting in 2019), but before that there was the 1040A (short form) and 1040EZ (the easy form). To be honest, I would use the 1040, because it ensures you do not miss any potential deductions, and it's not that much more difficult than the A or EZ, even if you qualify for using them.

When ready to start writing on your tax form, read the general instructions, and then follow the line-by-line instructions. Do not assume that you know what goes where! Write legibly and carefully—start in pencil! When you are done, check all your calculations TWICE, and then copy the numbers in pen. Then check it again. Sign the return, attach required forms (W-2, 1099R, anything with tax withholding – use the instructions) and mail it to the appropriate address. The instructions will tell you where to send it based on where you live, and if you are getting a refund or owe money. Make sure to put the right postage on it and mail it by the due date (generally the 15th, unless that falls on a holiday, then it is the following Monday.) If it is in a mailbox, before the postman picks up at that box on the 15th of April, you are good. Keep a copy of the return and all information forms for yourself!

Online Software. For online software, you need to do a few more things before you start. First, pick a good provider. Most of you already have one you're satisfied with, but, if you are just starting, or think you might want to change, I would suggest using one of the big boys—you know who they are. Check reviews to decide which one you like, then stick with them. Switching providers can result in loss of carryover information from the prior year. This not only creates more work for you, it could cause you to screw up your tax return. While you're at it, check irs.gov to see if you qualify for Free File. Depending on your income, you might be able to file your federal taxes for free! Income limitations and other restrictions are set by the IRS, so you can be comfortable that if the service charges you, it is because you didn't qualify, not because they are trying to rip you off (actually...I think TurboTax is getting sued for doing exactly what I just said they would not do). In fact, one of the nice changes in 2018 is more aggressive policing of these Free File agreements. You will most likely have to pay for your State taxes, even if the Federal is free. Which reminds me, many providers will lure you in with a free federal, and then stick you with a state fee. This is common practice, but make sure you know the state fees before you buy. Military personnel can check with Military One Source to see if you can have your taxes prepared online for free.

Once you have decided who to use, you are ready to start. First, do not use public Wi-Fi! Are you insane? This is identity theft gold for those evil bastards! Do it at home, and make sure your internet connection is secure. This is the only real difference between online and at-home software. With this method, everything you do goes over the internet. With home software, just the actual filing goes over the internet. You should be able to trust the connection between you and the software provider. They have enough incentive to make sure it is secure. You just need to make sure it's secure at your end. Second, I would have IRS Publication 17 downloaded and ready to review just in case you have questions.

Now you just follow the software prompts, making sure you enter your information accurately. The key here is to not just answer the questions off the top of your head. Use your documents and think! This is the biggest problem with software. It says, "How much did you pay for uniforms?" and you enter how much you paid for those logo shirts your company makes you wear. But they are not deductible! Even military uniforms are mostly non-deductible. Starting in 2018, no employee business expenses are deductible, but you get the point. Generally, the software will have somewhere you can click for more information. ALWAYS click it! At least for your first time through. In subsequent years, you can be a little more casual when your situation stays the same. Be VERY careful if you find yourself entering a given form a second time. This usually means you are deducting something twice in different places, such as mortgage interest on both your personal Schedule A and on your Rental Property – this is a big no-no!

Another note of caution: most programs will provide values for Goodwill type contributions - they are CRAP! Check the charitable deductions chapter for more information—that is probably where this book will make people the most money with their refunds.

Once you finish your Federal return, the software will do some sort of review, and prompt you to check some things (maybe). Then it is time for State. For the most part, State will be dragged directly from your Federal, without a lot of input from you. Having said that, State is where software starts to really show its weaknesses. Federal gets all the attention by the software developers, and the States get the leftovers. Even the amazingly expensive professional software I use to prepare taxes has its shortcomings regarding States, so you can imagine what you get for $14.99. Some States are more complicated than others. You need to be even more cautious navigating the State screens. If you have a complicated situation (more than one State, moves between States, military spouses) I would urge you to either have it prepared or checked by a professional.

Now we come to another major problem with software tax preparation: you do not get to review the return until you pay for it. Sure, it tells you your refund and you can look at what you put in, but you cannot look at the forms! Most people who use software never even look at the forms. They just electronically file and save a copy to their hard drive (or just rely on the online company to retain a copy). This is a MISTAKE! Go ahead and pay for your return, and, if possible, print a copy before filing. If you have to file before printing, go ahead and file and then print. Review your return line-by-line or have a professional do it. Then electronically file it (you can mail in a paper copy, but this will delay your refund). If you had to e-file and then you find a mistake, the software should have a method for correcting it. Now take the copy you printed and put it somewhere safe with all the documents you used to prepare it. I would also suggest making notes of anything you might want to remember about how you prepared it in case you are audited.

A note on guarantees: You'll see many a proclamation about the Maximum Refund Guarantee and Accuracy Guaranteed! Make sure to read the fine print. First, they generally only guarantee the software's programming, not the entire return. They will assume (correctly for the most part) that any error on your return was a result of you not following the instructions, mis-entering information, or misinterpreting the rules—they will not pay anything for this. If their software is wrong, you will probably hear about it on the news—it happens, but rarely. Even if their software is wrong, they generally only pay interest and penalties, with maybe a refund of what you paid for the software. They do not pay any extra taxes you owe, unless you pay for some magical extended guarantee with a fancy name.

Store-bought Software. For software you buy in a store, the process and problems are pretty much the same as with online preparation. You do all the preparation at home, and the only thing that goes over the Internet is the actual electronic filing. Follow the same suggestions I made for online software, and you will end up in the same place. Most of the at-home versions of a company's software are very similar to the online version. One good difference is that your work and final tax return are automatically saved on your home computer, vice just the company's servers. Another big advantage of store bought over online software is that it is easier to review your return before finalizing and paying for it. This actually is a big deal – one of the things that separates professionals is our ability to look at a tax return as we prepare it. You should do this as well. When you put a form into the software, you should review the output forms to see where it ended up. A professional who just inputs forms and assumes the output is correct is just as useless as an individual who does the same thing with store bought software.

IRS Direct File:

The IRS will be piloting a program in several states where you can file simple taxes directly with them. It will be limited to most states with no state taxes, California, New York, Massachusetts, and Arizona. The pilot is only for Federal taxes but the IRS would then send you to something set up by the states to file theirs.

It will be limited to W-2 income, Social Security/Railroad Retirement Income, Unemployment Compensation and Interest Income less than $1500. You must take the Standard Deduction (no itemizing). The only other deductions are Educator Expenses and Student Loan Interest. The only credits allowed will be Earned Income Credit, Child Tax Credit and the Credit for Other Dependents. They don't list Additional Child Tax Credit, which is weird because it dovetails right off the Child Tax Credit, but information is limited now.

The program will be rolled out in phases, so just because you meet the above criteria does not mean you will be able to use it, at least at the start of the tax season. Based on data from the pilot program, the IRS will evaluate its effectiveness and consider expanding it in scope.

Again, this is very early in the development of the program so not a lot of information is available and even the IRS says it is all subject to change.

Using a Professional:

Using a professional brings on a whole new set of concerns. The first step is deciding who to use. The IRS gives great advice on this subject, and I will mirror some of it here. To select a preparer, I recommend going online and searching for someone in your local area (though in the world of the internet, many preparers, including myself, now offer worldwide, remote preparation of U.S. tax returns).

Experience. You do not want someone with little or no experience providing the final look at your tax return. However, if nobody uses new preparers, how do they get to be experienced preparers? The mercenary in me says that is the problem of the people who don't know how to pick a good preparer. The tax preparer in me who works with and relies on new preparers to help staff an office is a little more understanding. The way my office handles new preparers is that we initially have them observe experienced preparers, then prepare under the direct supervision of an experienced preparer (sitting right there as they work), and then have them prepare tax returns that are thoroughly checked by an experienced preparer. How does this matter to you? If you find yourself in front of an inexperienced preparer, make sure that an experienced and qualified supervisor will thoroughly check your return. Always feel free to refuse an inexperienced preparer if you do not feel comfortable. As for volunteer services, such as Voluntary Income Tax Assistance for the Military and AARP, use the same criteria for evaluating them as you would a paid preparer. While I know some truly outstanding VITA volunteers, be prepared to not find any with extensive experience or ability. You do get what you pay for after all.

Qualifications. I highly recommend a licensed preparer. Shockingly, there is no requirement to be licensed to prepare taxes. You could register for a Preparer Tax ID Number, hang a sign on your door, and start preparing returns for money. There are two types of preparers with licenses you should look for (there are other registrations available, but they have no testing required so I do not consider them useful):
- Enrolled Agent. This is not actually a license to prepare taxes, it's a license to represent people in front of the IRS, such as at audits. The testing and continuing education are serious. You can be pretty sure that Enrolled Agents know their stuff about taxes.

- Certified Public Accountants (CPAs) are licensed within their state. CPAs must meet education and experience requirements established in their state of license. If you are running a complex business, you want a CPA to prepare your taxes. The catch is to make sure that they specialize in and are experienced in the areas you need. You do not want a CPA specializing in Trusts doing your Rental Property tax return.

The IRS has a handy discussion of Tax Professional Qualifications on their website here: https://www.irs.gov/tax-professionals/understanding-tax-return-preparer-credentials-and-qualifications. Clicking around in that area of their website will take you to additional advice on choosing a preparer.

Check online for reviews of their performance, check their LinkedIn profile, and figure out how long they have been preparing taxes. Five years is a minimum for me for an unsupervised preparer. I thought I was pretty awesome at five years—I was wrong.

Fees. My next piece of advice is to make sure that they will not charge you unless you are satisfied, at least for the first year. What I mean is that if you are trying out a new preparer, you should be able to see the results, and the fees, before deciding if you want to use them. Most preparers cannot quote you a fee until they see what they are getting into. Many of them charge by the hour. Do not be surprised if you ask how much, and they give you a ballpark, but tell you that there's no guarantee that's what the price will be. You just never know what's in a tax return until you're done. This is one of the toughest things to explain to potential customers. If your tax return is simple and easy, you will get a lower price. If it is hard, you get a higher one. Even when I've been sure the return I start is simple, I often discover new items along the way that dramatically complicate things. Many of these will improve the results, but all of them will increase the price. You don't want $100 worth of effort on a $500 return!

My policy has always been to do the whole tax return, tell the client the results, and tell them the price. If they do not want to pay, I give them their paperwork back and send them on their way. No hard feelings. I would expect that policy from any preparer for at least their first year working with you – think of it as a trial period. The point is, ask up front to make sure. The next chapter of this book is about average fees for professional preparation.

Transparency and Communication. The next thing you want to check is to make sure the preparer you researched is the one preparing your taxes. If you sit through the whole preparation process, this is obvious. However, if you drop off your paperwork and leave, you need to ask who will prepare your taxes. I have people assist with my preparation, but I always disclose that to the clients affected, and I always go over EVERYTHING myself before presenting it to my clients. That is what you want your preparer to do.

If you drop off your paperwork and leave, make sure you establish how you will communicate and a basic time frame when it should be done. Do not expect a guarantee of when your taxes will be done—sometimes a client's tax issues are more complicated than they originally appeared. Also, if they need more information from you, this often means the return goes to the end of the work line, especially if you do not reply in a timely fashion. Make sure you and the preparer review what you drop off to make sure it is as close as possible to everything they need, though do not be mad if it turns out they still ask for more, since this is not an exact science. Reply to questions as quickly as you can while still being careful that the information you provide is correct. Many preparers will have you fill out a questionnaire for dropping off, and have you sign an engagement letter or client service agreement. Make sure to read these carefully.

Guarantees and Representation Practices. The last things to consider before deciding who to use are their guarantees and representation practices. At a minimum, and this is the industry standard, they should pay interest and penalties that result from a mistake they made – this is generally provided through insurance they pay for, called Errors and Emissions Insurance and the preparer is not always in control of what gets paid. If you fail to disclose something or forget to bring in a form, that is on you (with some consideration for if they should have known to ask for something based on other information you provided). You have to pay extra for an extended guarantee if you want your preparer to be financially accountable for any tax shortfall due to their error. Whether to get it or not is a tough question, though I lean toward getting it, if only for the support you receive from the company when you have it, especially if you use a big box company. Big national tax chains are notorious for crappy year-round support, using it as an opportunity to charge you additional fees. If they aren't on the hook for the taxes the IRS is chasing you for, they have little motivation to help. That said, preparation fees cover tax preparation, not hours of responding to letters, tracking your refund, or calling the IRS on your behalf. Many tax preparers will do their best to help you with this, but you should recognize that it is above and beyond what you paid for. If your preparer is making a lot of judgment calls, paying for the extended guarantees might be a good idea.

As for representation, we are talking about what happens when you get a letter from the IRS or have to be audited. Most preparers will charge you hourly for this kind of work, and it is not included in the price of preparation. It is also very expensive – junior lawyer expensive. Some will review letters and provide limited assistance as part of the price, basically interpreting the letter and suggesting how to respond. Going to an audit with you or for you is almost always extra (a lot extra) but sometimes that is included free if you pay for the extended guarantees. Keep in mind, face-to-face audits are very rare, and letters are certainly not common, but they can be a NIGHTMARE when they happen. Make sure you know what you get, preferably in writing, before you agree to use a preparer.

Once you have chosen a preparer, make sure to give them EVERYTHING. They should provide a checklist or discuss it verbally with you. Include a copy of last year's tax return if it was not prepared by them. When in doubt, include it. Try to be organized. Many preparers charge extra for sorting through a grocery bag of receipts. Whether dropping off or sitting face-to-face, the preparer should communicate with you as necessary to ensure they have complete information, and they should review the tax return with you before filing it. Be wary if you just drop off a package and then get results with no intermediate questions, unless you have been working with the preparer a while and they understand your situation. There are too many places that just enter your data and assume you mentioned everything pertinent, despite the fact that THEY are the expert. Obviously they can't ask about every little thing, but they should ask a lot of questions, either at the beginning or the end to ensure they covered all the bases.

I would suggest filing electronically, for speed of refund, and because the IRS requires professionals to do it unless you give them written authorization not to. Plus, e-filing avoids humans, which can be a good thing with taxes.

I'll close with a brief discussion of time to get refunds (see the How Fast Can I Get my Refund chapter for more). If a preparer promises to get you your refund faster than someone else, they are full of crap, and possibly breaking the law. No preparer can get you your refund faster than any other preparer, assuming you e-file. When a tax return is sent to the IRS and accepted, the timing is in the IRS' control, and no bank or tax preparer can change this. Some places will give you a loan as an advance on your refund, but this is not your refund, and they are not allowed to say it is. It takes 6 to 21 days to get an e-filed refund, just wait for it.

My Advice:

1. Have your tax return checked by a professional at least once every four years. This ensures that it is still possible to correct a mistake.
2. Always use the instructions and basic publications when preparing your taxes even when using software.
3. Strongly consider the extended guarantee if you use a national tax company unless your return is extremely simple. Chances are you will never need it, but if you do, you will wish you had gotten it. Most non big-box preparers do not offer these types of guarantees, and they generally do not need to offer them.
4. Make sure the free preparation service you use is competent and understands your situation. I am talking about VITA and AARP here mainly.
5. Take the time to select an experienced and capable preparer. Get referrals and read reviews of their service. Only use a licensed professional (EA or CPA).
6. Give your tax professional EVERYTHING and, if they don't ask you a lot of questions about your situation, make sure you take the time to tell them what has been going on in your life. I ask all of my clients to provide a synopsis of their financial life for the year we are preparing tax returns for.

Military: Look for free military editions of popular software, though the warning about paying for state tax returns still applies. Be careful of VITA free tax preparation; some are awesome, others not so much. I would strongly consider having a professional check your tax returns, especially the State.

4. How Much Should Tax Preparation Cost

2023 Update: The last few years have been a nightmare for tax professionals. Due to last minute law changes, extended tax seasons, stimulus payments and a myriad of other things, preparers have been spending more time per return, answering many more calls and emails, and generally working harder for the same income. We saw big price increases for 2022 and I expect some of them to continue for 2023. I have reviewed a number of industry publications and projections to come up with the 2023 numbers beyond what I normally do. Because of this, the numbers are much more variable, and probably not perfectly accurate, but are a good starting place. Not every preparer or company is going to jump prices in one year, but expect numbers to creep up towards this level rapidly. The good news is that you are getting more for your money, and the value a good preparer provides, often in literally real dollars in results, is worth every penny.

This chapter is specifically about tax preparation with professional assistance of a paid preparer and not volunteer services such as VITA or AARP. They also assume you are not using one of the "car dealer" preparers where you pay a small price but have to apply your refund to a purchase.

The primary purpose of this chapter is to let you know what to expect, and how much is "fair". An important and interesting side note is appropriate here: I surveyed a lot of preparers in a lot of places to verify these numbers and almost NONE charged these numbers. Almost all were 20 to 30 percent higher or lower, making the averages "accurate" but unusual. You should be concerned if you find someone charging more than 30 percent more or less, though it is not necessarily a perfect indicator of a bad tax professional. While there are some great Mom and Pop firms that still do quality tax prep for around $150, there are many others that don't stay on top of new rules, are just trying to churn simple returns for fast money or are criminally negligent (two local firms in my area have been busted for fraud in the last decade – both were deep discount preparers).

Remember ANYONE can be a tax preparer with very little effort. On a similar note, many big box companies spend more time marketing and selling add-ons than they do making sure their preparers are competent. The same applies to being over-charged for work that another preparer could perform for costs closer to average.

Bottom line, finding a good preparer value is about finding an INDIVIDUAL you can trust, regardless of where they work (though you want to be absolutely sure there will be off-season assistance available.) Following my advice about having a different preparer check your return every 3 or 4 years is made more valid by this information. Make sure to read the previous chapter's advice on choosing a preparer and what method you should use for preparing them.

The below estimates are my aggregates of information provided by the IRS, the National Society of Accountants and my personal research into big box company prices, as well as checking of small firms. They are MY best guess and are not truly scientific. The numbers can vary widely from state to state and return to return. Also, some returns that seem uncomplicated, such as people getting Earned Income Tax Credit (EITC) or Education Credits, as well as those filing Head of Household, are more expensive due to the increased due diligence requirements, liability issues and non-tax complexity issues. Anything involving children is more expensive due to some of the above issues, as well as the potential for more Advance Child Tax Credit and Stimulus shenanigans.

The national average for ALL returns, of all types, using all ways of filing is $335 for the Federal return only. Since this includes pen and paper, as well as software, it is a lot lower than what paying a professional will cost. With a State return the average would be closer to $375.

The rest of the numbers below are for a Federal 1040 including one State return. Even if you are from a State with no income tax, the averages are pretty close since the preparers in those States seem to charge more for a Federal return. The fees do not include probable surcharges for tax professional due diligence concerns caused by EITC, ACTC and Education Credits. They are also for tax preparation only, not accounting or record-keeping, which some places charge extra for. They only include the more common forms, accounting for the more unusual forms as a part of the averages. The more unusual tax forms you have, the more you will likely pay.

These are what the listed forms letters and schedules refer to, with a brief explanation for each, since you may not know them off the top of your head:

A: Schedule A: Itemized deductions like taxes, home mortgage interest, charity and medical.

B: Schedule B: This won't be separately stated on this list since there is often no charge for simple entries and non-simple entries count as "unusual" as discussed above.

C: Schedule C: Business Tax Return that is included on your personal return (not partnerships or corporations). This assumes a single business. Multiple businesses will increase the fees. How complex the business is affects this a lot. A simple business with just a few lines of income and expenses and no depreciation, car usage or other complications can be cheaper, while a big complicated business using a lot of forms such as office in home can be a lot more.

D: Schedule D: Sales of investments (not business property). If you have a lot of individual sales, these charges can go up by a LOT. Cryptocurrency and day trading can make this very expensive. The price calculated in the table assumes less than 10 trades.

E: Schedule E: Rental Property and Royalties (assumes a single rental property – will increase for each additional).

ACA: You got insurance through the Health Care Marketplace.

Remember – these include 1 State tax return:
1040: $335
1040 + A: $375
1040 + C: $535
1040 + D: $455
1040 + E: $470
1040 + A + C: $575
1040 + A + D: $575
1040 + A + E: $510
1040 + A + D + C: $675
1040 + A + D + E: $620
1040 + A + C + D + E: $780
1040 + ACA: $375
1040 + A + ACA: $425
1040 + C + ACA: $575
1040 + D + ACA: $495
1040 + E + ACA: $510
1040 + A + C + ACA: $615
1040 + A + D + ACA: $615
1040 + A + E + ACA: $550
1040 + A + D + C + ACA: $715
1040 + A + D + E + ACA: $660
1040 + A + C + D + E + ACA: $820

Depending on where in the country you live, you could pay significantly more or less. The following states or regions vary from the average. If a state or region is not listed, it runs about average:

New England: About 20% higher
West Coast: About 15% higher
NY, NJ, or PA: About 5% higher
IL, IN, MI, OH, WI: About 10% lower
AL, IA, KY, KS, MS, MN, MO, NE, ND, SD, TN: About 20% lower

Things that will crank up your fees:

Multiple State tax returns (about $45 to $90 per State)
Schedule K-1 from partnership investments, trusts or estates ($75 to $150 each)
Trusts and Estates returns ($700 each)
S Corporations returns ($1200 each)
Partnerships returns ($1000 each)
Lots of individual investment sales (often a couple dollars per reportable trade above a certain amount)
Multiple businesses or rental properties (very roughly around $100 per rental and $200 per business though this varies widely with complexity)
Alternative Minimum Tax
Early retirement withdrawals
Foreign Earned Income Exclusion
Unusual dependent situations
Depreciating a lot of assets
Unsorted receipts in a grocery bag

Two categories that will tend to differ from the above:

1. Very simple returns with just W-2's and no additional credits or deductions can usually be found for between $99 and $200 including one State. Also, simple returns filed just for stimulus payments or Advance Child Tax Credit payments can often be done for free or around $50.

2. A simple return like the one above that includes children will often have significantly higher prices than average, especially if they include Head of Household, or any children credits (Earned Income Credit or Additional Child Tax Credit) that produce a refund that exceeds withholding amounts. Basically, many of these returns get back more money from the government than they paid in, and all of these require additional due

diligence paperwork from the preparer, extra record-keeping requirements, and the possibility of being fined if the preparer is not "suspicious" enough of unusual situations. These returns can cost between $320 and $510 dollars, with the higher end kicking in as more "due diligence" items are added. Another reason these fees tend to be high is because the refunds tend to be very large, and they are often bundled with loan products to get some money (not your refund) in your pocket faster. It is ILLEGAL for a company to claim they are getting your refund faster than normally available.

3. Many preparers will offer free or discounted preparation for your dependents. ALWAYS get your children's W-2's from them and provide them to your preparer. Do NOT let your kids file their taxes before you do! They will often make a tiny mistake that will cause you endless trouble. Ask your preparer what their policy is (if you file at the last minute, they are unlikely to offer you a discount but if you file early and tell them it is no rush the kids might be free).

One New 2021 Category:

In the past, if you had children, but no Earned Income, there was no reason to file a tax return since you weren't required to, and there was no refund to get. In 2021, you can get $3000 or $3600 per child 17 or under, even if you have no income. These returns will be both simple and need a TON of due diligence as required by law. They will also be very likely to reject or have other time-consuming issues. While many returns of this type could be completed in 10 to 30 minutes, it will be impossible to tell which ones will cause problems. I expect many preparers to weigh this when deciding what to charge, probably landing in the $250 to $350 range. Others will aggressively market low prices for these, but I suspect they won't be there if your return doesn't fly through easily.

To expand on this, drifting from true tax rules and into personal experience and analysis, kids are worth a LOT of money on tax returns. This means that children with a valid SSN don't generally NOT get claimed, whether legal or not. Obviously, as a tax preparer, I do my best to ensure my clients only claim children they are legitimately entitled to, and I am required by law to take a lot of additional steps to ensure this. That said, it isn't very difficult to claim kids wrongly, and, unless someone else claims them as well, it often slips through. So, a lot of people's kids are probably getting claimed, sometimes legally and sometimes not, sometimes with their knowledge and sometimes not. When they go to claim this child for the first time, their return might be rejected, or drama might ensue as the person who "normally" claims them rejects. So, you can see why legitimate tax professionals might want to "average out" the costs between difficult returns and easy returns, since you don't know which is which.

You should pay the $275 to $425 range and expect the preparer to be there if it runs into difficulty. Don't assume the $150 person will do this. Of course, some expensive preparers provide crap service as well…

My Advice:

1. Feel free to ask about fees upfront, but do not be upset if the quoted fee changes as long as there is a reasonable explanation. Also don't be surprised if they refuse to quote a fee, even in a ballpark, mainly because it causes more trouble than it is worth when things inevitably change.
2. Along the same lines, make sure your professional has some sort of satisfaction guarantee policy, at least for the first year, or is willing to reasonably abide by their quote.
3. The combination of an unwillingness to even attempt to reasonably estimate fees AND the lack of a guarantee that you will not be charged if you are not happy with the results is a good reason to walk away from a preparer (not providing an estimate is perfectly reasonable if they guarantee you can refuse to file with them if you are unhappy).
4. Ask for military discounts but do not be upset if they do not have them. Many firms charge the minimum they are able to in order to remain competitive, which does not allow a lot of room for special discounts.
5. Be wary of overly cheap tax preparation. Always ask about seasonal training, experience, and licensing.
6. Always use a CPA or an Enrolled Agent with at least 5 years of experience.

Military: There are VITA preparers on most bases worldwide. Some of them are phenomenal, some are awful. Ask how long the preparers have been doing taxes, and if it is not several years, or at least there is a supervisor with several years, run away.

Always ask for a military discount, though the big box companies will usually only allow them for their on-base offices. Big, busy offices and preparers will be less likely to offer these discounts, and it should not be a deal breaker, but it never hurts to ask. Keep in mind that a military tax return is likely to be more complicated than a local's (due to different States and strange military rules) so giving you a discount may hurt more than you think. I am retired Navy, and I always ask, but I don't get offended if the answer happens to be no.

Since your State return is probably different from the State you are living in, it might cost more, and will also be a very likely place for errors to be made. Be VERY careful checking the State returns.

5. Ten (or more) Simple Pieces of Tax Advice

Here are a few of my best pieces of advice when it comes to taxes, in no particular order:

1. If you are doing something just for the tax benefit, you are probably making a mistake. Buy a house because it is the right time, not for the tax break. Buy equipment that makes your business more profitable or efficient, not to get the deduction. By all means, take the deduction, but do not make it a critical part of the decision.

2. When in doubt, donate it. If you have stuff you do not want, and you are not sure if it is worth the trouble of selling, give it to charity. Make sure to deduct its REAL fair market value, not what Goodwill is selling it for. Clothes and other used items should be valued based on what a for-profit thrift store would sell it for. If you have a garage sale, do not give in to the temptation to mark everything down to nothing at the end. Ask a fair price, dicker a little, but don't just give it away. After the sale, while everything left is still on the tables, take pictures of it all, load it in the car, and take it to a charity. With the new tax law, donations are harder to make work to your advantage since itemizing is rarer. If you do not normally itemize, accumulate stuff for a few years and then donate a CRAP TON to Goodwill in one year.

3. Depreciate your rental property. This is not advice—it is a NO BRAINER! Some people do not depreciate because they don't realize they can. Other people don't because they know that they have to pay taxes on the depreciation when they sell (called depreciation recapture), but they are messing up. You cannot avoid depreciation recapture by not depreciating the property. You have to recapture depreciation that is taken OR ALLOWED! I have no idea how software does not have a giant, flashing red diagnostic box anytime there is a rental return without depreciation. This is unconscionable! The number of rental property returns prepared using at home software that do not have depreciation on them that I see drives me CRAZY!

4. Have your taxes checked by a professional, or a different professional once in a while. Especially have it checked after some big changes have happened. You can usually find someone to check them for free. You would be stunned at the errors I have seen made, and the money left on the table. You have three years after the due date to fix it, so do not wait too long. An alternate trick is to use a professional for tax preparation every

fourth year and bring in your prior year's taxes for a quick review when you have the current year done. You don't have to do this if I am your tax preparer – I am perfect – the Tax Unicorn.

5. Do not cheat or lie. Claim all income. Do not make up deductions. Stretch the rules as far as you can, but do not break them. Obviously, how much you stretch depends on your ability to absorb the taxes and penalties when the IRS decides to argue and asks for the money back.

6. Along those lines: Do not be afraid of the IRS. If you're not cheating, you have very little to worry about beyond money and a little bit of hassle. Professionals like to scare you with the IRS, and, if you are cheating, you should be scared. I prefer to scare people with the prospect of not getting all they deserve. 2022 Update: The Inflation Protection Act had a lot of money in it to increase IRS enforcement. It is supposed to only affect "the rich" but it will increase overall enforcement actions. This still doesn't mean you need to fear the IRS.

7. Don't count on getting your refund when promised. You probably will, but do not have things depending on getting the money. The IRS gives estimates of 6 to 21 days from e-filing. However, this gets screwed up enough to make it worth being aware of, and nothing stops them from reviewing your return and adding delays. That is also 6 to 21 days from acceptance, and there are a number of reasons a return might not be accepted the first time it's submitted. Returns with American Opportunity Credit, Earned Income Tax Credit, and Additional Child Tax Credit will not be accepted until February 15th, delaying refunds until 6 to 21 days AFTER that. 2020 tax season had a larger than normal number of returns help up for 30 to 60 days. On the IRS refund status page, it just said "Processing". It appears that most of these were a result of reporting the wrong amount of stimulus payment on the return. There was stimulus AND Child Tax Credit advances to be reconciled on your 2021 tax return so make sure you know EXACTLY how much the IRS sent you in advance (deposits will be from "US Treasury").

8. Do not over-complicate your records, and don't obsess about organizing every receipt. Keep a good notebook, or series of notebooks that document income and expenses and deductions. Keep them up to date and save your receipts where you can find them. They do not have to be in perfect order—the odds that you ever need them are pretty slim. If you get audited, you can match up your receipts with your books. Odds are good you will

only have to do this once in a lifetime (literally).

9. Do not claim kids that you are not legally entitled to claim, even if the parent gives you permission. Your tax professional can tell you what the rules are to claim kids, as they apply to your situation, and, if you do not meet them, do not claim the child.

10. Pay your child support and your student loans. The number one reason I see for people not getting refunds is delinquent student loans and unpaid child support. If you're marrying someone with kids from a previous marriage, make sure they're up to date on their child support because their problem is about to become your problem, and it's not that easy to get around it (though not impossible). A weird 2020, COVID-19 aside here: During the Coronavirus pandemic, the IRS had suspended collections of all debts EXCEPT child support out of tax refunds and stimulus checks. Then they changed it for some stimulus payments and tax refunds. That fact does not make this advice any less important, especially since we do not know how long this will last.

BONUS: Don't believe everything you hear about taxes. The myths out there are LEGION. Talk to a professional or look them up on the IRS website.

DOUBLE BONUS: Change your address with the IRS every time you move. Your tax return updates your address, but between tax filing you have to use Form 8822. This ensures that letters from the IRS get to you in an efficient manner so that you can respond to them before they expire. This is even more important in a world where the IRS is sending stimulus payments and advance Child tax Credit payments, along with letters informing the taxpayer of the amounts sent. You do NOT want your stimulus check or advance Child Tax Credit check going to the wrong address. Here is a link to the IRS web page on changing your address and the appropriate form:

https://www.irs.gov/forms-pubs/about-form-8822

TRIPLE BONUS (I'm going to have to bite the bullet and change the chapter title one of these days): If you haven't already done it, go to the IRS website (irs.gov) and click the "Sign into Your Account" button. Now click the big blue "Sign into your Online Account" button. Have your picture ID and phone ready and follow the steps to create an IRS account. Both you and your spouse should do this. This is the future of the IRS and an active account is going to be critical within a few years. Get ahead of the power curve and create one now. Check it every few months for letters and balance dues, just in case you missed something.

Military: The advice about not doing something for the tax benefits does not apply if you have the opportunity to tie a big bonus to when you are in a combat zone. The bigger the bonus, the more benefit you can get from receiving it in a combat zone.

6. Common Tax Myths

There are a lot of myths and confusion out there, and I am going to try to clear a few of them up. Some are a big deal while others are a bit nitpicky. All of them come up very frequently and most of them will cause you some trouble.

1. You do NOT have to buy a new house in order to exclude the gain from the sale of your personal residence. I have a whole chapter on it: I Sold My Home. Basically, if you owned and lived in the home for 2 of the last 5 years, never rented it out and never used it for a business, you can exclude $250,000 of gain ($500,000 if Married Filing Jointly and both of you meet the timing rules) regardless of what you do after selling. There are timing rules on how often you can do this, but they are pretty easy to meet.

2. Moving up tax brackets is a good thing. It means you made more money! Only the part of your income that is in the higher bracket is taxed at the higher rate, everything else is taxed at the lower rates based on what bracket THAT income falls into. The only real trick about crossing tax brackets is when your household has multiple sources of income. If all your (and your spouse's) jobs fall into the 12% tax bracket, but together you hit the 22% bracket, your withholding is not going to keep up very well. This is a source of endless frustration for people using software that updates their refund constantly. I talk to a lot of people who put their income information into the software, and then freak out when the really big refund plummets as they put their spouse's income in. The refund is only useful as a number when you are done – do not look at it along the way.

3. Deductions are nice, but not spending money on things you don't want or need is better. Just because you can deduct something does not make it a good idea – you are only getting pennies on the dollar back in taxes.

4. The following arguments are bunk: the income tax is voluntary, the 16th amendment was never ratified, the income tax is illegal or any other scheme that avoids taxes altogether. The IRS refers to them as frivolous tax positions and you can be fined just for using the arguments in IRS proceedings. Most of these have been thoroughly litigated through Federal courts, many all the way to the Supreme Court ruling on them or refusing to review a lower court ruling against them. Here is the IRS page on the subject: https://www.irs.gov/pub/taxpros/frivolous_truth_march_2018.pdf

5. Individual Retirement Accounts (IRAs) are not an investment; they are a shelter AROUND an investment. This may not seem like a big deal, but it matters because a lot of times people open IRA's and think that means they have worthwhile investments in them. If you open it at a bank, this will often be a money market account or Certificate of Deposit which is wholly unsuited as a retirement investment for most people. The process of opening an IRA involves setting up the account AND determining what an appropriate mix of investments is for the account. You can have almost any common investment in your IRA: Stocks, bonds, mutual funds, publicly traded partnerships, exchange traded funds, closed end funds and much more. An IRA should be opened with the help of a competent financial professional or after you have done a lot of personal investment research. You should also consult your tax professional to make sure there are not income limitations regarding how much you can invest. You can read my chapter on IRAs: I Have Tax Sheltered Investments.

6. Head of Household means something different for taxes. In life, you can be the head of your household, but it does not mean that is your tax filing status. For taxes, Head of Household means you are unmarried and are taking care of a certain type of qualifying child for a certain amount of time. The rules are covered in the Filing Status chapter. Starting on 2018 returns, the IRS is going to be taking a harder look at Head of Household and fining tax preparers who do not exercise due diligence when determining if their clients can file as Head of Household. This is a big deal, because in most cases I can believe anything you tell me and not get in trouble. There are very few things that I can be fined for if I am not being suspicious enough regarding what a client tells me – Head of Household is one of the things I can be.

7. Social Security is taxed in a weird way. Also, if you retire before reaching your full retirement age, you have to pay back Social Security if you make too much money from a job or business – this has NOTHING to do with taxes and your tax pro isn't going to be much help with this. People confuse these things repeatedly. Here is the tax stuff: up to 85% of your Social Security can be subject to tax if you have other income. I cover the details in this later chapter: I am Receiving Social Security. This calculation of taxability applies no matter how old you are. Having to pay back Social Security if you make too much money only applies when you are below full retirement age, and the numbers are a lot stricter, though this is NOT my area of expertise.

8. Tips are taxable income. You are responsible for reporting them to your employer so it can be included on your W-2 and have various taxes withheld from your paycheck to cover the tip's taxes. Even if your employer does not insist that you report them (or actively discourage you from reporting them) this does not relieve you of the responsibility to report them. I am not your Mother or Father, so do what you want, but recognize that failing to report tips is tax fraud and may be other types of fraud if you receive other benefits or subsidies based on your income. I have a chapter on tips: I Get Tips at Work.

9. This is pure tax professional nit picking here: You file a tax RETURN to determine the amount of REFUND you get or your BALANCE DUE that you have to pay. The money you get is not your "return" it is your "refund". You only get a refund if you have too much in taxes withheld from your paycheck and/or you qualify for a refundable credit such as Earned Income Credit, American Opportunity Credit, Electric Vehicle Credit, Solar Credit etc. I have actually had clients who thought a tax refund was some kind of free money from the government vice a reconciliation of taxes withheld versus what is actually owed.

7. The IRS is Having Problems

This was a new chapter for the 2022/2023 edition

The IRS was limping along before COVID-19 and the pandemic pushed them over the ledge. Closing their offices was devastating to their ability to do the work and put them massively behind. At one point they were well over 10 MILLION returns backlogged, almost all paper returns. They didn't man their phone lines, so calls went unanswered. Stimulus checks and Child Tax Credit Advances only worsened things. Enormous amounts of resources were diverted to process these and handle problems with them. Call volume exploded. They honestly did a great job with the stimulus, but everything else suffered.

Anything done by hand was particularly affected. Paper filed returns and amendments went from taking months to taking who knows how long (many are still pending). Any return requiring a hand review, including purely random checks, went months without being resolved or any notification provided. The IRS sent letters suggesting changes to taxpayer's tax returns and then left the taxpayer's response unopened even as they sent more demanding letters and started collection activities. It was a mess.

If you could get a hold of the IRS on the phone, the answer they provided was often incomplete, unhelpful or flat out wrong. Which means it is important to point out that doing what an IRS agent says is okay on the phone is not a defense if it turns out wrong!

The Inflation Reduction Act has a lot of money for the IRS. A lot for additional enforcement, but some for modernization and to hire new people. It is going to be a while before that helps anything, but it's a start. The real question is if the enforcement money changes how likely you are to face an audit or review. Promises are one thing…I'm waiting to see reality. Even if it does increase enforcement for everyone, it is still going to be very rare that the IRS comes looking at you unless you make an obvious, computer identifiable error.

Even the Taxpayer Advocate, who used to be a great resource is overwhelmed since part of the requirement to qualify for their help was excessive delays, which now is pretty much everyone.

So why did I write this chapter? It isn't to bash the IRS, but just to let you know what to expect if you are forced to deal with the IRS. They do the best they can with what they are given, and almost all of them care about getting the return correct, not about winning. It is also an excuse to push setting up an account with the IRS for you AND your spouse.

As of the start of 2023, the IRS is starting to clear the backlog, and is hiring a lot of new employees. There is a large push to improve things and it appears to be working.

My Advice:

1. Always electronically file your tax return if at all possible.
2. Set up an IRS account at irs.gov. It is fairly easy. Usually, they have a big button with "Sign in to My Account" on their front page. Clicking it will eventually lead to a way to set up your account. Have a phone with a camera handy, at least an hour of time, your photo ID and either your Social Security Card or Passport.
3. Only call the IRS if you have a letter with a specific number to call for your situation and you have no other options. Otherwise, try everything else, including consulting a professional before you call.
4. Keep organized copies of all letters they send you and you send them, with dates and notes. Make notes of all other actions taken, including phone calls and keep in a safe place.
5. Be patient, polite and professional when communicating with the IRS.
6. If you have questions, ask a professional and not the IRS.

8. How Fast Can I Get my Refund?

This is the most common question I get, and the answer, despite anything anyone tells you is: "I don't know."

Anyone who promises to get you your refund faster than someone else is, as I said before in this book, full of crap. There are things you can do to make sure it doesn't go slower: file electronically, make sure it's accurate, don't owe any government agencies money, and use direct deposit. Owing the government agencies money means delinquent student loans, child support, government benefit agencies, and of course, back taxes. If you do owe these things, the government can, and will, take the money out of your tax return, and it often delays the return as well. If you ever get less money from the Feds than the amount you expected, this is a likely culprit. Check out the Where's my Refund chapter for more information if this happens. You can call 1 (800) 304-3107 to see if an agency (other than the IRS) is going to take your refund. It is automated and easy. Make sure to call the number for both your and your spouse's SSN.

I am sure the answer above is not very satisfactory, so I'll expound on it. The IRS says you can expect an electronically filed, direct deposited refund in 6-21 days assuming there are no issues. In fact, the IRS will not even talk to you about your refund status unless it had been at least 21 days. This pisses a lot of people off, but I agree with the IRS (this time). People start calling the IRS after 14 days and tie up the lines that should be getting used to answer real questions and deal with real problems. Do yourself and everyone else a favor and don't worry for 21 days. You can check the status of your refund at www.irs.gov using a prominently marked, "Refund Status" button. You need your SSN, filing status, and your refund amount. If you use a professional that takes your fees out of your refund, make sure you use the original refund amount, not the amount you will be getting after fees. The honest truth is that most people will get their money in 6 to14 days, and the vast majority within 28 days. If it takes longer, either you (or your preparer) did something wrong, the IRS is taking a longer look (nothing you can do about this) or the IRS is messing up (not too likely, but it happens). The Where's my Refund system at irs.gov should give you an update as to the cause of the delay, and sometimes tell you what to do. You will also generally get a letter if the IRS decides to take an extended look.

Tax Identity Theft has become a big deal, and the IRS keeps trying to stop it while still getting the majority of people their refunds within 21 days.

Even so, more and more people are facing delays as a result of these scumbags. For 2016 and later years, Congress passed a law requiring certain types of refunds to have their processing delayed until February 15th. Those are refunds that include Earned Income Credit or Additional Child Tax Credit. These are the common types of returns that the identity thieves make up. If you get back more money than you pay in, and it is not because of college, you will probably see this delay. February 15th becomes the date that the 6 to 21-day clock STARTS, so you are looking at some time between the 21st of February and the 8th of March for a normal refund time frame. The good news about this is that, at least in our office, it seems that tax identity theft is way down. States are also taking it far more seriously as well. Dozens of states delayed refunds last year and I expect more to follow suit this year. Some of these delays are weeks and months. Check out your state's tax website to see how this might affect you.

Having said all of the above, those dates are from the time the return is accepted and are the timeframes for your money to get to the bank. Your bank can legally hold a direct deposit for up to 5 days after receiving it, but if they do, I would find a new bank. When you send your return to the IRS electronically, they do a number of checks immediately, and, if they fail, it is rejected. The following are common causes for returns to be rejected:

- Names, SSNs, or birthdays on the return do not match IRS records
- Identification numbers on W-2s or other forms do not match IRS records.
- A person on the return has already been claimed or already filed a tax return.
- Last year's AGI that you provided to software isn't correct or you did not file a tax return in the prior year (this rejection should not occur if you use a professional to prepare your tax return since this is a Tax ID Theft prevention tool).
- The First-Time Homebuyer Credit payback was not included on the return when required.

There are literally hundreds of other reject causes, but suffice it to say, the clock in the paragraph above does not start until you correct the problem and resubmit. Most rejection problems are easy to solve, and, if you use a professional, they should walk you through solving them. Keep in mind, though, that they cannot work miracles and will often need information from you. I would say that 80% of my client's rejected returns are resolved over the phone in 24 hours. Another 10% require modifications to the return that affect the refund. About 5% require the return to be mailed in, and 5% do not get resolved because the client disappears or is unable or unwilling to make the changes required to the return.

If your return is rejected, don't panic. Your software support or tax professional should be able to help. Also, a rejected return is not considered to have been filed, so whatever mistake you made to cause it to be rejected will not get you in trouble with the IRS. You also get a 5-day grace period at the tax deadline to correct rejected returns.

Now let's mention a few wrinkles that some tax companies will introduce. The first one is a system for withholding your tax preparation fees from your refund. The way this works is that you agree to have your refund deposited with a bank that the tax company has contracted with who immediately forwards the money (minus fees) to your bank account. The main thing to understand about this is that they have no control over the speed of your refund. They don't send you your money until the IRS sends it to them. If the IRS sends you less, you get less. If the IRS does not send enough to cover the fees, the company will expect you to make up the difference. They will also take any back fees that you owe them from prior tax returns, and any money you might owe the bank. Also, if you are a careful tax return reviewer, you might panic that the direct deposit information on the 2nd page of the Form 1040 is wrong. That is because it's the bank's information, and that's okay – your information will be on a document the tax company provides. There is almost always a fee for this service, but it is usually not too much. My mantra is that the fastest and cheapest way to get your tax return from a professional is pay the fee up front, electronically file, and use direct deposit.

The last thing is getting your money faster than the IRS sends it. No matter what your tax professional calls it, this is a LOAN. They are required to disclose this fact, but not all companies are as conscientious about this as they should be. Most of the really bad loan products have been eliminated, so mostly the remaining bad ones are paystub-based advances, and a new wrinkle: In the last couple of years, some of the big players have been offering smaller loan products with no fees and no requirement to pay it back if the IRS keeps your refund. The reason they are doing this is because the competition between tax preparation companies is intense and these are a way to lure customers. Unlike the loans I started talking about, these are pretty neutral as to quality, and the main caveat is to make sure you understand EXACTLY what you are getting, what it costs, and what happens if the IRS keeps your money.

One other bonus piece of advice: Make absolutely sure that the routing and account number on your tax return is correct. Get it from a CHECK, not a deposit slip. If you get it online make sure the routing number is for DIRECT DEPOSIT and not wire transfer. If you get this wrong, best case is a delayed check mailed to you and worst case is weeks or months of delays tracing the deposit and getting the money sent to you.

2020 Update: The IRS didn't start accepting tax returns until much later than normal due to late changes to tax laws. This was a cause of some abnormal delays.

2021 Update: Failure to accurately report the amount of stimulus payments received caused a very large number of tax refunds to be delayed for 30 to 60 days as the IRS corrected the refund with accurate numbers. Make absolutely sure you report the correct numbers for your stimulus payments. In addition, the IRS has been directed to send some of the expanded amounts of Child Tax Credits in advance starting in July of 2021. These payments will need to be reconciled on the 2021 tax return. The IRS is supposed to have a lookup tool available and is also required to send a statement to you by 1/31/2022. I would not rely on these and instead would track all the payments I received and report them on my tax return. The deposits generally come from the US Treasury.

A COVID-19 aside: From mid-March 2020 up until late 2021, the IRS was basically not processing anything on paper. This meant amendments and paper filed tax returns, as well as returns held for hand review or requiring faxing of additional documents just sat there, piling up. Refunds waiting on these were SIGNIFICANTLY delayed. This only serves to highlight how important it is to not rely on getting your refund for any reason. The IRS is STILL not cut up on this – but getting better.

Military: No real changes here for you, though you may not be eligible for some loan products due to the Soldiers and Sailors Civil Relief Act and similar legislation. Update your address with the IRS every single time you move!

9. Where's my Refund?

I'll answer that question with a question: Has it been at least 21 days since you electronically filed your return and the IRS accepted it (28 days if they are mailing you a check)? If not, wait. This is the normal processing time, and you should not call the IRS or your tax preparer until this much time has passed. You will probably know people who filed after you and got their refunds faster, but that is because the timing can vary, between 6 and 21 days, and there is no way of knowing who gets it when. For the first 21 days, the best way to track it is at irs.gov using a prominently marked, "Refund Status" button. You need your SSN, filing status, and your refund amount. If you use a professional that takes your fees out of your refund, make sure you use the original refund amount, not the amount you will be getting after fees. You will be given the status of your return and contact information if they need you to do something. If there is a problem, they'll let you know, though they may not tell you anything useful besides that. If they indicate there is a problem, now is the time to call your tax preparer or contact the IRS at the number they give you when you check the status. Be prepared to wait, and wait. The IRS phones are VERY busy during tax season.

2020/2021 Update: Reporting incorrect amounts of stimulus payments or advance Child Tax Credit payments received is likely to result in a significant delay in getting your money. Be absolutely sure you report correct amounts.

Now let's talk about a few of the more common reasons you might not get your refund on time:

The IRS is taking a harder look at it: The timing guidelines from the IRS are not obligations. They sometimes pull a return for additional review. Sometimes this is quick, sometimes it can take a long time. If it takes more than a few days, they will usually send you a letter telling you they are doing it, but not always. Feel free to harass the IRS for answers if you have the patience.

You owe the IRS or other government agency money: This is called an offset. If you have delinquent student loans, Veterans Administration overpayments, military credit card delinquencies, back child support, back taxes, and/or many other things, they can deduct the payment from your refund. "Where's my Refund?" will tell you if an offset was deducted and give you a number to call to find out what organization they took it for and their phone number. Make sure to check with your spouse to make sure it was not their offset. If it was taken for your spouse's debts, you may be able to file as an Injured Spouse to get some of the money back—contact a professional for help. If you think this has happened, or may have happened to you, you can call 1 (800) 304-3107 and this automated system will tell you if you have offsets, and who to contact about them. That number only includes non-tax offsets, so you may have to contact the IRS if it was Federal Taxes. **A COVID-19 aside**: At various times, Congress has directed the IRS to suspend collections of various debts other than delinquent child support from tax refunds and stimulus payments. There are also various rules for the new 2021 credits regarding what can and can't be collected.

You owe your tax preparer (or their bank) money: When you use a preparer and have them pull your fees out of the refund, you generally give them permission to collect any debts you owe them or their bank. Check the paperwork, the permission is in there.

You gave them bad Direct Deposit information: Make sure you get the Routing and Account numbers right. Check your actual checks and match them to your tax return. If you had your fees pulled from your refund by your preparer, the numbers will not match the return, since your money goes to the preparer's bank first. Check the paperwork for pulling the fees out: your direct deposit information should be in there somewhere. If you made a mistake, chances are that you will simply get a check mailed from the IRS, or, if you had fees withheld, your preparer's company will process a check for you using their own processes. It should not be more than a couple weeks of delay. The worst case is if your direct deposit error matches an actual account for someone else. In that case, you have a long road of pain ahead—though you will get your money. Contact the IRS or your preparer for help. You can help prevent this by bringing your checkbook to your tax appointment or getting numbers directly from you banking app. Both you, your preparer, and/or your wife should verify these numbers. DON'T MESS THIS UP!

The IRS corrected your return and you do not get a refund: Sometimes the IRS finds errors and corrects them on the spot, sending you the proper amount of money. If this results in a balance due, you will not get any money—you'll get a letter asking you to pay.

The return you filed includes a credit subject to a delay designed to prevent Tax ID Theft: Tax Identity Theft has become a big deal, and the

IRS keeps trying to stop it while still getting the majority of people their refunds within 21 days. Even so, more and more people are facing delays as a result of these scumbags. For 2016 and later years, Congress passed a law requiring certain types of refunds have their processing delayed until February 15th. Those are refunds that include Earned Income Credit or Additional Child Tax Credit. These are the common types of returns that the ID thieves make up. If you get back more than you pay in, and it's not because of college, you will probably see this delay. February 15th becomes the date that the 6 to 21-day clock STARTS, so you are looking at some time between the 21st of February and the 8th of March for a normal refund time frame. The good news about this is that, at least in our office, it seemed that ID theft was way down. The timelines listed above have been wildly inconsistent, with some taxpayers getting their refunds well in advance of those timelines, but you should assume that if the above credits apply to you that March 8th is the date to be focused on.

The amount you reported for stimulus payments does not match the IRS records (2020 and 2021): The IRS explicitly stated that not reporting accurate amounts for stimulus payments will delay refunds. I can say, anecdotally, that this turned out to be true and the delays can exceed 60 days. The payments aren't taxable, but you have to report them so the IRS can ensure you received the proper amount. If you got less than you deserved, they send the excess with the tax return. When your return indicates that you should be getting more, but the amount you reported doesn't match, this requires a human to reconcile things, and possibly make corrections. When humans get involved, things slow WAY down.

For 2021 Only: The amount you reported as Advance Child Tax Credit payments don't match IRS records: This is a presumption on my account, but I expect failing to report the right amount will have the same impact as reporting incorrect stimulus payments. The IRS will have a method to lookup your amounts received, and you should use it.

My Advice:

1. Wait at least 21 days after your return is accepted before contacting anyone.
2. Use the Refund Status function on the IRS or state website as your first source for checking the status (you do not have to wait 21 days to do this).
3. Never count on your tax refund until you have it.
4. Keep up on payments for student loans, taxes, child support and other debts subject to Federal collection activities.

5. Always enter direct deposit information directly from the bottom of your checks (do not include the check number) or your banking app. Make sure you use the direct deposit routing number and not the Wire routing number.

6. Be aware that there is very little that your tax professional or software can do to get any more information on a delayed refund.

7. Make absolutely sure that the amounts of stimulus payments and advance Child Tax Credit payments that you report are accurate. When possible, try to use the IRS tools to get accurate amounts.

Military: Delinquent bills to military charge cards for travel or exchanges can be collected from your refund.

10. I Owe Taxes and Can't Pay

This situation sucks. I see it all the time and it can be nerve racking. You do not want to owe money to the IRS because they have some of the most effective methods of getting money from you and can do a lot more than other creditors can. That said, don't freak out. The IRS can be understanding and does have a number of programs available to you, especially if this is the first time. Also, you need to immediately take the steps laid out in the next chapter to ensure you do not owe again next year. This can be a double whammy, because anything you do to lower your tax bill next year will generally lower your take-home pay just as you are trying to pay the IRS for this year!

Here are some general considerations. First, pay them what you can as soon as you can. Send every penny you can afford in with your tax return (or the voucher you will get printed if you're e-filing) by April 15th. You can also pay online, which I highly recommend. Second, do not try filing an extension to avoid this. It is an extension of time to file, not time to pay. Third, do not ignore the IRS. If they send you a letter or a bill, you need to reply, preferably with some money and an explanation.

A word on those tax resolution companies you see advertised on television. While I am sure that some of them are honest and helpful, I think most of them are one step above con artists. Some are one-trick ponies who will try to file an Offer in Compromise for you, the vast majority of which are not approved. They are telling you the truth when they say they can stop garnishments and levies, but what they do not tell you is that this is only while the IRS considers your Offer in Compromise. Be very careful and do your due diligence if you try to use one of these firms.

Keep in mind that it is highly unlikely that you can avoid paying the taxes you owe, and that the IRS will charge interest, and often penalties, on the amount that you don't pay by April 15th. You should consider all sources of money that are available to you in order to make the payment (though talk to a tax professional before pulling money out of a retirement account). By the way, even if you file before April 15th, you do not have to pay until April 15th.

Here are some details on what the IRS has available as options when you cannot pay:

1. The most common solution used when you can't afford to pay right away is the installment agreement request. There is a fee to apply, but the IRS has to accept an installment agreement that will get the taxes paid within 5 years, as long as you have filed and paid your taxes on time in the past and owe less than $50,000. Interest and possibly a late payment penalty will still be assessed. You can go to irs.gov and on their front page there is a button that says "Pay". You will find the installment agreements there. Keep in mind that the IRS has a limited time it is allowed to collect money from you and an installment agreement extends this time. This should not be an issue unless you are planning on avoiding the IRS for a long time.

2. You can pay your taxes with a credit card, though the IRS uses third-party vendors who will charge you a fee and it can be annoyingly high. Information on them is available at https://www.irs.gov/payments/pay-taxes-by-credit-or-debit-card.

3. You can file for a payment extension. You can ask for up to 6 months, and, if approved, you will not pay a penalty if paid by the extended date. You will still owe interest the entire time. DO NOT apply for one of these if you are not sure you can pay by the extended date. Make sure to apply for the extension before April 15th. You file for the extension using Form 1127.

4. You could try for an Offer in Compromise (OIC). These are difficult and not approved very often. The IRS will generally accept an Offer in Compromise in only two situations. One is a scenario in which it is unlikely that you will ever be able to pay the amount due. You will need to PROVE this with tons of financial documentation, as well as substantiation as to why your financial situation will never improve. The other reason is if there is doubt as to whether you owe the money. This normally comes up when you are fighting the IRS over something on your tax return. The IRS may accept less than what's owed if there is a possibility that they might lose a fight in court on the issue in question. You should seek some professional advice before filing an OIC, even if you are going to file it yourself. You will save yourself a lot of trouble talking to an EA or CPA to ensure you at least stand a chance.

I want to reiterate two points here: pay as soon as possible and fix your tax situation so you do not owe again.

Here is a thought that is not conventional wisdom, and doesn't really align with the rules, but I have found tends to work out fairly conveniently (just don't tell the IRS I suggested it). If you will be able to pay your full bill within the first week of May, just send it in when you have it. If your balance due is small, it might not be worth the trouble of applying for extensions or installment agreements. The IRS might not even notice. Just recognize that you could be charged some non-payment charges and interest. If you owe a lot of money – ignore this suggestion.

My Advice:

1. File early in the tax season so that you can see what the damage is. You still do not have to pay until April 15th, and this gives you time to gather the money before it is due. You do NOT have to PAY before the deadline even if you FILE before the deadline. Also, filing a tax return starts various clocks that limit how long the IRS can go after you.
2. Pay as much as you can by April 15th, even if you cannot pay it all. This will reduce any interest and penalties and indicates to the IRS that you plan on paying the balance due.
3. If you set up a payment plan, use a payment amount that you are sure you can make – leaving some room for unforeseen circumstances, but pay as much as you can, when you can.
4. Use auto draft from your checking account for your payment plan and track EVERY payment that comes out.
5. If anything weird happens on a payment plan, such as a missed payment or unusual amount, follow up early and aggressively. DON'T IGNORE IT! The payment plan only works for the IRS as long as you stick to it and make the payments on time, every time.
6. Make your payment online and use your IRS account to pay it.
7. If you are paying online, make sure you make the payment for the correct year AND make the payment under the primary (first on the return) Social Security Number. I absolutely prefer people to pay online, preferably through their online account setup per the instructions in the 10 Simple Pieces of Tax Advice section under TRIPLE BONUS. In 2022 the IRS had some trouble with guest payments made through their website, so please set up an account. Print out and save proof of your payment and the confirmation number provided.

8. Chances are if you owed in one year, and it wasn't something unique to that year, you are going to owe again in the next year. You need to fix this! Get your withholding squared away, even though it sucks to have a payment plan AND more money coming out of your paycheck for taxes.

Do it anyway. This situation can snowball out of control if you don't stay on top of it!

Military: If you are on active duty, or National Guard called up for more than 30 days for an emergency, you can request a deferral for the time you are on duty and have interest capped at 6%. You will need to talk to an expert about this. There are also payment deferral programs for active-duty military, but they are complex and confusing, so you will want to seek expert advice.

The Soldiers and Sailors Civil Relief Act allows PRE-SERVICE debt to be capped at an interest rate of 6%. Up until recently, the IRS interest rates were below that, so it never came up and I didn't look into it. I am having difficulty determining if it applies now and am continuing to research but it is worth asking the question if you have IRS debt from before joining the military.

11. I Owe Taxes and Want to Get a Refund Next Year

This is a tough situation to fix with accuracy and certainty. You usually ensure that they withhold enough from your paycheck by filling out a W-4 and providing it to your employer. The problem is that the W-4 form is pretty much a piece of crap. If you were anything other than a single income family, it struggles to get you the right answer. To add to that, even though a new one has been out for like 5 years, most people don't realize it, including payroll people! So everyone keeps talking about Single and 1 and Married and 3, when that isn't how it works anymore.

One thing the IRS does have that can help is a Tax Withholding Estimator, which can help you to track the status of your estimated refund throughout the year.

The W-4:

The "new" W-4 appears to be designed to make the chances of owing near zero if filled out correctly, while at the same time generating a fairly modest refund. Unfortunately, the form is a bit confusing, and payroll companies and HR departments seem to be messing them up more often than they did with the old form.

The form is divided into 4 parts. It has a number of tables that you can use for unusual situations, but most people will be able to get their W-4 correct without using the tables.

Here is a link to the new W-4 page, which includes instructions, Frequently Asked Questions, and the Withholding Estimator:

https://www.irs.gov/forms-pubs/about-form-w-4

Step 1 is for Filing Status (remember, there is a chapter on just that!) As a general rule, checking the box matching the filing status on your tax return will work, if everyone involved pays attention. One exception is that putting Single down for a little side job when you are married can keep the withholding up on that job. As with the old form, it is unusual or extra sources of income that make the W-4 process break down.

Step 2 is the complicated, or insanely easy step, depending on your situation. If you have only one source of income, skip this step. If you are married, and your spouse works, and those two jobs are the only jobs, check Box C. Otherwise, you need to use all the tables and worksheets, or the Withholding Estimator to help you fill out the rest of the form. Sometimes, a small side job or steady extra source of income can be simply accounted for without using the Estimator or Tables, but most often the estimator is going to be the way to go.

Some payroll companies are struggling with Box C, or have two check boxes on their website rather than just having Box C. The two boxes are generally: "I am married, and my spouse works" and There are only two incomes (or W-2s)". Check both of these to effectively check Box C.

Another option for a multi-income household is to ignore Step 2 entirely and put Single in Step 1. It literally does the exact same thing, and your employer can't mess it up.

Step 3 is where dependents are counted. Every qualifying Child under the age of 17 gets you $2000 and every other dependent gets you $500. You just add it all up here. VERY IMPORTANT: The end of Step 2 tells you to only fill out the rest of the form for the HIGHEST income source. Only ONE job gets to account for the kids. You and your spouse need to coordinate this and ensure you do it right. There are very good reasons why the kids go with the highest income, mainly that the higher income is going to tend to be over withheld, while the lower income will be under withheld, so this balances it. It is also possible that the lower income will run out of income before getting full benefit for the children. Including the same child on multiple W-4's is the single biggest reason why withholding gets messed up!

Step 4 accounts for the wildcards. You can add extra income here if you want to make sure it gets accounted for in the correct bracket. You can account for deductions above the standard deduction here as well. This is also where you tell your employer to take a little extra out of every paycheck.

Here is the deal. If your situation can easily be accounted for without using the Tables, go ahead and do it. If you need to futz with the Tables or a lot of weirdness in Step 4, use the Withholding Calculator (discussed below).

Here are some easy scenarios and what to do:

A Single person with one job just checks Single in Step 1 and stops. This also works with multiple jobs as long as they aren't worked at the same time (meaning it works if you change from one job to another but not if you are working two jobs).

Someone filing Head of Household with one job checks Head of Household and accounts for the child (or children) in Step 3.

A Married couple each with a job checks Married Filing Jointly, checks Box C in Step 2 and accounts for children in Step 3 for the HIGHER income W-4 ONLY. They can also both check Single and ignore Step 2.

Any of the above with a consistent amount of extra taxable income slaps it in Step 4 for the HIGHER income earners W-4 ONLY. This can even be used to account for a side job by going exempt on the side job and putting the full annual salary in Step 4 of the big earner's W-4.

Any of the above with a consistent amount of deductions can account for them in Step 4 for the HIGHER income ONLY. Even inconsistent amounts can be partially accounted for by using conservative numbers.

Anything more complicated than the above, use the Estimator. Even if you don't use the Estimator to fill out your W-4, you should use it to check and make sure you didn't mess it up. You can even fill out your W-4 for a complicated situation using a best guess, and then use the Estimator to tweak it after a few pay periods.

I Guess we Need to Talk about the Estimator:

I have played around with the Estimator A LOT, and I have to say that I am pretty impressed. It is not perfect, and the pre-filled W-4's only use Filing Status and extra withholding to accomplish the desired result, but if you take the time to use it correctly, it can be very accurate and is very good at anticipating your refund.

The above said, many of my clients have struggled with it. It is by no means simple and you need to have some understanding of how your taxes work. Your tax pro can help, but will likely charge extra to do the calculator.

You can use it to get a very detailed result, accounting for all your deductions and credits, or you can just put the most basic information in to get a good SWAG estimate.

The most important thing is to fill it out with pay stubs or statements from ALL your income sources. This allows the Estimator to use actual withholding for the year to get its best estimate. The estimate will be most accurate later in the year, but you will have less time to correct if the results suck.

I recommend using the estimator regularly, both to keep on top of your tax status, and to get to the point that you can knock an estimate out in just a few minutes. Here are some times to use the Estimator:

A couple pay periods after you made a change in withholding.
After you get your tax results, and you are not happy with them.
Between August and October of EVERY year.
When you get a new income source or have a change in income.

Here are a few additional considerations to consider:

1. Tax withholding is a zero-sum game. Any change you make to get a bigger refund is going to reduce your paychecks by EXACTLY the amount your refund goes up. Make sure your budget can sustain the changes you make, and if it cannot, work on your budget.
2. Don't try making less money. Making less money very rarely improves your tax situation more than it hurts your paycheck. In fact, one of the best ways to fix this is to make MORE money and have the extra income (or a lot of it) withheld and sent to the IRS.
3. Don't try to be perfect. People will tell you that a refund is an interest free loan to the government, but I can tell you based on thousands of tax returns that getting a $5,000 refund is infinitely preferable to owing even $500.
4. You are already behind on this. Every paycheck you received during the year before filing your taxes and seeing that you are screwed had the wrong withholding. The changes you make now, if you make them exactly right for a full year, will still be short for the part of the year you were not paying enough. The later you filed your taxes, the worse this is, which is why you should at least PREPARE your taxes as soon as possible (you can wait to pay until the due date).
5. No matter what you do, you should be able to see if it is working by using the IRS' Tax Withholding Estimator after a few pay periods have passed.
6. The more things that change your income, the more difficult it is going to be to get this right. Make bigger adjustments if a lot of stuff is changing.

7. If you want to be more exact, you can make estimated payments. Estimated payments are made on April 15th, June 15th, September 15th, and January 15th of the next year. You can make them more often if you want to. I used to hate this idea, because you had to send a check, but now you can make estimated payments online at irs.gov. To do this simply take your balance due and divide it by 4. Make those payments on the above dates. *

8. Keep in mind that using your prior year's balance due as the basis for changing withholding or making estimated payments will not be perfect unless your income and tax rates (and tax laws) stay the same. The more your income changes, the more error will occur. You can account for some of this by being more aggressive and having them withhold extra, or sending in larger estimated payments. Worst case is that you get a bigger refund of the money withheld from your paycheck. Obviously, you need to be able to afford the lower paycheck…

9. Some payroll managers will automatically match your State withholding to your Federal withholding, so make sure you see what is happening on the State side as well on your paycheck.

My Advice:

1. Use the IRS Withholding Estimator regularly, making sure that you have all of your current and former pay stubs handy while doing it. Take your time and put in everything as accurately as you can. Print out or write down the results. It can be helpful to make notes the first few times you do it to make it easier later times.

2. Do a withholding checkup with the Estimator in August, September, or October to make sure you are still on track.

3. Remember that unless you are adjusting withholding in January, you are already behind the power curve and will need to be aggressive to make sure you catch up, though the calculator will do the opposite, making certain you are good to go for the current year, and making you over withheld for the next year.

4. As hinted just now, if you use the calculator late in the year and make a big swing to get a refund in the current year, it is going to be overkill for the following year, so you can make another adjustment at the beginning of the new year to get some of that extra money withheld back into your paycheck.

5. If you make an adjustment to your W-4, do a checkup with the Estimator a few paychecks later to make sure things went the way you expected them to go.

6. Always follow up when you submit a new W-4. The amount of money coming out of your paycheck and the net amount you receive should change. If it doesn't they may not have implemented your requested changes.
7. If you are a multi-income household, I advise ignoring Step 2 and filing Single on the W-4. Read on for the why:

Why put Single if I'm Married?
And why can't we both include our kids?

So, the new W-4 form looked great, but, unfortunately, either taxpayers or payroll still seem to get it entered wrong for two income married couples. The form has a system for taking the below problem into account, but, too often, it isn't getting entered properly and withholding is not correct.

The numbers below are rounded for demonstration purposes and do not reflect the real numbers:

Married couples are entitled to a $25,000 standard deduction
Single people get $12,500. Married couples enter the 22% tax bracket at $80,000 (everything below this is taxed at 12% or lower and everything above is taxed at 22% or higher). Single people enter the 22% tax bracket at $40,000

When you put married on your W-4, you are telling the system to deduct $25,000 from YOUR calculated annual pay and to tax it at 22% only when YOUR income reaches $80,000. The payroll system at YOUR job has no idea what your spouse makes. If your spouse does the same thing, you are telling the systems to give you $50,000 in deductions and effectively not start taking 22% out until income reaches $160,000

This will obviously mess things up. Checking Single corrects it all and puts it on the right table that all the other checkboxes were trying to do anyway.

Likewise, if you have kids, and you both put them on your W-4, you are claiming twice as many kids as you actually have. Only the higher income should claim the kids on their W-4 (you can split them if incomes are similar).

A 3rd job worked at the same time as your main job basically needs 22% coming out for Federal and usually around 5% for state. This is easiest to get by adding additional withholding in Step 4 of the W-4 to get to these amounts. This applies to pensions as well, which comes up a lot with military retirees.

Military: You can see your withholding on MyPay and can make changes there. Be careful making changes in years when you get promoted or transferred. That said, when your pay goes up due to advancement or moving to an area with COLA or higher BAH, this is an opportunity to increase withholding without taking a big hit in take-home pay.

When you retire, if you will continue to work, manually calculate 22% of your monthly pension and add enough additional withholding to your pension to ensure that amount is getting pulled out every month. Way too often I have military retirees get a big shock when they file that first tax return! The Married and Single stuff on MyPay for retirement assumes you will actually be RETIRED and no longer working. 22% might not be enough, but the next tax bracket is only 24%, so the 2% difference won't mess you up too bad. As always, talking to a tax pro is the best way to ensure you get this right.

Obviously, the "Pay Stub" we talk about in the above paragraphs refers to your Leave and Earnings Statement (LES).

*One weird caveat to this that most people do not understand: The IRS expects you to pay taxes on money you earn AS YOU EARN IT. This means you cannot make one big estimated payment at the end of the year and be okay. Strangely, this does not apply to withholding. You can have ZERO withholding January through November, and then GIANT withholding in December, and the IRS will consider it like you had paid it evenly throughout the year. I have no explanation for why they do it, but it is a good thing to note that withholding is given a presumption of timeliness, while estimates are not.

12. I Get a Big Refund and Want a Bigger Paycheck

Other than the first paragraph and a few tweaks, this is the same chapter as the previous chapter since the principles are mostly the same.

The main difference between trying to avoid owing and trying to get a big refund is that if you go to far trying not to owe, you end up getting a big refund. If you mess up trying to lower your refund, you can end up owing. This means you want to be a little more careful trying to lower your refund. Also, due to refundable credits, people with lower incomes and/or a lot of children may not be able to get there refund close to zero. Once they stop taking any money out of your check, that is as far as you can go.

The other difference is that, unlike with the old W-4, you basically have to reset your withholding to a standard amount (which generates a smallish refund) and then use the Estimator to tweak your refund back up if you want a medium sized one.

The W-4:

The "new" W-4 appears to be designed to make the chances of owing near zero if filled out correctly, while at the same time generating a fairly modest refund. Unfortunately, the form is a bit confusing, and payroll companies and HR departments seem to be messing them up more often than they did with the old form.

The form is divided into 4 parts. It has a number of tables that you can use for unusual situations, but most people will be able to get their W-4 correct without using the tables.

Here is a link to the new W-4 page, which includes instructions, Frequently Asked Questions, and the Withholding Estimator:

https://www.irs.gov/forms-pubs/about-form-w-4

Step 1 is for Filing Status (remember, there is a chapter on just that!) As a general rule, checking the box matching the filing status on your tax return will work, if everyone involved pays attention. One exception is that putting Single down for a little side job when you are married can keep the withholding up on that job. As with the old form, it is unusual or extra sources of income that make the W-4 process break down.

Step 2 is the complicated, or insanely easy step, depending on your situation. If you have only one source of income, skip this step. If you are married, and your spouse works, and those two jobs are the only jobs, check Box C. Otherwise, you need to use all the tables and worksheets, or the Withholding Estimator to help you fill out the rest of the form. Sometimes, a small side job or steady extra source of income can be simply accounted for without using the Estimator or Tables, but most often the estimator is going to be the way to go.

Some payroll companies are struggling with Box C, or have two check boxes on their website rather than just having Box C. The two boxes are generally: "I am married, and my spouse works" and There are only two incomes (or W-2s)". Check both of these to effectively check Box C.

Another option for a multi-income household is to ignore Step 2 entirely and put Single in Step 1. It literally does the exact same thing, and your employer can't mess it up.

Step 3 is where dependents are counted. Every qualifying Child under the age of 17 gets you $2000 and every other dependent gets you $500. You just add it all up here. VERY IMPORTANT: The end of Step 2 tells you to only fill out the rest of the form for the HIGHEST income source. Only ONE job gets to account for the kids. You and your spouse need to coordinate this and ensure you do it right. There are very good reasons why the kids go with the highest income, mainly that the higher income is going to tend to be over withheld, while the lower income will be under withheld, so this balances it. It is also possible that the lower income will run out of income before getting full benefit for the children. Including the same child on multiple W-4's is the single biggest reason why withholding gets messed up!

Step 4 accounts for the wildcards. You can add extra income here if you want to make sure it gets accounted for in the correct bracket. You can account for deductions above the standard deduction here as well. This is also where you tell your employer to take a little extra out of every paycheck.

Here is the deal. If your situation can easily be accounted for without using the Tables, go ahead and do it using the W-4 instructions. If you need to futz with the Tables or a lot of weirdness in Step 4, use the Withholding Calculator (discussed below).

Here are some easy scenarios and what to do:

A Single person with one job just checks Single in Step 1 and stops. This also works with multiple jobs as long as they aren't worked at the same time (meaning it works if you change from one job to another but not if you are working two jobs).

Someone filing Head of Household with one job checks Head of Household and accounts for the child (or children) in Step 3.

A Married couple each with a job checks Married Filing Jointly, checks Box C in Step 2 and accounts for children in Step 3 for the HIGHER income W-4 ONLY. They can also both check Single and ignore Step 2.

Any of the above with a consistent amount of extra taxable income slaps it in Step 4 for the HIGHER income earners W-4 ONLY. This can even be used to account for a side job by going exempt on the side job and putting the full annual salary in Step 4 of the big earner's W-4.

Any of the above with a consistent amount of deductions can account for them in Step 4 for the HIGHER income ONLY. Even inconsistent amounts can be partially accounted for by using conservative numbers.

Anything more complicated than the above, use the Estimator. Even if you don't use the Estimator to fill out your W-4, you should use it to check and make sure you didn't mess it up. You can even fill out your W-4 for a complicated situation using a best guess, and then use the Estimator to tweak it after a few pay periods.

I Guess we Need to Talk about the Estimator:

I have played around with the Estimator A LOT, and I have to say that I am pretty impressed. It is not perfect, and the pre-filled W-4's only use Filing Status and extra withholding to accomplish the desired result, but if you take the time to use it correctly, it can be very accurate and is very good at anticipating your refund.

The above said, many of my clients have struggled with it. It is by no means simple and you need to have some understanding of how your taxes work. Your tax pro can help, but will likely charge extra to do the calculator.

You can use it to get a very detailed result, accounting for all your deductions and credits, or you can just put the most basic information in to get a good SWAG estimate.

The most important thing is to fill it out with pay stubs or statements from ALL your income sources. This allows the Estimator to use actual withholding for the year to get its best estimate. The estimate will be most accurate later in the year, but you will have less time to correct if the results suck.

I recommend using the estimator regularly, both to keep on top of your tax status, and to get to the point that you can knock an estimate out in just a few minutes. Here are some times to use the Estimator:

A couple pay periods after you made a change in withholding.
After you get your tax results, and you are not happy with them.
Between August and October of EVERY year.
When you get a new income source or have a change in income.

Here are a few additional considerations to consider:

1. Don't try to be perfect. People will tell you that a refund is an interest free loan to the government, but I can tell you based on thousands of tax returns that getting a $5,000 refund is infinitely preferable to owing even $500.
2. No matter what you do, you should be able to see if it is working by using the IRS' Tax Withholding Estimator after a few pay periods have passed.
3. The more things that change your income, the more difficult it is going to be to get this right. Make bigger adjustments to your W-4 if a lot of stuff is changing.
4. If you want to be more exact, you can make estimated payments. Estimated payments are made on April 15th, June 15th, September 15th, and January 15th of the next year. You can make them more often if you want to. I used to hate this idea, because you had to send a check, but now you can make estimated payments online at irs.gov. To do this simply take your balance due and divide it by 4. Make those payments on the above dates. *
5. Keep in mind that using your prior years refund as the basis for changing withholding or making estimated payments will not be perfect unless your income and tax rates (and tax laws) stay the same. The more your income changes, the more error will occur. You can account for some

of this by being more aggressive and having them withhold extra or making larger estimated payments.

6. Some payroll managers will automatically match your State withholding to your Federal withholding, so make sure you see what is happening on the State side as well on your paycheck.

My Advice:

1. Use the IRS Withholding Estimator regularly, making sure that you have all of your current and former pay stubs handy. Take your time and put in everything as accurately as you can. Print out or write down the results.
2. Do a withholding checkup with the Estimator in August, September or October to make sure you are still on track.
3. Remember that unless you are adjusting withholding in January, you are already behind the power curve and will need to be aggressive to make sure you catch up.
4. If you use the calculator late in the year and make a big swing to get a smaller refund in the current year, it is going to be overkill for the following year, so you can make another adjustment at the beginning of that year to get some of the money back into your paycheck.
5. If you make an adjustment to your W-4, do a checkup with the Estimator a few paychecks later to make sure things went the way you expected them to go.
6. Always follow up when you submit a new W-4. The amount of money coming out of your paycheck and the net amount you receive should change. If it doesn't they may not have implemented your requested changes.
7. If you are a multi-income household, I advise ignoring Step 2 and filing Single on the W-4. Read on for the why:

Why put Single if I'm Married?
And why can't we both include our kids?

So, the new W-4 form looked great, but, unfortunately, either taxpayers or payroll still seem to get it entered wrong for two income married couples. The form has a system for taking the below problem into account, but, too often, it isn't getting entered properly and withholding is not correct.

The numbers below are rounded for demonstration purposes and do not reflect the real numbers:

Married couples are entitled to a $25,000 standard deduction

Single people get $12,500. Married couples enter the 22% tax bracket at $80,000 (everything below this is taxed at 12% or lower and everything above is taxed at 22% or higher). Single people enter the 22% tax bracket at $40,000

When you put married on your W-4, you are telling the system to deduct $25,000 from YOUR calculated annual pay and to tax it at 22% only when YOUR income reaches $80,000. The payroll system at YOUR job has no idea what your spouse makes. If your spouse does the same thing, you are telling the systems to give you $50,000 in deductions and effectively not start taking 22% out until income reaches $160,000

This will obviously mess things up. Checking Single corrects it all and puts it on the right table that all the other checkboxes were trying to do anyway.

Likewise, if you have kids, and you both put them on your W-4, you are claiming twice as many kids as you actually have. Only the higher income should claim the kids on their W-4 (you can split them if incomes are similar).

A 3rd job worked at the same time as your main job basically needs 22% coming out for Federal and usually around 5% for state. This is easiest to get by adding additional withholding in Step 4 of the W-4 to get to these amounts. This applies to pensions as well, which comes up a lot with military retirees.

Military: You can see your withholding on MyPay and can make changes there. Be careful making changes in years when you get promoted or transferred.

Obviously, the "Pay Stub" we talk about in the above paragraphs refers to your Leave and Earnings Statement (LES).

*One weird caveat to this that most people do not understand: The IRS expects you to pay taxes on money you earn AS YOU EARN IT. This means you cannot make one big estimated payment at the end of the year and be okay. Strangely, this does not apply to withholding. You can have ZERO withholding January through November, and then GIANT withholding in December, and the IRS will consider it like you had paid it evenly throughout the year. I have no explanation for why they do it, but it is a good thing to note that withholding is given a presumption of timeliness, while estimates are not.

13. I Get a Big Refund, Is That Okay?

That depends on who you ask.

I understand the arguments both ways, but you almost always hear the "No" side, and never the "Yes" side. So, this chapter has a few reasons why a big refund is okay, and one time that it definitely is not.

I know what everyone says, "A refund means you made an interest free loan to the government!" And they are right, but really, have you seen interest rates lately? Okay, inflation has made interest rates go up, but short term savings of a big refund ain't gonna earn you much money, especially since we will all just spend it as it arrives.

I'm not here to argue that their opinion or facts are completely wrong. To be honest, they are pretty much spot on. But that doesn't mean it's the whole story. I'm here to reassure you that you should not feel guilty about the big refund, and I'll tell you why. First, however, let me tell you when a big refund really would be bad:

If you're really struggling to make your monthly bills, barely getting by paycheck to paycheck, but get a big refund, you really should adjust your withholding to cut down the struggles. In addition, there is nothing wrong with trying to minimize your refund, and there are a lot of great reasons to ensure you don't let the government keep too much of your money during the year. Information about that is easy to find, so this chapter isn't about that. Do what you want, but here are a few reasons a big refund is okay:

1. Interest rates are still pretty mediocre. If saving the money for a big purchase is your plan, you really aren't losing much letting the government keep it and getting it on your refund. If you are saving for long-term things, such as retirement, then you should get it in your paycheck rather than the refund (or contributing to a 401k or similar account directly from your paycheck). If you are saving for short-term goals, there's not much of a difference. Combined with a few more of the following reasons, you can make a compelling case for a big refund.
2. Most Americans (myself included) suck at saving. We tell ourselves that we'll save the money, and maybe we even set up an account to do it. Then the money is there: mocking us, tempting us. So, we spend it! Or even more likely, we never get around to setting that account up, or we end up "needing" it for "just this one time." Next thing you know, we've saved bupkis!

3. Getting a big refund is a good way of ensuring you can catch up if you have a bad year with bills. You get a little behind because, like most Americans, we are not really great at budgeting. The credit cards build up a little more than we wanted and are maybe even get a little hard to pay, then BAM! It's refund time and we can do a reset. Now I am not recommending this as a planning method, but I see a lot of reality in the tax office, and this is a big helper for a lot of people.

4. It is really difficult getting a small refund without ending up going too far. I can say with absolute certainty that virtually every person I do taxes for would consider a $500 balance due as nearly end-of-the-world bad. It SUCKS owing the government money. Even the ones who want to get a small refund would rather get too big a refund than owe one thin dime! Trying too hard for a small refund risks the evil balance due.

My Advice:

1. Relax. Tell the naysayers to mind their own business. If you want a big refund, that is fine with me.

2. Never assume your refund will be as high as the previous year, or that you will get one, or that it will be on time. Always assume zero and hope for the best.

3. Adjust your withholding if you get a big refund but struggle to make your monthly payments.

Military: The variability of military pay can make the act of getting a small refund even more difficult. One good thing is that MyPay makes it easy to adjust your withholding allowances as often as monthly. Just make sure to pay attention as you make changes and be especially attentive when you do a PCS move or receive a big bonus.

14. I Get a Big Refund and Don't Know What to Do with It

These are some ideas for making your big refund work for you. They are a little preachy, but I think its good advice (though it is purely my personal opinion, and not really tax advice):

1. If you are behind on any bills, please, for the love of God, catch them up and keep the bill collectors at bay. After that...
2. If something important, like your car or your HVAC system is broken, get it fixed. After that...
3. If you do not have $2,000 dollars saved for an emergency, open a savings account and put $2,000 dollars in it. Please, for the love of God, **DON'T TOUCH IT**, unless you have an emergency. After that...
4. Spend some of it, no more than 20%, on you or your family for something that makes you, and them, happy. You should enjoy the fact that you have accomplished steps 1 through 3. That is more than many families will accomplish in their lives. A $2,000 emergency fund is a BIG DEAL, and you should be proud of it. After that...
5. Increase the emergency fund to the point that it could pay two months' worth of rent, mortgage, critical utilities, car payments, insurance, and food. After that:
6. Pay off credit card or other high interest debt. All of it. After that...
7. Pay off student loan or car debt. After that...
8. Increase the emergency fund from Step 5 to three to six months of expenses. Leave It Alone! It is for emergencies. After that...
9. Feel free to spend the rest on something you want, or a vacation you desire. If you have accomplished Steps 1 through 8, you probably have a good budget, and a good plan for your future. Everything that follows is optional, and you can do any of the steps in any order. If you want...
10. Fully fund your Individual Retirement Account (IRA) for the year. You have until April 15th. Or...
11. Sock some money away for the kid's college fund...maybe a 529 plan. Or...
12. Put a big chunk towards the house. Big payments early increase the power of the normal payments you make. Do not listen to the morons who say you should always have a mortgage. They don't know what the hell they're talking about. The Super Tax Genius rules say NEVER do anything just for the tax benefit and owing money to the bank qualifies as one of the dumber things you can do. Or...
13. Upgrade the house. Maybe new counters, new bathroom. Whatever. You have demonstrated that you're smart enough to spend your money the

way you want. I would probably jump on Step 12, but if you've got 1 through 8 done, you don't need me to nag you.

14. One aside: Your refund can be used to purchase up to $5,000 of I-Bonds. I-Bonds are beyond the scope of this book, but your refund is one of the few ways to purchase more than the $10,000 per year, per person allowed. Ask your financial advisor or research them yourself if you are interested.

If some of these ideas seem familiar, that's because many of them were inspired by listening to Dave Ramsey. I don't think his advice is absolutely necessary for everyone, but if you have tried to get your financial life in order and failed, you should follow his plan, TO THE LETTER. If you are out of debt and your retirement plan is on track, you probably don't need all of his advice, though we can always learn something.

Military: No real changes for you on this subject, except that all of the above advice applies to any bonuses you get.

15. I Want to Lower my Taxes

Don't we all! There are a lot of guru's out there claiming they can lower your taxes. They range from frauds, kooks, and one trick ponies all the way to legitimate tax experts.

Avoid the scam artists like the plague.

You can always tell who the scammers are because they over promise and make it sound easy. The fact of the matter is that it is hard to lower your taxes without causing problems with your life. As I said in my advice chapter, you should rarely be doing anything just to lower your taxes. Sure, buying a house can lower your taxes, but you should buy a house when it makes sense for your life - not just to lower your taxes. So, I won't be talking about things that might lower your taxes, but that should be done based on other factors.

I am going to cover two types of things here. Things that directly lower your taxes and things that defer your taxes. Deferring taxes is usually good, unless you will pay taxes at a higher rate later. Even then, deferring taxes is often the right plan, especially over a long timeline.

I am going to try to put things in the order of best to worst, based on my opinion, and the extent to which they are likely to apply to more people. Some of them I will advise based on things other than just taxes, though I might not specify why - it is kind of like my personal preference. There are probably more ways than these, but these are the ones that apply most often, or that do not require 7 CPA'S to make happen.

Last thing before the meat - some of these require you to itemize. If you do not normally itemize, some of these things will not help you unless big numbers are involved. I will identify these with a "Requires Itemizing" closing sentence.

I lied – one more thing – **Make More Money**. It is often easier and more time efficient to focus on making more money than it is saving on taxes. I'm serious about this. Too many people are obsessed with paying less taxes when they should be obsessed with making more money with less work. That's the secret to financial success (one of them).

1. The first thing you should do if you want to save on taxes is talk to a tax professional and have them review your last three years' tax returns. Many

will do this for free and only charge you if they find some more money for you. A good tax pro will not only use the review to find you money in the previous years, but also use what they learn about your tax situation to give you advice for the future.

2. Funding tax deferred accounts such as 401k's and Individual Retirement Accounts is almost always a good idea. Talk to BOTH a tax pro and a financial advisor to figure out what types of accounts are best for your situation. If your employer matches contributions to your 401k, investing up to the match is a no brainer. For accounts with your employer, you might not see the reduced taxes reflected in your paycheck, since the withholding will drop with the reduced taxable income. To be clearer, if you put $1000 in your 401k, and are in the 22% tax bracket, your paycheck should only drop by around $780, the $220 difference is your tax savings. These numbers will not be exact for you, because how you set up your withholding will drive how much you see on your paycheck, and how much you see on your refund. This is also one of the few ways to lower your AGI, which might make you eligible for tax benefits you might otherwise not qualify for due to income limits.

3. Health Savings Accounts are another great option for deferring taxes on current income. My enthusiasm for these has gone through the roof as I have seen the benefits of them making my clients lives better. A lot of people call these "triple tax advantaged". What they mean is that you don't pay taxes on the money that goes in, the money grows tax deferred, and you do not pay taxes when you take the money out for medical expenses. Add to that the fact that you do not lose the money if you don't use it, and these become an amazingly powerful vehicle for long term growth. A lot of my clients max these out. Most times your employer puts money in for you, but you can put your own money in through either payroll deduction or direct investment. Their plan is to get it to grow to the point that they can retire before age 65 (when Medicare kicks in) and use the accumulated money to pay for health insurance until they hit 65. See My Advice below for my exact directions for these. It is better to have the employer put money in if possible, rather than do it yourself. You save money on Social Security and Medicare taxes that way. Still – when your employer stops, try to get it up to the limit with your money.

3. Giving stuff to charity is a great way to save on taxes. One of the things I like to tell people is that anything you pay that reduces your taxable income (mortgage interest, state taxes, etc.) is money out of your pocket. The return on your deduction is whatever your state and federal tax rate is; so, it's a net loser. Cash contributions to charity work exactly like that, however, non-cash donations, are like the proverbial free lunch. You give away crap you don't want to someplace that will do good with it, and you

pay less in taxes. I have a whole chapter on this: I'm Donating to Charity. Requires Itemizing except that in 2020 and 2021, some cash (or equivalent) donations to qualified charities can be deducted whether you itemize or not.

4. Selling investments that are in non-tax deferred accounts for a loss during the year can help a bit. You can do this both to offset taxable capital gains and you can deduct up to $3,000 of net capital losses right off of your other income ($1,500 if Married Filing Separately). Do this only if it makes good investing sense. Also, don't try to sell for a loss and buy it right back - that's called a wash sale. You have to wait more than 30 days after selling in order to deduct the loss.

5. There's a weird trick on Capital Gains, but you might need your tax pro's help with it. If you have investments that you have held more than a year, and are worth more than you paid for them, you have unrealized long-term capital gains. If you are in or near the 12% or lower tax bracket, you might be able to sell some of those investments and be able to pay ZERO taxes on the gains. As long as the now realized gains don't move your income above $44,625 (Single and MFS), $89,250 (MFJ) or $59,750 (HH), the long-term tax rate on capital gains is ZERO! You will not see a direct reduction on your current taxes, but you will NEVER pay taxes on those gains, even if you buy the investment back the next day. The wash sale rules discussed in the last step only apply to losses, not gains. This is the most under-utilized tax strategy out there. I do not recommend doing this without the help of a tax pro, because there's a lot more to it than I can discuss here.

6. Some deductions come with a threshold you have to be above before you can deduct them. Medical expenses are the main one. If you do not normally get above the threshold but have an unexpected expense in one year that puts you above it, this strategy can help. Once you know you will be above the threshold, move any planned expenses for early in the next year into the current year. For medical this might mean moving physicals or procedures up or buying new glasses or contacts. For job expenses, you might move a business trip or big purchase up into the current year. This also applies to itemizing itself. If you are below the standard deduction, but close, donate to charity every few years, instead of every year. This will allow you to get some use out of the donations. Requires Itemizing.

7. Keep better records. You cannot deduct something you forgot about. I like notebooks that are always at hand. In the car, on the desk, in your purse, in your shirt pocket. Write things down right away!

8. Don't miss mileage deductions. Keep a mileage log in the car and write down the mileage after every trip. Mileage mostly applies to home

businesses, medical trips and charity trips. Requires Itemizing (except businesses).

9. If you have children in private school, and your state offers a deduction for 529 college saving plan contributions, you can funnel the tuition through a 529 plan and get the deduction. You can do this for up to $10,000 per child, per year, but you should talk to a local pro to make sure what the rules are in your state.

10. Do NOT just assume that using 529 plan money for the full amount of college tuition is a good idea. There are a million complications and tax advantaged options surrounding college, so get advice BEFORE taking money out of the 529. Often times the American Opportunity Credit provides better advantages than using 529 money.

11. Take advantage of credits for solar panels, electric vehicles, vehicle charging stations, high efficiency wood stoves, energy efficient home improvements, adoption, going to college and other items that the government wants to encourage you to do by giving you money. Just don't go into these things blind and NEVER believe the salesman when they tell you what the benefit is, especially solar salesman. Do the math on the purchase price, benefit and reward, and then factor in taxes. Many of these items have income limitations and other restrictions that may reduce the amount you get. Many also cannot reduce your tax liability below zero, so some things you might do together: solar panels, electric vehicle and car charger, for example, may make more sense to be done in different tax years. This is definitely an area where a consultation with a tax professional can be worth its cost.

12. Expounding on college, talk to a tax professional about a year ahead of sending your kids to college to ensure you align the tuition and funding sources in the most advantageous way. A mistake in this area can cost $10,000 over 4 years of college, so check out the I'm Going to College section well in advance of sending your kids to school.

My Advice:

1. You should have a plan for contributing to your 401k and/or IRA with the goal of ultimately maxing these accounts out. Talk to your financial advisor and a tax professional to decide on what to invest in, and whether to use a Roth or Traditional version. When you get a raise – give your 401k a raise!

2. In coordination with the 401k discussion above, you want to work toward maxxing out your HSA. Do not use the money in the HSA for medical expenses unless they are truly unaffordable. Especially don't use it for small copays or prescriptions. The HSA is the best place for your

money, so leave it there until you retire if at all possible. Your HSA is probably invested quite conservatively. Once you have enough money in the account to cover about 150% of your maximum annual deductible, start investing in things with a higher return. Your financial advisor can help you with this. Try to get your employer to put more money in whenever negotiating for a higher salary.

3. If you have stocks that no longer meet your investment objectives and are lower in price than what you paid for them, sell them late in the year to get the losses, especially if you have gains to offset. In addition, EVERY year you are below the thresholds for a 0 percent long-term capital gain rate, sell appreciated stock to get to that threshold and buy it back the next day. Keep in mind that you only factor the GAIN (price sold for minus price paid) to determine the gain.

4. If you normally do not itemize, pick a year to go nuts with charity and other itemized deductions. Accumulate stuff until you are a bad weekend away from being on an episode of Hoarders, and then give it all to charity, making lots of moderate sized trips. Combine medical expenses and taxes with flexible due dates into this same year.

5. If your kids are going to private school, talk to a local tax pro to see if funneling the money through a 529 plan to save on State taxes makes sense for you. You should also be able to do this with student loan payments as well.

6. If you or your children are going to college and are getting scholarships or grants and/or you have a 529 plan, talk to a tax professional before paying the tuition. The I'm Going to College chapter will talk more about this, but, properly managing how you pay for college can be worth $10,000 over four years.

Military: If you can reenlist in a combat zone for a bonus, do it. If this involves taking a smaller bonus, talk to a tax pro to see if the taxes saved is more than the bonus given up. The Thrift Savings Plan qualifies as a tax deferred account as discussed in suggestion #2.

The Thrift Savings Plan qualifies as a tax deferred account as discussed in suggestion #2.

You can't have a Health Savings Account so ignore that section.

16. I Can't File by April 15th

First things first, relax. This is not as big a deal as most people make it out to be. In fact, for most people, this is an absolute non-event. I am going to start by clearing up some myths and explaining some important things everyone should know about the filing deadline:

1. If you are getting a refund, for all intents and purposes, the IRS doesn't give a crap when you file, and, there is very little they can do to you if you don't. Almost worst case, you get a letter telling you to file, you file, and they send you your refund. No penalties, no jail, no yelling. So, if you are SURE you are getting a refund, you really don't need to do anything. You can file an extension to avoid letters and hassle for six months, but you probably don't need to. Now, to be 100% accurate, there are some possible issues for not filing - so you should file as soon as you can. These are the issues: they can hold up another refund until you file, they might calculate a tax return for you that says you owe money and send you a bill (but your tax return for a refund as a response will fix it), you might need the return filed to get a loan, job or security clearance, and, if you wait more than three years from the deadline to file for the refund, the IRS won't give it to you.

2. You can get an extension of time to file for an extra six months, and its approval is almost automatic, but...BIG BUT, it is an extension of time to FILE, not time to PAY. When you file the extension, you are expected to estimate your balance due, and send the money with the extension. Failing to send the amount you owe will result in interest and failure to pay penalties. The extension avoids failure to FILE penalties. So, if the reason you cannot FILE by April 15th is really that you can't PAY by April 15th, then you are in the wrong chapter. You want: I Owe Taxes and Can't Pay Them.

3. As a corollary to the above, even if you can't pay your taxes, you don't need to wait to file. Your money is not due until April 15th, even if you file in January or February. Filing early to see the damage makes a lot of sense and there is a chance you might be due a refund!

All that covered, what to do if you cannot file by April 15th depends on why you can't file, and when you can file. Here are a few reasons, with suggestions for what to do:

Waiting on paperwork: This is the most common one, and, the one that ticks me off the most. I am not mad at you, I'm mad at companies that make people wait for paperwork. Assuming you keep places up to date with your address, there is no excuse for this. Keep calling and harassing them to get the paperwork. I really can't provide much better advice than that. If the paperwork will not be received by April 15th, complete your tax return as much as you can, including a best guess for the numbers from the missing paperwork. Then file an extension using the estimated balance due and send the extension with payment by April 15th. Make sure that when you finally file the tax return that you include the payment amount as part of the tax return, so you get credit for it in the final results. Make sure to file the tax return by October 15th. Your tax pro or tax software should handle this smoothly, and you can probably e-file the extension. If you are getting a refund, don't send any money with the extension. One other little thing: if you can get 100% accurate numbers for the document, it doesn't include any Federal withholding, and it's not a W-2 or 1099-R, you might be able to file without getting the actual document - check with a tax pro.

Waiting on Spouse availability to sign: If your spouse is unavailable temporarily, you can try to file on time by getting a Power of Attorney, getting his or her signature on the documents via fax, email or something else, or your tax pro may have ways of helping. Otherwise, complete your tax return then file an extension using the tax return data, and send the extension with payment by April 15th. Make sure that when you file the tax return that you include the payment amount as part of the tax return, so you get credit for it in the final results. Make sure to file the tax return by October 15th. Your tax pro or tax software should handle this smoothly, and you can probably e-file the extension. If you are getting a refund, don't send any money with the extension.

Waiting on Spouse availability to provide needed information: In this case, you can obviously attempt to get the information, but I am assuming that you already tried that. Depending on the amount of missing information, the extension might be just a little off, or wildly inaccurate. You need to work with your spouse to get the tax return done as much as possible, before filing the extension. If you KNOW you are due a refund, you can wait for them to get you the missing items and file without bothering with an extension or you can send an extension in with 0 as the balance due. If your spouse is more permanently unavailable, you will need to work with a tax professional on what options you have. If they are deceased, I'm sorry for your loss, but I have a chapter on that: My Spouse Died.

Divorce or Separation Issues: This can be tough. You can always file Married Filing Separately or Head of Household (if qualified). Read the chapters I'm Getting Divorced and I have to File Married Filing Separately first. Otherwise, you should talk to your divorce lawyer AND a tax professional to cover your options. You really need to do both since there is no way I can cover this well enough to help you with all possible scenarios in this book.

You are waiting on a new child's SSN: This should only be an issue if the child was born outside of the United States. In this case it is IMPERATIVE that you be proactive in getting the SSN as soon as possible! It is also critical that you file extensions if you won't have the SSN by the normal due date. If you fail to do this you may not be entitled to some of the more lucrative tax credits for having a child.

Don't have time: This one really doesn't work. In order to file an extension, you practically have to do the whole tax return in order to know how much to send them, so you might as well do the whole thing and be done with it. Seriously, no one has time for annoying things like filing taxes, but the IRS could not care less. Make time for this and get the damn thing done. There is no reason to have the IRS hanging over your head for any longer than necessary.

My Advice:

1. Plan ahead and be ready to file early in the tax season. Being ready makes filing on time easy, even if you decide to wait.
2. If you are married, both spouses should have access to the information needed to be able to file your taxes. This means both spouses need to know where all the paperwork is, what paperwork to expect in the mail and what deductions you plan on taking.
3. Have a plan if you will not be available during tax time. Either have a plan for an extension to be filed or plan for someone to prepare and file your taxes for you using a power of attorney.
4. ALWAYS make sure you have electronic access to your tax paperwork from your job, your mortgage company, your student loan, your investments, etc. Make sure you know all the passwords AND have a good password reset system setup with each company.
5. If you are getting divorced, discuss tax filing with your lawyers early in the process, especially if you won't be divorced by the end of the tax year. You generally want to avoid filing Married Filing Separately, so agreeing on how, when, where you will file, and how to split the refund or balance due is very important. Keep in mind that many lawyers tax knowledge is very incomplete so you should talk to a tax professional as well.

6. Even if you think you are going to owe, get your taxes done early so that you can begin planning how to pay it. If you owe, this usually means that you need to make an adjustment to your withholding that will lower your paycheck, making it doubly hard on your budget. Starting the planning early limits the impact of this.

Military: The IRS and all states will accept a military Power of Attorney as long as it authorizes the filing of taxes, regardless of whether it comports perfectly with state laws for POA's. When stationed outside the U.S. at the time the tax return is due you get an automatic 2-month extension of time to file (not time to pay) and this applies even if only one spouse is overseas. If you are in a combat zone, you get an automatic extension that lasts until 180 days after you exit the combat zone. If your spouse is deployed to a combat zone when the return is due, you can sign the return FOR them and attach a statement to the return explaining that they were in a combat zone.

You may request an extra two-month extension to December 15th IF you already filed for the automatic 6 month extension to October 15th. This extension is NOT automatic, and you need to send a letter requesting the extension and explaining why you need it. They will not respond if the extension is approved but are supposed to respond if it is denied. The Armed Forces Tax Guide (Pub 3) available on the IRS website has specifics for the extension and the address you send it to.

Having a child overseas and needing to wait on the SSN is common for military and you should follow the instructions detailed above and also file the above 2-month extension to December 15th if you still don't have the SSN.

17. How do Taxes Work?

You probably know a lot of this intuitively, simply by having filed taxes before, but I want to review the basic tax process, so we have all the terms right when I discuss them later. In the age of software tax preparation, it is way too easy to let the program do magic without knowing what is happening behind the data entry, so this will help a bit.

You start with INCOME. For most people, this is their wages, which come from their W-2's. It also includes business, rental and investment, pension and retirement, unemployment and other miscellaneous income. In addition, alimony (before Trump Tax Changes), disability and Social Security income might be taxable. Add all that together and you get your TOTAL INCOME subject to tax.

Now we take some magic deductions, many of which have special rules or income limitations, such as student loan interest, moving expenses, some alimony paid, teacher expenses, traditional IRA contributions, a bit of charity, etc. and deduct these to get a very important number: ADJUSTED GROSS INCOME (AGI). These deductions are often called "above the line" deductions because they do not require you to itemize in order to subtract them. Knowing your AGI for a tax year can be very important, since most income limitations are based on it, and you often provide it as proof of identity when accessing your data or filing a tax return.

We are about to hit the part of taxes where FILING STATUS matters. See the next chapter if you are not certain what yours is.

Now we get to STANDARD or ITEMIZED DEDUCTION. To keep people from having to keep track of every little deductible expense, the IRS gives you a very large STANDARD DEDUCTION that you can take even if you do not actually have that much stuff to deduct. This is a good deal, and a major feature of the Trump Tax Change was to expand this number to reduce the amount of people required to itemize. For 2023, the STANDARD DEDUCTION is $13,850 for Single and Married Filing Separate Filers, $27,700 for Joint Filers and $20,800 for Head of Household Filers. If you add up your itemized deductions, made up primarily of state and local taxes paid, mortgage interest and charitable contributions, and it exceeds the STANDARD DEDUCTION, you take that bigger number and you have ITEMIZED your DEDUCTIONS.

Now you take your STANDARD or ITEMIZED DEDUCTIONS and subtract them from your AGI to get TAXABLE INCOME. It is exactly what it sounds like...this is what you pay taxes on.

Most people will look their TAXABLE INCOME up on a tax table to get the amount of taxes, but certain income is taxed at lower or higher rates, so you might need a worksheet...way too much info for here, but I need to take another aside and talk about Tax Brackets. As your income increases, you move up tax brackets. Most people think that when you enter the 22% tax bracket, all your TAXABLE INCOME gets taxed at 22%. That is not how it works. Here's how it really works, using rounded numbers for illustration only (not the actual tax bracket break points). For a Married Joint filer, the first $20,000 of income is taxed at 10%, $20,000 to $90,000 is taxed at 12% and ONLY the portion above $90,000 is taxed at 22% (unless the income enters one of the other 4 higher tax brackets) but the principle continues. Jumping a tax bracket is a GOOD thing!

So, after this calculation you have the amount of TAX.

At this point, we can lower the TAX by taking CREDITS. These reduce the tax amount dollar for dollar and are AWESOME! The most common is the $2,000 per child under 17 Child Tax Credit. There are also Education Credits, Child Care Credits, Saver's Credits and Foreign Tax Credits. These are also called non-refundable credits because they cannot reduce your tax due below zero.

Now we have ADDITIONAL TAXES. These are basically taxes that are not fully related to income taxes. The most common is self-employment tax, which business owners pay instead of Social Security and Medicare taxes. Take a look at your W-2 or pay stub. You see Federal Income Tax withheld, which is what a Federal tax return is all about, but you also see Social Security and Medicare taxes (also called FICA). Those taxes are GONE, and not even a discussion on your tax return. That said, the IRS is used to get those taxes from people who do not have an employer withhold them, or people who get the majority of their income from tips, such that there isn't enough paycheck to cover them. Other things you might see here are penalties for early retirement withdrawals and a bunch of Affordable Care Act (Obamacare) taxes.

Add these ADDITIONAL TAXES to your base TAX and you have TOTAL TAX. For most people, you compare your FEDERAL TAX

WITHHELD from your pay to this number to get your REFUND or BALANCE DUE.

But wait! There are also REFUNDABLE CREDITS and ESTIMATED PAYMENTS. Estimated payments are basically exactly like withholding from a job, except that you sent it to the IRS directly, to make sure you did not owe. REFUNDABLE CREDITS are CREDITS that can get you back more money than you paid in. The most common are Earned Income Credit, Additional Child Tax Credit and the American Opportunity Credit (an Education Credit). Basically, they treat all these items just like the withholding from your paycheck to get your REFUND or BALANCE DUE.

One last thing, if you owe more than $1000, and do not meet an exception, you have to pay a PENALTY. You were supposed to have paid taxes on your income as you earned it, not after you filed your taxes. Poop...

18. What is My Filing Status?

This is the first decision you need to make about filing your taxes, though for most people they don't have a lot of choice. This is sometimes the easiest question to answer, and sometimes the most complicated. I'm going to try to put the facts you need down, in an order that will help you make the decision as easily as possible.

2023 Update: Qualifying Widower was changed to Qualifying Surviving Spouse but none of the actual rules surrounding it were changed.

Just to make things easy, here are some situations that are pretty cut and dried:

- If you are unmarried, have no children and live alone, you're probably going to file SINGLE.
- If you're married and live with your spouse, you're going to file MARRIED FILING JOINTLY (MFJ) or MARRIED FILING SEPARATELY (MFS).
- If you are a single parent of your own minor child and it's just you and your children in your home all year, you're probably going to file HEAD OF HOUSEHOLD (HH).

Here are the details:

1. There are five filing statuses available. They are SINGLE, MARRIED FILING JOINTLY (MFJ), MARRIED FILING SEPARATELY (MFS), HEAD OF HOUSEHOLD (HH) and QUALIFYING SURVIVING SPOUSE (QSS).
2. If you are married and not legally separated on December 31st of the tax year, you are MARRIED. This means you have to file MFJ or MFS, unless you meet very unique requirements to file HH by being considered unmarried for tax purposes (covered next). Legal separation requires the involvement of the courts and is governed by the laws of your state.
3. If you aren't divorced or legally separated, you can be considered unmarried if ALL the following apply:
   a. You did not live with your spouse after June 30th of the tax year. This doesn't count if it's a temporary absence, such as school or military orders. The idea is that they left and aren't coming back.
   b. You paid over half the costs of maintaining a home, which was the main home for your child, stepchild or foster child

for at least 6 months and a day of the tax year. A foster child must be placed with you by an authorized placement agency or court. Note that the relations are VERY specific. One way to think of it is that you as a parent have been forced to take care of a child for whom you are responsible due to being the birth parent, step-parent or foster parent. I should also note that step-relationships established by marriage do not end by divorce or death.

   c.   You claim that child on your tax return as a dependent, unless you could claim the child, but are allowing the child's other parent to claim them under special rules for divorced or separated parents (which I will discuss in the I'm Getting a Divorce chapter).

4.   The requirement of paying more than half the cost of maintaining a home discussed in this chapter are different from most times we will talk about paying more than half the costs for kids. In this case, it is just for the home. You include taxes, interest and rent paid (later situations will talk about Fair Rental Value—here it is rent PAID). You also include utilities, repairs and insurance for the home. Other than that, it's food consumed in the home, and not much else. You need to have paid more than half of that total during the period of time the child lived with you (at least 6 months and a day).

5.   If you meet all the requirements in 3 above, you can choose to file HH. You can also file MFJ if the other spouse agrees. If you file HH, the other spouse must file MFS, unless they meet the requirements of 3 above with a different child.

6.   If you are married as discussed in 2 and don't meet the requirements of 3 (or are simply happily married), you can file MFJ or MFS. Generally, MFJ is better, but you can figure out your taxes both ways and choose the one that gets better results. I have a whole chapter on MFS, but I'll list a few reasons to consider that MIGHT make you want or have to file MFS:

   a.   You don't want to be responsible for your spouse's taxes. If you file MFJ, you have to sign the return saying that everything is true under penalty of perjury, and the IRS will hold you accountable for what's on the tax return, even if all you did was sign it. It is very difficult to get the IRS to accept that you are not responsible for a joint return you signed (though there are ways). By filing a MFS return, you are taking responsibility only for the information on YOUR tax return.

b. You might have to go MFS if you can't get your spouse to file jointly with you. You can't make them. This happens sometimes because your spouse doesn't want to be responsible for YOUR tax return, or during divorces or separations.

c. Your spouse owes debts that will be collected out of their refund, such as back child support, student loans or taxes. If you file separately, they won't take it out of your refund if you weren't responsible. There are ways to avoid this without filing MFS, but you should get professional help in these cases.

d. There are certain tax situations that do work out better MFS. Mainly they involve big differences in income, and either medical expenses or job expenses. You'll have to run the numbers both ways to be sure.

e. You are making student loan payments with an Income Based Repayment Plan. Filing MFS means the payments are calculated only based on YOUR income. MFJ they include both spouse's income and your payments will be higher (if your spouse has income).

7. If your spouse or child died during the year, you may consider them to have lived with you and/or been married to you through the end of the year. If your spouse died during the year, you will still file MFJ or MFS with them. However, if you get remarried during the same year, you have to file MFJ or MFS with your NEW spouse, and you will file your deceased spouse's tax return as MFS.

8. If you have never had any children, and aren't married, your filing status is SINGLE.

9. If you aren't married, you may be able to claim HH if you pay half the costs of maintaining a home for someone who lived with you for more than half of the year. I discussed paying half the costs of maintaining a home in 4 above. The person has to meet very specific requirements:

a. If they are your parent, they don't have to live with you, but you have to pay the costs discussed in 4 above for the home they live in (can be a nursing home). You also have to meet the requirements for claiming them as a dependent on your tax return, and you have to claim them to qualify for HH.

b. If they are your son, daughter, stepchild, foster child (foster child must be placed with you by an authorized placement agency or court), brother, sister, stepbrother or stepsister, or a direct descendent of one of them (meaning nieces, nephews, grandchild, etc.) they must meet the following requirements:

1. They must have lived with you more than 6 months and a day,
2. You must claim them as a dependent,
3. They must be under 19, or between 19 and 23 if a full-time student for at least five months, or if older, permanently and totally disabled, and
4. They must not have provided more than half of their own support.
5. (You'll learn more about this when you read the chapters that apply to you with regard to claiming people as dependents.)

   c. If you don't claim the relative just above only because they are married, someone else can claim them and does, or you allow the other parent to claim them under rules for divorced or separated parents (covered in I'm Getting a Divorce chapter) they still count for HH.

   d. For people who live with you who don't meet the relationship or age requirements above, they may still qualify if they are the following relationships: son, daughter, stepchild, foster child (foster child must be placed with you by an authorized placement agency or court), brother, sister, or a direct descendant of any of those, father, mother and any sibling or descendent of them, a stepbrother, stepsister, stepparent, son-in-law, daughter-in-law, brother-in-law, sister-in-law, or parent-in-law. You must also provide more than half of their support (discussed in chapters you will read about trying to claim them as dependents) and be able to claim them as a dependent on your tax return.

10. If none of the requirements for MFJ, MFS and HH apply, you are Single, with one major exception, covered next under 11.
11. If you were married and your spouse died during the year, we've already discussed what to do for the tax year they died in. However, there are special rules that might apply for the next two years AFTER the year their death, if you have dependent children. You must not have remarried, the dependent must be your child or stepchild (not foster child), they must have lived with you ALL year, you must claim them as a dependent, you must have paid over half the cost of maintaining the home (discussed in 4 above) and you must have filed a MFJ return with the spouse in the year they died. If all those requirements are met, you file as QSS, which

basically gives you a lot of the benefits of being married, even though you technically aren't.

12. When discussing living with you in the above discussions, temporary absences for school, work, military, etc. still count as living with you.

My Advice:

1. If you get married, plan on filing jointly if at all possible. Run a rough estimate of your taxes shortly after getting married and make withholding adjustments as necessary. Talking to a professional is also a good idea.
2. If you get married and one of you is on Income Based Student Loan Repayment, one of you owes back taxes or other Federal Debt, or there are other unusual situations, talk to a tax professional as soon as you can before or after getting married.
3. Do NOT change withholding allowances to Married just because you got married. Chances are, if children are not involved, your combined tax results will be very similar for a two-income household with no kids and leaving them Single is a good start. If one of you was a Single Parent, there are significant differences between you and your spouse's income, or other complications, use the tax withholding calculator at irs.gov to figure out what change to make or talk to a professional.
4. The IRS is looking hard at Head of Household. Make sure that you meet the requirements for using that filing status AND be sure that you can access paperwork to PROVE that you meet the requirements, especially relationship and living status information. This paperwork can be birth certificates, divorce records, adoption papers, school and doctor records.
5. Be careful with filing status especially if you do not fall into one of the obvious categories. If you are getting divorced or your spouse dies, make sure you understand the impact on your tax return.
6. Get a formal, court approved separation agreement in place as soon as possible once your marriage separates so you can avoid having to file Married Filing Separate.

Military: Being separated from your spouse due to being deployed does not count for not living with your spouse for purposes of claiming unmarried for tax purposes (though geographical bachelor probably does). If your dependent lives with you at the time you are deployed, they continue to count as living with you during the deployment, even if you send them to another household (such as your parents) for the time you are deployed. Some people might debate this, but a good rule of thumb is that a non-permanent deployment or assignment does not change the living situation for taxes so long as the intention is for the dependent to return to the pre-deployment living situation when the deployment or temporary assignment ends (sending the child to your ex-spouse who is the child's parent, however, might be trouble). Geographical bachelor or Permanent Change of Station orders would not count as "temporary".

19. The Long Sordid Tax Forms Tale

NOTE: None of this should be construed as a political statement for or against a specific political party, though there is a bit of fun made at general government and politician incompetence.

Back before Trump Tax, there were three main tax forms. The 1040 Long Form, the 1040A Short Form and the 1040EZ. Most people could get away with the 1040A, and only people with very simple tax lives could use the 1040EZ. Everyone could use the 1040, but it was LOOOONG. Which is why it was called the Long Form – weird, I know.

During the Obama years, Congress decided that seniors needed their own EZ tax form, so they mandated that the IRS develop the 1040SR form. The mandate for this form was that it be as easy to use as the 1040EZ, but still allow all the things most seniors had: Social Security income, retirement income on 1099R Forms, investment income from 1099 forms, etc. These instructions were, of course, completely contradictory, so they gave the IRS a bunch of money, and a few years to get it done, so they were diligently working on it when Trump came into office.

The Trump tax reform envisioned one, super easy tax form for everyone, so they simplified the 1040 (mainly by moving everything off the 1040 onto schedules) such that the 1040 was basically a half sheet of paper, front and back, like a postcard. Not that anyone printed it as a half sheet front and back, but it was important to the politicians that it could be called a postcard. This allowed the elimination of the 1040A and 1040EZ, so for 2018 taxes we had one tax form, and 6 schedules.

But nobody remembered to eliminate the 1040SR, or they still wanted it, so in 2019, the 1040SR was revealed. It looked suspiciously like the regular 1040, with two main differences: it included a table of standard deductions right on the form, and the font was bigger. In my system, the bigger font was easy to miss, but when I saw the pre-printed forms from the IRS, the print was HUGE!

They also eliminated 3 of the schedules in 2019, so for 2019 tax year we had a 1040, 1040SR and 3 schedules. The two forms were pretty much interchangeable, and, best as I can tell, home software and professional preparers are not distinguishing between the two when it comes to fees. It just happens that if you meet the requirements for the 1040SR, your printed return has a standard deduction table on it, and bigger print.

What about later years? It looks like the politicians have finally settled down and have quit mucking with things. Maybe we can just keep using the basic 1040 Form (or 1040SR) and the 3 normal schedules for a while. I will keep you posted about this on my website.

20. Can I Use Itemized Deductions?

So…the answer is: Maybe. To help answer that question, this chapter has generic information about itemized deductions. I am going to cover more details of the various deductions during chapters on specific life events or situations. For example, I'll cover charitable deduction requirements and details in the I Give to Charity chapter. Here I'm going to go over the broad strokes and the overall way that itemizing works.

There were major changes made to itemized deduction in 2018, the main one being the elimination of Employee Business Expenses and a bunch of other deductions in a category that was subject to a 2% income limit. For the last few years, I have left the old information in the book, but this year I am yanking it out. Probably a terrible idea since a lot of the provisions expire in a couple years, but they were bogging the book down and making it more complicated to read than necessary.

The first thing you need to understand is that for every filing status, the IRS gives you a deduction that you can take, without having to prove anything or save any receipts. This is called the standard deduction, and it's pretty generous. If you don't have enough qualifying itemized deductions, you generally take the standard deduction. However, there are situations where itemizing is done even though you are below the standard deduction (mainly if it saves you more money on the state return). The standard deductions are (2023 values): $13,850 for Single, $27,700 for MFJ and QSS, $20,800 for HH, and $13,850 for MFS (there are caveats to this so make sure to check the MFS chapter if this applies). You also get an additional $1,850 for being over 65 or blind if you are not married, and $1,500 for each one of you who is over 65 or blind if you are married. There are special rules for children and people being claimed on other person's tax returns, but I will cover those in the relevant chapters.

As you can see by the numbers, you need quite a few deductions before it is worthwhile not taking the standard deduction. I often have people bring me $200 worth of deductions, not realizing it will not make a difference. I tell them about it, but don't make a big deal of it. I would rather have them keep track and not need them, than not keep track and then need them. Here's why: Say you don't keep track for the first ten months, and then an opportunity comes along, or you end up with a huge deductible expense that gets you over the limit. Now all those deductions you did not keep track of are either gone, or a big pain in the butt to reconstruct. That's why you keep all your potentially deductible receipts, even if you're pretty sure you won't itemize. It is also why you bring things you think are deductible to your tax pro and let them tell you they're not deductible. Better to ask and be told no, then not to ask when it would have been deductible.

Here are some general categories of itemized deductions:

Medical expenses: Medical deductions are available, though there are also many caveats. These are limited to the amount that exceeds 7.5% of your AGI. That 7.5% number has been changed and unchanged many times over the last several years but has pretty much been 7.5% straight through and is 7.5% going forward. If you hear someone saying 10%, they are probably incorrect. Check out the I Have Medical Expenses chapter for more.

Taxes: You can deduct real estate taxes, state income tax withheld from your check or paid with your return, personal property tax that you pay to register your car (not the fees, just the taxes) and sales tax. If you deduct state taxes withheld, your refund will generally be included as income next year (this is very confusing, but it does make mathematical sense). The maximum total amount of these that you can deduct is $10,000.

Mortgage Interest: You can deduct the mortgage interest you pay on a first and second home. You can also deduct points paid with some restrictions (these restrictions mostly apply to refinancing or home equity lines). There are limits on the amount of debt you can deduct interest on, but I'll cover those in the I'm Buying (or Already Own) a Home chapter. You can deduct the interest on up to $100,000 of home equity debt, but only if it is used to build or improve your home.

Charitable Contributions: You can deduct contributions made to properly established charities. You can deduct cash and non-cash donations, but not the value of your time. There is a maximum contribution that you can deduct in a single year that varies between 20 and 60% of your AGI, but any not allowed can be carried over to the next year. See the I Donate to Charity chapter. For 2021, you can deduct up to $600 in cash or equivalent donations to qualified charities without having to itemize. The AGI percentage for 2020 was also changed due to the Coronavirus to 100% for cash equivalent donations (not goods or property).

Casualty and Theft Losses: The rules for this have changed significantly since the Trump/GOP Tax Law was passed and vary depending on which disaster and which year. The one common thread is that they now have to be Presidentially declared disasters – no more theft or personal losses like home fires. Read The Disaster Losses Chapter.

Gambling Losses: You have to keep good records and can only deduct them up to how much you won (which you should have claimed as income).

Investment Income Expense: Investment INTEREST is deductible. All other investment expenses are not deductible.

My Advice:

1. Keep track of, or at least save the receipts for medical expenses and charitable contributions even if you do not think you will be itemizing. Also track your medical and charitable mileage. It is easier to have them and not need them than need them and not have them.
2. Do not let your software just assume you can't itemize. Use this list and add up your numbers (at least a ballpark) and see where you are.
3. If you are close to itemizing every year, move charitable deductions, tax payments and other things around to one year and itemize in that year. Go crazy on charity (especially Goodwill type) in the itemizing year and then just accumulate things in other years until you can itemize again.
4. Keep track of who owns your mortgage. If you refinance with a new company, you will need a 1098 from the old AND new company. If your mortgage company sells your mortgage – same thing. Even if they don't sell your mortgage, sometimes they change servicers. USAA did this a few years ago and a lot of service members were quite surprised.
5. Compare deductions that do not change a lot (taxes, mortgage interest) to the prior year's number to make sure you found everything. If the numbers are way off, it is time to find out why. This is a good idea to do even when someone else prepares your return. Check the year over year numbers and make sure you know why they changed.

Military: Generally, you will not have medical expenses since it should be mostly covered, but fertility treatments will sometimes get you there. Make sure to include non-taxable allowances and combat pay when calculating your sales tax deduction. Don't miss the VA funding fee as mortgage insurance (this deduction keeps disappearing and then getting reinstated retroactively so make sure to check if it is deductible in the current year when filing taxes). Your December LES will have a year-to-date charity amount for your CFC and other payroll deduction charity. Uniforms are generally not deductible. If you have to repay a bonus, the Claim of Right repayment discussed above might apply, but not as an itemized deduction – see a tax pro if this applies to you.

21. I am Getting Married

Congratulations!
We have a lot to talk about.

For this chapter, I am going to assume that you are marrying a U.S. citizen and that you plan on living with your new spouse. If the marriage falls apart quickly (let's hope not) you'll want to read this chapter and the chapter on divorce. That's because for this chapter I'm going to assume that your marriage actually lasts through 12/31 of the year with you both still living together. The nice thing about this chapter is that the vast majority of situations are going to apply to most people, so there won't be a lot of hopping around for you. The not so nice thing is that marriage has a lot of tax surprises if you're not prepared. That's one of the things that separates this book from others. If you are doing it right, you're reading this chapter well before tax time, so you'll be ready.

MOST IMPORTANT STUFF! (will be repeated in detail later)

Do NOT just change your W-4 withholding from Single to Married. If both of you are working, it is best to simply leave your W-4 as it is until you see how it affects the next tax return. If only one of you works, that person can safely change their W-4 to married and account for any children in the household as normal – the W-4 works best for a single income household.

If your situation is weird – single, working parents marrying, multiple income sources, it is best to either 1 - work with a tax professional, providing copies of pre marriage tax returns to them or 2 – Use the IRS withholding calculator: https://www.irs.gov/individuals/tax-withholding-estimator.

Make sure that children are only accounted for **ONCE**, between all W-4 forms.

Filing Status:

You only have two choices now: Married Filing Jointly (MFJ) and Married Filing Separately (MFS). I am going to tell you now to plan on filing MFJ. You can run the numbers both ways just in case, but MFJ is usually best. The only reason to file MFS if it doesn't get you a bigger refund is if there is some reason you need to keep your finances separate from your spouse's, you are doing Income Based Student Loan Repayment or they owe money that will be taken from their tax return. If you are considering filing MFS for a reason other than a bigger refund, read the chapter: I Have to File Married Filing Separately.

Note for Picky People: As I said above, this chapter assumes you are married and living with your spouse on 12/31 of the tax year, that's why Head of Household is not an option in this chapter, where it might be for some different and weird Married tax return situations.

Tax Effects:

As a general rule, two basic Single tax returns combined into a MFJ tax return will be mostly unchanged AS A COMBINED RETURN. If one person gets a big refund, and the other a balance due on a Single return, the combined return will be a disappointment to one, and an improvement for the other. I am about to list a lot of reasons why your combined tax return might change, but, if none of them apply, you should be okay with your current withholding. One of the biggest mistakes newlyweds without kids make on taxes is changing their withholdings to Married. This lowers your withholding and causes the combined refund to be lower than the combined refunds were when they were Single tax returns. If you DO change to Married, and your spouse also works and earns income, make sure both of you check Box C in Step 2 of the new W-4 form.

The following factors should be considered, as they may cause refunds to change:

1. Head of Household (HH): If one of you is filing HH before you get married, at the very least, the combined standard deduction and tax tables will not be as good MFJ. I will talk about kids next, but you obviously have at least one if someone filed HH. The MFJ standard deduction and tax tables are pretty much double the Single tax tables: you would see no difference going Single/Single to MFJ if nothing else applied. HH has a higher standard deduction and better tax tables than Single, so going HH/Single or worse, HH/HH to MFJ, is going to impact the tax return. For middle income couples, HH has higher limits at which various benefits start phasing out, though most are the same as Single. Retirement Savings Credit is an example of one where you might get hurt.

2. Children: The big thing with children is Earned Income Credit. I am not going to run the numbers for every scenario but suffice it to say that a combined income is going to hurt when compared to an individual income.

I cover the exact numbers for EIC in the I'm Having a Child chapter. EIC involves BIG numbers that can be dramatically affected by marriage, and you cannot avoid them by filing MFS. A person with a child and an income of $13,000 per year who marries a person making $50,000 is going to see a refund drop in the THOUSANDS! I often say to emphasize that there's no support test for EIC: "You can live with Mark Zuckerberg and still get EIC. However, you can't MARRY him and get EIC." The point being that you can live with someone and they do not affect your EIC (generally), but you can't MARRY them without having it affect your EIC.

3. AGI Limited Items: Itemized deductions are the best example of this, where medical expenses are limited based on a percentage of your AGI (7.5%). If one person has the deductions, the combined income will make them less deductible. The limit for charitable deductions (in most cases) is no MORE than 60% of your income (for 2020, the limit was increased to 100% for cash contributions to charity), so if you give a ton to charity, the combined income might let you deduct more.

4. Federal Debt: If one of you owes back taxes, student loans, child support, excess VA payments, or a number of other things, they can be taken directly out of your federal refund. Talk to your future spouse to find out about these things BEFORE you get married. You can file an Injured Spouse claim to prevent the entire refund from being taken, but it is a bit of a pain. I would get professional help BEFORE filing if this is the case and you are considering filing separately or using an Injured Spouse Claim. During the Coronavirus pandemic, collections from refunds for everything other than Child Support was suspended and then various stimulus payments had different rules for what can be taken.

5. Others: Most of the rest of the tax provisions are affected by filing MFJ, but the numbers are usually exactly doubled, so they rarely make a big difference. It's possible that if one of the newlyweds has something that's affected but the other doesn't that the increased limit might be helpful. A good example is that a Single person can exclude up to $250,000 of gain on the sale of a main home, while a couple can exclude $500,000 (there are a lot of other rules so be aware that this is just an example).

There might be a few things I'm missing, but those are the big things. If none of the reasons that cause refunds to change applies to you, and you're happy with the total that your previous year's Single tax returns would get you (assuming no other big changes), leave your withholding alone.

Withholding:

So, the question is: Do you adjust your withholding?
The answer is: maybe?

If none of the discussions above apply to you, I would leave things alone and see what happens. Sometimes you can be too proactive.

If any do apply and you feel a need to adjust your withholding, read Chapters 10 or 11 about getting a bigger or smaller refund (they are basically the same just from differing perspectives. They will link you to the IRS withholding calculator and also give instructions for filling out the brand-new W-4 form for many common scenarios.

A good trick is to run a fake return for you as a couple using the information from your previous year's returns. If you use software, you can probably just add your new spouse to your last year's return. Make sure to save a copy of the original!

I'm sorry that this is so nebulous, but withholding is not an exact science.

My Advice:

1. Do not change your withholding until you have filed your first tax return as a married couple. If you do change your withholding, do not forget Box C in Step 2 if you both work. If you are a single income household, changing to married will be fine.
2. Make sure children are accounted for on only ONE W-4 form. You only get one credit for each of them on your tax return, so you don't want multiple credits used on your withholding estimate.
3. I now have a few years of experience with people and human resources using the new W-4 form and payroll people are continuing to mess it up. I have generally started advising my two income families to ignore Step 2 and Box C and just file as Single when both spouses work. Also, to be redundant because I can't say this enough, make sure kids are only accounted for on ONE W-4 (generally the highest income source). All other W-4's for different jobs or your spouse should have no kids on them.
4. Do not change the name on your Social Security Card within a month before filing your tax return. It takes a while for a name change to work its way through the system, so your return might reject if it has not been updated. If your return rejects following a recent name change, just change the name on the return to your maiden name and refile. There is no

problem or worry doing this, and it should get through without a lot of trouble.

5. Unless your tax situation is simple, it might not be a bad idea to take the tax returns you most recently filed and run a simulated tax return using the same documents as a joint tax return, just to see if it's going to have a big effect. The easiest way to do this is to ask a tax pro to do it (if either one of you already uses a tax pro just bring the new spouses prior return to them). If you use software, just pull up one of your returns and add the spouses information to it (make sure you can use a "what-if" mode or can save the original return. If it doesn't allow you to do this, make note of everything you add and then go take it back out. Print a physical copy of the return FIRST!

6. Do not file your tax return as Single if you are married, even if the tax changes are devastating. Just don't. Note I'm talking about the TAX RETURN, not your W-4 form for withholding. The W-4 can be Single, your tax return has to be married if you are.

7. If you use tax software, it generally will have an estimated refund that updates as you add information. Do NOT look at it! You will add one piece of income and see a huge refund, get excited, and then add more income and watch it plummet. That information is useless until ALL your data is in.

Military: If you are going to be deployed, make sure to get a Power of Attorney (POA) that covers taxes. A POA prepared by the military must be accepted even if it does not fully match state requirements. You can adjust your withholding on MyPay, usually as often as once a month. There are a lot of other military things that are affected by marriage, but most of them aren't tax related. Ask your Chain of Command for help.

Military Spouses Residency Relief Act: The spouse of an active-duty military member has two choices for state of residency: The state they live/work in, or the military member's state. They must be in their current state only to be with the service member and the military member must be stationed in the state you live/work in on PERMANENT orders. Some states can be enormous pains in the ass about this, and (for example) at one time, Louisiana believed that you HAD to select Louisiana even if you no longer live there, so be wary of ANY communication from the state about this. They can be extremely, and stubbornly wrong in a ton of different ways. Some states, such as South Carolina, have a much more liberal view, such that your spouse could be stationed in GA, while you work in South Carolina, and you can still claim the military member's state. Check with a tax professional if your situation is weird like this. (For 2017 and before, there was an additional test where, in order to choose the military member's state, the spouse must have at some time established a domicile/residency in that state – but it was eliminated for 2018 and later).

The choice is not as easy as it sounds. Obviously, if the military member is from a tax-free state like Florida or Texas, it's a no brainer. Be careful if they are from a state that is tax free FOR MILITARY. Also, be aware that some states (like California or South Carolina) treat military spouses very well. Consider seeking professional help to make the decision.

Recent changes to the Soldier's and Sailor's Civil relief Act made explicit the idea that a service member might choose their SPOUSE state of residency as their ultimate, post service destination and that might affect the choice of state of residency. It allows a service member to elect the spouse's state of residency if they choose. The big difference between this and the Military Spouses Residency Relief Act is that the service member can, and should, change residency using DD Form 2058. This changes state of residency, but not home of record, and primarily affects taxes. Even if you neglect to file DD Form 2058, you can probably file as a resident of your spouses state, as long as you are consistent in later years and ultimately file DD Form 2058 – basically, you might not know this is an option until your tax pro tells you – or you read this book.

Make sure your state of residency for taxes is the state you register and vote in. Car registration, driver's licenses, etc. are beyond the scope of this book, and are a state law issue, but voting and residency go hand in hand.

22. I am Having (or Already Have) a Child

Congratulations! Kids are just about the best tax deduction out there; unfortunately, they are going to cost you a lot more in life than they save you in taxes!

I'm going to spend a lot of time talking about weird situations involving children later in the book, but for this chapter, I'm going to assume a traditional parent/child/family situation and go over what's available from start to finish. I am also going to assume that you and the child are U.S. citizens living in the U.S., and that at least one of the following applies:

- You are either married to the other parent,
- The other parent is not in the picture, or
- The other parent does not have custody and has no rights to claim the child.

MOST IMPORTANT!! (Details repeated later)

Protect your child's Social Security Number. Don't share it with anyone who doesn't absolutely need it.

Make sure that when you add the child to your W-4 forms that they are only added on ONE job. Otherwise, you are claiming more children than you have and tax time will be a bummer.

Recent Tax Changes:

Let me go over a bunch of things that have changed in the last few years, just so you can realize how crazy things have been, and to help you understand what applies in what year:

2018 Trump/GOP Tax Law Changes: This chapter was dramatically affected by the new tax law.

- You no longer get a deduction for your child. It was $4050 in prior years but now is zero.
- Instead of the previous deduction, they doubled the Child Tax Credit (what you get for children until they turn 17) to $2000 and give a credit of $500 for all other dependents. To be clear, it is EITHER $2000 or $500. You don't get both for kids under the age of 17.
- The income above which you lose the Child tax Credit was dramatically raised. For example, in 2017, the limit was $110,000 – after 2018 it is $400,000.

- 529 plans can now be used for private K-12 school tuition of up to $10,000 per year, per child. This does not eliminate taxes on the withdrawal, just the penalty.
- The Kiddie Tax was dramatically simplified, such that children's investment income above $2200 is now taxed at Trust/Estate rates instead of at the parent's rate. This simplifies things, but the tax rates are bad. This requirement has been repealed retroactively, but you don't have to go back and change things if you don't want to, but the old rules are used for 2020 and later.

2019 and 2020 Changes:
- You can use up to $10,000 from your 529 plans to pay off student loans without paying taxes on the earnings.
- You can take $5000 out of retirement accounts penalty free in the year after having or adopting a child. Each parent can do this, so you can get $10,000 out. You can put it back within the year and owe no taxes on it. If you do not you pay taxes on the withdrawal, but no penalty. I don't recommend doing this if you can avoid it, and seek assistance form a good tax dude or financial advisor if you do decide to try this.
- The Kiddie tax rules discussed above were retroactively eliminated.
- There is a $500 and a $600 stimulus check for each child under 17 that you claimed on your 2020 tax return and a $1400 stimulus payment for all dependents you claim on your 2021 tax return, regardless of age (paid in advance based on your 2019 or 2020 tax return). Parents who swapped children year over year often got extra payments for the same child, and these payments are not required to be paid back.

2021 Changes (affect 2021 ONLY):

- The daycare credit was significantly improved for 2021 only. In the chapter on daycare forthcoming, I am going to provide a comparison of the 2020 and 2021 credit to help you understand how big the changes were.
- The Child Tax Credit discussed later also had significant modifications which will also be discussed in this chapter when we go over it. Highlights include: 1. Increasing the credit by $1000 ($1600 for children 5 and under) though to get the full benefit your AGI needs to be below $150,000 for MFJ, $112,500 for HH and $75,000 for all other filing status. 2. Raising the qualifying age to

17 (one year older). 3. Making the entire amount refundable vice only $1400, meaning you can get the entire credit available after taxes reach zero. They also eliminated the income for qualifying for this refundable amount. 4. Up to 50% of the credit will be sent in advance, starting in July, based on 2020 or 2019 tax returns. The advances will be reconciled on the 2021 tax return and excess payments will be deducted from the 2021 tax return except for individuals with income below a threshold (discussed in detail later in this chapter).

- You can calculate 2021 Earned Income Tax Credit using either 2019 earned income or 2021 earned income, whichever results in a higher credit.
- The Earned Income Tax Credit was slightly modified by raising the Investment Income Limit. Previously, you could not get Earned Income Credit if you made more than $3650 in investment income. This number was raised to $10,000. Unlike the previous changes discussed, this applies to all subsequent years and not just to 2021.

2022/2023 Changes: I just added this to clarify that most things are back to normal regarding children. No advances of tax credits and no super big credits, but the permanent changes from 2018 – 2020 are still in effect, such as the $2000 per child Child Tax Credit and $500 for all other dependents.

Here is the rest of the chapter:

First big piece of advice—get them a Social Security Number (should be automatic unless you are living abroad), keep it safe and secret, and make sure you know how to spell their name exactly as it appears on the Social Security Card and make sure you remember their birthday (you probably think this is obvious, but do a few thousand tax returns and you would be surprised how many people mess this up). If you do not have the SSN by the tax deadline, File an extension BEFORE the deadline or you might lose some credits.

The name, SSN and birthday on the tax return must match the Social Security Card and IRS records EXACTLY. This is one of the most common causes of problems on tax returns. Also, as I said, protect the SSN. If someone else has their name, SSN and birthday, there is nothing stopping them from claiming your child before you do, and that will create big problems for you to deal with.

NOTE: Support is discussed periodically below and is usually obvious and straightforward. I have included a Support Worksheet in Appendix A if you need more details.

I'm going to cover things chronologically, starting with the things that disappear first. Before that, some fine print:

1. If the child is born before midnight on 12/31 of the tax year, they count as living with you all year.
2. This one is a little depressing, but if the child dies before 12/31 at midnight, they still count as living with you all year. Be careful on this though—file early if your child dies. For some stupid reason, it is extremely easy for identity thieves to get a deceased child's information and fraudulently claim them. You can recover, but it is painful.
3. Even more depressing, if your child is born and dies in the same year, you still get to claim them. This applies for any amount of time. If the child is born alive, even if it immediately dies, you may claim the child. You have to make sure to get a SSN and birth certificate, which will unfortunately be the last thing you will be concerned with if this happens to you. If the child is stillborn, you may not claim the child.

Claiming the child as a dependent: Generally speaking, the assumptions we talked about for this chapter will make claiming the child a slam dunk, at least for the first 16 years or so. Claiming a child is actually one of the more complex tax things, but, when you are the parent and the child lives with you, most of the requirements are covered right there. Starting in 2018, you no longer get a deduction for your child (was $4050 in 2017). Instead, the main thing left is the Child Tax Credit (discussed shortly) if they are under 17, or a $500 non-refundable credit if they are 17 or over.

There are a few things to be aware of:

1. The child must live with you for at least 6 months and a day during the tax year (calendar year really). They can be absent for vacations, school, medical care and even detention in a juvenile facility—those still count as days living in your household.
2. The child cannot have provided more than half of their own support (Appendix A Test 1). Note that this does not mean that YOU have to support them, they just can't provide more than half of their own support. This test changes if they are too old based on item 3 below. If they are too old, then YOU (together with your spouse if MFJ) must provide over half of the child's support (Appendix A Test 2). More details below under 5 - 7.

3. They must be under age 19, or under age 24 if a full-time student for at least 5 months, or any age if disabled. If not, additional tests must be met:

     a. Support test listed under bullet 2 above changes as noted in the bullet (YOU have to pay half their support vice them just not paying half themselves).

     b. The child's income cannot exceed $4,700 (the test says "gross" but it is effectively "taxable" – see a pro if your child has sources of income other than Social Security that exceeds $4,700). Sometimes a child receives Social Security benefits due to a deceased parent. Social Security benefits will not affect this test because even though it could be taxable, the income levels that make it taxable would be higher than $4,700, so you would have already failed the test.

4. Note that when a child starts making their own income, turns 18, or goes to college, things start to change. A child can simply move out once they're 18, and no divorce decree, custody document or anything else can get you back to claiming them (assuming they move out before July 1st). They also start messing with who provides over half their support. I have a number of chapters coming up about your child's life events, so keep an eye out and read them as your child gets older.

5. Support **from** the child includes: wages, investment income, scholarships, student loans that the child is obligated to pay back, unemployment income and savings withdrawals. Any of the above that are not spent for support (generally this means added to savings) don't count as support from the child.

6. Support **for** the child includes: cost of the home (fair rental value of the home plus utilities, repairs, taxes, insurance and other household costs divided by number of occupants), education, entertainment, clothing, medical, travel and other necessary expenses.

7. If the child is young enough that 3 above doesn't apply, you simply determine if the support **from** the child (total from 5) is less than half of the support **for** the child (total from 6). If the child is old enough that 3 does apply, then you determine if YOU (together with your spouse if MFJ) provide over half of support **for** the child (total from 6).

Daycare (also read 2021 updates at the end of this chapter for specifics for that year only): Up until your child turns 13 (to the day—not the age on January 1st), you can get a credit of between 20 and 35 percent of any daycare expenses that you pay while you work or look for work (though you must ultimately earn income if looking for work). If you are married and filing jointly, both you and your spouse must be working or looking for work, though one of you may be a student or disabled. Being self-employed counts as work, as long as you make a profit. What happens is that you take either your income (and your spouse's if MFJ), how much you pay for daycare, and the limit for how much the IRS allows, whichever is **smaller**. You then subtract any money you get from your job for daycare (will be reported on your W-2 in Box 10), and then multiply it by a percentage between 20 and 35, depending on your income. This amount comes right off of your taxes due but cannot reduce them below zero. If you are a student or disabled, you obviously don't have income, so the IRS allows you to use $250 per month ($500 for 2 or more qualifying children) for every month you are disabled or a student as your income (one spouse must be working and have earned income, the other may be a student or disabled).

I often get questions on if it is better to use a Child Care Flexible Spending Account (FSA) or your own money for daycare, due to the tax credit. The answer is that, unless your income is pretty low, the FSA account is almost always better because it avoids the 7.65% in Social Security and Medicare taxes, in addition to your regular taxes. If you are like most people, in the 12 or 22% tax bracket or somewhere in between, you will get a 19.65% to 29.65% benefit from the FSA (plus possibly a state benefit) as compared to the 20% credit you will most likely get from the credit. When in doubt, do the FSA.

Now for the fine print:

1. The 13-year age limit is waived if your child can't take care of them self due to a disability. You will need to back this up with a doctor's statement.
2. The limit for how much you can get a credit for is $3,000 if you have one child under 13, and $6,000 if you have two or more. They don't both have to be going to daycare, they just have to qualify based on age. This is a common source of lost refund money by allocating the expenses to the child it is paid for – this is not required, total the expenses for ALL qualifying children, and take the expenses up to the limit based on if you have one or two children.
3. You cannot get this credit if you are filing MFS.
4. It has to be daycare, not school. You don't get squat for private school or home school. You can get credit if you pay for after school care, even if it is to their regular school. It just has to be separately stated from other payments.
5. Speaking of statements, you should get a receipt from the provider. You will need the amount paid, the name and address, and their Employer Identification Number (for a professional) or their SSN (for an individual).

6. That said, make sure that the person taking care of your children gives you this information up front. It is a very awkward conversation at tax time when you find out your provider won't give it to you because they don't plan on claiming the income on their taxes! This would be illegal, of course. You generally don't need to worry about this if they are a professional daycare provider, such as a Child Development Center.

7. You generally cannot claim the credit for money paid to your children, your spouse or the child's parent, even if they aren't your spouse.

8. Day camps can count, but not overnight camps. The day camp can be activity related, like band camp, and still qualify.

9. If you get daycare money from your job in excess of what you spend on qualified daycare, it's taxable income and is reported on the same line as your wages. If your job reimburses more than $5,000 of daycare expenses, the excess is taxable income. (Most software handles this smoothly if you enter everything from your W-2 right.)

10. If you have a live-in nanny or housekeeper, you can claim payments that are specifically for childcare. If the primary purpose is childcare, and they do some minor household tasks, you can take the entire amount paid. Be aware that if you pay a live-in nanny more than $2400 per year, you may have to pay them as an employee and withhold taxes. This is a mess! See a pro or a company that handles nanny tax issues for you.

11. If the daycare provider provides transport, you can include that expense. You cannot include cost of transport you provide.

12. Unemployment compensation is not earned income for determining eligibility for this credit.

13. You generally must claim the child as your dependent (discussed in previous paragraphs).

14. The child must live with you for at least 6 months and a day (they can be away at school, on vacation and other temporary absences and still count as living with you, they basically just can't be living with someone else).

For 2021 ONLY: The Coronavirus relief bill passed in late 2020 had major changes for the daycare credit that are significant. Rather than list all the changes, I am going to do a quick comparison of the 2020/2022 and 2021 credits here:

Here is the 2020/2022 calculation:

$3000 max in expenses for one child. $6000 for two children. Get a credit for 35% of expenses if income (technically AGI) is below $15,000, then it drops quickly by 1% every $2000 of income until it hits 20% of expenses, where it stays forever. You cannot use this credit once your taxes hit zero.

Here is the 2021 calculation:

$8000 in expenses for one child. $16000 for two children. Credit of 50% of expenses if income is below $125,000, then it drops to 20% as income goes up to $185,000, where it stays until income hits $400,000, where it quickly drops to zero as income gets to $440,000. Here is the **BIG DEAL**: You can get this credit even after your taxes hit zero.

So, if you are good at math, most people get a maximum credit of $1200 for two children in 2020/2022, and once they hit zero taxes, it no longer helps. In 2021, the maximum credit for most people with two children will be $8000, and you can get the credit even if your taxes hit zero.

Child Tax Credit (CTC) (also read 2021 updates at the end of this chapter for specifics for that year only): Up until the year your child turns 17, you get a $2,000 credit off of your taxes. This credit cannot reduce your taxes below zero, but once you hit zero, another credit immediately appears. This additional credit has a confusing name that makes no real sense—the name is a carryover from when the credit was different (it is called the Additional Child Tax Credit). Anyway, I prefer to treat it as an extension of the normal Child Tax Credit. Basically, you can get $2,000 for every child you have under 17 with no limit on the number of children (there is an income limit, discussed later). You calculate your taxes, and then reduce them by all your credits, in a certain order (most are taken before the CTC, leaving a lot of it behind to potentially reduce your taxes below zero). You take whatever wasn't needed to get you to zero, and do a calculation based on your income to figure out how much you get back from the government even when you are already at zero taxes owed! Here's the fine print:

1. The credit phases out by $50 for every $1,000 your AGI exceeds $400,000 if MFJ, $200,000 for other filing statuses.
2. Don't look for a loophole around age 17, there isn't one. This is one of the few times when there is no exception to the age rules. You get 16 years of Child Tax Credit per child, no more.
3. The child must live with you for at least 6 months and a day (they can be away at school, on vacation and other temporary absences and still count as living with you, they basically just can't be living with someone else).

4. You must claim the child as a dependent (discussed in the first few paragraphs).

5. The credit can exceed your total taxes if your earned income (generally wages or business profit) exceeds $2,500. After reducing your taxes to zero, you take your earned income minus $2,500, multiply it by 0.15, and take the smaller of that number, and the amount of credit that was left after you reduced your taxes to zero. There is a maximum of $1,500 per child that can be refundable.

6. Refunds with refundable Child Tax Credit can take until after 2/27/18 to arrive.

For 2021 ONLY:

1. The qualifying age is raised by one year to 18.

2. The credit is made fully refundable, regardless of income.

3. The credit is increased to $3000 for children age 6 and older and $3600 for children 5 and under. This applies only if AGI is below $150,000 when filing Married Filing Jointly, $112,500 filing Head of Household and $75,000 for all other status. Above these incomes, the credit is reduced by $50 for every $1000 of income above the limit, but not below the normal $2000 credit (unless income exceeds the "normal" limits discussed above).

4. The IRS is going to use a very complicated system to send up to 50% of your Child Tax Credit to you in monthly payments starting in July of 2021 until the end of the year. Full details have not been released, but they will use your 2020 tax information (2019 if you haven't filed 2020) to determine these amounts. They will also use other sources to adjust for born or died children, as well as create a system to allow you to opt out. Advance payments have to be reconciled on 2021 tax returns, so if they overpay you, you have to pay the excess back, unless your income is below $60,000 (MFJ/QSS), $50,000 (HH) or $40,000 (Single/MFS).

The above advance payments of the Child Tax Credit, as well as the income limits for the extra amounts, create numerous complicated situations that can impact both year's of tax returns. If your income will be close to the applicable AGI limits, maximizing traditional 401k and Health Savings Account contributions can make a major difference. If the number of children you claim varies due to birth, death, divorce or other family changes, you can find yourself with some real trouble when you get too much advance credit. Talk to your tax person (or consult with one if you self-prepare) to save you a LOT of trouble with this. Keep an eye on the IRS website for details on the new rules.

Earned Income Tax Credit (EITC or EIC): If you have kids under age 19 (24 if in school half time or more for at least 5 months out of the year, or disabled), and don't make a lot of money, EIC is a HUGE benefit. Because of this, there is a ton of fraud, including those people trying to steal your kid's identities. The IRS is focusing a lot of attention on the credit, and there are a lot of hoops to jump through. The idea of EIC is to encourage people with children and limited income to work more and earn more money. In return for this, the IRS gives them a tax credit against their tax due. (It gets better, the EIC can reduce your taxes below zero, resulting in free money from the government). In order to do this, the Credit works weirdly with income. If you have no Earned Income, you get no EIC. As you make small amounts of money, the EIC goes up until it reaches a point where the government thinks you're doing okay, so it levels off for a while as your income goes up, and then, when you are earning even more income, it starts to go down until finally it fades away. You get a higher amount of credit for every child up until three, then you get the same for more than three as you get for three. I'll cover the specific ranges in the details so you can get an idea how much we're talking about.

For 2020 and 2021 only: You can use 2019 earned income to calculate Earned Income Credit if the current year income is lower than 2019 and it results in a better credit. For 2020, you had to be able to say that the lower income was due to COVID-19. For 2021, this is not a requirement.

1. If you are self-employed you cannot manipulate your business expenses to qualify for more EIC. This is an area the IRS takes seriously, and you can expect your tax pro to ask you a lot of probing questions on the subject. The reason for this is that we can be fined for not being suspicious enough. Believe it or not, we can just take your word on most things with no real risk to ourselves – this is not one of those things.
2. Your child cannot file a joint return with their spouse unless they are not required to file and are only filing to get back their withholding. Your child can be married, but they must still live with you.
3. There is no support test for EIC. I state this because many people will fail to claim EIC because they don't support the child. You can live with Mark Zuckerberg and still get EIC! Though if you marry him it's all gone.
4. The child must live with you for at least 6 months and a day (they can be away at school, on vacation and other temporary absences and still count as living with you, they basically just can't be living with someone else).
5. You cannot get EIC no matter how little you earn if you have investment income of over $11,000 for the year. Investment income includes taxable and non-taxable interest, dividends, royalties, capital gains (profits from

selling investments) and other income reported on Schedule E (rents and royalties). You also include your children's investment income if you are subject to Kiddie Tax (discussed later).

6. Your earned income is generally your wages and business income (self-employment income) from your tax return. If you had taxable scholarships, you subtract them off. If you had non-taxable combat pay, you may include all or none of it, whichever is better for you. If you have non-earned income, such as unemployment compensation or retirement income, you get the lower EIC amount calculated when including it and not including it (in other words, most unearned income can hurt, but not help EIC).

7. Speaking of unemployment, the following are NOT earned income: unemployment compensation, pensions, annuities, Social Security, alimony, child support, welfare benefits, workman's comp, VA benefits, non-taxable military allowances, investment income and tax-free foster care payments. Disability payments may or may not be earned income. You'll want to ask for help with this if you are receiving taxable disability payments.

8. The IRS is serious about EIC fraud. Don't claim it if you don't qualify. They do want you to get it if you deserve it. Don't be surprised if your paid preparer asks a lot of questions about your life situation when discussing EIC. The IRS puts extra due diligence requirements on us for EIC, and we can be fined if we ignore things that make an EIC claim questionable. Also, if you claim EIC when not entitled to it, the IRS can require you to file additional forms for subsequent years. They may even bar you from claiming EIC for a child for 2 to 10 years, depending on how flagrant you were.

9. You cannot get EIC if you file MFS. Starting in 2021, the rules were relaxed on this if you did not live with your spouse the last half of the year, or you were legally separated (through the courts) and did not live with your spouse on the last day of the year.

10. Everyone needs a valid Social Security Card (parents and children).

11. You cannot be filing Form 2555 for the Foreign Earned Income Exclusion and also get EIC.

12. Refunds with EIC can take until after February 27th of the filing year to arrive, even if you file early in January. This is to prevent Tax Identity Theft and seems to have been very effective.

13. EIC amounts vary depending on how many children you have (one, two, and three or more), your income, and your filing status (one amount for MFJ, another for all the rest. Here's a rundown.

      a. If you have one child and are MFJ, the credit goes up from 0 to a maximum of $3,995 as your income goes up, and then starts to go back down as you make more money until it is gone at an income of $53,120.

b. If you have two children and are MFJ, the credit goes up from 0 to a maximum of $6,604 as your income goes up, and then starts to go back down as you make more money until it is gone at an income of $59,478

c. If you have three or more children and are MFJ, the credit goes up from 0 to a maximum of $7,430 as your income goes up, and then starts to go back down as you make more money until it is gone at an income of $63,398.

d. If you have one child and are not MFJ, the credit goes up from 0 to a maximum of $3,995 as your income goes up, and then starts to go back down as you make more money until it is gone at an income of $46,560.

e. If you have two children and are not MFJ, the credit goes up from 0 to a maximum of $6,604 as your income goes up, and then starts to go back down as you make more money until it is gone at an income of $52,918.

f. If you have three or more children and are not MFJ, the credit goes up from 0 to a maximum of $7,430 as your income goes up, and then starts to go back down as you make more money until it is gone at an income of $56,838.

College Savings Plans: You can contribute to a college savings plan for your child. There are two kinds: Qualified Tuition Programs (QTP) and Coverdell Education Savings Accounts (ESA). QTPs are set up by individual states and are sometimes called 529 plans or college savings plans. ESAs are set up by an individual for the benefit of their child. I'm not going to go into a ton of detail because you should discuss these with your financial advisor, but I will hit some high points:

1. Contributions are not deductible (though your state may allow you a deduction on your state taxes for contributions to your state's QTP).
2. There is a $2,000 per year limit for contributions to an ESA. There is no limit for QTPs (except as established by individual states – usually related to what it costs for 4 years of college).
3. Contributions grow tax deferred (earnings are not taxed).
4. You do not need to be related to set up and contribute to a QTP for someone. An ESA is limited to parents and children.
5. Withdrawals are subject to taxes and penalties if not properly used for education (only the earnings). ESA contributions must be withdrawn when the beneficiary turns 30. If properly used for education, amounts withdrawn from either type of these accounts are not taxed or penalized. For 2018 and beyond, qualified expenses for 529 plans include private

elementary and secondary schools. Starting in 2020, you can withdraw up to $10,000 from a 529 plan to pay off student loans without having to pay taxes on the earnings.

6. Talk to your financial planner AND your tax professional before setting up one of these or withdrawing from one.

7. Many states offer a tax deduction for contributing to one of their 529 plans. Many also have no rules regarding the timing of withdrawals as long as they are used for education expenses. This means it's possible that even if you already have money for tuition outside of a tax deferred account, you might get a state tax deduction by contributing it to a 529 plan in your state, and then immediately pulling it out to pay the tuition. Talk to a tax expert in your state before trying this.

Education Credits and Deductions: If you can still claim your child while they attend college, you can get an education credit or deduction for them. I'll cover them in more detail in the I (or my Spouse or Child) is Going to College chapter.

Student Loan Interest Deduction: You can deduct student loan interest you pay of up to $2,500 per tax return for student loans that you are obligated to repay. This means that if you pay your child's student loan for them, you cannot deduct the interest. I'll cover them in more detail in the I am Paying on Student Loans chapter.

Kiddie Tax: Having kids isn't all roses and sunshine for tax purposes. The dreaded Kiddie Tax is designed to prevent you from shifting your investments to your child's name so that you can pay taxes at a lower rate (since your kid probably doesn't have a high tax bracket). This sucker is COMPLICATED, but I'll do my best to put it in plain English. Kiddie Tax kicks in when your child has unearned income of more than $2,200. Some people call this investment income, but that's really not true. For Kiddie Tax, unearned income is ALL taxable income that's not wages, salaries, tips, or payments for services (like running a lawn mowing business). That means it includes unemployment, Social Security payments (if taxable— which happens if the child has a lot of other income), and investment income (also Alaska Permanent Fund Dividends). Kiddie Tax applies until the child turns 18, but if the child doesn't provide more than half of their own support at age 18, the Kiddie Tax applies in that year as well. Also, if the child is a full-time student, Kiddie Tax applies until they turn 24, unless they provide over half of their own support. There's more, but I'll hit it in bullets now:

1. The Kiddie Tax applies even if you're not claiming the child. Many people try to avoid this for older children by just not claiming them, but, if you qualify to claim them by the rules – the Kiddie Tax applies even if you don't do it.
2. The Kiddie Tax works by taxing your child's income above $2,300 at YOUR tax rate. If they have no earned income, the first $1,100 of their income is tax free, the next $1,150 is taxed in the 10% tax bracket, and the rest is taxed at YOUR highest tax rate (though they still get a standard deduction).
3. You calculate their tax using Form 8615, which will take their income, and calculate taxes based on your tax rate.
4. You can elect to include the child's income on your tax return instead of filing Form 8615. You do this by filing Form 8814 with your tax return.
5. There's more about who has to claim the income in weird parental situations, but this chapter isn't about that—Thank God.
6. I'm going to add this just to be clear: If your child has a small amount of investment income in their name, as long as the earnings don't exceed $1,150, you don't have to do anything with it (unless the child has a job that requires them to file, of course).

One thing to note: The Trump Tax Law changed this to require taxes be paid at Estate and Trust rates, rather than the parent's rate. This was changed retroactively so the old law applies in all years. If you paid taxes at Estate or Trust rates in 2018 or 2019, you may amend the tax return to get any excess taxes paid back.

Itemized Deductions: You can claim itemized deductions paid on behalf of your children.

1. You can claim medical expenses you paid for your child while you are still claiming them as a dependent.
2. Even if you aren't able to claim them as a dependent, you can still take medical expenses you pay for them if the reason you can't claim them is they filed a joint return, or their gross income was over $4,700 (see above on claiming your child as a dependent if you don't understand why these matter.) There are other exceptions but they'll be covered in the I'm Getting a Divorce and various I'm Living with... chapters.
3. You can generally take a charitable deduction when you give away your child's stuff while they are under 18. After that, it's a bit shaky. However, if you paid for it while they were a child and they left it behind, I'd deduct it.
4. Other itemized deductions that you pay on behalf of your child will depend on a case-by-case basis. If you buy your child a car, titled and

registered in their name, and pay the personal property taxes on it for them, they are probably not deductible. If the car was titled and registered to you, even though you considered it their car, you probably can deduct them.

The next chapter dovetails directly from this one, and it's about your child getting a job!

My Advice:

1. Don't claim kids you don't fully qualify to claim. Just don't.
2. Don't let people claim your children if they aren't entitled to do so. It's not okay, and, as I see all the time, they will continue to do it even after you tell them not to.
3. Pay attention to your children's ages and be prepared for the tax hits. No daycare credit once they turn 13, $1500 less in Child Tax Credit the year they turn 17, EIC goes away at 19, or 24 if they are in school.
4. Get a daycare provider's SSN or EIN up front.
5. If someone takes care of your children in your home, make sure that you handle the taxes correctly as discussed above. Do not ignore them or try to circumvent them. I am not saying this just to be a tax rules psycho, but because the implications for you and your employee are a big deal and should not be trifled with.
6. If you paid Kiddie Tax in 2018 or 2019, check to see if you can get some of the taxes paid back by using the parent's tax rate versus the Trust and estate tax rate.
7. If you have children in private school, look to see if your state has a deduction for 529 plan contributions. You might be able to funnel the tuition through a 529 plan and save on state taxes. Get help from a tax professional if you think this will work for you.
8. When your child goes to college, get professional tax help if they are receiving tax-free scholarships or you are using a 529 plan to pay the tuition. You can lose $10,000 in tax credits over 4 years of college if you don't plan these things out correctly.
9. When in doubt, do the daycare Flexible Spending Account (FSA). I often get questions on if it is better to use a Child Care Flexible Spending Account (FSA) or your own money for daycare, due to the tax credit. The answer is that, unless your income is pretty low, the FSA account is almost always better because it avoids the 7.65% in Social Security and Medicare taxes, in addition to your regular taxes. If you are like most people, in the 12 or 22% tax bracket or somewhere in between, you will get a 19.65% to 29.65% benefit from the FSA (plus possibly a state benefit) as compared to the 20% credit you will most likely get from the credit.

Military: If a child lives with you at the time you are deployed they continue to count as living with you during the deployment, even if you send them to another household (such as your parent's) for the time you are deployed. Some people might debate this, but a good rule of thumb is that a non-permanent deployment or assignment does not change the living situation for taxes so long as the intention is for the dependent to return to the pre-deployment living situation when the deployment or temporary assignment ends (sending the child to your ex-spouse who is the child's parent might be trouble). Geographical bachelor or Permanent Change of Station orders would not count as "temporary".

Combat pay can be all included, or all excluded for EIC and most AGI limitations.

If you are stationed outside of the U.S. that still counts as living in the U.S. including for your family.

Not discussed: Unusual parental situations.

23. My Kid Is Getting a Job

Like the previous chapter, I am going to assume a traditional parent/child/family situation. I am also going to assume that you and the child are U.S. citizens living in the U.S., and that at least one of the following applies:

- You are either married to the other parent,
- The other parent is not in the picture, or
- The other parent does not have custody and has no rights to claim the child.

I'm going to start with the first and most important thing, even though it's not technically a tax law: As long as your child lives at home (even if they go away to college for a while) make them get their W-2 come tax time and IMMEDIATELY give it to you. Under no circumstances are they to file their taxes without going through you! Way too many tax returns are screwed up by a child filing their taxes without consulting their parents. Now it may turn out that you cannot claim them, but that doesn't mean they don't affect your tax return (see medical expenses in the previous chapter). The only way to be sure the returns are both done correctly and the most advantageously is to compare the documents side by side. This applies even if your child has children of their own (especially if they have children of their own!) As long as they live at home, taxes go through you. Many tax professionals will prepare your dependent's tax returns free or at a discount.

NOTE: Support is discussed periodically below and is usually obvious and straightforward. I have included a Support Worksheet in Appendix A if you need more details.

Now that we have covered that, let's talk about you and your kid's taxes:

Dependency: The first thing to consider is whether you can still claim them as a dependent. Let's revisit the requirements and talk about where their getting a job might impact.

1. The child must live with you for at least 6 months and a day. They can be absent for vacations, school, medical care and even detention in a juvenile facility—those still count as days living in your household. This shouldn't be a concern unless they move out permanently before July 1st.
2. The potential dependent cannot have provided more than half of their own support (Appendix A Test 1). Note that this does not mean that YOU

have to support them, they just can't provide more than half of their own support. This test changes if they are too old based on item 3 below. If they are too old, then YOU (together with your spouse if MFJ) must provide over half of the child's support (Appendix A Test 2). More details are below under 5 - 7. Now that they have a job, you have to take their income into account and compare how it applies to the support test.

3. They must be under age 19, or under age 24 if a full-time student for at least 5 months, or any age if disabled. If not, additional tests must be met:

a. Support test listed under bullet 2 above with changes as noted in the bullet.

b. The child's income cannot exceed $4,700 (the test says "gross" but it is effectively "taxable" – see a pro if your child has sources of income other than Social Security that exceeds $4,700). Sometimes a child receives Social Security benefits due to a deceased parent. Social Security benefits won't affect this test because even though it could be taxable, the income levels that make it taxable would be higher than $4,700, so you would have already failed the test. Obviously, this is where their getting a job has the biggest chance to impact you, once they reach the age where this test applies.

4. Note that when a child starts making their own income, turns 18, or goes to college, things start to change. A child can simply move out once they're 18, and no divorce decree, custody document or anything else can get you back to claiming them (assuming they move out before June 30th). They also start messing with who provides over half their support.

5. Support **from** the child includes: wages (this is what we're talking about!), investment income, scholarships, student loans that the child is obligated to pay back, unemployment income and savings withdrawals. Any of the above that are not spent for support (generally this means added to savings) don't count as support from the child.

6. Support **for** the child includes: cost of the home (fair rental value of the home plus utilities, repairs, taxes, insurance and other household costs divided by number of occupants), education, entertainment, clothing, medical, travel and other necessary expenses.

7. If the child is young enough that 3 above doesn't apply, you simply determine if the total support **from** the child (5 above) is less than half of the total support **for** the child (6 above). If the child is old enough that 3 above does apply, then you determine if YOU (together with your spouse, if MFJ) provide over half of support **for** the child (6 above).

Earned Income Credit: Their income will not affect EIC, assuming they qualify under all the other requirements.

Kiddie Tax: Kiddie Tax is not significantly affected by getting a job. The Kiddie Tax is based on unearned income, but if your child gets laid off and receives unemployment income, that is considered unearned income and is subject to the Kiddie Tax.

Now They Might Need to File: The other major item to consider is them filing their tax return. You could just review all the chapters of this book to do their taxes, but that would be cruel. I'll cover the gist here. If you can't claim them as a dependent, all the usual rules for filing taxes apply. I'm assuming in the bullets below that you are still claiming them and that they are not married, and have no children of their own:

1. Generally if they make less than $13,850 of total income, they will not owe any income tax (assuming no Kiddie Tax). They might have to file anyway, and should, if there was any state or federal withholding on their W-2, so they can try to get some of it back.
2. Make sure that they check the box on Form 1040 indicating that they are being claimed by someone else (they should have 0 exemptions).
3. Their filing status will be Single.
4. If they have education expenses, you get the credit or deduction, even if they pay them. This is because the education credits go with the exemption, and we assumed you are claiming them.
5. To determine if they need to file, you need to know their earned income, unearned income (investment income, unemployment, annuities, etc.) and the total. They have to file if their unearned income was over $1,250, their earned income was over $13,850 or their total income was larger than their earned income plus $400, or $1,250, whichever is larger (basically if they have earned income and more than $400 of unearned income, they have to file.)
6. Just to be safe, in case you mess up, electronically file your tax return before you e-file your kids. That way, if you accidently have the kid claim themselves, their tax return will be rejected, and yours will go through. Don't sweat a rejection in this case, there's nothing you can be held accountable for since a rejected return isn't considered to be a filed return. The IRS cannot hassle you for incorrectly filing it. Just correct it and e-file it again.

My Advice:

1. As long as your child lives at home, their W-2 comes directly to you, and you coordinate with them to get their taxes filed when the time comes. File yours first.

2. Walk your child through filling out their first W-4 form and make sure they understand how it works. They will probably file Single in Step 1 and everything else blank except their personal details and signature. else0 (2018 and before), but make sure they understand why. This is also a good chance for you to refamiliarize yourself with the brand new for 2019 overly complicated and ridiculous W-4 form.
3. If you have opened a bank account in the child's name, they are collecting Social Security from a deceased parent, or have any other sources of income, make sure you help them get the documents and include them on their tax return.

Military: If your child joins the military, for active duty, and leaves for boot camp before July 1st, you probably cannot claim them. If they leave on or after July 1st, their age and income will determine if you can claim them. Talk with them about this before they leave!

24. My Child had (or is having) a Child

Congratulations Grandparent (feel old yet?). If your child is off on their own, and do not live with you or receive significant support from you, then relax, nothing has changed about your taxes. If they live with you or you support them, read on...

Like the previous chapter, I am going to assume a traditional parent/child/family situation. I am also going to assume that you and the child are U.S. citizens living in the U.S., and that at least one of the following applies:
- You are either married to the other parent,
- The other parent is not in the picture, or
- The other parent does not have custody and has no rights to claim the child.

Hopefully, you have read the previous chapters on children and have some pretty good ideas about how the rules affect you claiming your child. The questions to be asked now are, does this affect me claiming my child? Can I claim my Grandchild? Are there any other effects?

I am not going to rehash all the requirements for claiming a child since you should have been through them for your kid before they had your grandchild. If not, please reread the chapters on having a child. I'm going to highlight the things that change or are weird about your child having a child:

1. If your child and/or grandchild both move out permanently such that they do not live with you for more than 6 months during the tax year, you're pretty much done and need not worry about the rest of this. You cannot claim much of anything for either of them, even if you're sending a bunch of money their way.
2. If your child moves out, leaving their child with you, such that your grandchild spends more than 6 months with you, but NOT more than 6 months with either parent (even if some or all of the 6 months is in your home), then you treat the grandchild just like it was your child. The previous discussions about having a child fully apply despite it being a grandchild. You will still list the child as your grandchild, but all the rules for dependency, education and daycare apply to a grandchild, just like your child. Again, this assumes that you (and your spouse if married) are the ONLY ones that the child lived with for more than 6 months out of the year.

3. In contradiction to what I just said, the one time that a grandchild isn't exactly like a child in the scenario above is if you are married and trying to be considered unmarried in order to claim the Head of Household (HH) filing status. A grandchild does not qualify for that exception.

4. If you live together with your child and grandchild in your home, that complicates things. The fact that your child had a child does not change any of the requirements for you claiming him or her, and, generally if you still qualify to claim your child, your grandchild will fall right in line to be claimed by you.

5. That said, it is possible that you might not end up claiming the child. The parent of a child has a higher claim than a grandparent, so, if there is a dispute about who gets to claim the child, you have to run through some scenarios and tests. It is generally a good idea for people to be agreeable about determining who claims a child, and, in a lot of cases, you can decide who gets to claim the child based upon what are the best financial results overall.

6. For the claiming dependency, if there is a dispute, the parent gets to claim the child over the grandparent. If you and your child agree, either can claim the child for tax purposes.

7. For EIC, if there is a dispute, the parent gets to claim the child, unless the parent of the child meets the requirements for you to claim them for EIC. You cannot get EIC if you are the qualifying child for EIC of another person, so, since we've already discussed that your child lives with you, and they are your child, the only question is age. If your child is under age 19, or under age 24 and a full-time student for 5 or more months during the year, or your child is any age but permanently and totally disabled, they are a qualifying child for EIC, and they CAN'T claim their child for EIC, and you should generally claim them both. If you want to be agreeable and put the child on the tax return that gets the best EIC, you first need to check the age thing we just talked about, and then, if the child qualifies for both of you, you can only put the child on your tax return if your AGI is higher than your child's.

8. For Head of Household (HH), only the person who pays more than half the cost of maintaining the home can be HH, and they must claim the dependent on their tax return to get it. So, if you agree that your child will claim the dependency exemption, but you pay more than half the cost of maintaining the home, neither you nor your child gets HH (unless there are other children).

9. For all of the above discussions, if the other parent of your grandchild lives with you, you need to include them in the determinations (keeping in mind that they won't be your qualifying child for EIC since they aren't your child). If they are married, see the next chapter...

My Advice:

1. If your child and grandchild are living with you, and there is any question as to who can claim what, I highly recommend paying a professional to help you. A professional can run through every scenario, determine what is allowed, figure out what is best for everyone and even help you determine how to divide refunds if that is what you want.
2. Do not just assume that because you pay a bunch of your kid and/or grandkids bills that you qualify to claim them. Follow the rules discussed above and if it is not clear, seek professional help. If you use software to file your taxes, read the questions about the children very carefully and answer them accurately and honestly.

Military: If a child lives with you at the time you are deployed they continue to count as living with you during the deployment, even if you send them to another household (such as your parents) for the time you are deployed. Some people might debate this, but a good rule of thumb is that a non-permanent deployment or assignment does not change the living situation for taxes so long as the intention is for the dependent to return to the pre-deployment living situation when the deployment or temporary assignment ends (sending the child to your ex-spouse who is the child's parent might be trouble). Geographical bachelor or Permanent Change of Station orders would not count for as "temporary".

25. My Child is Getting Married

I hope this is a happy situation! If your child is off on their own, and do not live with you or receive significant support from you, then relax, nothing has changed about your taxes. If they live with you or you support them, read on...

Like the previous chapter, I am going to assume a traditional parent/child/family situation. I am also going to assume that you and the child are U.S. citizens living in the U.S., and that at least one of the following applies:

- You are either married to the other parent,
- The other parent is not in the picture, or
- The other parent does not have custody and has no rights to claim the child.
- None of the relationships in the household violate State or Local Law (I have never seen this and don't want to imagine what would cause this situation.)

NOTE: Support is discussed periodically below and is usually obvious and straightforward. I have included a Support Worksheet in Appendix A if you need more details.

The real question that comes up here is can you still claim your child once they get married. The answer is yes, but a few more potential roadblocks come up. The biggest one is that you generally cannot claim your child if they file MFJ (though there are a couple of exceptions). You should definitely go over the filing requirements chapter of this book with your child and their spouse, and while you're at it, you should be preparing your taxes at the same time as them, so you can evaluate the positives and negatives to both tax returns. There is also the question of your child's spouse. If they are living with you, can you claim them? The answer is not as easy as it is to claim your own child, though it is actually easier to figure out. You also have to consider your child's spouse's income sources and how they affect you supporting your child.

Let's revisit claiming your child, and add how their marriage affects it:

1. They must live with you for at least 6 months and a day. They can be absent for vacations, school, medical care and even detention in a juvenile facility—those still count as days living in your household. This should not be a concern unless they move out permanently before July 1st.

2. They cannot have provided more than half of their own support (Appendix A Test 1). Note that this does not mean that YOU have to support them, they just can't provide more than half of their own support. This test changes if they are too old based on item 3 below. If they are too old, then YOU (together with your spouse if MFJ) must provide over half of the child's support (Appendix A Test 2 and their spouse's income now comes into play as a source of support not from you). More details below under 5 through 7.

3. They must be under age 19, or under age 24 if a full-time student for at least 5 months, or any age if disabled. If not, additional tests must be met:

    a. Support test listed under bullet 2 above with changes as noted (again, their spouse's income can count against this calculation).

    b. Their gross income cannot exceed $4,700. Sometimes a child receives Social Security benefits due to a deceased parent. Social Security benefits won't affect this test because even though it could be taxable, the income levels that make it taxable would be higher than $4,700. If your child is 19 or older, and not in college for 5 months out of the year, or 24 or older, regardless of school, they can't make more than $4,700 and you still claim them as a dependent. This does not apply if they are permanently and totally disabled, but you'll need a doctor's statement to that effect.

4. Note that when a child starts making their own income, turns 18, or goes to college, things start to change. A child can simply move out once they're 18, and no divorce decree, custody document or anything else can get you back to claiming them (assuming they move out before June 30th). They also start messing with who provides over half their support.

5. Support **from** the child includes: wages, investment income, scholarships, student loans that the child is obligated to pay back, unemployment income and savings withdrawals. Any of the above that are not spent for support (generally this means added to savings) don't count as support from the child.

6. Support **for** the child includes: Cost of the home (fair rental value of the home plus utilities, repairs, taxes, insurance and other household costs divided by number of occupants), education, entertainment, clothing, medical, travel and other necessary expenses.

7. If they are young enough that 3 above doesn't apply, you simply determine if the total support **from** the child (5 above) is less than half of the total support **for** the child (6 above). If they are old enough that 3 does apply, then you determine if YOU (together with your spouse if MFJ) provide over half of the support **for** the child (6 above).

8. The biggest one is that they can't file a joint return with their new spouse. This means they must file as MFS (or not file a return) in order for

you to claim them. The only exception to this is if they are only filing MFJ in order to get back ALL of their withholding. In essence, this means that they are not required to file due to low enough income and are only filing to get back money that was withheld from their paychecks.

Now let's see about claiming their spouse:

1. Since they are not your biological child, they do not meet a relationship test to be a qualifying child so YOU must provide more than half of their support (as discussed above).
2. They have to live with you ALL year (January 1 through December 31), though the temporary absence rule for school, temporary jobs, etc., still applies.
3. They cannot be the qualifying child of another taxpayer. This means that if they lived with you all year in order to meet the above test, then a relative of theirs must also have lived with you in order for them to fail to meet this test for you. This would be someone like their parent, sibling, aunt, or uncle.
4. Their gross income cannot exceed $4,300. Sometimes a child receives Social Security benefits due to a deceased parent. Social Security benefits will not affect this test because even though it could be taxable, the income levels that make it taxable would be higher than $4,300. This test applies to the spouse regardless of their age, due to not being YOUR child.
5. They cannot file a joint return with your child that they married. This means they must file as MFS (or not file a return) in order for you to claim them. The only exception to this is if they are only filing MFJ in order to get back ALL of their withholding. In essence, this means that they are not required to file due to low enough income and are only filing to get back money that was withheld from their paychecks.

My Advice:

1. Claiming your child's spouse is worth basically $500. If it is close...don't do it. For 2020 and 2021, the stimulus payments changed this calculus, so talk to a pro to see what is best.
2. If your child and their spouse are living with you, and there is any question as to who can claim what, I highly recommend paying a professional to help you. A professional can run through every scenario, determine what is allowed, figure out what is best for everyone and even help you determine how to divide refunds if that is what you want.
3. I think, generally, that, other than the year of marriage, the only obvious scenario for claiming a married child and/or their spouse is if one or both

are disabled to the point that they cannot work. Most other scenarios would be tough to justify and (my personal opinion) you should be working to end the dependency situation by getting your child and their spouse on their feet and able to support themselves (even if they still live with you).

Military: If a child lives with you at the time you are deployed they continue to count as living with you during the deployment, even if you send them to another household (such as your parents) for the time you are deployed. Some people might debate this, but a good rule of thumb is that a non-permanent deployment or assignment does not change the living situation for taxes so long as the intention is for the dependent to return to the pre-deployment living situation when the deployment or temporary assignment ends (sending the child to your ex-spouse who is the child's parent might be trouble). Geographical bachelor or Permanent Change of Station orders would not count for as "temporary".

26. I am Getting Divorced (or already am)

This chapter assumes that you and your spouse separated at the time you decided to divorce or shortly thereafter and that you do not continue to cohabitate during divorce planning and/or after the divorce.

MOST IMPORTANT! (details later):

For divorces settled in 2018 and before, alimony is generally deductible by the payer and taxable to the recipient. For divorces settled in 2019 and later, alimony is not taxable to the recipient nor deductible by the payer. Divorces from 2018 and before that are relitigated or resettled the taxability of alimony is presumed to remain the same as the prior settlement unless it is EXPLICITLY outlined in the new decree that it has changed.

Your divorce lawyer probably does not understand how divorce affects taxes and you should consult a tax professional in addition to a divorce lawyer.

Now the rest of the chapter:

Tax issues for divorcing couples have become more complex every year, and recent tax law changes have made it even more imperative that good preparation and advice be given during and after a divorce is final. Tax planning begins at the moment of separation (or even before). Many individuals are unprepared for the effect that separation has on their tax situation. Most only discover the difficulty when they go to file their taxes and discover that they cannot file as Single. Keep in mind that marital status is determined on 12/31 of the tax year in accordance with the laws for marriage established by your state. If you are still married and living together on this date, all the stuff about custodial vs. non-custodial parent does not apply. Children are claimed via standard tie-breaker rules (# nights, then AGI, which we will discuss later).

Couples who are still married generally can only file MFJ or MFS. This is why it is critical to get a legally binding separation agreement that is accepted in accordance with the rules of your state. Your divorce lawyer can help you with this. Failing to do that, MFS versus MFJ becomes the problem. MFS has significant disadvantages due to disallowed deductions and lower income thresholds. It is rarely a good way to file (I have a full chapter on <u>MFS</u>). In order to avoid this quandary, you have limited options (listed in general order of preference):

I. The custodial parent (the one the child spent more nights with—forget what the divorce court says—more later on custody) may be able to file HH if they meet all the following requirements:
(The non-custodial parent would be MFS, unless they had another child)
  A. You are unmarried or "considered unmarried" on the last day of the year.
      1. You are considered unmarried on the last day of the tax year if you meet all the following tests:
         a. You file a separate return (not necessarily MFS, just not MFJ).
         b. You paid more than half the cost of keeping up your home for the tax year.
         c. Your spouse did not live in your home during the last 6 months of the tax year.
         d. Your home was the main home of your child, stepchild, or foster child for more than half the year. (Once you are the step-parent of a child that status does not change, even due to death or divorce from the child's "natural" parent.)
      2. You paid more than half the cost of keeping up a home for the year (this may seem repetitive, and it is, but this is a test for being "considered unmarried AND a test for HH).
      3. A "qualifying person" lived with you in the home for more than half the year (except for temporary absences, such as school). However, if the "qualifying person" is your dependent parent, he or she does not have to live with you. (Keep in mind that if your parents live in their own home, the Fair Rental Value of the home counts as support provided by them, even if they pay no mortgage or rent.) You also pretty much have to meet this "HH" test in order to qualify as "considered unmarried".
      4. You must be able to claim an exemption for the child. However, you meet this test if you cannot claim the exemption only because the noncustodial parent can claim the child using the rule for divorced or separated parents (or parents who live apart). We will discuss the rule for divorced or separated parents later.

II. They may file Single if they obtain a divorce or separation agreement prior to 12/31 of the tax year (this must meet the requirements of your state's laws.)

III. They may file MFJ with their spouse and divide the refund. A tax pro can help you understand how a refund should be divided based on your input and agreements with your ex spouse.

Once divorced or separated there are a number of issues to consider. I will start with the biggie: Children.

Who can Claim the Child?

The IRS uses many of the same terms that lawyers and laymen use, but they do not mean the same thing. Many people believe that custody as granted in a divorce decree is custody for taxes. It is **NOT**. The IRS defines custodial parent as the parent the child spent the most nights with during the tax year. In the event of a tie, the parent with the higher Adjusted Gross Income is the custodial parent. Nights are counted based on spending them with the parent or in the parent's home. If the child is not with either, the night counts for the parent who would normally have the child in their home. This could happen for sleepovers or when the parent is deployed while in the military, resulting in the deployed individual's family taking care of the child or for a child in college.
Again, the IRS does not care what the divorce decree says. A divorce decree cannot force a parent to grant the exemption to the non-custodial parent (except decrees before 1985). After 1984 and before 2009, a divorce decree may be used for the non-custodial parent to claim the exemption if it provides the following:

- Gives the claim to the non-custodial parent WITHOUT ANY ADDITIONAL REQUIREMENTS (such as up-to-date on child support).
- States that the non-custodial parent can claim the child and that the custodial parent will not for specified years.
- Signature by the custodial parent is on the decree (judge's signature not required).

After 1985, only the custodial parent can release an exemption—the divorce decree was simply the method by which it was done. The exemption can be revoked by providing (or in good faith attempting to provide) written notification to the non-custodial parent that the custodial parent is revoking permission for the non-custodial parent to claim the exemption. This notice and proof of attempted delivery must be enclosed with the tax return. After 2008, only a signed IRS Form 8332 or similar statement may release the exemption. There is some argument as to whether a judge can compel a parent to provide an IRS Form 8332;

prevailing opinion is leading to the idea that a judge cannot. However, a judge can hold YOU accountable for failing to provide this form if you are ordered to do so.

My recommendation to the non-custodial parent is that they get a Form 8332 signed at the signing of divorce papers. The form should specify all years that the non-custodial parent may claim the child. Form 8332 is still revocable, but this is the best way of making clear what is intended for all future years. If I was representing the custodial parent, I would recommend they not provide the form upfront, rather that they provide it each year. Obviously, the tenor of the divorce will affect this decision.

The non-custodial parent will have to attach this form to their return. Normally, when e-filing, you actually mail the 8332 in attached to IRS Form 8453, which your software or tax pro will print out for you. If you use a tax professional, they will generally mail the 8453 and 8332 for you. You need to do this every tax year that you claim a child that does not live with you as a result of divorce or legal separation.

Who can Claim What for the Child:

This is vitally important and regularly done wrong. When the non-custodial parent is claiming the child, it is vital that BOTH parents file the child correctly. They are "splitting" benefits. As a general rule, the non-custodial parent only gets the Child Tax Credit (and Additional Child tax Credit if applicable) or the Credit for Other Dependents if the child is 17 or older. The custodial parent is the ONLY one who can get Earned Income Credit (EIC) and the Daycare Credit, as well as file as HH based on that child – though they may qualify using other children or parents. All of these tax benefits require that the child live with you for more than half the year with no exceptions for divorced couples – that's why a divorce decree can't give these away – it would violate THE LAW. Even when the non-custodial parent makes too much money to get EIC, they must still file as the non-custodial parent. No divorce decree, judge or lawyer can change this.

Other items are less obvious...

- Medical Expenses go to who paid them.
- Education Credits go with the exemption (custodial, unless Form 8332 signed).

Child Support and Alimony:

Child Support is never taxed or deducted. Alimony is generally also neither deducted by the payer or taxed to the recipient EXCEPT if the divorce was finalized in 2018 or before, in which case the opposite applies and taxes are generally paid by the recipient and the payments deducted by the payer. It is important to remember that the rules are determined by the date of the DIVORCE, not the tax year being filed.

Renegotiating a 2018 or older divorce decree does not alter the taxability of alimony unless it is explicitly agreed to in the new divorce decree. The requirements to do this are very specific, so do not assume your lawyer fully understands the rules.

Three Final Points:

First, make sure you have your children's and ex (or soon to be ex) spouse's SSN and birthday—you will need them for taxes!
Second, do not assume your divorce lawyer understands taxes—they probably do not.
Third, get copies of your joint tax returns—you are entitled to them and might need them.

My Advice:

1. Try to get a divorce or legal separation by 12/31 of the tax year to avoid all the complications of MFJ versus MFS.
2. Keep track of the number of nights your child spends with you on a calendar or in a journal. Keep copies of school, medical or other records that show that the child lives with you. 20 years doing taxes and I can assure you that a lot of people will try to claim children they are not entitled to. Don't assume it's going to happen but be prepared if it does. In the world of cell phones, a daily picture of the child in your home can be helpful, though not a slam dunk.
3. If you are the non-custodial parent, get a Form 8332 signed at the signing of divorce papers for all years that you are allowed to claim the child. Form 8332 is still revocable, but this is the best way of making clear what is intended for all future years. If you can't get the form up front, have the divorce decree specify that the form be provided, and try to get a requirement that it be provided no later than January 31st of the tax year.
4. If you are the custodial parent, provide the 8332 form each tax year that you are allowing, or required to allow the other parent to claim the child.

Do not provide them up front and file your taxes early if possible. Provide the form AFTER you file.

5. Get your ex-spouses SSN and birthday, as well as this information for all children, even if you will not be claiming them.

6. Get copies of the last 3 year's tax returns if you filed jointly. During the divorce or via the divorce decree is often the easiest way to do this rather than waiting.

7. Do not assume your divorce lawyer understands taxes. Talk with a tax professional unless things are absolutely clear. The judge may not understand taxes. Judges often order a joint return be filed but I am pretty sure you cannot be made to sign a return since signing it makes you responsible for the entire return and you may not trust your spouse or have all of the information. If a joint return is ordered and you are unsure, talk to your lawyer, a tax expert and if ordered to file jointly have a statement added that explicitly identifies information you are uncertain about and that you are signing the return only due to a court order.

8. If division of retirement accounts is on the table, talk about it with a tax professional BEFORE negotiations get serious.

9. The following is non-tax advice but is the result of experience dealing with lots of divorced clients. I am not an expert in this area: If you are getting pension from your ex-spouse that does not include a provision that it continues for you after they die, try to get a life insurance requirement in the divorce decree such that your ex-spouse has to cooperate with you getting a life insurance policy on them sufficient that it would account for the loss of the pension if they were to die. Normally you would be required to make the payments, they just have to participate with reasonable requirements for medical exams and other such necessities. You are likely going to be relying on these pension payments going forward, and it isn't unreasonable to ask someone to help protect yourself against their loss, but in divorce, assuming someone is going to be cooperative for the rest of your life is not a good assumption. Getting the requirement in the divorce decree protects both of you.

10. Try to discuss things that affect your taxes up front and do not just assume that everyone understands how things should be done. Obviously, this requires that your ex-spouse be a reasonable person...

11. Change passwords for any tax filing accounts you have or have your tax professional set up new accounts for future years. Do not just continue filing with the same accounts you used prior to the divorce to ensure that your ex does not have access to your future tax returns.

Military: If a child lives with you at the time you are deployed they continue to count as living with you during the deployment, even if you send them to another household (such as your parents) for the time you are deployed. Some people might debate this, but a good rule of thumb is that a non-permanent deployment or assignment does not change the living situation for taxes so long as the intention is for the dependent to return to the pre-deployment living situation when the deployment or temporary assignment ends (sending the child to your ex-spouse who is the child's parent might be trouble). Geographical bachelor or Permanent Change of Station orders would not count as "temporary".

If you send military retirement benefits to your ex-spouse, they might be alimony, but this is complicated. Normally, DFAS should be sending the payments to your ex-spouse (as long as you were married for at least 10 years while you served). In this case, your 1099-R will reflect only what you receive, and your ex-spouse will get their own 1099-R. This avoids all the alimony questions. If you have to make the payment yourself, my fellow tax pros THINK you can still deduct it and the recipient pays taxes on it, but it's not 100% clear this is the case.

27. My Spouse Abandoned Me and/or Our Children

I'm sorry about that. The main concern here is the effect on your filing status and claiming of the children. For the purposes of this chapter, I'm assuming you were legally married and that they're GONE, as in no or limited contact and things like filing taxes will not involve the spouse. I'm going to cover things very simply based on the date of abandonment, and then go over the details. You should definitely read the details to make sure these apply to you, but the initial scenarios will help you understand what you should be thinking.

Scenario 1: Abandoned between January 1st and June 30th of the tax year: Assuming the children remained with you and qualify to be dependents, you will most likely file as HH and claim the children.

Scenario 2: Abandoned between July 1st and December 31st of the tax year: Assuming the children remained with you and qualify to be dependents, you will most likely file as MFS and claim the children.

Scenario 3: Abandonment after December 31st of the tax year: For the tax year before the abandonment, you will most likely file MFS, and the parent with the higher income (AGI) will claim the children. This applies even if your spouse was not the biological parent of the children. The next year you will most likely file HH and claim the children. To be clear, if you are abandoned January 15th of 2022, you will likely file MFS for 2021 and HH for 2022.

Here are the details you should understand:

1. If domestic violence was involved in any way, go to the police and file a police report. I'm not saying this to be preachy and to tell you what to do in your personal life, but because domestic violence victims have some special tax protections (though not a ton) and a police report is good evidence if needed with the IRS. I'm also pretty sure there are a lot of non-tax things that make this a good idea. One of the biggest non-tax issues has some big effects on taxes anyway. If you've been abandoned, you need a divorce or legal separation in order to remove the specter of MFS from over your head. More about that later.
2. As for the children, assuming you were abandoned before the end of the calendar year (December 31st), and the children lived with you all year, you have a slam dunk, higher right to claim them than the spouse who abandoned you. That said, this does not mean he/she will not try to claim

them anyway. Document the date he/she left, making sure to notify people, such as schools and doctors and (I would suggest) a good divorce lawyer. File your taxes early and if the other spouse claims them—fight. See the chapter titled <u>Someone Claimed my Child</u> if that happens.

3. If your spouse left after December 31st, you have a bit of a problem. In this case, standard tie-breaker rules apply. This means that if you lived together all year, the person with the higher income (technically AGI) gets to claim them. If that's not you, don't try to claim them, even if morally you feel you have the right. Wait until next year.

4. The biggest issue you have to face is Filing Status. Marital status is determined as of December 31st of the tax year, so you will probably still be legally married for tax purposes in the year they abandoned you. If they left on July 1st or later, you have to file MFS. If you have no children, you pretty much have to file MFS. Married Filing Separately sucks. I have a whole chapter on it, so make sure to read the <u>I have to File Married Filing Separately</u> chapter. If you have children, you can be considered unmarried if ALL the following apply:

      a. You did not live with your spouse after June 30th of the tax year.

      b. You paid over half the costs of maintaining a home, which was the main home for your child, stepchild, or foster child (foster child must be placed with you by an authorized placement agency or court) for at least 6 months and a day of the tax year. Note that the relations are VERY specific. One way to think of it is that you as a parent have been forced to take care of a child for whom you are responsible due to being the birth parent, step-parent, or foster parent. I should also note that step-relationships established by marriage do not end by divorce or death.

      c. You claim that child on your tax return as a dependent.

Note that the requirement of paying more than half the cost of maintaining a home discussed in this chapter are different from most times we will talk about paying more than half the costs for kids. In this case, it is just for the home. You include taxes, interest, and rent paid (later situations will talk about Fair Rental Value—here it is rent PAID). You also include utilities, repairs, and insurance for the home. Other than that, it is food consumed in the home, and not much else. You need to have paid more than half of that total during the period of time the child lived with you (at least 6 months and a day). If you meet all the requirements, you can choose to file HH.

5. Some of the MFS problems can be avoided if you were a victim of domestic violence. The one that is likely to come up is if you get an Affordable Care Act (Obamacare) subsidy. MFS really messes up this subsidy and can cause you to pay back all or most of it. There is an exception for victims of domestic violence, but you should seek a tax

professional's help to get it right. This is a good time to re-mention that if you are a victim of domestic violence, a police report is very useful. I can't speak to dynamics other than taxes, but for taxes, that report means a lot.

My Advice:

1. Make note of the last date your spouse last lived with you.
2. Keep track of the number of nights your child spends with you on a calendar or in a journal. Keep copies of school, medical or other records that show that the child lives with you. 20 years doing taxes and I can assure you that a lot of people will try to claim children they aren't entitled to. Don't assume it's going to happen but be prepared if it does.
3. File a police report if domestic violence occurred.
4. File your taxes as early as you can.
5. In contradiction to what I said earlier about not claiming your child if the abandonment occurred after 12/31 and your spouse had a higher AGI: Consider talking to a tax professional about what your options might be. This is not absolutely cut and dried and the facts of your specific situation might make it worth the money to have this consultation.
6. Do not sign a joint return that you are not confident in the accuracy of unless you are directed to do so by the court. At the same time, if a joint return results in the best net tax return, and there is no reason to question the accuracy, the court could very well penalize you for a willful refusal to file a joint return. State court decisions are split on this aspect of taxes, and I am NOT a lawyer, but courts seem to be concerned about the negative impact of a separate return on the marital assets and takes a dim view of spiteful refusal to file jointly. Similarly, they may require monetary compensation from the one refusing to file. That said, when there is a reasonable reason to choose to file separate, the courts are much more amenable. Examples are refusal of one spouse to share documents supporting the return, history of fraudulent filing, and attempts to shift tax burden to the other spouse using joint filing – the classic example of which was one spouse liquidating retirement accounts, spending the money on themselves, and then trying to get half the penalties and tax paid by the other spouse through joint filing.

Military: A military spouse deploying would not normally be considered abandonment. If a child lives with you at the time you are deployed they continue to count as living with you during the deployment, even if you send them to another household (such as your parents) for the time you are deployed. Some people might debate this, but a good rule of thumb is that a non-permanent deployment or assignment does not change the living situation for taxes so long as the intention is for the dependent to return to the pre-deployment living situation when the deployment or temporary assignment ends (sending the child to your ex-spouse who is the child's parent might be trouble). Geographical bachelor or Permanent Change of Station orders would not count for as "temporary."

28. My Spouse Died

I'm very sorry to hear that. Take a few weeks and don't worry about taxes, or much of anything other than taking care of yourself. Come back when you are ready (but don't take forever).

Okay. Let's first remind ourselves that this is a tax book, so this isn't about estate resolution, finances, or other complexities—talk to the experts. Also, there are situations where you should talk to an expert rather than relying on this book. Here are a few:

1. Your (or your deceased spouse's) net worth is in the millions (near or above 10 million).
2. Trusts are involved.
3. Other heirs beside you will get more than a few personal items or some money (especially Real Estate and/or retirement accounts).
4. There are disputes about the estate.
5. You were estranged from your spouse or there were other unique factors, such as separate finances or businesses.

Also, read the next chapter I Inherited Money or Property.

For the most part, the tax implications for a surviving spouse should not be too complex. Most of their assets should automatically transfer to you or be specifically laid out in their will. Bank accounts and investment accounts are probably joint tenant accounts or have a designated beneficiary, which means they automatically become yours. This may require paperwork, but the transfer is tax-free. I will cover specifics of things that don't quite work that way.

If you are the beneficiary for your spouse's retirement plan accounts (i.e., IRAs) and/or pension plans (i.e., 401k's), the good news is that you can treat your deceased spouse's accounts as your own. You just contact the plan administrator and they will tell you what you need to do. If you are not the beneficiary, the beneficiary should talk to BOTH an investment advisor you can trust, and a tax expert before pulling the money out of these accounts. There are a lot of rules that apply to withdrawal, depending on the relationship to the original owner. You generally must take the money out within a certain period of time, which can have big tax implications. (Just to ensure this isn't confusing, you, as the ex-spouse, can treat the money as your own, and leave it in the account. Anyone else will have restrictions requiring them to eventually pull the money out.)

For a house (or houses) in both your names, you may increase your BASIS (your "investment" in the home—usually what you paid for it—that is used to determine gain or loss when sold). If you live in a community property state, your BASIS becomes the value of the house on the date of death—get an appraisal! In non-community-property states, YOUR half of the house keeps its original BASIS, and your spouse's half goes up to the value on the date of death. Again, get an appraisal. The math on this is to take half your original BASIS and add it to half the appraised value. This is the new BASIS. If you did not own the house 50/50, get expert help.

Also, if you plan on selling the house you both lived in at the time of death, you get the MFJ Principal Residence exclusion for two years after the date of death. See the I Sold my Home chapter.

For other items that pass on to you, such as investments that were in their name only, you get the stepped-up basis discussed in the next chapter: I Inherited Money or Property.

The last thing to worry about is actually filing your tax returns. If you do not remarry before the end of the year, you can file a joint return you're your deceased spouse, and get all their deductions as if they were still living. You will sign the return as surviving spouse. For years after that your filing status will be based on your new situation, without considering your deceased spouse, UNLESS you have dependent children. In that case, for the next two years, if you meet the following requirements, you can file as a Qualifying Surviving Spouse: you have not remarried, the dependent is your child or stepchild (not foster child), they lived with you ALL year, you claim them as a dependent, you paid over half the cost of maintaining the home and you filed a MFJ return with the spouse in the year they died. This gives you almost all the tax benefits of being married.

My Advice:

1. Shortly after your spouse passes (within about a month) have any real estate that wasn't solely in your name appraised and save the appraisal with the rest of your house documents (the big package they gave you at closing).
2. Make sure to record the value (on the date of death) of any investments that were solely in your deceased spouse's name. You do not have to do this right away, but generally within a few months makes it easy to find the information.

3. Talk to an expert if the estate situation has anything that is not discussed in this chapter.

Military: The Thrift Savings Plan is a retirement plan that you can treat as your own as discussed above.

29. I Inherited Money or Property

First things first. if any of the following occurred, you should seek the advice of a competent tax expert, financial advisor, and/or an attorney:

1. You are the executor of the estate.
2. You inherit more than a few million dollars' worth of stuff.
3. You inherit real estate property that will not be immediately liquidated or occupied by the person inheriting it.
4. You inherit retirement accounts (unless you are the spouse of the owner).
5. You inherit an on-going business.
6. You inherit from a trust account.
7. You inherit anything significantly different than the things I discuss below.
8. Money, property or investments are inherited by a minor. This would not include small value personal type items or even higher value items that don't appreciate in value. A basic car would probably be fine but shares of stocks, collectibles or real estate would require tax help.

Second thing—a misconception—if you inherit money, you are not responsible for estate taxes. The estate should pay the taxes BEFORE it sends you money or property. This is why I say if you are handling the estate (as executor) you should get help from an estate attorney. This means that, generally, when you get money or property from an estate, you will not have any tax issues, except in a couple cases discussed later (selling property and tax-sheltered accounts).

So, let's talk about what you should do or know if you inherit the following:

Cash: This includes bank and money market accounts, and term life insurance proceeds. In general, you simply receive a check from the estate or assets are transferred to your name. You can be almost certain that this cash is yours, free and clear with no tax implications. The only thing to be sure of is that the estate did not liquidate tax-sheltered accounts and send you the money (they should absolutely NEVER do this, but you want to make sure.)

Stocks or Bonds: You do not pay any taxes on these when you inherit them, and you don't pay taxes on any increases in value until you sell them. Any money they earn for you after they become yours (dividends and interest) is taxable in the year you receive it (even if it is reinvested). If you inherit a lot of stocks or bonds, this can be a big addition to your taxable income that will affect your taxes for the year, so make sure you understand how much they earn, and how it will impact the tax return. Adjust your withholding if necessary. The biggest thing you need to do when you receive these is to know their value on the date of death (of the person you inherit them from). The brokerage house that holds them for you can tell you this, and you should get the information and save it. When you sell them, you only pay taxes on the increase in value (or take a loss if they go down in value). This is why you need to know the value on the date of death (this is your BASIS). *

Real Estate (Personal Residence): We're talking about the house the person who died lived in when they died (or just before). Make sure the estate had the property appraised and get a copy of the appraisal. If they didn't get it appraised, have one done immediately. If you plan to live in it, this appraisal will tell you what your BASIS is in the property, which will be important when you sell it or convert it to business use. Essentially, this value acts the same as the price you pay for a home, had you bought it. It's your "investment" in the property. Similarly, if you plan to sell it, this BASIS determines if you have a gain or loss on the property. Generally, if you sell the property immediately, you should not have any appreciable gain on the sale of the property, and any loss would not be deductible. If you hold it for a while, or make improvements to it, the gain on the sale is taxable and the loss deductible (subject to limitations). Read the chapter on I Sold a Home that wasn't my Principal Residence and it will tell you everything you need to know, just remember that the BASIS discussed there is the appraised value we just talked about. *

Real Estate (Investment Property): This is mostly the same as we just talked about for Personal Residence, so go ahead and read that, then come back here...Okay. The main difference is that if there is a loss, it is deductible (subject to limitations). The idea is that you don't get to deduct a loss on "personal" stuff, just investment and business stuff. When you inherit someone's "residence" it is "personal", at least for a while. Here it never was personal. Now if you move into it, it becomes personal for you, and you treat it just as if you had bought it to live in it. The appraised value is like your purchase price, becoming your BASIS for the future. If you don't sell the property right away, and don't move into it, talk to a tax expert. *

Collectibles: In a lot of ways, these are just like stocks. They have a value, which you need to know at the time of death. The problem is that there is no broker to tell you what that value is. If the estate appraised them, get a copy of the appraisal. If you sell them right away for as much as you can get for them (not to a relative – get help if you do this), you can pretty much assume they were worth what you were paid for them and that you have no gain. If it's not a lot of stuff, not worth much money, and you're hanging onto it, you can probably not worry too much about it. You can deal with it when/if you eventually sell it. If there's a lot of value, get it appraised and keep copies of the appraisal. Just be aware that when you sell it, you pay taxes on the increase in price, but you can't deduct a loss (subject to limitations) if it goes down in value (if you are in the business of buying and selling collectibles this does not apply to you and you need expert help). *

Personal Items: If you are keeping them, then treat them just like all your other stuff. You will probably never face any tax implications. If you are selling them and sell them right away, you can pretty much assume you sold them for what they were worth, and thus have no taxable gain. *

*Okay. For all those things with an asterisk I've said a lot of complicated things, so here's the simple explanation: you basically treat all those items as if you had bought them, on the date of death, for what they were worth on that date. You also consider them as held long-term for capital gains purposes. If you think about it that way, it gets pretty simple.

Tax Sheltered Accounts: These include IRAs, Pension Plan Accounts (401k, 403b, pension, etc.), Tax Sheltered Annuities, and any other accounts that had contributions or earnings sheltered from taxation. The reason that these types of accounts matter is because the previous owner avoided taxes on some or all of the money in these accounts. Now the government wants those taxes. You should talk to BOTH an investment advisor you can trust and a tax expert before pulling the money out of these accounts. The applicable tax rules depend on your relationship to the original owner. You generally must take the money out within a certain period of time (except when it was your spouse that died). I will give you my best, generic advice on what I think should be done:

     1. Talk to the experts discussed above to determine if and/or when you have to take the money out.
     2. Make a plan for the money before you get it.

3. Unless you have a pressing need for the money, leave it in the accounts as long as possible without breaking the rules and/or spread the withdrawals over as long a period as possible. Leaving it in and taking it out at the last minute allows it to grow tax free, but taxes will be higher. Spreading it out keeps the taxes lower, but you lose some tax free growth. A professional is a really big help on this.

4. When you take the money out have your tax pro estimate the tax liability and either have that amount (plus a little extra) withheld, make an estimated tax payment for that amount, or save that amount until tax time. This is "found" money, so there is no need to spend it until you are sure how much you get to keep. My favorite plan is to put the money in an account until after you file your tax return for the year.

5. You'll get a tax form (probably a 1099-R) that you will use when filing your taxes. This form seems simple but in reality can be incredibly complicated.

My Advice:

1. See directly above where I discuss tax sheltered accounts and follow that advice. If you have already liquidated an account, ask the company that held the account if they will be issuing a 1099R and if so, what the taxable amount and any withholding was. Immediately check with a tax professional to see if you should be setting money aside for taxes.

2. It is always a good idea when you get a big windfall of money to avoid spending a significant amount of it until after you file your taxes, just in case there is a big tax bill that you didn't expect. Also, a big windfall is time to create a really well funded emergency fund, which everyone needs.

3. Have any real estate, jewelry, collectibles or other valuable items appraised as soon as possible if the estate did not already do it. If the estate had them appraised, get copies of the appraisals.

4. Note the value of any stock you inherited as of the date of death and keep these in a safe place. If possible, work with the brokerage company that holds the assets to ensure that they record the value on the date of death as the basis for them such that when you sell them, the 1099B reporting the sale has an accurate basis reported to the IRS.

5. Seek tax advice before selling highly appreciated items or liquidating tax advantaged accounts. It is generally better to spread these things over several years if possible.

6. This is non-tax advice but it is based on some hairy problems at the tax desk. If there is property in the estate, try to have the executor dispose of it before the estate is liquidated, or have it transferred for consideration within the estate to the final owner. This is complicated, and a lawyer

should be consulted, but, my point is that things get troublesome when several people end up on the deed for a property and then can't agree on how to handle it with regard to selling, rental, or keeping. Getting things handled and finalized while there is still an estate and an executor can avoid some problems that I have seen drag on for decades.

7. Always, ALWAYS, ALWAYS!!!! Make sure all of your investment, retirement and bank accounts have a designated beneficiary and update it immediately when things change.

Military: The Thrift Savings Plan is an example of a Tax-Sheltered Account.

30. I am Buying (or already own) a Home

I am assuming you are purchasing the home to use as a personal residence and that you and/or your spouse will be the only owners. Seek professional help if this isn't the case.

Subsequent Tax Law Changes:
- The deductibility of Mortgage Insurance Premiums, including FHA and VA Funding Fees has phased in and out. Currently, it is deductible for 2018 through 2021, but not 2022. I would not be surprised for it to be reinstated for 2022. To give an indication how likely it is to be reinstated, this chapter last year had the exact same wording regarding 2021 not allowing the deduction, and the deduction was ultimately allowed.
- The ability to exclude cancelled debt from home foreclosures has also been off and on allowed. Currently, it is allowed through 2025.

Now on to the chapter:

Buying a home is normally the final hurdle that gets someone from claiming the standard deduction to itemizing (though higher standard deductions in 2018 and beyond will make it even harder to itemize). In the course of this discussion I am going to spend some time talking about how owning a home affects itemizing. You need to read the Itemized Deductions chapter to make sure that you get all the deductions that you are entitled to.

I first want to talk a little bit of taxese. I know I promised to try not to, but there is some information about owning a home that you need to calculate and track: BASIS. Basis comes up all over the tax world and applies in this instance to the house you just bought. Simply put, Basis is the amount of money (or value of property) that you put into something, minus what you take out of it. You need to know the basis of your house. You won't use it for a while, but it will come up when you sell it, or if you convert it to business or rental use. (This is a good time to say that if you bought this house for a reason other than personal use, such as a first or second home, then you are in the wrong chapter.) The good news here is that the basis of your house is usually easy to figure out. All the information will be in your closing packet, so put the closing packet in your files, label it as "house" and have it available for your tax professional if you sell the house or convert it to rental or business use. Assuming that you purchased the home with a standard mortgage (or cash) and that there weren't any really weird things involved (like the loan for the house was also used to buy a car, or you paid expenses for the seller) your basis is the cash you paid for the house plus the mortgage you took out on the house, including amounts for settlement costs that weren't a part of getting the loan or placed in escrow for future insurance or tax costs. It's more complicated than that in Taxese, but all the details of basis are pretty much encapsulated within the cash, plus mortgage calculation. If you traded properties or did anything weird with the purchase contract, you'll want to talk to a tax expert, but this cash plus mortgage gets you a good basis to start with. If possible, you'll want to know how much of that basis represents the value of the land, which you can usually find in the appraisal paperwork. Going forward, you want to track things that change your basis (putting money in or taking money out). Generally, the only things that will change the basis are home improvements; assessments the government makes you pay to improve sidewalks, sewers or streets; or money the government pays you to use your land (such as an easement to widen the road). If you pay it, it is added to basis; if they pay you, it's subtracted from basis. Also, if there is a big fire or other accident, the event will likely affect your basis. If anything like that happens, put the receipts in your "house" file. An improvement is something that increases the value, like redoing the kitchen or floors. Repairs and upkeep are not improvements, unless you upgrade the item repaired to a more expensive type that increases the value. Put receipts for this in your "house" file. If keeping track of the basis seems like too much trouble, just keep the file up-to-date with the paperwork and let your tax professional do the math if the house is sold or converted to rental or business use.

Sorry about that paragraph, but it could save you a lot of trouble later. Now just to be clear, you do not get any current benefits for home improvements (unless they meet a very narrow list of energy efficient home improvements, discussed later in this chapter), but you need to track them. The next thing to talk about if you just bought a home is the Master Settlement Statement. This form is usually one of the first forms in the stack of crap that they made you sign when you closed on your home. Go through the big folder they give you and look for this form. It is the one with two columns about paid by buyer and paid by seller. You want to set aside a copy of this form for when you do your taxes. Sometimes you'll get multiple copies, other times just the one. Make a separate copy for this year's taxes and leave one with the big package of crap. This form is going to detail where every dollar of your down payment and what you financed went toward. It will also document everything that the money the seller provided went toward. We're going to need this as we try to figure out what you can deduct from your home.

You are going to get at least one, and maybe many 1098 forms with information discussed below. The information from the Master Settlement Statement that you need SHOULD be sent to you on a 1098, but, since the company that you get your mortgage from normally sells it off within a nanosecond to another company, it often gets lost in the shuffle. You should track ALL of the people who own your mortgage (or companies that manage the payments for them) and ensure you get a 1098 from every one of them. You don't absolutely need a 1098 to claim it on your taxes, but the IRS computer matching program is getting more aggressive in sending letters out when mortgage information doesn't match the 1098's it receives. The limitations discussed below will normally be properly accounted for on your 1098 if you only own one home.

The main deductions you get from your home are mortgage interest and real estate taxes. Most years, it is easy to get these numbers since your lender is going to send you a Form 1098 that will generally have all of these numbers. Some banks, like Bank of America, make you search for the real estate taxes on a second page, but they will be there. I highly recommend getting online access to all of your mortgage accounts so you can get copies online if needed. The other wrinkle in the year of purchase is that sometimes the Form 1098 does not report everything that you paid. In that case you need to go through the Master Settlement Statement from closing AND your 1098's to make sure you take every penny you are entitled to. Be careful not to duplicate deductions reported on multiple forms.

As a general rule, the 1098 will have everything that is included on the Master Settlement Statement, but you need to double-check to be certain. Some commonly missed items are various points, discount points, and other prepaid interest items. Again, you can use the Master Settlement Statement if they aren't on the 1098. Also, you sometimes won't even make a payment to the original lender, but there will still be a 1098 form so make sure that you get a 1098 from the lender listed on the Master Settlement Statement or use the numbers directly from the Master Settlement Statement. If you use any numbers that differ from the 1098's you receive, or your name (or spouse's if MFJ) or SSN are not on the 1098, you must attach a statement to your return explaining why. Most tax software has a system for doing this. It can be a good idea to have a professional assist you if your 1098 numbers don't match what the Master Settlement Statement says.

Having said all of the above, here are the details on deducting mortgage interest and taxes:

Mortgage Interest:

1. You can deduct mortgage interest on a first or second home, but no more. If you have more than two homes or buy a third or replace one during the year, you have special rules to follow on selecting which home to deduct. The main rule is that you cannot change which home you count as your second home unless you change your primary home or buy or sell your second home.
2. On the original loan, you get to deduct points immediately—if you paid them. If you had a no money down loan, you probably have to spread the points out over the life of the loan (divide by loan term in months and multiply by months you paid the loan in the tax year). Generally, you will either get all or none of the points right away, but it is possible to get a portion if you put some small amount of money towards closing costs. You get points even if the seller pays them, though they would have to be spread out since you did not pay them. The 1098 from the original lender (the 1098 is from the same lender that appears on the Master Settlement Statement) can generally be relied upon to accurately reflect the points you can take right away. Just make sure to compare the Master Settlement Statement to the 1098 and spread any points not on the 1098 across the life of the loan as we just discussed.
3. You can elect to spread the points out over the life even if you qualify to deduct them immediately. This is a good idea if you buy the house late in the year and do not end up with enough deductions to itemize.
4. Points might be called discount points, loan origination fees, maximum loan charges, loan discount and a few more unusual things but they are the same thing.
5. Points cannot be fully deducted on a mortgage that is 15 years or fewer if the points are more than 4%. On a mortgage that is 15 years or longer, points cannot be fully deducted if they are more than 6%, unless the loan amount is less than $250,000.
6. You cannot fully deduct points on a loan of more than 30 years. If the loan is 10 years or more, the terms must be similar to other

loans in your area (you can't be getting some special magic loan from your brother's bank, or a desperate seller).

7. To deduct points or interest the loan must be secured by your home, meaning that if you don't pay the mortgage, you lose the home.

8. You can deduct interest on a construction loan for up to 24 months before you move in, but you have to move in by that 24-month point. You don't have to start deducting the day you take the loan out; you can choose any day as long as it's within 24 months of you moving in (this might apply if it's going to take 2 years or more to build your home).

9. You can deduct late payment fees and prepayment penalties.

10. The loans must be to buy, build or improve your home.

11. If the total loans on both homes exceed $750,000 ($375,000 if MFS) you only get to deduct the interest on the first million. Starting in 2018, this limit is $750,000 – but only for NEW loans as of 2018.

12. Home equity debt not used to buy, build or improve your home can be deducted on equity debt up to $100,000. If it is used to build, buy or improve your home the usual $750,000 limit applies.

13. Your mortgage must comply with all the various laws of your state or locality.

14. If your home is destroyed you can continue to deduct the interest on your home as long as you rebuild it or sell the land within a reasonable time (reasonable time is nebulous, but as long as the delay is not primarily procrastinating, you can usually meet reasonable time. Reasonable can be 10 years or more if you are fighting to rebuild the home against opposition from neighbors or government). If you just let it sit there and make no effort to rebuild or sell, you are going to run into problems with the IRS.

15. Your first or second home can be a boat, mobile home, condo or RV/fifth wheel as long as it has sleeping, toilet and cooking facilities.

16. You must own or co-own the home or be legally liable for making the interest payments.

17. For low-income taxpayers, there is a Mortgage Interest Credit you can get if you set it up during the purchase. You get it by following the rules for your state that involve location and income requirements set by them. It is set up BEFORE closing so you need to work with your real estate agent and bank to see if you qualify. If you get the credit, you cannot use the same interest paid

for the credit and the deduction (but any excess interest above what is used for the credit can be deducted).

18. You generally have to be the one who pays the payment, but there are situations where that might not be true. If you are divorced, see the I'm Getting Divorced chapter. If you get government assistance paying it, seek professional help with your taxes.

19. When you refinance your home, you generally have to spread any points you pay on the refinancing out based on the life of the refinance. Any unused points from before the refinance are spread out over that same period. If you do a cash-out refinance and use the proceeds to substantially improve your home, you can take the points immediately. If you use some for improvement and some for other things, you can pro rate the points based on the use of the money and deduct the portion related to the improvements.

20. Any points not previously deducted can be taken in the year you sell the home.

21. If you receive a refund of mortgage interest in the same year you paid them you only include the amount that was actually kept by the bank as a deduction. If you receive a refund in a later year, you must include the refund as income in the year you get it, but only to extent that it benefitted you. If your itemized deductions were only $100 above the standard deduction the year you deducted them, and you receive a rebate of $500, you only include $100 as income since you would have gotten the full standard deduction anyway.

22. Military and clergy housing allowances do not affect the deductibility of mortgage interest, even if it covers your full mortgage payment.

Real Estate Taxes:

1. You can deduct real estate taxes if they are based on the value of your home, are similar to others in your area, and are not used to provide you special benefits that others do not get.

2. They will generally be reported on the Form 1098 from your lender if they are paid through your escrow account via your monthly payment. If you pay through escrow and they are not reported on your 1098, you probably had your mortgage sold and the other bank handled them. Again, make sure you get all of your 1098 forms. If you don't have a mortgage, you will use your own records of paying them to determine the amount (if you don't have a mortgage you get a tax bill to pay just like other bills.)

3. When you buy your home, no matter who pays the real estate taxes, you only get to deduct the taxes based on the dates you owned the home. The Master Settlement Statement will normally indicate which taxes were attributed to you. If they are not broken down on the Master Settlement Statement, you ratio them based on the days of ownership to the entire year.

4. You can only deduct taxes based on the value of your home. The transfer taxes and tax stamps that will be riddled through your Master Settlement Statement are not deductible.

5. If you receive a refund of real estate taxes in the same year you paid them, only include the amount that was actually kept by the government. If you receive a refund in a later year, you must include the refund as income in the year you get it, but only to extent they benefitted you. If your itemized deductions were only $100 above the standard deduction the year you deducted them, and you receive a rebate of $500, you only include $100 as income since you would have gotten the full standard deduction anyway. If the limitation discussed next affects how much benefit you got, it will also reduce how much you include as income in the following year.

6. Starting with 2018 tax returns, you can deduct a MAXIMUM of $10,000 in real estate taxes AND state and local income or sales taxes AND personal property taxes COMBINED.

Energy Efficient Home Improvements:

Due to recent changes in this area that take effect in 2023, adding both sets of rules to this chapter would dramatically expand it, and it is already long enough. If you are considering adding new doors, windows, insulation, HVAC systems, wood stoves, solar, wind power, geothermal or anything else energy efficient. Read the I Made Energy Efficient Home Improvements chapter.

If you got the First-Time Homebuyer Credit:

The last big thing to discuss about your home is if you bought it in 2008 and took the First-Time Homebuyer Credit. If you did, you should have been paying it back at the rate of $500 per year as a part of your tax return. As long as you own and live in the home, you will pay the $500 each year until you pay the whole amount back. Here are a few more things to be aware of:

1. If you sell the home you have to pay back the remaining amount you hadn't paid, up to your gain on the sale. The gain is figured by taking the sales proceeds, minus expenses of the sale, and subtracting the basis. The basis is discussed above but is reduced by the unpaid portion of the credit.
2. If the home is condemned or destroyed, you have two years to buy a new home. If you do, you continue to repay at $500 per year. If you don't, you pay back the remaining amount on the tax return in the year that the 2 years ends, up to gain as discussed in 1.
3. If the home is transferred in a divorce, the credit issues go to the spouse who gets the house.
4. You don't have to repay the credit if you die. If there is a surviving spouse who was on the return when the credit was taken, their repayment amount is cut in half (the spouse who died takes half the issue with them to the grave).
5. If the house ceases to be your main home, you must repay the remaining credit that tax year.
6. If you are transferred on PCS orders as a member of the military you don't have to repay the credit immediately, unless you sell the home. You just keep paying the $500 per year. This also applies to Foreign Service employees sent on extended official duty.

Areas not fully explored here that may require more research for you: A foreign home, mortgage assistance payments, divorce issues, short-term financing, gifts and transfers of houses other than arm's length sale, reverse mortgages and if you cohabitate and share payments with someone other than your spouse.

My Advice:

1. Start a home folder. Use a folder color that you can write on. A manila folder with pockets is perfect! Put your Master Settlement Statement in the folder. After that, if you do something that affects the basis (mainly improvements) write the date and amount on the front of the folder in a nice column, and then put the paperwork supporting it into the folder. You will probably never need any of this information, but you will be really glad that you have it if you end up needing it. Likely reasons for needing it would be if you sell the home for an enormous profit or you convert the home to rental or business use.
2. Make sure you get a 1098 form from every lender who help your mortgage and/or every servicing company who managed your

payments. A few years ago, USAA changed servicing companies and many taxpayers had no idea that they should have gotten two 1098's since they knew their loan was still with USAA.

3. Get online access to your mortgage accounts and keep passwords and account recovery options up to date. Check each account for a 1098 before filing your tax return.
4. It is a good idea to at least consult with a tax professional when you have bought a home. They can help you assess what you need to track to allow you to take full tax advantage of being a homeowner.
5. When you move into your new home, give excess stuff to a Goodwill type charity. Be aggressive with clearing things out, take photos of the items donated and get a receipt. There's a chance you might be itemizing this year, and this is a HUGE potential deduction that most new homeowners only figure out AFTER it is too late.
6. Check with your state or county to see if you need to do anything about your real estate taxes. Some states assume a property will be used commercially anytime it is sold and jack up the taxes until YOU prove to them that it is your personal residence. South Carolina is one of these states. Getting a higher than expected tax bill will totally screw up your escrow account!
7. If you paid Mortgage Insurance Premiums 2020, check to see if you should amend that tax return, since these weren't deductible during the time you would normally file the return, but were retroactively restored. You need to file the 2020 amendment before 4/15/24 or you will not get the money refund as the time limit will have expired. 2018 and 2019 had the same issue, but those are now "closed" years for the purpose of getting refunds.

Military: Basic Allowance for Housing and Cost of Living Allowances do not affect the deductibility of any of the above items for your home. The VA Funding fee is mortgage insurance for the purpose of taxes. You are not required to pay the VA Funding Fee if you have a disability rating (seek help on this – I am NOT an expert). If you pay a VA Funding Fee and subsequently get a disability rating backdated to before you bought the home, go to your LENDER to get it rebated or applied to the loan principle.

Do NOT buy a home with a VA mortgage while on terminal leave if you are putting in a disability claim. The claim will likely be backdated to the date of discharge, NOT the date you started terminal leave! Take your time finding a home and close AFTER your real discharge date. In fact, the best advice I can give you is to talk to a mortgage broker who is experienced with VA loans well before your discharge if you plan on buying a home shortly after getting out.

31. I Made Home Improvements

Let me first say that if they are energy efficient home improvements, they MIGHT qualify for a credit. Check out the next chapter to see if they do. If not, read on...

Home improvements are not a tax deduction for your personal residence.

Sorry.

That does not mean you shouldn't track them.

One of the goals of this book is to not talk in taxese, but sometimes you have to talk some basic tax terms that most people have never heard of. One of those terms is "Basis." Basis, to put it in layman's terms, is how much you've put into something. Generally, we're talking about money. At its most simple, basis is what you pay for something. Everything you own has some sort of basis, and the IRS actually thinks you're going to track this for everything you own, just in case it ever comes up on a tax return. That said, there are a few things you really need to know, or be able to figure out, the basis of. One of these is your investments: stocks and bonds, but that's for a future discussion. The other is your house. Someday you will probably sell your house, give it away to your family, or convert it to business or rental use. You'll need to know the basis in that case.

Figuring out that basis can get VERY complex. For most people, it's what you paid for the house plus the cost of improvements that you make. A lot of other things might affect it, such as taking a home office deduction, having to pay special assessments for sewer improvements, or getting paid by the city so they can take part of your property and build a sidewalk on it. If these come up, or any other thing that appears to affect the value or money you have at stake in your property, either talk to an expert, or keep all the paperwork in your "home" file.

You do have a "home" file, right? If the answer is no, immediately find that big package of crap they gave you when you closed on the house and put it in a file labeled "home." Into this file you will put all records of things we just discussed, as well as paperwork documenting the cost of any home improvements. Improvements raise the value of the home and increase the basis. Repairs maintain the home, and don't increase the basis. Put repair receipts in the file anyway, just in case. The file isn't just for tax stuff. If you refinance or take out a home equity line of credit, put that paperwork in there, too.

My Advice:

1. Start a home folder. Use a folder color that you can write on. A manila folder with pockets is perfect! Put your Master Settlement Statement in the folder. After that, if you do something that affects the basis (mainly improvements) write the date and amount on the front of the folder in a nice column, and then put the paperwork supporting it into the folder. You will probably never need any of this information, but you will be really glad that you have it if you end up needing it. Likely reasons for needing it would be if you sell the home for an enormous profit or you convert the home to rental or business use.

Military: Not much different for you here.

32. I Made Energy Efficient Home Improvements

So, this chapter is basically going to be two chapters because the Inflation reduction Act made major changes to these credits that take effect in 2023. Since it is so late in 2022, comparing the relative benefits of the two years before making a decision isn't really helpful, though, in general, delaying to 2023 is the going to be the best idea. So I am going to leave the 2022 information right where it was, just below this paragraph, and then put all of 2023's brand new information completely separately to follow it. This way I don't have to intermix the rules and talk about name changes and everything else.

Here is the 2022 and before info:

The two credits for energy efficient home improvements are quite restrictive. I will cover each credit separately, but there are some common items to consider:

1. They must be for your MAIN home, the one you live at most of the time. That home can be a house, boat, RV, fifth wheel, condo or houseboat.
2. You must own it (you can still be paying a mortgage).
3. You must reduce your basis that we discussed in the I'm Buying a Home chapter by the amount the credit lowers your taxes.
4. Costs are considered paid when the work is complete, or when you move back into the home if you had to leave while the work was completed.
5. Most of the time, if you are having a home constructed, the builder will take any credits for energy efficiencies associated with the home, especially if you are buying a tract home from one of the major builders in a planned community. If you are having a custom house built, communicate with your builder, and your tax professional, to ensure it is clear who is qualified to take and who is taking any credits available.

Here are the details on the two credits:

Residential Energy Efficient Property Credit:

1. This is the big one, and the hard one. To get this one, you need to have installed truly alternative energy sources as a part of your home. Examples are solar power, wind, geothermal, fuel cell, or solar hot water. For 2017 and beyond, only solar power projects

get the credit. Work with the installer and your tax professional to determine if you qualify and get documentation from the installer. Taxes and government subsidies are a big part of determining the cost effectiveness of these type of projects, so you need to do more than just read this chapter.

2. The credit was up to 30% of the qualified costs, with each type of improvement having its own maximums. Starting in 2020 the credit started to phase out. The percentage is 26% in 2020 through 2022, 22% in 2023, and the credit is gone in 2024 (not really – it is now a new credit as discussed at the beginning of the chapter).
3. This credit is available for new construction.
4. If you share the house with someone other than your spouse, you get the credit based on what you paid, and the maximum is applied based on the percentage paid by each occupant.
5. The credit cannot reduce your taxes below zero, so it may take many years to get full benefit from the credit. Many solar sales companies aggressively market, or worse, make loan payments based on these credits. Make sure you understand how, when and how much you will be getting back on your taxes BEFORE you sign a contract or take out a loan.

Non-business Energy Property Credit:

1. This is the much more common credit, so I'm going to provide more details.
2. The Non-business Energy Property Credit is 10% of qualifying costs, with a LIFETIME maximum credit for all costs of $500.
3. The LIFETIME maximum credit for windows is $200 (this is inclusive, not in addition to the $500 limit; if you take $200 for windows, you only have $300 for the rest of your life for other things).
4. They are subject to AGI limitations for 2014 that were unavailable at the time this book was being published.
5. The credit is available for insulation, exterior doors, windows, skylights and roofs that are SPECIFICALLY designed to reduce heat loss or gain.
6. It also applies to water heaters, heating systems, and air conditioners that are near the most efficient available at the time of installation.
7. The instructions for the current year form will identify the standards to be met, but the manufacturer or installer can also tell you. They must provide, and you must maintain, documentation to

prove that it meets these standards. I recommend that you make the contractor or salesman SHOW you the documentation and proof that it meets the standards. Energy Star doesn't mean crap—these items have to be really high quality (and generally more expensive than non-qualified items).

8. If you share the house with someone other than your spouse, you get the credit based on what you paid, and the maximum is applied based on the percentage paid by each occupant.
9. If you and your spouse have separate main homes, there are extra hoops to jump through and you will need a bit of professional help to be safe.

Here is the 2023 and later info:

There are still two credits for energy efficient home improvements, one based primarily on improving the efficiency (insulation and more efficient systems) and the other for generating power (wind, solar, geothermal and wood stoves). There are certain requirements you must meet to claim either, detailed here:

1. They must be for your MAIN home, the one you live at most of the time. The only exception is for the Heat Pump (electric, not gas), Heating and cooling systems, Electric Hot Water Systems as well as Wood or Pellet Stoves, which have a separate, maximum credit of $2000 that does not count against the $1200 annual limit. These only require that the home be used by YOU as a residence, but you don't have to own it (you can be a renter) and it can be a second home.
2. That home can be a house, boat, RV, fifth wheel, condo or houseboat.
3. You must own it (you can still be paying a mortgage). Except as noted above for Heat Pumps etc…
4. You must reduce your basis that we discussed in the I'm Buying a Home chapter by the amount the credit lowers your taxes.
5. Costs are considered paid when the work is complete, or when you move back into the home if you had to leave while the work was completed.
6. Most of the time, if you are having a home constructed, the builder will take any credits for energy efficiencies associated with the home, especially if you are buying a tract home from one of the major builders in a planned community. If you are having a custom house built, communicate with your builder, and your tax

professional, to ensure it is clear who is qualified to take and who is taking any credits available.

7. You can generally rely on the manufacturer's certification that the specific energy efficient item qualifies for the credit. In later years, there will be specific requirements and code numbers for claiming the credit that they will provide. Their certification does NOT mean that you qualify for the full credit based on your taxes, or that the home you installed them in is your MAIN home as required. It just certifies that the item is energy efficient enough or of the proper type to qualify for the credit. ALWAYS consult a tax professional before investing large sums of money in an improvement that you are planning to get a big credit for. Do this BEFORE signing any contracts.

The two credit names are pretty self-explanatory:

Energy Efficient Home Improvement Credit.

1. Applies primarily to insulating products and energy efficient HVAC and hot water systems.
2. It is 30% of the cost of the item with some limitations applied.
3. There is a $600 per item limit and a $1200 per year total maximum credit limit which is changed and/or modified for certain items as discussed in further areas.
4. Equipment must meet specific requirements (Energy Star for doors, windows and insulation and specific, ever-increasing criteria for the rest) but you can rely on the manufacturers certification that it qualifies – SAVE THIS! In 2025 and later they must provide Qualified Product Identification Number and you will include these with your tax return.
5. An Energy Efficiency Audit has a maximum credit of $150.
6. Doors have a maximum, per door credit of $250 and a $500 per year total limit.
7. Exterior Windows and Skylights have a per year total credit maximum of $600.
8. Heat Pump (electric, not gas) heating and cooling systems, Electric Hot Water Systems as well as Wood or Pellet Stoves, have a separate, maximum credit of $2000 that does not count against the $1200 annual limit.
9. So you can get $1200 from insulation type stuff and $2000 for bigger heating and cooling stuff for a total maximum annual credit of $3200 if you do everything right. Paying attention to these

limits and doing things in the right order, for the right amounts to maximize the credits can be pretty important.

Residential Clean Energy Credit:

1. This is the big one, and the hard one. To get this one, you need to have installed truly alternative energy sources as a part of your home. Examples are solar power, wind, geothermal, fuel cell, or solar hot water. This also includes battery power storage technology. Work with the installer and your tax professional to determine if you qualify and get documentation from the installer. Taxes and government subsidies are a big part of determining the cost effectiveness of these type of projects, so you need to do more than just read this chapter.
2. The credit is up to 30% of the qualified costs, with each type of improvement having its own maximums. Starting in 2033 the credit starts to phase out. The percentage is 26% in 2033 and 22% in 2034 and theoretically expires after that. Be aware that these dates have been creeping outward so they may be extended further into the future. Based on political reality surrounding climate change I find it highly unlikely that an incredibly popular credit like this, which is also an easy political point, will ever go away.
3. This credit is available for new construction.
4. If you share the house with someone other than your spouse, you get the credit based on what you paid, and the maximum is applied based on the percentage paid by each occupant.
5. The credit cannot reduce your taxes below zero, so it may take many years to get full benefit from the credit. Many solar sales companies aggressively market, or worse, make loan payments based on these credits. Make sure you understand how, when and how much you will be getting back on your taxes BEFORE you sign a contract or take out a loan.

My Advice:

1. Be aware that the Solar Credit is not refundable. This means that it cannot reduce your taxes below zero so it may take several years to get the full advantage of it. It is a good idea to look at your tax return from the prior year and see what the number on Line 24 was (on the 2023 Form 1040 – this is your total tax – might be a different line for older years). If everything (except the Solar) stayed the same, this is a decent estimate for the maximum tax

benefit you would get in the first year after installing the panels, and then you can divide your total credit by this amount to see how many years it will take you to get the full credit.

2. If you are expecting a state tax credit, make sure you fully understand the rules. For example, South Carolina has a 25% credit, which the sales companies LOVE because they could say you only pay 45% of the cost of the panels. But in SC, you can only cut your taxes in half with the credit (vice eliminating them for the Federal Credit) so it can take WAY longer to get the full benefit. Check your state rules and make sure you FULLY understand how you will be getting your tax credit, and how long it will take.

3. Some states (like Massachusetts) have plans whereby you can get paid for generating alternative energy. Generally these payments will be taxable income but you often will not get a specific tax form from them. As with all unusual sorts of income, contact a tax pro to be sure whether you have to claim them.

Military: Not much different for you here.

33. I am Considering an Electric or Alternate Fuel Vehicle

2022 Update: There were a lot of changes made to credits for Electric Vehicles with the Inflation Reduction Act passed in 2022. The majority of these changes either went into effect immediately or change which cars qualify and how much you can get. Because determining what cars qualify is so complicated, it is best simply to reference a list available on the IRS website or ask a car dealer. You can rely on a car dealer's written certification that a car qualifies for the credit.

The IRS is still finalizing regulations related to 2024, so some of the information provided here might change. Use the IRS FAQ linked below to stay up to date. The rules changed mid-year, but only the new rules apply at this time, so I am not including any of the old rules because you either already bought an EV, or you didn't, so you only need the new rules.

The credits are "non-refundable" meaning they cannot reduce your taxes below zero, and thus, it is important to review your tax return or discuss with your tax pro how much credit you REALLY get. The credits do not carryover so buying multiple cars and/or installing chargers or other credit worthy items could cause you to miss out on all or some of the credit. That said, it appears that if you allow the dealer to collect the credit in return for selling you the car at a lower price, the tax liability limit does not come into play – though income limits do!

This is a link to the IRS Frequently Asked Questions on this topic: https://www.irs.gov/newsroom/topic-a-frequently-asked-questions-about-the-eligibility-rules-for-the-new-clean-vehicle-credit-under-ss-30d-effective-112023
Note that there is an index with additional questions in the right hand column.

New Vehicle Credit:

1. The credit for new electric and alternate fuel vehicles is capped at $7500 and is based on a complex calculation using the type of energy, where it is manufactured, where the components are sourced and a few other things. Again, the dealer can tell you exactly how much the credit is worth for the vehicle you want (though they cannot tell you how much will actually be available on your tax return due to the non-refundable nature of the credit as well as income limitations).

2. You can also look up specific vehicles by make, model and year here: https://fueleconomy.gov/feg/tax2023.shtml

3. The credit is only available if your current or prior year Adjusted Gross Income is $300,000 or less if filing jointly, $225,000 or less filing Head of Household and $150,000 or less for all other filing statuses. Using prior year income allows car dealers to directly reduce the price of the vehicle by the amount of the credit (plus a bit extra) starting in 2024. If you took the Foreign Earned Income Exclusion or have Puerto Rico or American Samoa income your AGI will need to account for any excluded income.

4. You have to provide the vehicles VIN number with your tax return.

5. The credit is NON-REFUNDABLE so make sure you have the tax liability to take advantage of it.

6. Starting in 2024, your car dealer can directly reduce the price of the vehicle by the credit amount (or other negotiated amount). If you do this, you have to report the information on your tax return just as if you were taking the credit yourself, and, if your income is too high, you might have to pay some of the credit back – though is your income was low enough in the year BEFORE you buy the car, you are safe to take the credit because you can use the year you buy the car's income, or the year prior. It does appear that the tax liability limit does not apply to a dealer taken credit, so if you don't pay a lot of taxes, using a dealer might be the best choice.

7. There was a limit where the credit was eliminated for a particular vehicle after 200,000 were sold. That has been eliminated in favor of a standard based on source of materials, type of power, place of manufacturer etc.

8. The vehicle must be purchased, not leased.

9. The vehicle must be primarily used in the United States.

10. The vehicle cannot be bought for resale.

11. You have to "place the vehicle in service" to qualify for the credit – basically, buy and use the vehicle. Things get twitchy if you return the vehicle.

12. The vehicle manufacturers suggested retail price must be $55,000 or less unless it is a van, pickup truck or SUV in which case the limit is $80,000.

13. The dealer should provide you with information required to claim the credit or reconcile a credit the dealer takes for you.

14. Make sure to look the VIN up yourself before trusting a dealer – just to be safe.

Used Vehicle Credit

1. The credit for used electric and alternate fuel vehicles is 30% of the sales price with a maximum credit of $4000. Again, the dealer can tell you exactly how much the credit is worth for the vehicle you want (though they cannot tell you how much will actually be available on your tax return due to the non-refundable nature of the credit).

2. The credit is only available if your current or prior year Adjusted Gross Income is $150,000 or less if filing jointly, $112,500 or less filing Head of Household and $75,000 or less for all other filing statuses. Using prior year income allows car dealers to directly reduce the price of the vehicle by the amount of the credit (plus a bit extra) starting in 2024.

3. You have to provide the vehicles VIN number with your tax return.

4. The credit is NON-REFUNDABLE so make sure you have the tax liability to take advantage of it, however, if the dealer takes the credit for you, you can get the full credit regardless of your tax liability.

5. Starting in 2024, your car dealer can directly reduce the price of the vehicle by the credit amount (or other negotiated amount). If you do this, you have to report the information on your tax return just as if you were taking the credit yourself, and, if your income is too high, you might have to pay some of the credit back – though is your income was low enough in the year BEFORE you buy the car, you are safe to take the credit because you can use the year you buy the car's income, or the year prior. It does appear that the tax liability limit does not apply to a dealer taken credit, so if you don't pay a lot of taxes, using a dealer might be the best choice.

6. The car must be sold by a dealer (I am sure that some enterprising car dealers may find a way to play intermediary on a private sale to allow for the credit. It might be worth your time to investigate this if you are involved in a private sale of an otherwise qualifying car. I am NOT stating that this will be legal – I have no idea. That said, if it turns out to be a legal loophole, taking advantage of it is a no-brainer.

7. You must be the SECOND owner.

8. The vehicle must be 2 or more years old.

9. The sales price of the vehicle, before the credit, must be less than $25,000.

10. The vehicle must be purchased, not leased.

11. The vehicle must be primarily used in the United States.

Car Chargers:

1. There is a credit of up to $1000 for installing fueling systems in your home, generally a car charger, though check with the installer.
2. The credit is 30% of the cost of installing.
3. This credit is also non-refundable so buying an electric vehicle and installing a charger in the same year increases the chance that you will lose some of the credit.

My Advice:

1. Talk to your tax professional before you buy the vehicle. Give them estimates for changes to your return from the prior year so they can estimate how much of the credit you will qualify for.
2. The credit is awesome but don't let it impact your vehicle purchase decision too much. These cars are more expensive even after the credit so make sure you are buying this kind of car because it makes sense in your life, and not because of the tax credit.
3. Get the proof of qualification from the dealer IN WRITING before finalizing the sale.
4. Make sure your income from the year before buying the vehicle qualifies you before you buy the car unless you are absolutely sure your income in the year you buy it will qualify.
5. If you aren't absolutely sure you will have the tax liability to take full advantage of the credit, consider allowing a dealer to take the credit for you and reduce the price of the vehicle by that amount.
6. Even if you claim the credit through dealer price reduction, you still have to report the credit on your tax return to ensure your income qualifies. I suspect the IRS will be rejecting tax returns missing the credit and this will be a source of trouble for this year.

34. I Have to File Married Filing Separately

I hope that you are filing MFS because you want to, but let me open this chapter by saying that MFS should be avoided except in a few very specific circumstances. These are:

1. You have no choice (you are married, do not meet the HH requirements and can't convince your spouse to file jointly)
2. You do not want to be responsible for your spouse's taxes
3. You will get better refunds because of MFS (generally this means that one of you has medical expenses and a lower income).
4. You are paying on student loans using Income Based Repayment and your spouse's income makes the payments truly unaffordable.
5. Either you or your spouse owe debts that will be collected out of your refund (delinquent child support, student loans etc.). This is actually not a good reason, but I included it to explain why. You can file an Injured Spouse claim to get the portion of your refund attributable to the spouse who does not owe the dept. Also, the debt probably is not going away, so a refund getting yanked is an effective way of getting it paid off – but you can make that call based on your own life situation.

If you think the third reason applies, run your tax returns both ways and see which one works out better. If the first applies, but there's wiggle room on the part of your spouse, consider running your tax returns both ways and see if the change in results makes them change their mind (you might need to make a financial compromise if it improves yours and hurts theirs).

If the fourth option applies to you, filing separately means only your income counts toward the calculation. Make sure that the negative tax effects do not outweigh the lower student loan payments. Do not try MFS if both you and your spouse are on IBR.

One of the things that is sometimes hard about filing MFS is that you need your spouse's name (spelled right), SSN and often their birthday. If you don't have it, you will have to attempt to get it (awkward conversation, I know, I've listened to them a lot). If you can't get it, you will have to paper file the return, which will delay your refund.

I am not going to discuss every detail of the differences between MFS and MFJ. You should review the chapters of this book that apply to you in conjunction with this chapter to fully understand the effects (though if this chapter says you don't get some or other deduction or credit, there's not much point in reading the chapter on it).

One thing I want to make clear is that living in a community property state (AZ, CA, ID, LA, NV, NM, TX, WA, WI) can have dramatic effects on how you file—expert help should be sought if you are MFS in a community property state. Specific rules for the treatment of community property vary from state to state and are too detailed to cover here. To give an example, in most cases you include half of your income and half of their income, instead of just your own. Separation agreements only make it worse. Trust me, get professional tax help in these cases.

You can go from a MFS return to a joint return with no special restrictions under the usual rules for amending returns, but you generally can't file a MFS return after filing a MFJ return once the due date for the return has passed. The IRS really does not like MFS returns (my opinion). If you don't agree, see the following list of what they do to you when you file MFS:

1. If one spouse itemizes deductions, the other spouse must as well. This means if the other spouse has no deductions, they get zero for a standard deduction.
2. You get half the standard deduction ($13,850), home mortgage interest limitations ($375,000), capital loss limitation ($1,500), exclusion of gain on sale of main home ($250,000), and Alternative Minimum Tax (AMT) exemptions. The tax brackets shift at exactly half the income they would for MFJ.
3. The income thresholds for the phase-out of the following are cut in half from MFJ thresholds: Child Tax Credit and Retirement Savings Contribution Credit.
4. You are not allowed the Earned Income Credit (starting in 2021 there are relaxed rules on this that basically apply to the imminently divorcing), Elderly or Disabled Credit (unless you lived apart all year), Child and Dependent Care Credit, Adoption Credit, and neither Education Credit (Lifetime Learning and American Opportunity).
5. You cannot take deductions for student loans.
6. You cannot exclude U.S. Savings Bond interest used for higher education.
7. You cannot make deductible or Roth IRA contributions if you have an AGI over $10,000 unless you and your spouse lived apart all year (you cannot have spent a single night with them).

8. Your Social Security benefits become taxable at $0 of income unless you and your spouse lived apart all year.

9. If you and your spouse lived together at any time during the year, you cannot deduct any Rental Real Estate Losses using the exception for Active Participation. If you lived apart, the limit for deduction is $12,500 and starts phasing out at an income of $50,000. (This will make a lot more sense when you read the chapters on renting out your home, former home or investment property.)

10. When claiming deductions, the spouse claiming it must have paid it and meet the requirements for deducting it. If the payment is made from a joint account into which both spouses put earnings into, it is presumed to be paid half by each spouse, unless you can prove otherwise. If one spouse pays for something, but the other spouse is the one who meets the requirements for deducting it then NOBODY gets to deduct it.

11. Medical expenses for your children may be deducted even if you don't get to claim the exemption.

12. You can claim medical expenses for your spouse if you paid them or the services were provided while you were married.

13. If you file a separate state and/or local return, you deduct the taxes you paid. If you file a joint return, you ratio the taxes based upon your income (your deduction is equal to your income, divided by the total income, multiplied by the tax paid).

14. If you own more than one house, you can only deduct interest from one of them, unless the other spouse consents in writing to allow you to deduct both.

15. If you made joint estimated payments, you may divide them in any way you can agree on with your spouse. If you can't agree, you ratio them by income in the same manner discussed under 14. If you divide payments made, you write "DIV" under the word payments to the left of line 62 on your tax return. If your spouse is filing HH, they need to write your name and SSN on their return just like you had to as discussed above. If you make separate estimated payments you just include them as normal.

16. Dependent Care Benefits paid by your employer become taxable above $2,500, vice $5,000.

17. If you got an Affordable Care Act (Obamacare) subsidy you might have to pay the full amount back.

18. The maximum amount of state and local income tax that you can deduct as itemized deductions is $5,000.

My Advice:

1. Do not file MFS if you can avoid it.

2. ALWAYS run the numbers jointly and separately to see if the reason you are filing MFS is worth the refund reduction. Remember that you have to pay for two tax returns when doing MFS so take that into account.
3. If you are making student loan payments, especially under an Income Based Repayment Plan, be certain that you understand how your filing status affects your taxes and repayments. If the payment plan doesn't save you a ton of money, the loss in tax benefits might overcome the reduction in student loan payment amount.

Military: Don't file MFS just because your military spouse is deployed. Either get a Power of Attorney or get an extension.

35. I Have Medical Expenses

2018 Trump/GOP Tax Law Changes: Between the Affordable Care Act and the Trump Tax Law, the percentage of income above which you are allowed to start deducting medical expenses bounced back and forth between 7.5% and 10%. It has now been permanently returned to 7.5%. I'm leaving this here just to alleviate any confusion.

Subsequent changes:
- COVID-19 expenses, including disinfectant supplies and personal protective equipment such as face masks were made deductible as medical expenses. They remain deductible going forward so make sure to include them as expenses.

Medical expenses are one of the itemized deductions you are allowed, though they are subject to limitations. You should review the general Itemized Deductions chapter as well as this chapter since you might need other deductions to get over the standard deduction. The biggest questions about medical expenses are, what can I deduct, who can I deduct it for, and what stupid rules apply. I'll start with the first stupid rule, then tell you what's deductible, who it's deductible for, and the rest of the stupid rules. The first stupid rule is that you can only deduct medical expenses that exceed 7.5% of your AGI. You actually include all of your deductible expenses, but then you subtract 7.5% of your AGI from it, before deducting what's left (or nothing, if 7.5% of your AGI is more than your expenses). The theory behind this is, I believe, to prevent most people from having to track their expenses unless something catastrophic happens to them. As usual, this completely fails to accomplish its goal, since you don't know if something big will happen to you late in the year, so, to be safe, you need to track all your medical expenses that would suddenly be deductible once this happens.

My advice is to apply the drawer system. Toss all your medical bills in a drawer, with the date paid. At the end of the year, find out what 7.5% of your AGI is and, if it's close, pull them out and add them up. Otherwise, empty the drawer out and start over with the New Year. You can also just throw them out if it's pretty obvious your other deductions won't get you above the standard deduction even with medical expenses added.

The idea of medical expenses is that they have to identify, prevent, cure, improve, or alleviate the symptoms of a SPECIFIC medical condition. They can't be just for general health, and they generally must be prescribed or supervised by a doctor or other qualified medical professional (I'll specify when they don't with an *). They include equipment, supplies and diagnostic devices. That said, many things that are or are not deductible will seem that they don't quite meet these criteria, or they may seem offensive or violate your political or moral standards (for example, the first on the list is abortion). If I list it one way or another, you can be pretty sure that it's been fought over and resolved to reasonable satisfaction one way or another. I'll list a ton of specific yes's and no's, but won't try to justify them (many times I can't because there is little rhyme or reason to them). If they are maybe's, I'll discuss circumstances that help or hurt your chances—you might want to enlist an expert to help you make the right choice.

After the yes, no and maybes, I'll go into more details, other deductions and general rules for medical deductions. The lists are long and sometimes repetitive to make it most likely that something you're looking for is discussed. More and more alternative therapies are becoming accepted every day, so if one isn't on this list, consult a professional just to make sure.

Yes:

Abortion
Acupuncture
Inpatient alcohol and drug treatment, including meals and lodging
Travel to and from AA meetings if attending based on medical advice
Ambulance
Artificial limbs and teeth
Autoette
Bandages*
Birth control pills
Braces
Braille books and magazines* (the amount above regular price)
Breast pumps and supplies*
Chiropractor
Christian Science Practitioner
Clinics
Contact lenses, including cleaning and storage supplies
COVID related medication, vaccines, testing, masks, gloves and even cleaning and disinfecting supplies.
Crutches*
Dental (except teeth whitening)

Diagnostic devices, such as blood pressure or sugar test supplies*
Prescribed drugs that are legal in the United States and legally imported
Prescription drugs taken in a foreign country if legal in that country and the U.S.
Insulin*
Eye doctor, glasses and eye surgery
Fertility treatments, including sterility procedure reversal
Sterilization
Service animal for PHYSICAL disability including costs to maintain the animal
Hearing aids
Hospital services, including meals (inpatient care) and lodging
Lab fees
Lead-based paint removal (if it is covered, see Maybe #7)
Medical exams
Medical information plan used to provide information to physicians
Doctor visits and services (includes most medical practitioners)
Halfway house from mental institution (not home of relative)
Occupational therapist
Operations (not cosmetic unless medically prescribed to treat something)
Organ donor medical expenses
Osteopath
Oxygen and associated equipment for medical problems
Physical therapist
Podiatrist
Prosthesis
Psychiatric care
Psychoanalysis
Psychologist
Sex reassignment for treatment of gender identity disorder (this means not elective)
Stop smoking programs (but not non-prescription gums or patches)
Surgery
Telephone and television specially designed for hearing impaired
Therapy as medical treatment
Transplants
Wheelchair
Whirlpool baths ordered by doctor
Wig advised by doctor for mental health of patient losing hair due to disease
X-rays

No:

Babysitting or nursing care for a healthy baby
Car medical insurance not specifically for you and your family (dependents)
Teeth whitening, except as discussed under Maybe #2.
Illegal operations or drugs
Drugs illegally imported into the U.S.
Drugs taken in another country that are illegal there or in the U.S.
Maternity clothes
Dancing or other lessons used to improve general health
Health club dues
Meals that are not paid to a hospital or other institution during inpatient care
Non-prescription drugs other than insulin
Swimming lessons
Travel that is merely beneficial to general health
Vet fees, except for a service animal discussed in the Yes chapter
Expenses reimbursed by insurance or other sources.
Funeral expenses
Household help, except as discussed under Maybe #12 and #14
Payroll deductions for Medicare Part A (the deductions shown on your W-2 box 6 or pay stub under Medicare)
Employer-provided health care, unless they include it as wages (odds are they are not)
Surrogate parenting expenses
Bottled water

Maybe (or detailed explanation required):

1. Car medical insurance is deductible if it is for you or your family (dependents) and is separately priced in the policy from other insurance.
2. Cosmetic surgery is only deductible if it fixes a deformity you are born with, or that is caused by an accident, injury, illness or the treatment of an illness. Example 1: Breast enhancement for improvement of looks is not deductible but following breast cancer mastectomy it would be. Example 2: Scar removal would be deductible, but not skin treatments to correct common effects of old age.
3. Diaper service is deductible only if it is needed to relieve the effects of a disease.

4. Vitamins or supplements are only deductible if they are recommended by a medical professional for the treatment of a SPECIFIC disease. Never deductible for preventative care.

5. Personal use items are not generally deductible, but if you pay more than the normal price for something as a result of a specific disease, you can deduct the difference between regular price and the special price. An example would be the extra cost of Braille books over normal books.

6. Health insurance premiums are mostly deductible. If you take the self-employed health insurance deduction, you can't double deduct as an itemized deduction. Specifically, deductible health insurances are medical and dental coverage, membership in associations that give cooperative medical care, long-term care insurance (subject to limits based on age), Medicare Part A (only if not enrolled in Social Security—payroll deductions for Medicare Part A are not deductible), Medicare Part B, and Medicare Part D. Prepaid medical care insurance has special limitations.

7. Modifications to your house to accommodate a medical condition are deductible if they are primarily for the medical condition. If they increase the value of your home, you must reduce the deduction by the increase in value. The classic example is an elevator that costs $10,000 but increases the home's value by $6,000. The deduction would be $4,000. Maintenance, repair and operation expenses (including electricity if you can account for how much is used by the device) are deductible even if you couldn't deduct the installation due to it increasing the value of the home. If lead paint was mitigated by covering instead of removal, you treat it just like a home improvement and deduct the cost minus the increase in home's value.

8. Improvements to plumbing and fixtures in a home or apartment you rent to accommodate your medical condition are deductible.

9. If your car is modified to accommodate your medical condition or disability (such as hand controls) the cost of the modification is deductible. If you purchase a specially equipped vehicle, such as a wheelchair lift equipped van, or a car that is already modified, the difference in price between the modified vehicle and the same, unmodified vehicle is deductible. Maintenance and upkeep costs are not deductible (though you get mileage similar to any other vehicle, which we will discuss later).

10. Lodging is deductible when provided by the hospital or similar facility. You can deduct $50 a night for lodging not at a medical facility if it is primarily for and essential to medical care, the care is provided by a qualified physician in a hospital or equivalent facility, the lodging is not fancy, and there is no element of pleasure or vacation in the travel. This disallows deductions for "medical tourism" and the like.

11. Meal expenses are only deductible if provided by and paid to a hospital or similar facility.

12. Long-term care services are deductible if they are medically necessary to treat a chronic condition and are under the plan of care prescribed by a medical professional. Chronically ill must be certified by a physician that within the prior 12 months either the person could not perform at least two essential activities of daily living for at least 90 days due to a medical condition (these activities are eating, toileting, bathing, dressing, transferring and continence) or they require substantial supervision to be protected due to severe cognitive impairment (think Alzheimer's, dementia and the like).

13. Nursing home care is deductible if the primary reason for being there is medical. If the primary reason is not medical, only the expenses specifically for medical care are deductible.

14. Nursing services are deductible even if not provided by a professional nurse. Their lodging and meals are also deductible if the nurse lives with the person requiring care. If the nurse provides non-medical household services, the cost must be separated from the medical services. Nursing services include medical care, grooming, bathing, providing medication and changing dressings. Some non-medical household services may qualify as long-term care under 12 above. They may also qualify for the Child and Dependent Care Credit, which I discuss under the children chapters and chapters about caring for parents, family members and others. If you pay the nurse as your employee, you can include Social Security and Medicare tax matching, as well as any state employment tax or unemployment insurance.

15. Special education for children with mental and physical handicaps is deductible, including attending special schools, as well as meals and lodging at the school, so long as the schooling is recommended by a doctor. The deduction is allowed even if non-special-needs education is provided as well.

16. Transportation for medical care is deductible. For a car, this is either gas and oil, or the standard medical mileage rate (22 cents a mile – but can change at any time, though usually mid-year). Parking and tolls are deductible in addition to gas and oil, or the standard mileage rate. The travel must be primarily for medical care. Driving to and from work, even if by a medically special means, is never deductible as medical expense. Travel includes airfare, taxis, train, bus, rental cars, and other necessary means. Lodging is subject to the limits and restrictions discussed in 10, above. Travel to receive medical care for personal reasons, as opposed to medical (you want to get an operation in Las Vegas because you like the shows) is not deductible. Travel for improving your general health is not deductible. Travel expenses for a nurse travelling with you are deductible if you are travelling for care and can't travel alone. Transportation to visit a

mentally ill relative are deductible if recommended as part of the treatment. The expenses of a parent travelling with a child who needs care is deductible.

17. Weight loss programs are deductible if they are for the treatment of a SPECIFIC medical condition diagnosed by a physician:

- Membership in weight loss groups and meetings
- Separate fees for weight loss programs at gyms (but not general membership)
- Food costs above those of a normal diet if they treat or improve a specific illness, are not part of normal nutritional needs, AND the need is substantiated by a physician.

You cannot deduct gym membership, weight loss costs to improve general health and appearance, and costs for replacement foods for normal foods (such as low-calorie, low-fat diet foods or nutritional supplements).

18. You can deduct costs of attending (including travel, but not meals and lodging) seminars and conferences if they are about a specific medical condition that you or your dependent has. You have to spend most of your time attending classes, seminars or workshops about the condition. Beware the vacation disguised as a conference!

19. If you buy a test to check for a disease or to self-diagnose, they are deductible even if not suggested by a doctor.

20. Service dogs for mental disability or psychiatric treatment MAY be deductible. This one is very complex and should be discussed with a tax pro.

Here are the rest of the details:

1. You can deduct medical expenses in the year you pay them. If you pay by check or charge, the year is determined based on when you send the check or charge the card. Payments made with credit cards count even if you don't pay the balance off. If you pay with loan proceeds independent of the medical provider, you can generally deduct the amount you pay. If you finance through the medical provider, you can only deduct the payments you make to them, not the full bill.

2. Don't deduct expenses paid by your insurance company, your employer, or paid for with proceeds from a tax advantaged medical account, such as a Health Savings Account, Flexible Spending Account or Medical Savings Account. Also, don't deduct expenses that are reimbursed through a lawsuit or settlement (if you deduct expenses that are subsequently reimbursed in a later year, you have to include them as income to the extent they improved your tax return in the year deducted, just like your income tax refund – this can be complicated so consider seeking expert help with it and, if you are

involved in a lawsuit or insurance settlement, keep scrupulous records of what is paid, when, by whom and when reimbursed).

3. If medical expenses are reimbursed in a later year than the one you deducted them in, they are added as income in that year, but only to the extent they improved your taxes in the year deducted. For example, if the reimbursement amount would have dropped your expenses below 7.5% helped you. Similarly, if the reimbursement would have dropped your itemized deductions below your standard deduction, only the amount above your standard deduction helped you. This can be complicated if the numbers are close, so you might want to seek help if you are in this situation.

4. You can deduct medical expenses you paid for your spouse on your tax return as long as you were married to them either at the time the expenses were paid or the medical services provided. If you file MFS, there is a separate chapter for that.

5. You can deduct medical expenses you paid for your dependent included on your tax return as long as they were your dependent either at the time the expenses were paid, or the medical services provided.

6. You can claim expenses for someone who would be your dependent, and claimed on your tax return, but was not, as long as it was for one of the following reasons: They made more than $4,700, they filed a joint return, you waived the exemption to the child's other parent during divorce or separation, or someone else claimed you or your spouse as a dependent. The $4,700 and the divorce one are the biggest reasons. I discuss waiving the exemption in the chapter on Divorce. The $4,700 comes up as your child gets older but continues to live at home. It comes into play if they turn 19 and don't go to school or turn 24 regardless of school. In those situations, you lose the exemption when they make more than $4,700 (unless they are disabled), but you can still deduct medical expenses. They may also come up if you care for an aging parent who makes more than $4,700, even if they don't live with you. Make sure to review the specific chapters on people who live with you or taking care of your parents to be sure you follow the right rules for claiming them.

7. One other item for divorced or separated parents: If you or the other child's parent have custody and one of you claims the child, and you are divorced, legally separated or lived apart the last six months of the year, each parent claims the medical expenses that they paid, regardless of who claims the child's exemption. If there is a third party who provides custody or support for the child who is not married to either parent, this may not apply, and you should seek help in determining who claims what for the child.

My Advice:

1. Unless you have a high likelihood of exceeding the income limits discussed above, it is probably not worth tracking medical expenses.
2. If you are likely to deduct medical expenses (or you always do) make sure to track mileage for medical travel. A simple log book with date, purpose, location and miles driven is sufficient.

Military: You cannot deduct medical expenses if they would have been reimbursable, even if you elect to pay for service due to not wanting to wait for military or VA medical services. This means that most active military will have no deductible medical expenses unless they pay for fertility treatments.

Discussed elsewhere or not discussed: MFS, non-citizen parents or children, third-party support or custody.

36. I have a High Deductible Health Plan and/or Health Savings Account through Work

Coronavirus UPDATE: The CARES Act passed in early 2020 allows you to use your HSA for over-the-counter drugs like pain killers, allergy medicines etc. It also allows you to use it for menstrual related products. This change applies to 2020 and later years.

Autocorrect LOVES changing HSA to HAS and I am never confident in catching everyone so if you see HAS below, it probably means HSA. And yes, I know there is a way to stop it and know, I can't figure out how – I am a tax expert not a computer expert.

Everything below assumes your employer is handling all the details for your High Deductible Health Plan (HDHP) and Health Savings Account (HSA). That has become less true lately as people have figured out just how amazing an HSA can be. HSA contributions are what we call "Triple Tax Advantaged". The money contributed comes right off the top of taxable income, the earnings are tax deferred, and withdrawals are tax free if used for qualifying medical expenses. Add to that the fact that money put into a HSA is YOURS forever. Doesn't matter if you lose or quit your job. The money is yours, and you can use it or leave it in the account forever. As long as it only comes out for medical expenses you will NEVER pay taxes on it. If your employer does not contribute the maximum amount for you, you can contribute your own money (through payroll deduction and/or direct contributions) up to the maximums discussed in the rest of the chapter. Many of my truly savvy clients plan to max these out and leave the money in the account to cover insurance costs between the time they retire, and the time they are eligible for Medicare (age 65). This is a BRILLIANT plan! Employer contributions and payroll deductions are handled smoothly through your W-2. Direct contributions need to be manually entered as a deduction on your tax return.

Done right, a High Deductible Health Plan (HDHP) and Health Savings Account (HSA) through your employer should have no impact on your tax return bottom line and should be simple to put on your tax return (unless you're doing it by hand on paper). This chapter provides an overview of how HDHP and HSA affect your taxes, then goes into more detail for more complicated situations.

The theoretical idea of High Deductible Health Plans and Health Savings Accounts is that they should go hand-in-hand to provide predictability, affordability and tax advantages with regard to health care and insurance costs. The basic idea is that you get a health insurance plan that has a high, relatively fixed deductible. In return for this, you get two main advantages: the plan should be cheaper than low deductible insurance, and you can save money in a tax advantaged account to pay for health care costs up to the deductible. All the complicated rules and limits are designed to align with these ideas.

For most people, these rules and limits will be handled at the employer level. The health plan will be purchased through your employer, the contributions to the HSA account will be either made by your employer, or done through payroll deduction, or both. Most will even provide a debit-type card that will only allow you to use it for allowed expenses. In this situation, everything you need to file your taxes is included on your W-2 (a code W in box 12), a Form 1099SA from the HSA account administrator, and a Form 5498 from the same place. If all of these apply to you, the only thing you need to be careful about is to make sure that you stay in the plan for at least a year. If you do, you just input your W-2 and 1099 into the software (or provide to your tax professional) and indicate that everything taken out of the HSA was used for appropriate medical expenses. If your plan doesn't provide a card that prevents you from using the HSA for unauthorized expenses, you will need to know what's allowed, and ensure you only take money out for those things (discussed later). Having done all these things, your tax return should show no deductions, additions or extra taxes due to your HDHP and HSA. You will have a Form 8889, but nothing should carry to the main tax return. This may make you wonder where the tax advantages are, which is a good question. The tax advantages occurred as you were paid, and as the HSA earned money. None of the money put into the HSA is included as taxable income, so nothing gets withheld from it, and it doesn't appear on your tax return. In addition, you don't include any earnings from the HSA account in income. You don't have to use all the money you put in in the same year. You can let it keep growing until you really need it. There's no limit on how much you take out, except that it must be used for allowable medical expenses.

That is where the easy part ends. The rest of this chapter will cover all the nitty gritty, and other requirements and rules. If the previous paragraph covered your situation, you are done, but feel free to keep reading, and definitely read it when you leave your job or cancel your plan. Keep in mind that you do not have to have your HDHP and HSA through your employer. You can set these up for yourself or your family if you don't have other health coverage.

In order to have an HSA you must be covered under a HDHP and you cannot be covered by military medical, Tricare or Medicare, or other employer programs. Both will be defined in the details below, as well as other requirements.

HSA:

1. An HSA is an account set up with a custodian, such as a bank or financial institution. Contributions up to the annual limit are either not included in income (when contributed through your employer) or deducted off of your income when filing taxes if you make them yourself. Earnings are not taxed. Withdrawals can only be made (with a few exceptions) for qualified medical expenses (discussed later). These withdrawals are tax free.

2. Withdrawals that are not for qualified medical expenses are taxable and subject to an additional 20% penalty.

3. Contributions do not have to be used in any given year and can be used for qualified medical expenses even after you no longer qualify to contribute.

4. Contributions can be made by the taxpayer, their employer, or anyone else, as long as they do not exceed the total allowed amount of contributions for the year.

5. There is a maximum amount that can be contributed in any given year. This limit for 2023 is $3,850 for a person covered by a plan for only him or herself (single plan), $7,750 for someone with coverage for them self and at least one other person (family plan). This number is increased by $1,000 if you are over 55. If your employer doesn't put in the maximum amount, you can contribute your own money either through payroll deduction or direct investment up to the maximums we just discussed. This is often one of the best tax avoidance strategies out there.

6. If both you and your spouse have HSAs, the limit applies to the total amount contributed to the accounts, though if both of you are over 55 you get an extra $2,000 instead of just $1,000.

7. There are some provisions for rolling over money from IRA's and other tax advantaged health accounts, but you should talk to your tax professional before doing this.

8. Qualified medical expenses are those that are incurred after the account was set up and would be deductible as a medical expense (see the chapter on I Have Medical Expenses for details). The same rules for who you can deduct expenses for (such as spouse or dependent) apply for these expenses. In addition, qualified medical expenses include non-prescription drugs that are prescribed by a doctor. Insurance premiums don't count

unless you are over 65, unemployed or they are for long-term care. Medigap insurance does not count.

9. Medical expenses paid from your HSA that would have qualified except that they were incurred before the account was set up save you from the 20% penalty, but the withdrawal is still taxable.

10. When you die, you can leave your HSA to your spouse and it becomes his or her HSA. If you leave it to someone else, they must take the money out and pay taxes on it (but no penalty). If it is left to your estate, the money goes on your final return, and is taxable to the extent the amount in it exceeds any medical expenses you had in the year before your death—again, no penalty.

11. To qualify for an HSA, you must be covered under a HDHP (discussed below). You cannot have any other comprehensive health insurance except disability, dental, vision, or long-term care. You cannot be enrolled in Medicare. You can't qualify as someone else's dependent, even if they don't claim you. If your spouse has a non-HDHP plan, you can still have an HSA if you are not covered by your spouse's plan, and you have a HDHP.

12. If you are covered on the first day of December, you are considered covered for that whole year, as long as you maintain coverage for at least a year. If you don't maintain coverage for a full year, your contribution limit is 1/12 of the annual total, times the number of months in the year you were covered. If your coverage is ended before December 1st, you get to contribute an amount equal to your annual limit, divided by 12, times the number of months you were covered.

13. You cannot take a medical expense itemized deduction for expenses you paid with funds out of the HSA.

14. You cannot have an HSA and another active tax preferred medical account such as a Health Reimbursement Account or Flexible Spending Account (FSA). You can have an FSA if it is restricted from paying medical expenses.

15. You can make contributions for a previous year up to 4/15 of the next year.

16. Excess contributions are subject to a 6% penalty—take them and any earnings out by the due date of the return.

HDHP:

1. A HDHP is a plan that has minimum annual deductibles, and a minimum cap on annual out-of-pocket expenses for covered expenses. For a single person's plan, the deductible must be at least $1,500 and the annual cap at least $7,500. For a family plan (two or more people covered) the deductible is at least $3,000 and the cap at least $15,000.

2. The HDHP can have a prescription drug plan, as long as it doesn't start paying for drugs until the deductible is met.

3. If the plan is a family plan, but has separates deductibles for each individual, the individual deductibles must meet the requirements for a single plan, and the totals of the deductibles must meet the requirements for a family plan.

4. There are some other annoying rules on what does or does not qualify, but they are best handled by the insurance provider. They will generally be identifying HDHP's for you, so you know what qualifies you for an HSA.

My Advice:

1. Maximize your contributions to your Health Savings Account to the greatest extent possible consistent with your other savings goals. The limit to how much you can contribute includes both money your employer puts in and money you put in yourself. If your spouse has an HAS as well, the limit applies to BOTH of your contributions.

2. Avoid using HSA money for minor medical expenses that you can afford to pay for out of pocket. This includes the CARES act additions for over-the-counter medications and menstrual products.

3. Once your HSA is well funded, invest the balance aggressively based upon your age and risk tolerance. Professional advice may be wise in this situation.

4. Discuss with your financial advisor and tax advisor about how to incorporate your HSA into your larger financial plan. Get them to assist you in determining a proper balance between 401k and HSA contributions. Ultimately you want to hit the limits on all these accounts, though that does require a pretty large income.

5. It is better to have your employer make contributions to your HSA than it is to contribute to it outside of work because employer contributions avoid Social Security and Medicare taxes in addition to income taxes. Always try to get your employer to do the contributions if at all possible.

Military: Military medical care and Tricare are disqualifying from having an HSA.

37. I am Donating to Charity

A Summary of Changes in the last few years:
2018: The Trump Tax Law raised the percentage of AGI that you can contribute to 60%.
2020: The AGI limit for 2020 ONLY was raised to 100% for cash equivalent donations. Also, for 2020 only, you can deduct up to $300 in cash equivalent donations without itemizing. For 2021 ONLY, you can deduct up to $600 in cash equivalent donations without itemizing. Both of these have large penalties for cheating on a percentage basis, but on a dollars basis they are pretty minor. I'm not saying to cheat, just commenting on how stupid some rulemaking can be. Most people might see around $100 in tax benefits in 2021 so that's nice, but not worth lying about. Rules revert back to Trump Tax Law for 2021 and later.
Various: Often during a disaster, Congress will pass a law allowing deductions to be taken retroactively to a prior year or tweak other provisions for specific periods. I will not cover these here since they will all be expired or about to expire by the time I finish the book.

Now we can get to the details since this is my favorite subject!

I have said before, and I'll say it again: Don't do anything just for the tax benefits! Usually this is because when you spend money to save on taxes, you save a lot less on taxes than you spend. Charity contains one of the few exceptions to this: Non-cash contributions (think Goodwill). It's a total win for everyone! You give away stuff you don't want, the charity uses it to accomplish its mission, and you get a tax deduction! That said, charity has a LOT of rules and recordkeeping requirements, so, before I get into those, I'm going to give some simple rules to follow that will make your charitable giving simple and easy. Most people will be able to tailor their giving to meet these requirements and won't have to read the encyclopedia volume that follows. Before I do that, let me remind you that charitable contributions are a part of itemized deductions, so if you don't meet the itemized deduction threshold, you don't get any benefit from charitable giving. Read the Itemized Deductions chapter for more details.

Here is the simple system:

1. Give to established, mainstream charities who can confirm that they are allowed to receive tax deductible contributions and will provide you with a receipt.

2. Give less than $250 by check or charge (no cash) to any given charity, on any given day. (This means you can give your church or charity over $90,000 in a year without needing a written acknowledgement, and you can give to as many different organizations as you want. You can even give over $12,000 in weekly donations via $249 checks in the church collection plate.)

3. If you want to donate more to your church, make sure they provide a written statement acknowledging the donation and that it specifies that no goods or services were provided by them to you (intangible religious benefits such as church services don't count). The acknowledgement will usually cover the entire year. You must receive this acknowledgement before the due date of the tax return. You can't go back and get it later if you are audited.

4. Don't make donations with strings attached, designated for a specific person, or in return for something provided by the charity.

5. If you make non-cash contributions, take a picture of the donated items (save it on your computer, no need to print), make a list of the donated items, and get a receipt (unless dropped at a drop box—see below).

6. Do not donate more than $5,000 worth of items in a single day.

7. Do not donate more than $5,000 of a category of items (such as books) in a single year.

Follow rules 1 through 4 above and your cash contributions will be simple and easy. Rules 5 through 7 will simplify non-cash donations. The next four items are special cases that tend to come up, and/or cool tricks you can use.

1. The drop box exception. I have called this the loophole you can drive a truck through. You need a receipt if you donate non-cash items, with the exception of places that don't normally provide a receipt. The IRS publications specifically list drop boxes as an example. So, you can donate non-cash items to a drop box and make your own receipt. I still recommend taking pictures and making a list, and you may want to take a picture of the drop box. This exception is ripe for abuse, but don't lie to the IRS. Trust me on this. You will need the location of the drop box, the organization that placed it, their local address, the date you donated the items, the value of the items and a list of the items. From this, you can make your "receipt." During COVID, many traditional donation centers converted to drop-off only and no longer provided receipts. It is my firm belief that the "drop-box exception" fully applies and a traditional receipt is not required. This is NOT an excuse to game the system and pretend you donated things that you didn't. I expect pictures of non-cash donations to

be even more important now, and I would even encourage taking pictures or video of you actually dropping things off – though this is absolutely not required.

2. Garage sales. I like garage sales. What I don't like is when the vultures come around later in the day, offering you pennies for your items because they know you want to get rid of them. Don't do it! Sell your stuff for a reasonable price and then, while everything is still on the table after the sale, take pictures of it all, load it into your car, and drop off at Goodwill or another place that takes non-cash contributions. Or take them to a drop box like we talked about above. If you itemize, you'll do better on your taxes than the pennies you'll get from the late-comers.

3. Auctions, dinners, sporting events and shows: If you buy a ticket for an event from a charity, you only get to deduct the difference between what you paid for the ticket, and the value of what you receive. Good charities will provide this information. If the values are close, don't waste your time with the deduction, just be happy you're helping a good organization. Raffle tickets are not deductible. You cannot deduct a contribution if it gets you the right to buy tickets to a sporting event.

4. Volunteering. Your time is not deductible. Your legitimate expenses in providing your time are. Don't try comingling vacations and volunteering. Travel deductions for charity work are only deductible if charity is the sole purpose of the trip. If you travel for volunteering with no significant personal enjoyment involved (other than the joy of giving) you can deduct your travel expenses (airfare, lodging, mass transit). You can also deduct mileage (14 cents a mile – but this can change at any time – usually the middle of the year), meals when away overnight, and uniforms that aren't suitable for everyday use.

5. Here is one neat trick that I have my clients do for non-cash donations. Use your cell phone to take pictures, then back them up to your computer, and put the pictures on the phone in a separate folder by date of donation (so I don't have to look at all their other pictures.) Then they just hand me the phone and I determine values. No list required! Your tax dude may not do this for you, so ask first. I spend a lot of time at stores selling used items to obtain comprehensive lists of values for my area. A lot of tax pros won't do this.

If everything you do fits the above, you can stop reading; otherwise, here are the nasty details:

1. You have to donate to a qualified organization, for qualified purposes. Most major charities and churches qualify. You can verify that they qualify by going to www.irs.gov, click on tools, and then click Exempt

Organizations Select Check. This has a search function, as well as the ability to download the full list of exempt organizations.

2. Civic leagues, homeowner's associations, labor unions, clubs, lobbying organizations, political groups and candidates are not organizations for which your donation would be tax deductible.

3. You cannot place strings on your donation such that it is directed to a specific individual or group.

4. Your time has no deductible value, nor does your blood.

5. The charities have to be U.S. charities, though Mexican, Israeli and Canadian charities may be deductible under certain very restrictive conditions.

6. You cannot receive benefits from your donation unless you subtract the value of the benefit from the amount you deduct (if you buy tickets to a $10 movie from an organization for $15, you deduct $5). Token benefits, such as pens or religious services, do not have to be deducted. A donation that grants you rights to buy tickets to sporting events are not deductible.

7. Lottery, raffle or bingo ticket costs are not deductible.

8. You can deduct 14 cents a mile for travel related to volunteering or gift giving.

9. Any single donation of $250 or more in cash requires a written acknowledgement from the organization. This acknowledgement needs to include the organization's name, amount of the donation, and a statement as to whether any goods or services were provided in return for the donation and the value of those services. This statement cannot be obtained at a later date for an audit. You must get it before you file your return, or the due date of your tax return (including extensions), whichever is earlier. For donations less than $250, a bank statement or cancelled check is sufficient.

10. Non-cash donations must be in good used or better condition. This is a bit of a nebulous term, so I recommend taking pictures of any non-cash donations you make.

11. You deduct the fair market value of the non-cash donation. Fair Market Value is (standby for taxese) the amount that a willing buyer would pay a willing seller if both parties were knowledgeable of all facts and had no ulterior motives (I added the ulterior motives part because it matters and is obvious, but it's not part of the formal definition). This is NOT the price that Goodwill sells the item for (no profit motive) but really is the price a for-profit thrift store would sell it. You generally cannot deduct more than you paid for an item (or what it was worth when you inherited it).

12. You need a receipt for any non-cash donation, unless the drop box exception discussed above applies.

13. If you donate more than $5,000 worth of items at a single time, you will need a statement from a qualified appraiser as to the value of the items. This also applies if you donate more than $5,000 worth of similar items (such as books) in a year. You cannot deduct the cost of the appraisal.

14. You cannot deduct more than 60% (50% in 2017 and before) of your AGI in a single year, but the excess is carried over to the next year. Certain unusual contributions may be further limited. For 2020 ONLY, this limit is 100% for cash equivalent donations.

15. Non-cash donations exceeding $500 for the year require filing Form 8283 with your return. This form asks for additional information, such as how much you paid for the property and how you determined the value. I hate this form and think it is the perfect example of being completely unrealistic as to what the average taxpayer has the time or inclination to track.

16. If you donate a car, you get to deduct what the organization sold it for. They should provide a Form 1098-C with this value. If the charity uses the vehicle, makes improvements to it, or sells it to a needy individual below market value, you can deduct the Fair Market Value of the car at the time of the donation. Don't place strings on the use or disposition of the car.

17. Don't try to deduct a house donated to the fire department for them to burn down for training, especially if you retain title to the land. Someone tried this and lost in court.

My Advice:

1. I am not going to restate the simple system discussed at the beginning of this chapter, but that is great advice if I say so myself.

2. Do not be overly conservative with Goodwill type donation values. They are certainly worth more than Goodwill sells them for. Software values are equally useless. If you donate a lot, check out what for-profit stores sell them for. Big ticket items can be valued via Amazon, E-bay or other reselling sites. If you donate a lot of clothes, check out used clothing (for profit) stores to get an idea for values.

3. If you do not normally itemize, consider accumulating stuff until you can donate a ton in one year for a huge deduction. My wife and I do this. I like to joke with my clients that we accumulate crap until we are one bad weekend away from an episode of Hoarders and then donate almost everything we own in one year.

Military: You can get a Year-to-Date charity amount from your LES for payroll deductions to CFC and the like. Dues to your officer or enlisted associations are not deductible. Many veteran's groups are qualified organizations.

Not discussed: Donations of stock, investments, collectibles or IRA's. Charitable Remainder Trusts.

38. Let's Talk About Disasters and Coronavirus! (formerly Casualty and Thefts)

This Chapter is a **DUMPSTER FIRE**! Congress and the President have modified the rules around this so many times that you basically have to look up your specific disaster to know what rules apply. Everything below this paragraph talks about those individual changes and applicability, so this paragraph is the basic, general knowledge that you need to know. BUT if you suffer from a disaster, take the time to look up to see if any special provisions apply to you. Okay – the basic rules: It has to be a Presidentially Declared Disaster (thefts don't apply anymore except possibly Ponzi schemes which are a separate thing entirely). You get to deduct the following amount as an itemized deduction: Your economic losses or costs, minus any insurance reimbursement taken or allowed (you can't just not claim something because it is too much trouble), minus $100, minus 10% of your Adjusted Gross Income. This goes on Schedule A as an Itemized Deduction and MIGHT save you on taxes. Yes, this is overly simplified. Yes, you should seek professional help if you suffer from a disaster. Yes, the rules will probably be changed if your disaster is big enough.

Now for the Dumpster Fire:

Fix and Update for this book…a lot of this stuff is covered elsewhere as the changes impacted the individual chapters, but Casualties and Thefts underwent a big change under the Trump Tax Plan and has been modified for special circumstances ever since, the biggest of these being COVID-19 (Coronavirus). So, I put a bunch of it here for easy reference.

The 2021 tax year has its own, specific, one-time rules, so I won't be covering them here if they only apply to 2021. Everyone should read the 2021 chapter, especially if they have children.

This chapter is not comprehensive or in full detail. I have tried to include and explain to the maximum extent necessary for the average taxpayer. If this post leads you to think you can use the benefits, you should talk to a tax pro or research the actual law. For the love of all that is holy, do NOT rely on your software to get this right. I use some of the best tax software in the world for my clients and I will be watching it like a hawk to make sure it gets this right (it is not – but I have been making it work by manipulating my form entries such that the software spits out an accurate tax return that accounts for all these provisions.) I have not included provisions that only apply to good sized businesses or employers.

I have used Big Letters to identify when I am switching between Tax Changes, since this chapter has a lot of them. Some of these provisions rightly belong as a part of other chapters, and I included relevant information in them, but the bulk of everything included in the various bills is written about here as well. If I don't move on to a new Capital Letter, you are still reading things that apply to the specific law or set of disasters.

A. Trump Tax:

The Trump Tax Law Change to this was short and sweet, but it was a big deal. After that, Congress kept tweaking the rules for specific disasters or timeframes. I am going to cover each of them separately, even though a lot of it is going to be repetitive.

The basic rule established by the Trump Tax Law that applies to all disasters that do not have specific rules applied to them is this: Casualty losses are now only deductible if the loss was attributable to a disaster declared by the President. This means people stealing your stuff, swindles, accidents and all the normal stuff covered under casualties and thefts pretty much no longer applies. Big disasters are the only ones now – but there are a lot of them every year!

The only real advice related to this is to make sure you have home/car/renter's insurance that is solid and up to date. Which you already should have.

B. The Sneaky Tax Change included in the Budget Bills in December of 2019:

Congress has played around with these provisions A LOT. In December 2019, mixed in with the budget bill were the below described provisions. Read carefully, they apply in very specific periods, but a LOT of people will qualify for some of them. This is not a comprehensive list of changes, but is trimmed down to those provisions most likely to apply to normal people:

To determine if your disaster qualifies, you go to the FEMA website:

https://www.fema.gov/disasters

Search for "Major Disaster Declaration" under Declaration Type and narrow it with your state.

I included the SC Dorian page here for illustration...

https://www.fema.gov/disaster/4464#

...so you can see the map. If you are in the orange area, most of the rules apply to you. A few more esoteric rules require you to be in a red area (not applicable to Dorian in SC). The disaster declaration must have been made between Jan 1st, 2018 and Feb 18th, 2020 and the disaster must have started before December 20th, 2019. These dates are on the FEMA pages. Once you know the disaster applies to you, you can see what tax benefits you have. There are retirement account benefits, deductions, Child Tax Credit (EITC and ACTC) benefits, filing deadline extensions and charitable deduction provisions. The charity provisions apply to everyone who donates to the disasters, not just those affected by them.

Retirement Provisions (note these only apply until 6/17/20, but later bills apply to later dates, so keep reading): These generally require you to have suffered an economic loss as a result of the disaster, though it does not seem that the limits are tied to the amount of loss. Simply put, you would need losses that were not reimbursed by insurance - but check with your tax dude to confirm you qualify before futzing with your retirement accounts. I am going to use 401k here, but I mean all the 403b, Thrift Savings Plan, 457 etc. deferred compensation type plans.

1. You can avoid the 10% penalty on an early 401k or IRA withdrawal. The max is $100,000 per disaster. The withdrawal must be made after the disaster began and June 17th, 2020. You still have to pay taxes on the withdrawal but...

2. You can spread the taxes over three years starting with the year you took it out. Or...

3. You can put the money back within 3 years of the distribution date and owe no taxes.

4. If you took advantage of the normal $10,000 first time home buyer exclusion but the disaster prevents you from buying or building the home,

you can put the money back tax and penalty free. The withdrawal must have been made within 180 days before the disaster and 30 days after it ended. The money must be put back before June 17th, 2020.

5. The 401k loan allowed amount was doubled to $100,000. Payments due between the start of the disaster and 180 days after may be delayed until June 17th, 2020.

Disaster Loss Deduction: The rules for a disaster loss deduction are modified to eliminate the 10% floor and to allow the deduction to be taken even if you do not itemize. Basically, you take your losses, subtract any insurance reimbursement, subtract $500 (the new floor) and that is the amount deducted. If you itemize, just include it as an itemized deduction. If you do not, add it to your standard deduction. Make sure your software or tax pro handles this right.

Very rough, even (inaccurate) number example: Say your standard deduction is $12,000 and your house has $10,000 in damage done. Insurance reimburses $5000. So, your deduction is $10,000 minus $5000, minus $500 which equals $4,500. If you take the standard deduction, it would now be $16,500. If you had $15,000 in itemized deductions, the disaster loss would now make them $19,500.

Earned Income Credit and Additional Child Tax Credit: Here's where things get really weird. If your principal abode was in the disaster area, or you were displaced due to the disaster (these are weird so ask a pro if your home wasn't in the zone) and your earned income went DOWN, you can use the prior year's earned income in these calculations if it works out better. You basically have to run the numbers both ways to see which way is best. You can do this for any year that falls within the disaster dates. You have to use the prior year's income for BOTH credits or neither.

For Married Filing Jointly, only one spouse needs to be affected, but you have to use BOTH spouses' income from the prior year for the calculation.

I cannot see anything requiring the disaster to be the CAUSE of the reduced income.

Again, 2020 and 2021 have very specific rules for these. I have included them in the basic chapters on children, and the specific year chapters. For kindle or online readers, here is a link to the 2020 Chapter, and the 2021

Chapter. For physical book readers, feel free to use the Table of Contents – you do know how, right?

Filing Deadline Extension: You get a 60-day extension of any filing deadline that falls between the start and end of the disaster. The 60 days starts after the disaster is over. It applies to IRA contribution deadlines as well. It only applies to disasters occurring AFTER December 20th, 2019.

Charitable Contributions: This will likely not apply to very many people, BUT, if you contribute to a qualified charity benefiting one of the disasters between Jan 1st, 2018 and Feb 18th, 2020, in cash (credit and checks as well, just not goods) you can exceed the 60% of AGI limit normally applied to charitable deductions. That's right, if you already donated 60% of your income to charity, you can now donate more if it goes to benefit these disasters.

C. Coronavirus Tax Provisions:

At time of publishing, this was basically the CARES Act, The Biden Stimulus Bill and a lot of action by the Treasury Department. There were a few tax provisions sprinkled in other bills surrounding it, and I have included them here. If they pass some sweeping changes, I will add a new chapter, but minor tweaks will be included here. I am going to include everything Stimulus Check in a separate post, though hopefully most everyone has their money by the time this is published.

Retirement Provisions: You do not have to take your 2020 Required Minimum Distribution from your Retirement Account. This applies to people over the age of 70 and a half who have to take annual withdrawals from their tax advantaged accounts and pay taxes on them. This is an under-reported and under-appreciated big deal. I highly recommend taking advantage of this if you do not need the money from your account. Pulling money out during a dramatic stock market downturn is painful. People who inherited IRA money who are pulling it out as required over 5 years can extend this period by one additional year.

If you suffered economic impact from the Coronavirus, specifically, you or a family member you care for contracted the disease, or you lost your job or lost business or were laid off, or lost business income due to the virus, or your child's daycare closing caused you financial hardship, you can withdraw up to $100,000 from your retirement accounts without penalty and with the ability to pay the taxes due over three years, or put the money back and pay no taxes. The connection and calculations between the economic impact and the withdrawal amounts are not clearly defined.

Retirement plan loan limits were increased from $50,000 to $100,000 and you do not have to start paying it back for a year. This applies to loans taken between March 27th and September 23rd of 2020.

There are also changes to loan requirements and costs associated with making a hardship withdrawal. I DO NOT recommend doing this unless ABSOLUTELY necessary and only withdraw the minimum amount possible to keep your family alive. In fact, there are so many programs available to defer rent, mortgages and student loan payments that this should not be necessary.

Time Extensions and Suspension of Enforcement: Most of these no longer apply so I have deleted them.

The IRS had suspended pulling back taxes, delinquent student loans and other debts from tax refunds and stimulus payments. Delinquent Child Support withdrawals are still happening on a state by state basis. These have been reinstated for the most part.

Charitable Giving: For 2020 only, you can deduct $300 of cash, check or equivalent donations to normally qualified charities even if you do not itemize. You can deduct up to your entire AGI in charitable donations via itemizing, as opposed to the normal limit. Documentation requirements remain the same: donations under $250 require some record of your paying it, such as a cancelled check or credit card statement while $250 or above requires written acknowledgement from the charity. The $250 limit applies to INDIVIDUAL donations, not the total amount donated for the year.

For 2021 only, you can deduct $600 of cash, check or equivalent donations to normally qualified charities even if you do not itemize.

Health Savings Accounts and Flexible Spending Accounts: HSA, FSA and MSA funds may now be used for over-the-counter medications. They may also be used for menstrual care products. This change is permanent. You may also use them for Coronavirus related supplies such as disinfectant or face masks.

Student Loans: There are a number of student loan deferment programs implemented that are beyond the scope of taxes, but one is tax related. That one allows an employer to pay up to $5,250 of your student loans between March 27th and the end of 2020 without it being taxable income to you. You cannot deduct the interest paid by your employer.

Business Rule Changes: Most of these go beyond the scope of this book, applying mainly to employers or not being tax related. A non-exhaustive list includes the ability of self-employed people to collect unemployment for business income reduction, the ability to postpone paying payroll taxes, a dollar for dollar credit against payroll taxes for paying employees on sick leave, the ability to carry back 2018 to 2020 net operating losses, increased business interest deduction allowed, accelerating credits for prior year AMT, and numerous credits for retaining employees or paying for sick leave. There was also a permanent correction to allow immediate expensing of improvement property by making it a 15-year depreciable item.

Self employed people can get sick and family leave credits in 2020 if they were unable to work due to being sick, quarantines, government stay at home orders, school closures, daycare closures or family members having COVID-19. See the 2020 chapter for more details.

Things I do not know jack about: There is greatly expanded ability to get unemployment benefits if you have reduced income vice full job loss, and for self-employed people. There are amazing small business loan opportunities, some of which do not require paying back (go to sba.gov). There are programs that limit the ability to evict people based on non-payment of rent, guaranteed deferment of mortgage payments for government backed loans, and deferment of student loan payments.

IRS Operations: At the time of publishing last year's book, the IRS had suspended a significant amount of operations. They were not manning phone lines, many fax lines were turned off and they were not processing ANY paper tax returns, including amendments. Almost all local service centers were closed. Even the Taxpayer Advocate Service was operating on a very limited basis. At the time of publishing this book, they had started resuming most normal operations to try to clear the backlog, but, if you are struggling getting a return processed by the IRS, it is likely to be a long time before it is handled. Getting assistance with anything that cannot be handled using an automated phone line or online tool is still nearly impossible.

A bunch of links on my blog: There are a bunch of useful resources out there. I linked to a bunch of them on this post (there's some politics and news in there as well:

https://supertaxgenius.blogspot.com/2020/04/the-big-coronavirus-link-post.html

My Advice:

1. Just because you can take money out of your 401k or IRA penalty free doesn't mean you should!
2. Likewise, the expanded list of Health Savings Account qualified purchases should not motivate you to use your HSA more. Use your HSA only for truly unaffordable health costs, and let that sucker grow into your retirement.
3. Check irs.gov and my blog at least weekly for updates to the above information, as well as details of any new rules or laws passed.
4. Keep proof of all cash type donations even if you do not normally itemize.
5. Document economic costs you suffer from COVID-19, even if you do not currently qualify for any relief. We do not know what benefits may come AND you might be forced to withdraw from your retirement for other reasons, and COVID-19 economic losses will provide access to a number of benefits.
6. Seek professional assistance from financial advisors and tax professionals if you think some of the more complex rules might apply to you BEFORE taking irrevocable actions.

While we're on the subject of the Coronavirus…

39. Hopefully, You Already Have Your Stimulus Money...

I'm mostly killing this chapter as all the stimulus checks are done with.

If you did not get your $1400 third stimulus check, file a 2021 tax return even if not required.

Make sure to accurately report 3rd stimulus payments received to avoid delays.

If the government passes another stimulus bill, talk to a tax expert to determine when and how to file to maximize your payment.

One last thing:

Your tax pro did not know he was filing for your stimulus payment when he or she did your 2019 tax return. Stimulus payments were an enormous burden on tax pros, one that was completely unexpected and was not accounted for in determining fees. Dealing with upset clients over stimulus payments took an incredible amount of time and was very frustrating for tax pros, not because we didn't care, but because we did, and there was often very little we could do. That, plus all the extra planning needed to maximize the payments, and the planning needed due to the latest tax bill for 2021, means your tax pro is (or should be) doing a lot more work for you than in normal years.

40. I am Living with Someone Who Helps Pay my Bills

NOTE: Support is discussed periodically below and is usually obvious and straightforward. I have included a Support Worksheet in Appendix A if you need more details.

If you are living with someone who helps pay your bills, the main thing we are concerned with is whether you are their dependent and if they can file Head of Household (HH). We won't discuss if they are your dependent in this chapter; that's covered in the following chapters (this chapter assumes that you are not paying more than half of their support). If you are paying more than half the bills, read the next few chapters as they apply. If they are paying more than half the bills, read this chapter. If it's close, read all the chapters. The point for you is that if someone else can claim you, you can't claim yourself.

I am assuming they (and you for that matter) are an adult, who may or may not be related. I am also assuming you are not their minor child or child attending college (if you are, read the chapters on children—they are written from the parent's perspective, but they still apply. You should coordinate with your parents in filing when you live with them.). I'm also assuming you are not permanently disabled and unable to work. If you are married to the person you live with, this is the wrong chapter—you should be looking into MFJ or MFS.

In most cases where you live with someone unrelated to you, there will be no effect on your taxes. I am first going to cover situations where you cannot be claimed, then talk about other common situations, and lastly cover all the nit-picky rules. With luck, your situation will be covered before you have to read the detailed stuff.

Here are the simple situations where you cannot be claimed:

If you are married and file a joint return with your spouse, you cannot be claimed unless you are only filing to get 100% of your money back, and neither you nor your spouse would have owed any taxes if you filed separately (no taxes paid at all—not just getting a refund). For the remainder of this chapter, this rule applies, and I'm assuming when I say you can be claimed that you aren't MFJ.

If they are not related to you (parent, child, sibling, niece, nephew, aunt, uncle [including grands- and greats-, and steps-] or parent, child or sibling in-law) and they did not live with you the entire year, you cannot be claimed. Temporary absences for school, medical treatment, business, vacations, etc. can be included as living together during the year.

If you have gross income (wages, investment income, business income, taxable pensions or annuities) of more than $4,700, you cannot be claimed.

If you pay more than half of your support, you cannot be claimed (Appendix A Test 2). Support includes the rental value of your lodging (take what it would cost to rent the entire house or apartment and divide by the number of people sharing the place, including children), clothing, transportation, recreation, lodging, medical expenses, and other necessities. If what you earn from all sources, minus what you put away in savings, is more than half of this amount, you support yourself and cannot be claimed.

If you don't pay more than half of your support, but neither does the person you live with (meaning there is a third person, someone sends you money for your support, or you receive support from the government or charity), you cannot be claimed as their dependent.

Here are some other common situations:

Roommate: If you live with a roommate, you would assume that you would share in the bills, however unequally they are shared. Having a roommate is generally not a dependent situation. In fact, if one person owns or leases the property and makes the payments, depending on the situation, the other person might be a tenant. Usually, you just treat it as two people sharing the bills. If, however, you provide limited funds to the household, live there all year, make less than $4,700 from all sources (wages, investment income, business income, taxable pensions or annuities), and are unmarried, you need to determine if your roommate supports you (Appendix A Test 2). Support includes the rental value of your lodging (take what it would cost to rent the entire house or apartment and divide by the number of people sharing the place, including children), clothing, transportation, recreation, lodging, medical expenses, and other necessities. If what you earn from all sources, minus what you put away in savings, is more than half of this amount, you support yourself and cannot be claimed. Unrelated Roommates cannot use you to file HH.

Boyfriend, girlfriend or fiancée: This situation is actually almost identical to the roommate situation, discussed above, with two unusual exceptions. One is that in some states you may cross a line that makes you common-law married. This is actually pretty unlikely to happen accidentally, but you should be aware of the laws as they affect you in your state. You might actually be able to claim yourself as married, without a formal ceremony, but you should seek professional assistance, both in tax law and marriage law, before trying it. Second, it is also possible, though unlikely, that your living situation violates state law. The example given in the IRS publication is living with your girlfriend who is married to someone else— if this violates state law, you cannot claim or be claimed by them, regardless of whether you meet the other requirements. Unrelated Roommates cannot use you to file HH.

Adult child with parents: If you move back in with your parents, are older than 18 and not going to college, or are older than 23 regardless of college attendance, the usual rules for claiming a non-relative apply. If you live there six months or more, make less than $4,700 from any source and are supported by them (Appendix A Test 2), they can claim you as a dependent. Support includes the rental value of your lodging (take what it would cost to rent the entire house or apartment and divide by the number of people sharing the place, including children), clothing, transportation, recreation, lodging, medical expenses, and other necessities. If what you earn from all sources, minus what you put away in savings, is more than half of this amount, you support yourself and cannot be claimed. If the age and college situations apply, read the chapter on children and coordinate with your parents to file your taxes correctly. If your single parent can claim you, they may be able to file HH. (The determination of support for HH is different than the support test in that you do not include the fair rental value. Instead, you include actual rent, or mortgage interest and real estate taxes [not the whole mortgage payment]. You also include repairs, insurance, utilities, and food eaten in the home.)

Living in a friend's house: Treat this the same as the roommate section discussed above.

Living with a family member: Again, treat this like the roommate section, except that if they are your parent, child, sibling, niece, nephew, aunt, uncle (including grands-, greats-, and steps-) or parent, child or sibling in-law, then you don't have to live with them for the entire year. If they meet this requirement, you live with them more than half the year, and they are unmarried, they may be able to file HH (the determination of support for HH is different than the support test in that you do not include the fair rental value. Instead, you include actual rent, or mortgage interest and real estate taxes (not the whole mortgage payment). You also include repairs, insurance, utilities, and food eaten in the home.)

Here are the nit-picky details:

1. I don't include Social Security as gross income because it is only included as gross income if it is taxable. The amount of income required to make it taxable well exceeds the $4,700 we are concerned with. So, if it's included, you are already above $4,700. I include this comment only because someone will read the book and point out that I "forgot" about Social Security.
2. If you live with more than one person, they determine if they can claim you independently of each other. Mathematically, the support test will either eliminate one or both such that it can't result in both being able to claim you, or neither will be able to claim you.
3. It is possible for the situation in 2 above to result in no one paying more than half your support, even though together they do provide more than half. There is something called a Multiple Support Agreement (Form 2120) that would allow them to agree to combine support to allow one of them to claim the exemption. Seek professional help if this applies.
4. If there are divorced or separated parents involved in this, read the I'm Getting Divorced chapter in addition to this chapter, though if you are 18 or older it is unlikely to affect this.

My Advice:

1. In most of these situations, unless the requirements for dependency are met in a clear and obvious way, it is usually best if everybody just claims themselves. Remember, for adults, dependency nets you $500 unless Head of Household is on the table, and you have to be related in certain ways to qualify for HH.
2. HH has due diligence requirements for tax professionals and is subject to stricter attention from the IRS than other tax areas, so be sure you meet the requirements before you try to claim it. A tax professional can be very useful helping with this.
3. It is always a good idea to establish the tax parameters of a living situation at the beginning of cohabitation rather than after you have been there for a while. If dependency or HH is potentially available, talk about it and make sure everyone is on board. Talk about if you are establishing a tenant/landlord relationship from the start or are just sharing bills as friends. Again, a tax professional can be helpful here.

Military: If a person lives with you at the time you are deployed, they continue to count as living with you during the deployment. Some people might debate this, but a good rule of thumb is that a non-permanent deployment or assignment does not change the living situation for taxes so long as the intention is for the dependent to return to the pre-deployment living situation when the deployment or temporary assignment ends. Geographical bachelor or Permanent Change of Station orders would not count for as "temporary".

41. I am Supporting my Parents

2018 Trump/GOP Tax Law Changes: This chapter was affected by the new tax law.

- Claiming Head of Household (HH) is now subject to due diligence requirements. This means that tax professionals can be fined if they do not question situations that don't add up. This obviously means that the IRS is probably going to be paying close attention to sketchy HH situations.

NOTE: Support is discussed periodically below and is usually obvious and straightforward. I have included a Support Worksheet in Appendix A if you need more details.

The meat of the Chapter:

In this chapter, I am assuming everyone lives in the United States and that you are not a dependent of someone else (being Married and filing a joint return does not make you your spouse's dependent.)

The first thing we need to establish is whether you are truly (in accordance with IRS definitions) supporting your parents (Appendix A Test 2). Support includes the rental value of their lodging (take what it would cost to rent the entire house or apartment they are living in and divide by the number of people sharing the place, including children), clothing, transportation, recreation, lodging, medical expenses, and other necessities. If what they earn from all sources (including savings withdrawals), minus what they put away in savings, is more than half of this amount, they support themselves and cannot be claimed. Once you establish that, you need to check some other tests. I'm going to run down the normal situations that would allow you to claim them. There aren't a lot of additional details and tricks for this chapter, so I'm covering everything in this straightforward chapter. Included in the discussion is the potential for Head of Household (HH) filing status, which has some unique aspects with regard to parents.

To claim HH, you must pay at least half the cost to maintain the place they are living for at least half the year, be that their home, a nursing home, or other arrangements. This determination is different than the support test in that you do not include the fair rental value. Instead, you include actual rent, or mortgage interest and real estate taxes (not the whole mortgage payment). You also include repairs, insurance, utilities and food eaten in the home. Assuming this applies, and you meet the other tests to claim them, you would meet the requirements to claim HH (assuming you are unmarried). For a nursing home, you essentially include all the payments made to the home in this determination.

If your parents are married, they must not file a joint tax return, or, if they do, they must file only to get ALL their money back, and, if they had filed separately, they both would have gotten ALL their money back. It's useful to run all three tax returns using MFJ and MFS with and without you claiming the exemption to determine the best way for all of you to file.

Your parent's gross income must be less than $4,700. This includes wages, investment income, business income, and taxable pensions or annuities.

If you meet all the above, you can claim your parents as dependents.

If you meet all of the above requirements except the $4,700 income rule, you cannot claim them as a dependent, but you can claim any medical expenses you pay for them as an itemized deduction on your tax return.

If you and other family members share the support of your parents but no one pays more than half, you might be able to file a Multiple Support Agreement that would allow one of you to claim them (but not get HH). You file Form 2120, but I would seek professional help if this applies.

My Advice:

1. If your parent's only income is from Social Security, claiming them as a dependent is often possible, but if they live in the home they own, it is nearly impossible unless they have significant other expenses. If they have much of any other income (not Social Security), it becomes very difficult to claim them.
2. There are many reasons people might want to "quit-claim" deed a parent's house to their children. It is important to be aware that this has significant tax implications, including potential gift tax filing requirements and/or gift taxes owed. One BIG one is that if a house is gifted to someone, which a transfer for no or little money would be, the "basis" of the house transfers. This means when selling the home you figure gain based on what the parent paid for it instead of getting a "stepped-up" basis to the value on the date of death which is what normally happens for inherited property. If the parents owned the property for a significant amount of time, or through

one of the housing booms, this difference in basis can make an enormous difference in the amount of taxes paid when the house sells.

3. If you claim your parent's and the situation is not mathematically obvious, keep good records of their income and assets, as well as what you pay to support them.

Military: Not much different here for you.

42. I am Supporting an Adult Relative or Friend

2018 Trump/GOP Tax Law Changes: This chapter was affected by the new tax law.

- Claiming Head of Household (HH) is now subject to due diligence requirements. This means that tax professionals can be fined if they do not question situations that do not add up. This obviously means that the IRS is probably going to be paying close attention to sketchy HH situations.

NOTE: Support is discussed periodically below and is usually obvious and straightforward. I have included a Support Worksheet in Appendix A if you need more details.

The meat of the Chapter:

In this chapter, I am assuming everyone lives in the United States and that you are not a dependent of someone else (being Married and filing a joint return does not make you your spouse's dependent.)

Two big things need to be established before we can decide whether you can claim this person, and whether you can use the Head of Household (HH) filing status.

The first thing we need to establish is whether you are truly (in accordance with IRS definitions) supporting this person (Appendix A Test 2). Support includes the rental value of their lodging (take what it would cost to rent the entire house or apartment they are living in and divide by the number of people sharing the place, including children), clothing, transportation, recreation, lodging, medical expenses, and other necessities. If what they earn from all sources (including savings withdrawals), minus what they put away in savings, is more than half of this amount, they support themselves and cannot be claimed.

The second thing you need to establish is if they are a certain kind of relative. These are parent (previous chapter), child (have their own chapter), sibling, niece, nephew, aunt, uncle (including grands-, greats-, and steps-) or parent-, child- or sibling in-law. If it is one of these, the person does not need to live with you all year, and HH is a possibility. Otherwise, they must live with you the entire year, and HH is not possible. Temporary absences for school, treatment, business, vacations, etc. can be included in the year.

To claim HH, you must pay at least half the cost to maintain the place they are living for at least half the year, and that must also be your home. This determination is different than the support test in that you do not include the fair rental value. Instead, you include actual rent, or mortgage interest and real estate taxes (not the whole mortgage payment). You also include repairs, insurance, utilities and food eaten in the home. Assuming this applies, and you meet the other tests to claim them, you would meet the requirements to claim HH (assuming you are unmarried).

If they are married, they must not file a joint tax return, or, if they do, they must file only to get ALL their money back, and, if they had filed separately, they both would have gotten ALL their money back. It's useful to run all three tax returns using MFJ and MFS with and without you claiming the exemption to determine the best way for all of you to file.

Their gross income must be less than $4,700. This includes wages, investment income, business income, and taxable pensions or annuities.

If you meet all the above, you can claim them as a dependent.

If you meet all of the requirements above except for the $4,700 rule AND they are a relative as discussed above, you cannot claim them as a dependent, but you can claim any medical expenses you pay for them as an itemized deduction on your tax return.

If you and other persons share their support, but no one pays more than half, you might be able to file a Multiple Support Agreement that would allow one of you to claim them (but not get HH). You file Form 2120, but I would seek professional help if this applies.

My Advice:

1. The $4,700 rule above makes claiming an adult very difficult. Social Security income does not count, but almost everything else does.
2. It is generally a good idea to discuss with someone that you plan on claiming them as a dependent BEFORE you actually do it. The best time to do this is shortly after the potential dependency situation begins.
3. If HH is off the table, dependency is only worth $500 so if it is a close call, it can be best not to bother.

4. Often times, whose house you live in is the critical factor for support. If you live in someone else's house, you probably do not provide half of the support.

Military: If a person lives with you at the time you are deployed, they continue to count as living with you during the deployment. Some people might debate this, but a good rule of thumb is that a non-permanent deployment or assignment does not change the living situation for taxes so long as the intention is for the dependent to return to the pre-deployment living situation when the deployment or temporary assignment ends. Geographical bachelor or Permanent Change of Station orders would not count as "temporary".

43. I am Supporting a Minor who is not my Child

2018 Trump/GOP Tax Law Changes: This chapter was affected by the new tax law.

- Claiming Head of Household (HH) is now subject to due diligence requirements. This means that tax professionals can be fined if they do not question situations that don't add up. This obviously means that the IRS is probably going to be paying close attention to sketchy HH situations.

NOTE: Support is discussed periodically below and is usually obvious and straightforward. I have included a Support Worksheet in Appendix A if you need more details.

The meat of the chapter:

In this chapter, I am assuming everyone lives in the United States and that you are not a dependent of someone else (being Married and filing a joint return does not make you your spouse's dependent.)

This is a very complicated situation. Most people think it is obvious and fall back on the: "I support them so I must be able to claim them!" argument. But the rules are messy. The first thing I'm going to assume is that this is not a foster child placed with you by an authorized placement agency—that's a whole other situation. You should also be aware that if you are or were married to the mother or father of the child, you are the step-parent (which is exactly the same as biological parent for tax purposes), regardless of if you were subsequently divorced or the biological parent died (see I'm Having a Child and I'm Getting Divorced). If you live with and are married to the parent of the child, you should be filing MFJ and reading the I'm Having a Child chapter. Just a reminder that a child that is born or died during the year is presumed to have lived with the person with whom they were living at the time of birth or death for the whole year.

I'm going to break down some basic situations and scenarios, then go over the nitty gritty details. There are going to be a lot of scenarios, so standby:

You are related to the child in the following ways: Sibling or step-sibling, grandchild, niece or nephew or any of their descendants, and their parent lives with you.

First off, in this scenario, the child's parent (assuming they meet the other rules for claiming them) wins in a fight over claiming the child, period. If, however, the parent does not plan to claim the child, you can claim them if you meet some criteria. The child must have lived with you as a member of your household for more than six months (temporary absences for school, illness, etc. still count as living with you). The child can't provide more than half their own support (Appendix A Test 1). Support includes the rental value of their lodging (take what it would cost to rent the entire house or apartment they are living in and divide by the number of people sharing the place, including children), clothing, transportation, recreation, lodging, medical expenses, and other necessities. If what they earn from all sources (including savings withdrawals), minus what they put away in savings, is more than half of this amount, they support themselves and cannot be claimed. They cannot file a MFJ return unless they are only filing to get ALL their withholding back and the couple would both get ALL their money back if they filed separately. The child must be under age 19, or under 24 if a full-time student during at least 5 months, or permanently and totally disabled (doctor's statement must be provided). If you meet all those tests, you can claim the child as a dependent. The child will also qualify you for Earned Income Credit, Child Tax Credit, Dependent Care Credit and Head of Household (HH) if you meet the other criteria for them. I'm not going to rehash these here, but they are included in the I'm Having a Child chapter.

You are related to the child in the following ways: Sibling or step-sibling, grandchild, niece or nephew or any of their descendants, and their parent does not live with you.

You can claim them if you meet some criteria. The child must have lived with you as a member of your household for more than six months (temporary absences for school, illness, etc. still count as living with you). The child can't provide more than half their own support (Appendix A Test 1). Support includes the rental value of their lodging (take what it would cost to rent the entire house or apartment they are living in and divide by the number of people sharing the place, including children), clothing, transportation, recreation, lodging, medical expenses, and other necessities. If what they earn from all sources (including savings withdrawals), minus what they put away in savings, is more than half of this amount, they support themselves and cannot be claimed. They cannot file a MFJ return unless they are only filing to get ALL their withholding back and the couple would both get ALL their money back if they filed separately. The child must be under age 19, or under 24 if a full-time student during at least 5 months, or permanently and totally disabled (doctor's statement must be provided). If you meet all those tests, you can claim the child as a dependent. The child will also qualify you for Earned Income Credit, Child Tax Credit, Dependent Care Credit and HH if you meet the other criteria for them. I'm not going to rehash these here, but they are included in the I'm Having a Child chapter.

You are not related to the child as discussed above and their parent lives with you:

First off, in this scenario, the child's parent wins in a fight over claiming the child (assuming they meet the other rules for claiming them), period. If, however, the parent does not meet the criteria to claim the child, you can claim them if you meet some criteria. The child must have lived with you as a member of your household for the entire year (temporary absences for school, illness, etc. still count as living with you). You must provide over half the child's support (Appendix A Test 2). Support includes the rental value of their lodging (take what it would cost to rent the entire house or apartment they are living in and divide by the number of people sharing the place, including children), clothing, transportation, recreation, lodging, medical expenses, and other necessities. If you pay more than half of this amount, you support them. They cannot file a MFJ return unless they are only filing to get ALL their withholding back and the couple would both get ALL their money back if they filed separately. The child cannot have gross income of more than $4,700 from any source. This includes wages, investment income, business income, and taxable pensions or annuities. If you meet all the above, you can claim the child as a dependent. You cannot get Earned Income Credit, HH or Dependent Care Credit.

You are not related to the child as discussed above and their parent does not live with you:

You can claim them if you meet some criteria. The child must have lived with you as a member of your household for the entire year (temporary absences for school, illness, etc. still count as living with you). You must provide over half the child's support (Appendix A Test 2). Support includes the rental value of their lodging (take what it would cost to rent the entire house or apartment they are living in and divide by the number of people sharing the place, including children), clothing, transportation, recreation, lodging, medical expenses, and other necessities. If you pay more than half of this amount, you support them. They cannot file a MFJ return unless they are only filing to get ALL their withholding back and the couple would both get ALL their money back if they filed separately. The child cannot have gross income of more than $4,700 from any source. This includes wages, investment income, business income, and taxable pensions or annuities. If you meet all the above, you can claim the child as a dependent. You cannot get Earned Income Credit, HH or Dependent Care Credit.

For any of the above scenarios, if someone else (other than the child's parent) lives with the child, meets all the other criteria, and wants to claim them, you can either agree ahead of time who claims them, or apply tie-breaker rules. If you don't agree, and two people try to claim the child, the first electronically filed return will go through. The second return will be rejected, requiring the child to be removed, or the return filed on paper. When the IRS gets the second, paper-filed return, they will send letters attempting to determine who gets the child in accordance with the tie-breaker rules. They will award the child to the one who wins, and demand money back from the incorrect filer, if they already received it. The tie breaker rules are: Parent wins over non-parent. Higher AGI wins between two non-parents. If two *parents* are fighting over a child, the parent with whom the child spends more nights during the year wins, before applying the AGI test.

My Advice:

1. With Head of Household off the table in many of these situations, you are fighting for $500 maximum. Don't bother if it's a shaky scenario.
2. It is generally a good idea to discuss with someone that you plan on claiming them as a dependent BEFORE you actually do it. The best time to do this is shortly after the potential dependency situation begins.
3. Often times, whose house you live in is the critical factor for support. If you live in someone else's house, you probably don't provide half of the support.
4. If you live with the child's parents (or they live with you) don't try to claim their child without their permission, even if you assume that they won't be filing a tax return or claiming the child. Ask them first. You would be amazed at the chaos and conflict caused by someone claiming a child without approval. You may have the moral high ground, but you'll be wrestling in the muck even so.

Military: If a child lives with you at the time you are deployed, they continue to count as living with you during the deployment, even if you send them to another household (such as your parents) for the time you are deployed. Some people might debate this, but a good rule of thumb is that a non-permanent deployment or assignment does not change the living situation for taxes so long as the intention is for the dependent to return to the pre-deployment living situation when the deployment or temporary assignment ends (sending the child to live with their other parent might be trouble). Geographical bachelor or Permanent Change of Station orders would not count as "temporary".

44. Someone Claimed my Child!

I assume when you say someone claimed your child that, you either know from someone that it happened, or your tax return was rejected due to the child already being claimed. In either case, if you have the proper rights to claim the child, you can still claim them AND YOU SHOULD!

I see it all the time, where people do not want to cause trouble and just leave the child off of their tax return when someone else claims them (see Note 1 below). This is a mistake! Guess what's going to happen next year. Follow a few simple steps and you will eventually get your money. The person who claimed the child incorrectly will have to pay their extra money back, likely preventing this from happening again. The IRS also has some things that will help in the future if Earned Income Credit is involved, but you don't need to worry about that.

Here are the steps:

1. Make sure you are the proper person to claim the child. Reread the I'm Having a Child and I'm Getting Divorced chapters and be sure. Talk to your tax professional and be completely honest and upfront about the situation. Once you are sure you are in the right...

2. Gather documentation that shows the child's relationship to you, the fact that they live with you, their age, and their student status. Birth certificates, marriage certificates, school and medical records, statements from daycare and neighbors will all help. The IRS has a form, 886-H-DEP that has examples of documentation that is considered acceptable to prove that you meet the requirements to claim someone as a dependent. If you are reading the Kindle version of this book, the link will take you right there. If you are reading the paper version, it will come out right at the top of a google search for "886-H-DEP".

3. Print and mail in your tax return. You can do this before you have all your documentation from step 2, and you can send copies or not send copies of the documentation. I have seen it suggested both ways and can't honestly say if one way is better or not. The main problem you might run across with this is if you are using a professional and having your fees withheld from the refund. The pro may want to be paid upfront now, since your refund will be delayed and not e-filed. Make this happen! Do not let the cost stop you from filing!

Your refund may be significantly delayed, and you may get a letter from the IRS asking for the documentation we talked about in step 2. Keep at it, and you will win. There is no ambiguity on claiming children. Only one person has the right to claim a child and if that is you, you should have only minor speed bumps between you and your refund.

Note 1: If it was a family member or even your child claiming themselves, and you want to avoid trouble, you can run the numbers with and without the child and see how much money is involved compared to the hassle. Particularly if it is your own child (maybe a college or high school age child claiming themselves) have a pointed conversation with them about the next year - I always tell clients to tell their children that as long as they live at home, their tax documents go through YOU! Generally, when your child claims them self, you can usually still file Head of Household (if you are a single parent) using them as a non-dependent. It's possible in this scenario that you don't lose too much.

My Advice:

1. You can probably guess what I am going to say: "Follow the above advice and CLAIM YOUR CHILD!"

Military: No real differences for you here.

45. My Tax Return got Rejected by the IRS!

The first thing to do here is relax. Very often the fix for this is simple. Oftentimes your software or Tax Pro will be able to walk you through fixing the problem and resubmitting the return with little difficulty.

The second thing to understand is that the return has been rejected for ELECTRONIC FILING ONLY. It has not been audited. The IRS is not coming to get you. This does not mean you can't file. E-file rejection is simply the IRS' way of preventing certain kinds of fraud, ensuring only one return per person has been submitted and a few other things. A rejected return isn't even considered filed yet, so, no matter how bad you buggered it up, you aren't in any trouble at all. Worst case, if you have filed an accurate return, you might have to mail it in and wait a while to get your refund (if you owe, make sure to pay by April 15th even if you are still having trouble getting the return accepted!) You even get up to an extra 5 days added to the filing deadline if you file at the very last minute and it gets rejected.

All the above said, there are some very common reasons for rejected tax returns, and I am going to cover a lot of them, as well as some advice on correcting them. Your software or tax professional is the first resource for information, but it can be confusing. I will try to use the verbiage the IRS will use when informing you, but, since I'm lumping things together, they may not match exactly. You should be able to figure out what I'm talking about. I'm not going to use the code numbers (mostly) for the same reason. Once you correct the error causing the reject, you just resend the return. You can keep resending as many times as needed.

Prior Year AGI or PIN incorrect: As one step to prevent tax ID theft, the IRS requires tax software users to provide information from their prior year's return to help ensure they are who they say they are. You must provide your prior year's AGI or the PIN. Your PIN is a 5-digit code that you probably didn't even enter yourself when you filed your prior year return. This is a good reason to use the same software every year, since it grabs this information automatically. If you have your prior year return, fixing this is easy - get your AGI (Line 11 of the 2022 Form 1040) or your PIN (form 8879 next to your signature) and input it into the software and resend. If you do not have a copy of your tax return, things get hard. You can try 1 followed by the last 4 of your SSN as a PIN, you can pay a professional to file it (since they see you and your forms face to face they don't need this extra step), or you can paper file. You can also get a copy of your return from the IRS, or the professional who filed it.

Name, SSN or Birthday do not match IRS records: There are numerous rejects involving wrong personal information. Your software or tax pro should tell you which one is wrong (primary SSN is first name on return, Secondary is the spouse, and dependents are numbered in the order they appear on the tax return and are often identified by the last 4 digits of the SSN used on the return). Generally, this is as simple as checking the information and correcting it to match the Social Security Card and Birth Certificate. Sometimes, in the case of names with more than just first, middle, and last names, the Social Security Administration inputs what you consider to be their second middle name as their last name (just one example of many). If there are more than three names on the Social Security Card, you can try changing the information and resending (keeping in mind that the ORDER of the names stays the same - Joe Bob Billy Smith might be first name Joe, middle name Bob Billy, last name Smith, or could be first name Joe, middle name Bob and last name Billy Smith, but wouldn't be first name Smith, middle name Joe Bob, last name Billy.) If the return involves a recent name change due to marriage, try using the maiden name.

Primary or Secondary SSN has already filed: This is generally caused by one of four things:
1. You filed and forgot you filed (not likely, but I have seen it)
2. Your spouse (or boy/girlfriend, or ex-spouse) already filed a return with you as their spouse.
3. The preparer you used filed your return when you had not (or believed you had not) approved it.
4. Tax ID theft.

I am going to cover 4 (Tax ID theft) at the very end of this chapter, and 2 might also qualify as 4 if they did this behind your back and you didn't plan to file with them. If that is the case read the Tax ID theft part at the end of this chapter.
If number 1 above is the case, and the return you filed isn't right, you'll need to amend (Note 1) the original tax return (wait until the first one is processed, but make sure to get it done before April 15th.)
For 2, if it is not fraud or ID theft, what you do depends on your personal relationship with the person, and whether you are actually married. It could be a misunderstanding, manipulation, or a lot of other things. If you aren't married to the person, don't know the person, and/or did not intend to file

jointly, you should paper file your own, accurate tax return and include an explanation as to what happened (to the best of your knowledge.) If you are married to the person and intended to file jointly, verify the return is accurate and amend (Note 1) it if it is not.

For 3, you will have to deal with the preparer. I cannot really tell you what to do, since it depends on if it's a mistake, a misunderstanding, or fraud. Your action will depend on how long you have dealt with them and the level of trust you have. You might have to deal with the preparer, their boss, the corporation, or a lawyer. I will say that one thing I see, not often, but also not too rarely, is people who see a preparer and are unsatisfied with the results, so they walk out with or without their paperwork. The preparer then files the return and has their fees withheld, so they get paid for the work they did. This is ILLEGAL! If they do not have a signed Form 8879 (or equivalent) from you, they CANNOT file the return. I can't tell you what exactly to do, but I can tell you not to accept this and raise whatever hell you need to get it fixed. At the very least report them to the IRS.

Again, 4 will be covered later under Tax ID Theft.

SSN has already been claimed as a dependent on another tax return: If it's your child that's already been claimed, read the chapter: Someone Claimed my Child. If it is you or your spouse (primary or secondary SSN) you have some sleuthing to do. If you recently moved out from your parents (or another person) who may have been supporting you, contact them and see if they did it and work out what the proper thing to do was. Based on that, either fix your return to identify that you were claimed, or paper file your tax return as is (in this case the other party should amend (Note 1) their return to remove you as a dependent - but that's their problem, not yours.) If you have no idea who did it (or you know, and you know it's fraudulent) see the last part of this chapter on Tax ID theft.

Records say Form 8862 required: If you improperly claimed Earned Income Credit (EIC) in the past, the IRS requires you to file Form 8862 to provide additional information before allowing you to claim EIC. Simply fill out the form in the software and resend the return.

First Time Homebuyer's Credit Repayment: If you bought a house in 2008 or so and took the $7500 First Time Home Buyer Credit that was a loan to be paid back $500 per year for 15 years, you need to include the $500 repayment on your return. If you sold or otherwise no longer own the home, you need to indicate this on your tax return. The IRS messes this up a lot, especially where divorce, deaths or home transfers are involved. The

IRS has a tool you can use to find out what they expect to see on the return, and there is a phone number you can call if it is inaccurate, or the information isn't there. Here is a link for the information on the tool: https://www.irs.gov/credits-deductions/individuals/first-time-homebuyer-credit-account-look-up

Records indicate person deceased: This can be bad...real bad...especially if the indicated person is still alive. How to fix things when the IRS and Social Security Administration have decided you're dead is VERY difficult, and way beyond the scope of this book. In either case, whether the person is actually dead or not is irrelevant to filing this tax return. You will need to send the return in on paper.

F???-502, Employer Identification Number is incorrect: This means the Employer Identification Number (EIN) for the specified form is incorrect. The ??? above will have the form type, either W2, W2G, 1099R or 2439. Simply find the physical copy of the specified form (or forms) and verify that the EIN you entered matches the form. Correct any errors and resend. Some forms, W-2's in particular, can have the number in a weird place (Boeing is one I see all the time). Make sure you don't use the State EIN for the federal.

ID theft PIN not entered or incorrect: If your tax identity was stolen or at risk, the IRS may issue an ID theft PIN to ensure that you are protected from future fraud. You should know this happened and have a letter with the PIN. If you have it, add it to the return and resend. If you don't...use the IRS "Get an IP PIN" tool at irs.gov to recover it. If that doesn't work, call (800) 908-4490 between 7am and 7pm, Monday through Friday. If you moved from the address they had on file, be prepared for trouble. It is very difficult to get your ID theft PIN to an address other than the one they have on file. This sucks, but since ID Theft is involved, you can kinda understand why it can't be easy. Be prepared to paper file the tax return or spend some time in an IRS office. This is a good time to point out that you should ALWAYS update your address with the IRS when you move (Form 8822 – For e-book readers the link goes to the IRS information page on Change of Address).

Tax ID Theft: If your return was rejected because you, your spouse or children were filed as taxpayers or dependents on a return you don't know about, or that you know was fraudulent, that is tax ID theft. There is a bit of a line between outright tax ID theft (stranger or someone you know steals your information and uses it to claim a refund) and dependency disputes (ex-spouse claims child you were entitled to). ID theft requires a police report and ID theft affidavit (Form 14039). Disputes just require paper filing an accurate return with documentation submitted or available proving your claim (Note 2). If it's ID theft, go to IRS.gov and search for "ID theft" and follow their instructions (during tax season there is often a very prominent link posted right on the IRS front page about ID theft, so you can click it without searching.) The basic steps will involve filing a police report, filling out Form 14039 (ID theft affidavit), and sending your tax return in with the affidavit and copies of identification cards. There are also other steps to take for future protection, including getting an ID theft PIN, checking credit reports and reporting to the FTC. Your refund will be significantly delayed.

My personal guess for a new reject in 2024 – Form 8936 missing: In 2024, you will be able to claim an electric vehicle credit as a direct price reduction through the dealer when buying an electric vehicle. You have to report this on your tax return even though you already "received" the credit. This is to allow reconciliation of your income and other qualifications for the credit in case you have to pay some of it back. The only way I see the IRS tracking this is with a rejection, similar to the First Time Homebuyer Credit. But I could be wrong.

Note 1: Amending a tax return means filing form 1040X, where you report the original numbers, the correct numbers, and the difference, and include an explanation for the changes. You can now e-file most amendments and the processing time has gotten better, but can still take a LOOOOOOONG time.

Note 2: The IRS has a series of forms, called 886 forms, that give examples of documentation that will show that you meet various tests to claim someone. Form 886-H-DEP shows the ones for dependents.

My Advice:

1. Change your address using Form 8822 from irs.gov every time you move. This will prevent a lot of issues, not the least of which is getting your updated ID Theft PIN.
2. Always print a physical copy of your tax return and keep it where you can find it. This will ensure you can get your prior year's AGI and also prevent a lot of other problems. Needing a copy of a tax return is the #1 thing I deal with in the off-season.

3. Carefully enter identification numbers from your various tax forms. They may not seem like they make a difference, but they do.

4. Do not claim dependents that you aren't qualified to.

5. If there is any question as to whether ID Theft was an issue, include the ID Theft Affidavit, Form 14039, with the paper filed return. Lately the IRS is asking for this on any return where someone has already filed the applicable SSN. Best to send it before they ask for it.

46. I (or my Spouse or Child) am Going to College

This is a HUGE chapter with lots of possibilities, so I'm going to try to break it down as much as possible. Start reading with the very first part and then stop when you have your situation covered. The My Advice section at the end will have some useful information and ideas, so make sure to read that as well. Make sure that you don't use the same expenses for more than one credit or deduction. That's a serious no-no.

For this chapter I assume normal family situations and individuals going to school in the United States (including semesters abroad but set up through their normal U.S. educational institution.

1. Determine who you can claim expenses for:

You can claim education expenses and credits for yourself and your spouse if you are MFJ. You can also claim them for someone who you claim as a dependent on your tax return. You can claim the credits for a dependent even if they pay the expenses themselves, but you should revisit dependency in the appropriate chapters to make sure you can still claim them. Age and support start becoming issues at this point. In addition, student loans taken out by your dependent that they are obligated to repay count as funds available for their own support, so these can knock you out of dependency through non-support.

2. Gather your information and documents:

The school is going to (or should) send you a Form 1098T that details what they think you paid. Starting in 2017, you generally must have a 1098-T to claim the American Opportunity Credit, with very few limited exceptions. The 1098T is useful for a lot of things, but don't rely on it solely to determine what you paid. Verify that it matches what you think you paid, and you should get an account transcript from the school showing what was charged, what was paid, and how it was paid. The one nice thing about the 1098T is that it will tell you if you were more than half-time, if you were a graduate student, and it has the data needed to fill out your tax forms. Using the 1098T, your payment receipts and other documentation, get the following information for the student:

    A. Total tuition charged

    B. Total course-required books and fees—prior to 2017, these had to have been specifically required as a condition of enrollment in the college or a course. Starting in 2017, "required" was changed to "needed" which opened it up to a lot more expenses, the main one of which is a computer that is needed, and also tools and equipment for practical types of education. They can't be general study supplies, athletic fees and other things unless they are needed for a specific course of study. I expect this to be an area where people are going to be pushing the boundaries, and over the years we will see what things the IRS lets fly, what things they fight, and what the courts say when they do.

C. Total charges for room and board.

D. Total amount of scholarships and grants (tax free – we really don't care about taxable scholarships as they are treated the same as money you pay out of pocket).

E. Status of at least half-time (from 1098T).

F. Year of college as determined by the school (freshman, sophomore, junior, senior or graduate as of the BEGINNING of the tax year).

G. Whether the student has ever been convicted of a felony drug offense.

H. Total amount of U.S. Savings Bond interest used to pay for college.

I. Total amount of money from tax advantaged tuition plans, such as Coverdell Educational Savings Accounts, Qualified Tuition Plans, Prepaid College Plans, 529 plans or other state-sponsored plans used for education.

You'll notice we don't talk about student loans because the expenses are considered paid even if you use student loans or a credit card. Same with taxable scholarships and grants.

3. Determine if college expenses exceed scholarships and tax advantaged plan sources:

Take the total of A and B from above (your college expenses), and compare it to the total of D, H and I (your tax advantaged funding sources and scholarships). If your expenses exceed your tax advantaged funding sources and scholarships, you have the potential for a credit or deduction. If they do not, then you have a bit of a problem, and should probably talk to a tax expert. You need see if there is a way that you can make use of the tax advantages of the funding sources, manipulate them to generate a credit and/or determine if you have taxable income from scholarships. This will be discussed in later steps.

4. See if you can use the **American Opportunity Tax Credit** (AOC (formerly the HOPE credit)):

This is the best credit available because you get up to $2,500 of credit, with $1,000 refundable (you get it even after your tax is reduced to zero) on only $4,000 of expenses. Generally, you should always shoot for this one. I'm going to refer to the letters from 2, above, to move things along when available. This credit is the one that will come up for a student attending a standard two or four-year college with the intention of getting a degree or other certificate. You get it for the first four years of education (freshman, sophomore, junior, senior, as determined by the college, even if it takes you more than four years to progress through them). However, each student gets a maximum of 4 tax-years' worth of AOC in their life (even if it's their parents taking the credit). For the normal student, they will have 4 years of schooling spanning 5 tax years. Most students begin college in Fall of the same year they graduate high school; half of their college senior year will be in the spring of their fourth year—the fifth tax year of college. This means that you can take the AOC for any four of those five years. If the student takes 6 years to graduate, you still get any four of those six years. Many tax professionals will spend a lot of time trying to anticipate the best four years to take. My recommendation is to take it the first four years the credit is available—you never know what's going to happen in the future. The only caveat is that if you only have a couple hundred dollars of expenses in the first year, you might want to wait to start taking the credit the following tax year. Otherwise, you won't get much out of the AOC and one of your 4 years is wasted.

One other point: you can take as many AOCs as you have students on your tax return. If you, your wife and your three children all qualify, you can get FIVE separate AOCs. Here are the rules once you've figured out that the year qualifies:

    a. If college expenses determined in 3 (above) do not exceed scholarships and tax advantaged sources, you get nothing.

    b. If the answer to 2E is not at least half-time, you cannot get AOC.

    c. If the student has been convicted of a felony drug offense, you don't get AOC.

    d. The student has to be attending an eligible school with the intention of getting a degree or other recognized educational credential, which includes virtually every accredited postsecondary (post high school) institution. This can even include colleges outside the U.S. if they are eligible to participate in the U.S. Federal Student Aid program. The college can tell you if they are eligible.

    e. You cannot be filing MFS.

    f. If your AGI exceeds $180,000 (MFJ) or $90,000 (HH or Single) you cannot get AOC.

    g. If your AGI exceeds $160,000 (MFJ) or $80,000 (HH or Single) your credit will be limited. These income limits were increased in 2020 but have not been increased for inflation since, so it gets harder and harder to meet this threshold.

    h. Calculate your expenses for Form 8863. This number will generally be A + B - D - H - I (tuition plus course-related fees, minus scholarships, grants and tax advantaged funding sources). This is the number you will use when filling out Form 8863 or entering data in your software program (though software may ask for A, B, D, H and I through separate questions). You can sometimes pay taxes on a tax-free scholarship and not have to subtract it when calculating the AOC – if the scholarship allows this is almost always the best way to go if you meet the income limits and have a tax liability. In addition, you can sometimes move around what you use 529 plans to pay for in order to get more AOC. It can also be a good idea to use less 529 plan money such that you maximize AOC, since any 529 plan money not used is still, actually, money that can be used for future education expenses or really anything else with a small tax hit. You probably need a tax professional to help you navigate this.

5. If you don't qualify for AOC, see if you can get the **Lifetime Learning Credit** (LLC):

The LLC is a nice credit, but not as lucrative as the AOC. You get 20% of eligible expenses, up to $2,000 of credit. The expenses are more limited, but the rules for qualifying are less restrictive. This is the credit you would use if the student had already used 4 years of AOC, wasn't attending half-time, wasn't in a degree or credential program, was a graduate student, or already has a four-year degree. Another major difference is that while you can get an AOC for as many students as appear on the tax return, you can get a maximum of $2,000 of LLC, per tax return, regardless of how many students are on the tax return. Here's how we work the LLC:

    a. If college expenses determined in 3 (above) do not exceed scholarships and tax advantaged sources, you get nothing.

    b. If the answer to 2E is not at least half-time, you can still get LLC.

    c. If the student has been convicted of a felony drug offense, you don't get LLC.

d. The student has to be attending an eligible school with or without the intention of getting a degree or credential, which includes virtually every accredited postsecondary (post high school) institution. This can even include colleges outside the U.S. if they are eligible to participate in the U.S. Federal Student Aid program. The college can tell you if they are eligible. This includes truck driving school, welding school and other non-degree attaining schools.

e. You cannot be filing MFS.

f. If your AGI exceeds $180,000 (MFJ) or $90,000 (HH or Single) you cannot get LLC.

g. If your AGI exceeds $160,000 (MFJ) or $80,000 (HH or Single) your credit will be limited. These income limits were increased in 2020 but have not been increased for inflation since, so it gets harder and harder to meet this threshold.

h. Calculate your expenses for Form 8863. This number will be A - D - H - I (tuition without course-related fees, minus scholarships, grants and tax advantaged funding sources). This is the number you will use when filling out Form 8863 or entering data in your software program (though software may ask for A, D, H and I through separate questions). The tricks discussed at the end of the AOC paragraph to maximize AOC still apply here but are generally not worth it with the LLC.

6. If you don't get AOC or LLC, see if the Tuition and Fees Deduction will benefit you:

This deduction was eliminated for 2020 and later years. I am leaving the information here for older returns and the possibility of it being brought back later.

The tuition and fees deduction is usually the least beneficial of the education benefits; you get a deduction from income instead of a tax credit. It is an "above the line" deduction, which means it improves your taxes whether you itemize or not and may reduce your AGI for figuring other limitations. The expenses that you can deduct for this deduction are virtually the same as the AOC, except that books and course-related fees are only included if they MUST be paid directly to the education institution as a condition of enrollment. One big caveat on all this education stuff is that the AOC and the LLC have no effect on state taxes. This deduction often does, so when determining whether this is better than the LLC or AOC, make sure to check your state taxes as well. Here are the details:

a. If college expenses determined in 3 (above) do not exceed scholarships and tax advantaged sources, you get nothing.

b. If the answer to 2E is not at least half-time, you can still get this deduction.

c. If the student has been convicted of a felony drug offense, you still get this deduction.

d. The student has to be attending an eligible school with or without the intention of getting a degree or credential, which includes virtually every accredited postsecondary (post high school) institution. This can even include colleges outside the U.S. if they are eligible to participate in the U.S. Federal Student Aid program. The college can tell you if they are eligible. This includes truck driving school, welding school and other non-degree attaining schools.

e. You cannot be filing MFS.

f. If your AGI exceeds $160,000 (MFJ) or $80,000 (HH or Single) you cannot get this deduction.

g. You can deduct a maximum of $4,000 if your income is less than $130,000 (MFJ) or $65,000 (Single or HH). If your income is between $130,000 and $160,000 (MFJ) or between $65,000 and $80,000 (HH or Single) you can deduct $2,000. This is per tax return, not per person.

h. Calculate your expenses for Form 8917. This number will be A + B (if required to be paid to the institution as discussed above) - D - H - I (tuition with required course-related fees minus scholarships, grants and tax advantaged funding sources). This is the number you will use when filling out Form 8917 or entering data in your software program (though software may ask for A, B, D, H and I through separate questions).

7. If you have QTPs, ESAs, 529s, or other tax advantaged education savings, account for them:

Bottom line do not withdraw more from these accounts than your educational expenses. These are tuition, fees, and room and board (does not have to be paid through the college but cannot exceed what the college would have charged). Make sure your student is enrolled at least half-time. Lastly, make sure you don't include expenses paid with these funds when calculating any of the credits or deductions above.

Plan ahead if you have these funding sources and don't just use it to eliminate all expenses. The AOC is MUCH more lucrative than the 529 plan advantage so work out the best way BEFORE you pay for college. This is an area that an expert consultation can come in very useful. That said, not all tax advisors fully grasp the smartest ways to manipulate college expenses, nor do they understand how it impacts your children's tax return. Review this chapter and have a basic understanding of what SHOULD work so you can back up what the expert is saying and know if they fully understand or are just making stuff up off the cuff.

8. If you use Savings Bond proceeds to pay for education, figure out what's tax free:

When you cash in U.S. Savings Bonds, you normally pay federal tax on the interest (difference between what you paid for the bond and how much they pay you when cashing in), but no state tax. When you use it for education, however, you can exclude the interest from income. That said, it's actually one of the more complicated subjects with regard to education expenses, because the exclusion is limited by how much cash you get, and not just by the interest you received. I would suggest talking to a tax professional before cashing in bonds for education, but here are a few simple tips to keep you out of trouble:

    a. Make sure your AGI is below $137,800 (MFJ) or $91,850 (Single or HH) before you cash in savings bonds for education. Above this income your deduction starts phasing out (Completely gone at $167,800 (MFJ) and $106,850 (S/HH.)

    b. Make sure that you don't cash in more in bonds (not just interest) than the tuition you have to pay, less any other scholarships or tax advantaged education savings you are using. Room and board does not count. If you follow these rules, you should be safe.

9. If you get more in scholarships and grants than tuition, prepare to pay taxes on it:

Did that scare you? Good. Now we can determine if you need to pay taxes on it, but, before that, let me say one thing. If you can find a way to get scholarships and grants that exceed the cost of your tuition, you win. Seriously. You will have to pay taxes on the excess (maybe), but it's free money! Pay the taxes and be happy! First, take the amount from 2D (scholarships and grants) and subtract A and B from it. If the number is positive, it's taxable, and you add it to line 7 of Form 1040 (the same line as your wages from your W-2s). If it's negative, you do not need to include anything as income.

10. VA benefits. If you use VA benefits (or GI Bill) to pay for school, none of the benefits are taxable, including any housing allowances you get. However, you can't get deductions or credits for expenses paid by the VA

or with VA money. The benefits can interact weirdly with the credits and deductions, so I would check with an expert before filing.

My Advice:

1. You might be noticing a pattern of me suggesting a folder or an envelope as a record keeping method and this chapter is no different. As soon as you start dealing with college bills and financial aid, start keeping documents and receipts in a folder, and write the date, description and amount on the outside in neat columns as you add them. This will make filing taxes significantly easier and, since the AOC is one of the most likely things you will be asked to prove, having the records is important. Include tuition and fees charged, payments made, books bought etc.
2. If you are within the income limits for the AOC and meet the other requirements for half time attendance and number of years, there are many counter-intuitive strategies that you can use to maximize your tax benefits. $4000 of eligible expenses is worth $2500 in tax credits, so even the supposedly obvious idea of using 529 plan proceeds to pay for college is MUCH more complicated. PLEASE consult with a tax professional if you are eligible for the AOC but also have tax free scholarships and/or a 529 plan you could use. Mistakes in this area can cost you as much as $10,000 in lost tax credits!

Military: See 10 above about GI Bill and VA benefits. Also, if you use Tuition Assistance (TA) to pay for schooling, you cannot use that expense for a deduction or credit. Think of TA, VA benefits and GI Bill as scholarships except that they won't be taxable income if they exceed expenses. The 1098-T you get from many schools will not note the TA or GI Bill payments, making it look like you have valid expenses. Don't fall for this. The IRS will eventually catch on and it can get ugly. Use the calculations I talked about, including military education benefits as if they were scholarships and you will be okay.

47. I Have to Pay Things for my Job

Starting with 2018 and later years, this entire category of deductions has been eliminated, so unless you are in the reserves or national guard, don't bother reading if you are working on a 2018 return or making plans for 2018 or later.

Honestly I'm just leaving this chapter in forever because, despite this being an almost 4 year-old change, the idea of deducting work expenses just won't go away. Also, it still applies for certain military reservists. So, the below is here for everyone to read anytime they start thinking they can deduct work expenses:

Employees don't get deductions for work expenses as an itemized deduction.

Military: Most military members are fully reimbursed for their expenses so generally your only deduction will be for professional publications if you pay for them. The only real exceptions that most people will ever see is for reservists whose drill location is more than 100 miles from their home (details below):

National Guard or Reserves:

Members of the National Guard or Reserves, who travel more than 100 miles from home to their drilling or service location can deduct these travel expenses directly on Form 1040 rather than as an itemized deduction. This is a BIG difference that is great for the tax return! They are still accounted for on the same form as other job expenses (Form 2106 in their own column) but they carry directly to the 1040, reducing your AGI and improving many aspects of your tax return.

Deductible expenses are mileage, tolls, parking, ferry travel, lodging (must be actual expense and cannot exceed the federal per diem rate), meals and incidental expenses (can take the standard federal meals and incidental expenses per diem amount for the area rather than keeping records for specific meals).

You should have a mileage log for this and save receipts and records that prove your expenses as well as documenting the days you were required to travel.

Many states have benefits similar to this. Some states do not tax reserve pay and, in this case, you cannot deduct these expenses on those states (or must add them back for the state).

48. I Tele-Commute

Starting with 2018 and later years, this entire category of deductions has been eliminated, so don't bother reading if you're working on a 2018 return or making plans for 2018 or later.

Employees don't get to deduct work expenses as an itemized deduction. Despite the Coronavirus making far more people work from home, this hasn't changed.

49. I Work Overseas

This is not really a fully instructional chapter. It really is a "get a tax professional" chapter and a "don't listen to the too good to be true stories from your friends (or tax pro or employer)" chapter.

Essentially, there are a lot of ways in which the tax system is set up to avoid you paying taxes on your income to both the United States and a foreign country. The U.S. is unique in that it is one of the only countries that taxes **worldwide income**, regardless of source. Most other countries only tax income from sources within their country. This necessitates systems to avoid double taxation. The methods used to prevent double taxation depend on whether your employer is U.S. or foreign, what country you are in, how long you are there, whether you are a bona fide resident of the foreign country (not the easiest of questions), tax treaties in effect between us and them, and who's social security system is responsible for you. There are TONS of other factors, but these are the big ones.

Point is, get professional help for this, from someone who specializes in foreign taxes.

That said, many people, including your employer, co-workers, and overly aggressive tax professionals, will tout not necessarily true things about working tax-free in a foreign country. The gist is that if you work overseas for over a year, you don't pay U.S. taxes. This is sort of true, with a BUNCH of caveats. The biggest of which is that you need stronger ties to the foreign country than to the U.S. If you go overseas on a 1-year contract (these are often sold as tax-free contracts) you probably don't qualify, especially if you left behind a spouse, kids and/or home. Many people have been taking advantage of this and not getting caught, but the IRS is cracking down. In addition, it has a maximum to be excluded, and the remaining part is taxed at the rate it would have been if the other income is excluded. Using it also excludes you from a number of tax credits and deductions that would otherwise have been allowed.

There are a myriad of complexities to this! Get professional help!

My Advice:

1. One piece of advice I give in ALL these situations is to try to withhold from your taxes as if you were working in the United States. Worst case is that you get a huge refund.

2. Be prepared that if you are able to exclude all of your income you might have to mail your tax return in vice electronic filing.

Military: This pretty much does not apply to you, no matter how much time you spend overseas—though it might apply to your working spouse.

50. I Lost my Job

2020 Only Update: You can exclude up to $10,200 in unemployment benefits from income if you meet certain income limitations. The IRS will fix your tax return for you if you filed before the change. See the 2020 Chapter for more details.

The meat of the chapter:

That sucks that you lost your job and I am sorry it happened to you.

This loss brings up a lot of tax issues, many of which will seem like adding insult to injury. For example, almost any money you get to help you get through the unemployment period, like, say, unemployment compensation, will be taxable. I'm going to go over several things, but I want to say, loudly and emphatically, DON'T TOUCH YOUR PENSION PLAN! Accessing your pension plan should be an absolute last resort. Taking money out of your 401k (I'm going to say 401k to cover all the various retirement accounts that follow the standard rules for tax advantaged plans) should be done only if it's the difference between eating and not eating, keeping the lights on, or saving your mortgage (and sometimes not even then). We'll talk about what to do with the 401k that doesn't involve taking it out, but trust me, you don't want to just liquidate it. This also applies to personal retirement accounts, such as Individual Retirement Accounts.

The first thing to know is that almost any money you get is going to be taxable, within reasonable limits. This includes most disability, third-party sick pay, severance, unemployment compensation or any other lump sum or periodic payments. Generally, you'll get a W-2, a 1099R or other formal tax form in January or February of the following year. This is a perfect sign that they belong on your tax return. An example I give is Social Security: even Social Security Disability is taxable. Supplemental Security Income (SSI) is from the same agency but is not taxable. The sure way of knowing the difference is the receipt of the 1099SSA. The one exception is that if you get a W-2 with nothing in Box 1, and the "Third Party Sick Pay" box checked, it is not taxable and does not go on your tax return.

To keep the nitpickers at bay, when I say taxable, it does not necessarily mean you'll pay taxes on it, but that you will report it on your tax return and calculate the potential taxability. You can't absolutely rely on getting these forms as a way of knowing what to report, mainly because they may not make it to you if you have to move or they get the address wrong. The best way to be sure is to communicate with the agencies giving you money, and ensure you know what forms to expect. You should also have them withhold taxes, if possible. They often will under-withhold, so you need to be prepared for a tax bill. Life can really suck when you've been scraping by for a year, depleting your savings, and then you get a big tax bill at the end of the year. Preparation is key to staying ahead of this. You'll need to calculate your income from when you had a job, other sources of income while unemployed, and estimate your tax liability to ensure you have enough withheld. Otherwise, you need to set enough aside for Uncle Sam and his bastard step-children from the state you live in. Professional help can be useful for this.

Short term disability can be taxable depending on who paid the insurance premiums. You will almost certainly get a W-2, but, this is the one time when a W-2 MIGHT not go on your tax return. If the W-2 only has an entry in Box 12 with Code J, and not in Box 1 and/or 2, you can leave it off your tax return. Anything in Box 1 means it is taxable, and you need to enter the numbers.

If you take money out of CDs, the early withdrawal penalties are deductible against the interest earned. I'm not talking about retirement accounts here, just savings accounts that have a specified term for which you are supposed to keep them.

If you have to relocate for a job, read the next chapter on moving for a job, but be aware that moving expenses for non-military personnel are no longer deductible for 2018 and later years.

For your 401k, you will need to do something with it, though you are sometimes allowed to leave it with your former employer. I'm not a financial advisor, but my non-professional suggestion is to roll it over to an Individual Retirement Account with a financial services company. Seek professional assistance from a licensed financial advisor, or if you are good at handling your investments, do it yourself, but DON'T HAVE THEM SEND THE MONEY TO YOU! Do a trustee to trustee transfer, where you tell the destination financial institution to go get the money from your old employer. You don't have to do it this way, but trust me, this is the safe and easy way to do it.

If you absolutely have to take money out of your 401k or Individual Retirement Accounts (IRAs), take the absolute minimum out that you need to SURVIVE. Make sure they withhold the maximum (generally 20%) and realize that this probably won't be enough. You will probably pay a 10% penalty, plus your regular tax rate (probably AT LEAST another 12%). If you have a Roth IRA, you can look into taking some out of there first. You can actually take the amount you put into a Roth IRA out tax-free (I would be very careful about pulling out of a Roth, since once it is in the account it is your best investment...PERIOD. Leaving it alone will pay off in spades later in life), but I would seek advice from both your tax professional, and your financial professional before doing this.

My Advice:

1. This is probably closing the barn door after the farm equipment escaped, but: Have an Emergency Fund with at least 3 to 6 months expenses in it. I cannot over-emphasize the importance of this. A big refund is a GREAT time to get one of these funded.
2. Tighten the crap out of your budget IMMEDIATELY at the first sign that your job might be at risk. Start stashing money away and figuring out the EXACT priority in which your bills should be paid. Cancel the cable, Netflix, streaming services, etc.
3. Take money out of retirement accounts only if absolutely necessary and do it in small chunks as you need it. They may allow you to withhold more than 20%, and if they do, try to withhold your tax bracket plus 10%. Don't forget about state withholding. Retirement account withdrawals are for SURVIVAL not for having fun.
4. This may seem cold-hearted but using a retirement account to pay the mortgage isn't exactly a no-brainer. If you are going to lose the house anyway, throwing retirement assets at it is just compounding the loss. Also, falling behind on a mortgage is recoverable, so it can be a lower priority than lights, heat, water and food.

Military: See the next chapter for moving information.
If you retired, see the chapter titled: I Retired from the Military.

The discussion above about 401k's applies to your Thrift Savings Plan.

If you were kicked out and they recouped bonuses or pay, you may have a Claim of Right repayment deduction or credit. If you are making periodic payments on these, and you have control and can afford it, it is to your advantage to ensure that the total payments for a year exceed $3000. If the payment is less than or equal to $3000, your only option is to take it as an Itemized Deduction subject to a 2% of income limitation (which is not available for 2018 and later years). In this case, if you don't itemize, you're out of luck. If it's over $3000 you can deduct it (like the <$3000) or take a refundable credit equal to the taxes you originally paid on it. This is quite complex but can be lucrative. You basically redo the tax return for the year you received the money and see what the difference is. This is the credit you get, dollar for dollar, on the current year's tax return.

51. I Had to Move

Starting with 2018 and later years, moving expenses are no longer deductible and all moving reimbursements are taxable income. The only exception to this is military Permanent Change of Station moves, so don't read this if you aren't active-duty military.

Moving expenses should be simple, but the IRS insists on making them complicated. I will try to simplify the rules you need to qualify, go over the usual expenses, and then talk about reimbursement and other complicated crap.

You have to be moving on Permanent Change of Station Orders for you to deduct moving expenses and you either have to be doing a Do it Yourself (DITY) move or have expenses that aren't paid for by the military. Everything below is about DITY moves, for non-DITY moves, the deductible expenses will generally fall into the area of shipping pets or other items that the military refuses to move for you, shipping a second car, or excess weight above your allowance. Pet medical and quarantine expenses are not deductible.

Here is what you can deduct:

You can deduct only reasonable expenses for moving you, your family and your household goods. You must move by the most direct route and not take side trips or excess vacations. If you have some of your household at a different location, you can deduct the moving expenses for them, but not any more than it would have cost to move them by the direct route from your old home to new home. Make sure to save all receipts.

If you drive you can deduct 18 cents a mile, or actual costs for oil and gas ONLY. In addition to that, you can deduct parking and tolls.

You can deduct lodging, but not meals for you and your family members. You get lodging for the day you have to leave your old house, up to the day you get ANY lodging (including hotel) in the area of your new job. You can't deduct meals. You can deduct plane, rail or train fare for you and your family. You don't have to travel together, but you only get one trip per person. (You can't go back and forth moving kids and keep deducting your travel, but you can deduct each kid's plane ticket.)

You can deduct expenses for moving your household goods, if you pay them. This includes truck rental and supplies, or professional moving services.

You can deduct thirty days of storage either before or after the move (or combination of before and after, but not more than 30 days).

You can deduct the cost of connecting and disconnecting utilities (but not deposits or regular monthly charges).

Here's how to handle reimbursements: This is actually easy. For a DITY move, they will provide a W-2 on MyPay under Travel and Miscellaneous W-2 and you simply include it on your tax return. For a non-DITY move, there should be no reimbursement since expenses are paid directly to the movers or relocation company and none of that is reported on your tax return. You simply report excess expenses on Form 3903.

Expenses for a DITY move are reported on the appropriate lines of Form 3903.

If you do a DITY move at the end of one year and don't get reimbursed until the next year, you include the 3903 with expenses in the year of the move and the reimbursement on the next year's taxes. Don't move income or expenses between year's – everything goes on the year it happened!

COAST GUARD:

The above rules also apply to members of the Coast Guard except that their reimbursement is often included on their regular W-2, mixed in with the regular wages. This doesn't affect anything about how you report the expenses – you simply don't have another W-2 to enter for the reimbursement.

52. I Sold my Home

There is good news and bad news in this chapter. The good news is: you probably won't have to pay income taxes on the gain you might have. The bad news is: you probably won't be able to take the loss if you sold the home for less than you paid for it.

In this chapter I'm assuming that this is your home preferably your primary home. If the property wasn't your main home (say it was a vacation home or you rented it out) you're in the wrong chapter. You want I Sold my Rental Property or I Sold a Home that Wasn't my Principal Residence chapter. I'm also assuming you didn't have any strange events involving the government while you lived in it such as special tax assessments for local improvements or easements/eminent domains you were compensated for. Get help if that is the case (unless you are able to fully exclude the gain as discussed below).

You'll need to know some information about the house, and one piece of taxese that is almost as important as AGI. The information you'll need is the date purchased, price paid, cost of any improvements, date sold, sales price and expenses of sale. The taxese is BASIS. Basis is basically your investment in something. It comes up all the time in taxes. Simply put, it's what you put into a property minus what you took out. For a house, it's generally the price you paid, plus any improvements you made to it. Other things that can affect the basis are casualties (such as fire or flooding), payments for easements (a sidewalk or right of way), using the property for business purposes (results in a deduction called depreciation, which we will discuss later), First-Time Homebuyer Credit that hasn't been paid back, the bank wrote off some of your debt, and parts of the property have been sold off (such as part of the land). Some of these will require you to seek professional tax help. There are a lot of other things, but we won't cover most of them because they rarely come up. Maybe in a later edition...

Let's start with the easy scenario...

If you (and your spouse, if filing MFJ) owned your home for at least two of the last five years, lived in it for two of the last five years, never ran a business out of it, never rented it to someone else, and haven't excluded the gain on a principal residence in the two years prior to the sale *, you can exclude up to $250,000 of gain ($500,000 if MFJ). In fact, you probably signed a form during closing that attested to these facts. If so, the home sale won't even be reported to the IRS and you don't need to do

ANYTHING! If it is reported to the IRS, you'll receive a Form 1099-S and you'll need to report the sale on your tax return (Schedule D). You will need to back out any gain or loss with another line entry that cancels it out. To figure your gain, you take the price you sold it for, minus expenses of sale, minus your basis. Here are the details on calculating the gain and taking the exclusion (assumes you meet all exclusion requirements discussed above):

1. Figure out your BASIS: Using the Master Settlement Statement from when you bought the home (the long form with columns that identifies expenses paid by the buyer and paid by the seller), figure out the price you paid for the home. If the seller paid points for you, subtract that amount from the basis. Add (from the Master Settlement Statement) settlement fees, title fees, legal fees, recording fees, survey fees, transfer or tax stamps that you paid. Also add any amounts that the seller owed, but you paid. Now add any amounts you paid to improve the home. This is your BASIS. Now add to this any expenses you paid for the sale (use the Master Settlement Statement from the sale). Make sure to include the agent's commission since that usually makes a big difference. If any other weirdness occurred that affected the basis, seek professional help. Also seek help if you received the house as a gift or inheritance. This is the BASIS that you report for the sale (it is technically basis plus costs of sale).
2. Now figure out the proceeds from the sale. Use "Gross Proceeds" from the 1099S form if you received one. If not, use the sales price from the Master Settlement Statement. This is your SALES PROCEEDS.
3. Subtract the BASIS from the SALES PROCEEDS and you have the GAIN (if negative this is a LOSS, which you cannot deduct).
4. Report, on Schedule D in the Long-Term section, the date purchased, date sold, BASIS, SALES PROCEEDS and GAIN (or zero for gain if it was a loss).
5. On the next line of Schedule D, write "Section 121 Exclusion" in the description, and a negative number in the Gain/Loss column. This negative number is the SMALLER of the GAIN discussed above, and $250,000 if you are not filing MFJ and $500,000 if you are filing MFJ. Essentially, if the gain exceeds your exclusion ($500K MFJ, $250K not MFJ), you pay taxes on the amount that exceeds the exclusion. Otherwise, these lines should zero out.
6. If there is a gain that is not excluded, you'll pay taxes at a lower rate than normal (maximum 23.8), depending on your tax bracket. This is the Long Term Capital Gains Rate, plus some possible Affordable Care Act taxes, since we know you owned it longer than a year if you meet the 2 year

requirement we are talking about. When you sell the home and get the check from closing, you should run these numbers and see how much of the money to set aside from closing. Basically, saving 23.8% of the amount from line 5 above will cover you safely (for federal taxes though not necessarily state taxes).

* Let me expand on this: You can use this exclusion no more than once every two years to the DAY! If you exclude the gain on a sale on June 2nd 2023, you cannot exclude another sale until June 3rd 2025. You need one more day past two years to qualify. This applies even if your closing attorney determines that you qualify and thus does not report the sale to the IRS, and you subsequently don't have to put anything on your return. This still counts as "using" the exclusion.

Steps 3 through 6 may be handled by your software, but you want to make sure the results are as I discussed by reviewing the tax return before filing.

What if you don't meet the 2 of 5-year rules and/or non-business/non-rental use rules? Let's talk some scenarios...

If one of you (you or your spouse) does not meet the 2 out of 5-year USE rule (don't worry about ownership if at least one of you meets it), figure out the exclusion for EACH of you, as if you weren't married, and take the total of that amount as your maximum exclusion for line 5 in the discussion above.

If you rented the property out, check out the next chapter: I Sold my Rental Property. If you used the property for business, seek out some professional help.

Let's say you have to move out before you have owned and lived in the home for two years, do you get an exclusion? Yes, if you meet certain circumstances:

1. If you move due to a change in employment (you or your spouse), and the new employer is at least 50 miles further from the home than the previous employer was, you can take a reduced exclusion.
2. If you move and the primary purpose was for medical care for you, your spouse, parent (step and in-law included), child, foster child, adopted child, grandchild (including in-laws), sibling (including half-siblings, in-laws and step-siblings), uncle, aunt, niece or cousin, you may qualify for a reduced

exclusion. This has to be to treat an illness, disease or injury and can't just be for improving the well-being of the individual.

3. If you move due to unforeseen circumstances that essentially FORCE you to move, you are eligible for a reduced exclusion. This can't simply be a move that improves your life, it needs to seriously affect your ability to live. Examples include divorce, death, unemployment, casualty to the home, loss of the home, multiple births from the same pregnancy or natural or man-made disasters. COVID-19 opened an entirely new category of unforeseen circumstances that could apply here.

If you qualify for the reduced exclusion, you calculate it this way:

1. Figure out your BASIS: Using the Master Settlement Statement from when you bought the home (the long form with columns that identifies expenses paid by the buyer and paid by the seller), figure out the price you paid for the home. If the seller paid points for you, subtract that amount from the basis. Add (from the Master Settlement Statement) settlement fees, title fees, legal fees, recording fees, survey fees, transfer or tax stamps that you paid. Also add any amounts that the seller owed, but you paid. Now add any amounts you paid to improve the home. This is your BASIS. Now add to this any expenses you paid for the sale (use the Master Settlement Statement from the sale). Make sure to include the agent's commission since that usually makes a big difference. If any other weirdness occurred that affected the basis, seek professional help. Also seek help if you received the house as a gift or inheritance. This is the BASIS that you report for the sale (it is technically basis plus costs of sale).

2. Now figure out the proceeds from the sale. Use "Gross Proceeds" from the 1099S form if you received one. If not, use the sales price from the Master Settlement Statement. This is your SALES PROCEEDS.

3. Subtract the BASIS from the SALES PROCEEDS and you have the GAIN (if negative this is a LOSS, which you cannot deduct).

4. Report, on Schedule D in the Long-Term section, the date purchased, date sold, BASIS, SALES PROCEEDS and GAIN (or zero for gain if it was a loss).

5. Calculate your reduced exclusion: this is the days you met ALL tests divided by 730, multiplied by $500,000 if you are MFJ and $250,000 if you are not.

6. On the next line of Schedule D, write "Section 121 Exclusion" in the description, and a negative number in the Gain/Loss column. This negative number is the SMALLER of the GAIN discussed on line 4 above and the

reduced exclusion from line 5 above. You pay taxes on the amount that exceeds the exclusion. Otherwise, these lines should zero out.
should zero out.

7. If there is a gain that is not excluded, you'll may pay taxes at a lower rate than normal (maximum 23.8), depending on your tax bracket. This is the Long Term Capital Gains Rate, plus some possible Affordable Care Act taxes, if you owned it longer than a year. If you owned it less than a year, it is tacked on the top of your income and taxed at whatever tax bracket rate it falls under. When you sell the home and get the check from closing, you should run these numbers and see how much of the money to set aside from closing.

IMPORTANT!!! This exception does NOT get you out of the "you can only do this once every 2 years rule".

My Advice:

1. May be a little late: Start a home folder. Use a color that you can write on. A manila folder with pockets is perfect! Put your Master Settlement Statement in the folder. After that, if you do something that affects the basis (mainly improvements) write the date and amount on the front of the folder in a nice column, and then put the paperwork supporting it into the folder. You will probably never need any of this information, but you will be really glad that you have it if you end up needing it. Likely reasons for needing it would be if you sell the home for an enormous profit or you convert the home to rental or business use.

2. At closing when you sell the home, make sure that it is discussed that you qualify for the exclusion when you do. Your closing attorney or agent should be able to have you sign an affidavit that you qualify for the exclusion and thus not even report the sale to the IRS.

3. If you are not sure if the sale is fully excludable, it is a good idea to set aside a good chunk of the proceeds for potential taxes until after you file them. This is a good idea anytime you get a windfall of money. In fact, the more complicated the tax situation, the more you should set aside. There have been a number of times when I have recommended to a client that they just sit on the entirety of some potentially taxable money until they can get in to see me with all the paperwork.

Military: If you are on active duty for greater than 90 days and get stationed greater than 50 miles from the principle residence in question, you can extend the 5-year test period for the ownership and residence tests for up to 10 years. What this means is that when you buy a home in the military and live in it for at least two years, if they transfer you more than

50 miles away, you can exclude the gain as long as you sell it within 13 years of moving out (or 3 years after you get out of the military, whichever is sooner) and still exclude up to $500,000 of gain if MFJ and $250,000 if you are not. This applies even if you buy and move into a new house! If you convert the house to rental, this exception still applies, but see the next chapter, I Sold my Rental Property, for some other caveats.

For the purposes of the reduced exclusion for when you own and live in it for less than two years, a PCS move counts as an unforeseen circumstance.

Not discussed: Inherited or gifted homes. Vacant land adjacent to residence sale. Business or rental use of residence. Physically or mentally disabled persons. Deceased spouse home sale. Divorced person not living in home. Home co-owned by taxpayer and a non-spouse.

53. I Sold my Rental Property

Now we are starting to get complicated. First of all, if you converted your personal residence to rental use, and then sold it within 3 years of conversion to rental, you might be able to get the personal residence exclusion for some of the gain that we discussed in the previous chapter. For active duty military (and some other government employees on extended duty), that 3 years becomes 13 years or 3 years after you leave the military whichever comes FIRST. If this is the case, seek a tax professional to help you out. If not, read on...

This is a VERY complex situation, and, in general, I'm not a fan of doing it yourself or with software. You can get away with doing rental property with software, if you are very careful. The sale of the property however, can get pretty messy. If you insist on doing it yourself, please have a professional review the return before filing it. If you've had rental property for any length of time, most of the terms I'm using should be familiar to you; this chapter is going to be a bit over the head of the typical taxpayer. If you own rental property, and this still goes over your head, get professional help, and bring your past few years of taxes for a review.

The first thing you need to do is closeout the rental portion of your tax return, recording the income and expenses on Schedule E. You note the date of sale, and figure out the depreciation of the property, and any other assets that you've been depreciating. If, in the past, you have disallowed losses from the rental property due to income limitations, or not being an active participant, you will net these losses with the gain or loss from the current year and take that as a rental gain or loss on your Form 1040.

Now figure the gain or loss on the rental property:

1. Figure out your BASIS: Using the Master Settlement Statement from when you bought the home (the long form with columns that identifies expenses paid by the buyer and paid by the seller), figure out the price you paid for the home. If the seller paid points for you, subtract that amount from the basis. Add (from the Master Settlement Statement) settlement fees, title fees, legal fees, recording fees, survey fees, transfer or tax stamps that you paid. Also add any amounts that the seller owed, but you paid. Now add any amounts you paid to improve the home. This is your BASIS. If any other weirdness occurred that affected the basis, seek professional help. Also seek help if you received the house as a gift or inheritance. Now subtract the depreciation taken on the property through the years, including

the current year (note the total amount of depreciation for later as well). All of this information should either carry automatically to the appropriate form or be available on a depreciation worksheet. This is a big SHOULD. I have attempted to help people with this using typical tax software and even my vast knowledge is often not enough to get the stupid things to spit out the numbers that I KNOW are right.

2. Now figure out the proceeds from the sale. To do this you use the Master Settlement Statement from the Sale of the home. Take the sales price and subtract any expenses you paid. Make sure to include the agent's commission since that usually makes a big difference. This is the SALE PROCEEDS.

3. Subtract the BASIS from the SALES PROCEEDS and you have the GAIN (if negative this is a LOSS).

4. Report, on Form 4797 in the Long Term or Short-Term section (Long Term if owned more than 1 year), the date purchased, date sold, BASIS, SALES PROCEEDS and GAIN (or LOSS).

5. If there is a gain, you'll pay taxes at a higher rate up to the amount of depreciation we discussed in step 1. Above that, you'll pay taxes at a lower rate than normal (maximum 23.8%) depending on your tax bracket (if the sale was Long Term). When you sell the home and get the check from closing, you should run these numbers and see how much of the money to set aside from closing.

Steps 3 through 5 may be handled by your software, but you want to make sure the results are as I discussed by reviewing the tax return before filing.

If the home qualified as a personal residence (discussed in the previous chapter) the depreciation portion of the gain will ALWAYS be taxed as depreciation recapture (the higher rate) even if you can exclude the gain as personal residence. This is of course limited to the total gain on the property, so you pay taxes on the gain, or the depreciation, whichever is LOWER (assuming your personal residence exclusion is large enough to cover the gain on the sale).

My Advice:

1. I really recommend using a professional for at least the first year of rental property activity and the year you sell it. There are just too many mistakes that you can make, and way too much potential lost money.

2. Set aside a generous amount of the sales proceeds for taxes, unless you can calculate an accurate amount based on fairly exact income numbers for the year of sale. Better safe than sorry on this. If you can afford to, wait to

spend the money you get from selling until after you file your taxes for the year.

Military: For selling your home as discussed above for the main home exclusion, the 2 of 5 year rule is extended by up to 10 years while you are on active duty. When you are within 18 months of this exclusion expiring, you need to take a hard look at how much gain you can exclude, even if you love the property. If you can exclude $100,000 of gain FOREVER, it really makes sense to sell one and buy another. Talk to your realtor and tax professional for help.

54. I Sold a Home that Wasn't my Primary Residence

In this case I'm assuming that this is either investment property that you've held, but not rented out, or property that you acquired through inheritance. If the property is an inheritance and was investment property held by the person you inherited it from, it remains investment property. If it was the residence of the person you inherited it from (even if they didn't live in it at the time of death), it remains personal use property, unless you take action to convert it to investment or rental property (talk to a tax dude to help you understand what makes this happen - it's not as clear cut as we might like). The reason this matters is that you can't take a loss on personal property, but you can on investment property. I'll cover both scenarios below, as I tell you how to calculate your gain or loss.

1. Figure out your BASIS: Using the Master Settlement Statement from when you bought the home (the long form with columns that identifies expenses paid by the buyer and paid by the seller), figure out the price you paid for the home. If the seller paid points for you, subtract that amount from the basis. Add (from the Master Settlement Statement) settlement fees, title fees, legal fees, recording fees, survey fees, transfer or tax stamps that you paid. Also add any amounts that the seller owed, but you paid. Now add any amounts you paid to improve the home. This is your BASIS. Now add to this any expenses you paid for the sale (use the Master Settlement Statement from the sale). Make sure to include the agent's commission since that usually makes a big difference. If any other weirdness occurred that affected the basis, seek professional help. Also seek help if you received the house as a gift or inheritance. This is the BASIS that you report for the sale (it is technically basis plus costs of sale).
2. Now figure out the proceeds from the sale. Use "Gross Proceeds" from the 1099S form if you received one. If not, use the sales price from the Master Settlement Statement. This is your SALES PROCEEDS.
3. Subtract the BASIS from the SALES PROCEEDS and you have the GAIN (if negative this is a LOSS, which you cannot deduct).
4. Report, on Schedule D in the Long-Term section, the date purchased, date sold, BASIS, SALES PROCEEDS and GAIN or LOSS (if the property was personal use at the time of sale, you cannot deduct the loss.
5. If there is a gain and it's long-term, you'll pay taxes at a lower rate than normal (maximum 23.8%), depending on your tax bracket. When you sell the home and get the check from closing, you should run these numbers and see how much of the money to set aside from closing. Save 23.8% of the gain just to be safe. If short-term, it will be taxed as if it were regular

wages. That could be much higher, so set aside a BIG chunk of the proceeds.

Steps 3 through 5 may be handled by your software, but you want to make sure the results are as I discussed by reviewing the tax return before filing.

My Advice:

1. Set aside a generous amount of the sales proceeds for taxes, unless you can calculate an accurate amount based on fairly exact income numbers for the year of sale. Better safe than sorry on this. If you can afford to, wait to spend the money you get from selling until after you file your taxes for the year.

Military: Not a lot of differences for you here.

Not discussed: Other forms of property other than investment homes or inherited homes.

55. I Get Tips at Work

Tips.

Fricken tips.

I have to say that these are the bane of a tax professional's existence. The IRS has very straightforward and very specific rules for how to handle tip income. The problem is that literally no one does it the right way. The other problem is that the lack of compliance is often driven by employers not understanding and/or not caring about the rules. Now who is going to fight their employer over proper tip reporting? I guess the good news is that the IRS doesn't really seem to be focused on proper tip reporting. I hate to ascribe bad motives to employers, since I think most of it is pure ignorance, but the methods I see used mostly save the employer a lot of money in Social Security and Medicare matching payments. I'm going to go over the right way to do tips, as well as some rationale for doing it correctly. I don't expect you to fight your employer over these, since for most people having a job is more important than fighting over tax technicalities.

The right way to handle tips is to maintain a tip record. You don't have to record every individual tip, but you need to track it well enough to have a daily total of tips received. Your employer may provide an electronic way to do this, and that's okay, but you need to accurately record your total tips, both cash and credit. If you have to give some of your tips to other employees as a result of a tip sharing arrangement, record the amount you pay out to them. You only pay taxes on tips you keep. Separate cash, credit and non-cash tips. You need to report these tips to your employer by the 10th of the following month, if there is not an arrangement to report more often. By reporting tips to your employer, they should include all of them on your W-2, and you don't need to do any special reporting on your tax return. Check your W-2 to ensure it matches your records. If your employer reported a different amount, you can make an adjustment on your tax return to correct it to the right amount.

If you fail to report accurate tip numbers to your employer, you can be charged a penalty of 50% of the amount of taxes (including Social Security and Medicare) that you would have paid if you fully reported your tips. I have never seen this penalty assessed, but that doesn't mean that it hasn't, or won't be assessed. Tips are a very poorly enforced aspect of taxes, but since they now impact a lot of other things (such as Affordable Care Act subsidies) I can see this becoming a serious issue going forward. My advice, as always, is to report ALL your tips to your employer.

Employers can be a pain on this because many employers withhold Social Security and Medicare taxes from your wages and credit card tips, and then they match that amount of taxes out of their own pocket. Any cash tips that are reported cause them to have to withhold Social Security and Medicare taxes from your regular wages, and then match from their own pocket. This is at a rate of 7.65%, so there's a motivation by your employer to report the lowest tips possible.

Sorry that this chapter sucks, but reality, rules and practicality just don't line up very well in this area.

My Advice: I have been in this business long enough to know that this is likely to be a waste of time, but: do tips right.

Military: You should not be getting tips unless you work another job.

56. I Receive Benefits from the Government

There are many different programs that will get you money from the government, and some of them have tax implications. I'll list the ones that come up most often.

Aid to Families with Dependent Children, Food Stamps, WIC (Women, Infants, and Children) and other programs similar to these are not taxable and have no impact on your tax return (since most are state-run, they may have different names). In fact, the IRS makes it a point to state that receiving Earned Income Credit (EIC) has no impact on these programs, nor do they on EIC. The only time they tend to come up is during EIC due diligence (which is how the IRS ensures professionals do not ignore things that indicate EIC fraud). One of the indicators of potential fraud is claiming EIC when you do not appear to have sufficient income to support a child. This doesn't mean you can't get EIC—support is not a requirement for EIC, but it does bring up questions that need answered. So you may be asked about other forms of support that you have that allow you to care for your child, and these programs would be included. Don't worry about disclosing this information, it will not be used against you.

SSI and Social Security. I bring these up together because they are very often confused due to both being sourced from the Social Security Administration. SSI is a program to provide assistance to the low income, the disabled, the elderly and children with limited financial resources. It is not based upon contributions to the Social Security program that are withheld from your paycheck. SSI is not taxable and is treated similarly to the programs in the preceding paragraph. Social Security is paid based upon contributions to the Social Security program by a taxpayer, and those contributions generally must meet certain thresholds in order to receive benefits. It is paid to people who have met contribution requirements and who have reached at least 62 years of age, or are disabled. It may also be paid to survivors of contributors. Social Security is potentially taxable to the person receiving it. If your children receive Social Security due to a deceased parent, it is unearned income to them, and may impact tests for you claiming them as a dependent (see chapters on claiming children). Children's Social Security income may require them to file a tax return (if all they receive is Social Security they generally will not need to file). If you receive Social Security in your name, you must report it on your tax return, and a calculation based on your other income will determine if it's taxable. Here are the fine points:

1. SSI is never taxable and does not need to be reported.

2. Social Security is unearned income to the person who receives it.

3. Social Security should always be reported if you are required to file a tax return.

4. If you are not sure if you are receiving SSI or Social Security, you can tell because you will get a Form 1099-SSA for Social Security. The 1099-SSA can come quite a bit later than your W-2s, so make sure you wait for it.

5. Even if Social Security is not taxable, it can impact other areas of your tax return. In particular, Social Security will lower EIC, but not increase it.

6. Determining how much of Social Security is taxable:

    a. The first thing you have to do is figure out your income that will be used to calculate the taxability of Social Security. This number is all your taxable income, plus any tax-exempt interest, plus HALF of your Social Security income for the year (from your 1099-SSA).

    b. Figure out your "base amount" for comparison. This is $25,000 if you are Single, HH, or QSS filing status, $32,000 if you are MFJ, $25,000 if you are MFS and didn't live with your spouse for EVEN ONE NIGHT during the year, $0 if you are MFS and lived with your spouse anytime during the year. MFS sucks, as we've discussed.

    c. Compare the income from Step a (above) to the base amount from 2. If the income exceeds the base amount, some of your benefits are taxable. There is a complex worksheet to determine how much is taxable, but it will generally be between 50% and 85% of your Social Security income if your income exceeds the base amount. It gets to 85% pretty quickly, so if you are above the base amount you can expect to pay a decent amount of taxes.

The Coronavirus pandemic has increased the amount of unemployment that you can receive, so it bears mentioning that Unemployment Compensation, including the extra money from the CARES Act is fully taxable at the Federal level. It is also taxed by the state you are a resident of, and might be taxable to the state providing it, though often is not. Also, Unemployment Compensation is Unearned Income, so it does not help you get more Earned Income credit. In fact, it can HURT the amount you get, in that they calculate your Earned Income Credit with and without Unemployment Compensation, and you get the lower amount. If you are subject to Kiddie Tax, Unemployment counts as unearned income and is subject to Kiddie tax rules.

Exception to the above for unemployment:

For 2020, the first $10,200 received by an individual who's AGI was less than $150,000 was not taxable at the Federal level and many states followed suit. A married couple could EACH exclude $10,200. If you already filed, there is no need to amend your taxes and the IRS will recalculate your refund and send the difference. Most people should get this money by the end of July. In some very rare cases, where it lowers income to the point that you qualify for a new credit that wasn't on your original return, an amendment might be required. WAIT to file this amendment until the IRS sends you their calculation, then amend from that point. See the 2020 Chapter for more details.

Military: No differences for you here. Military pay and allowances are not benefits from the government in the way we are discussing them here.

Things not covered just yet: Housing/Rent Assistance, HAMP and HARP (foreclosure prevention programs). Probably a lot more programs that I've never heard of and/or don't affect taxes.

57. I Have Investments Outside of Work (non-tax sheltered)

2018 Trump/GOP Tax Law Changes: This chapter was affected by the new tax law.

- The incomes at which lower long-term capital gains rates are applied were decoupled from tax brackets with the new law. That said, they currently mostly coincide with where the brackets shift, but they technically have their own values.

This is going to be a LOOOOOOONG chapter, covering a ton of information about investments. As usual, I will try to cover the more common situations early, so that you don't have to read the whole chapter if you don't need to. To be clear, this chapter is not about investments through your job, or investments in tax advantaged accounts such as IRAs. The next couple chapters cover some of those. Even with this chapter being quite long, I can't cover every detail of every investment. I'll list the things I didn't cover at the end. I will also provide some quick hit information to provide some direction regarding more complex issues, or simply to direct you to seek professional help when applicable. One last thing before I go too far, I am not a financial adviser. None of the information in this chapter is meant as investment advice or advocacy of any particular strategy, except to the extent that it impacts your taxes. Investing should be done with thorough research on your part or the assistance of a reputable financial advisor—and that is not me.

A note for everyone: Your tax information will be reported to you on various forms of 1099s, many of which will be different from each other. Be very careful that you get all the data from your 1099s into your tax software or onto your tax return. If you have any doubts, have it checked by a professional, especially if you are new to investing.

Mutual Fund Investor:

If you have an account where all you do is put money in mutual funds and generally leave it there long-term (even if you shuffle it around once or twice a year) you really don't have a lot to worry about here. If you don't already know, mutual funds are one of the most common ways that we ordinary people invest our money. They pool our money with millions of other people's money and then invest it based on the criteria disclosed to us in the prospectus (you did read that, right). Generally, you pay taxes on the dividends and capital gains that the mutual fund makes on your behalf, even if the money gets reinvested. Dividends are the income that the mutual fund gets when the stocks they hold distribute some of their profits to their shareholders as cash. Capital Gains distributions are the gains the mutual fund has when it sells some stock it owns on your behalf at a profit (these are netted with stocks they sell at a loss, but if the net is negative there's no money to be distributed). Both Dividends and Capital Gains Distributions are yours. You can have the money sent to you on a quarterly basis, though most people simply have the money reinvested automatically in new shares of the mutual fund. Either way, you have to report and pay taxes on these on your return. Your investment company will send you a 1099-DIV (though they may send you a combined 1099 if you have other investments besides mutual funds, or you sell or exchange funds, but it will have the same information). The 1099 will report your dividends, qualified dividends (dividends that get a lower tax rate), and capital gain distributions. These are all reported directly into your software or directly on your Form 1040, Schedule B and/or Schedule D, and are fairly straightforward and easy to handle.

If you sold one mutual fund, even if just to move the money into a different mutual fund, they will send you a 1099-B. This will list your "proceeds from broker or barter transactions." This is a complicated way of saying, "how much you got for selling something." The key is that you need to report this, even if you sold it for EXACTLY (or less) than what you paid for it. Many times, the IRS gets just the amount you sold it for, not the amount you paid for it. You only pay taxes on what you made (difference between price paid and price sold), but the IRS may not know what you paid for it, so if you don't report it, they'll send a letter demanding an amount of taxes based on the full proceeds. This wrinkle is the source of many a jaw-droppingly scary letter from the IRS. The biggest problem for some people is figuring out just what you paid for it, especially if you only sold a portion. The good news is that many brokers are providing this information (it's required to be on the form they send you if you purchased it in the last few years, so this is getting easier every year). If the information is not on the 1099, you can either get it by reviewing the statements from when you purchased it (and every statement between then and the sale, since you add dividends and capital gain distributions to basis), contact your broker for help, or bring your records to your tax professional. I will add that if you are paying a full-service broker, they should be doing this for you. They may need records from a previous broker, but I would demand this from them.

The last couple of things you might see on your 1099 are "Non-dividend Distributions" and "Foreign Taxes Paid." Non-dividend distributions are essentially a return of the money you invested in a company. They are tax neutral, but they reduce the amount you "paid" for a mutual fund and will increase your gain when you sell. Hopefully your investment company is tracking this for you. You will generally see Foreign Taxes Paid when you invest in a fund that invests outside of the United States. This represents your portion of the taxes the mutual fund paid to foreign governments. You can get these taxes back on your tax return as a Foreign Tax Credit. If they are from mainstream mutual funds, you generally file a simplified version of Form 1116 and the taxes come back to you.

Individual Stock Investor:

The first warning I'll give you is to either make sure the companies you are buying are actually corporations or be prepared for the craziness that ensues from investing in non-corporations. What I'm talking about are Real Estate Investment Trusts, Publicly Traded Partnerships and the like. Thanks to technology, you can pop onto an investment web site and buy these just like a regular stock from a corporation. The old classic example would be Kinder Morgan Energy Partnership. You could buy a share in the partnership just like it was a stock, but late in the tax season (sometimes after filing your taxes) you get a Schedule K-1 representing your share of the various items from the partnership's tax return. This amazingly complicated form can drive you crazy and almost certainly requires a tax professional to file since it will often have a number of things that go in strange places on your tax return. This is not to say that these aren't great investments, many are, but you need to know what you are getting into. For the record, I believe Kinder Morgan has converted itself to a traditional corporation.

Having said that, the main differences between a mutual fund investor and an individual stock investor is that you won't have capital gain distributions, and you might get 1099-DIVs and 1099-Bs individually for your stocks or combined depending upon your investment company. When you invest in individual stocks, you only pay capital gains when you sell the individual stocks. It's also a lot easier to track basis since you don't have to track capital gain distributions. The separate or combined forms for 1099-DIV and 1099-B don't significantly impact how they are reported, other than using more lines on Schedule B, Schedule D or form 8949. Do be aware that anytime you sell an individual stock, you will have to report it on your tax return and pay taxes on the gain (or deduct some or all of the loss—capital loss deduction is discussed below).

Day-Trader

I'm not really interested in going into a huge amount of details on this, but the big thing to point out is that usually, EVERY single stock or crypto transaction needs to be reported on your Form 8949. As a guy who has done tax returns for day traders with thousands of transactions, this sucks. What you can do now is, if the investment company reports the basis to the IRS, you can do one line for combined short-term sales (less than one year from purchase to sale) and one line for long-term sales. You can tell the basis has been reported to the IRS because those transactions will be separated from the other transactions on the 1099-B and will state that basis was reported, or that they are "covered" transactions. The form will specifically say that the transaction's basis is reported to the IRS. You will need to send a copy of the 1099-B to the IRS, either with your mailed-in tax return, or attached to Form 8453 if you are electronically filing. For currency investors, YOU need to track every purchase and sale by date and amount. Use this information to report every sale, and its associated basis just like we discussed for stocks. KEEP GOOD RECORDS!

Read if you sold ANYTHING (or you get a 1099-B):

I kind of talked about this already, but it's important enough to reinforce. If you sell or exchange a mutual fund or stock, you should get a 1099-B. If you get a 1099-B, you absolutely MUST report it on your tax return, even if you broke even or lost money. Tons of terrifying IRS letters are generated from people not reporting transactions because "I didn't make any money." The problem is that the IRS may not know you didn't make any money. You need to TELL them you didn't make any money, by reporting the transaction on your tax return.

Capital Gains and Losses:

As discussed above, when you sell a stock or a mutual fund, you may have a gain or a loss. On tax returns, you need to separate these gains and losses based on "holding period." Basically, if you bought the stock or fund more than a year before selling it, it's long-term. Less than a year ago, it's short-term. The capital gain distributions we talked about from mutual funds are assumed to be long-term. Later I will clarify holding periods for weird situations. So now what you do is net your long-term gains and losses and your short-term gains and losses. If you have short-term gains that exceed your losses, you pay taxes at your normal rate. If you have long-term gains that exceed your losses, you pay taxes at a lower rate, depending on your income. If they net to a loss, you can deduct some of that loss, and carry over the rest to your future tax returns. It will then be your starting point for long-term or short-term capital gains or losses. The amount of loss you can deduct in the current year is $3,000 ($1,500 if you are MFS). If your gains are long-term, they are taxed at a maximum rate of 23.8%. The great news is that if your taxable income is below $83,350 (MFJ/QSS) or $41,675 (Single/MFS) or $55,800 (HH), then the gains are taxed at ZERO! Keep in mind that, your AGI is based on your income including your capital gain, so don't go overboard selling stock because you think you will be below those incomes.

Wash Sales:

A wash sale is an IRS term that is specifically designed to prevent you from selling a stock that is currently losing money, solely for the purpose of generating a taxable loss. As long as you sell the stock and don't re-buy it, you're good. If you buy it back within 30 days of selling it, you essentially ignore the sale for tax purposes. You report it, but don't take the loss; your basis (purchase price) remains the amount you originally paid for it. This only applies to assets sold at a LOSS.

Reverse wash sale (not a real term):

A reverse wash is my made-up term for selling and buying stock back to eliminate gains from potential taxation. First and foremost, if that if your taxable income (income after your deductions) is not below $89,250 (MFJ/QSS) or $44,625 (Single/MFS) or $59,750 (HH), stop reading. This won't work for you.

If you are below the above incomes, then you can cash in appreciated stock or mutual funds at a 0% tax rate so long as the gains do not put your AGI above those limits (even if you go above the limits, the sales income that gets you UP TO the limit is still taxed at zero, and the portion above at 15%, so you don't have to be perfect. You can then immediately buy the same stock back (if you want) and the new price will be what is later used to figure gain when you sell it again. You can do this every year and effectively eliminate gains from potential taxation! This is why I call it the reverse wash sale. Wash sales only apply to losses, not gains.

Here is a list of things to consider when determining if it's worth contacting your tax professional for help on this:

1. For 2023, your taxable income should be several thousand dollars below: $44,625 if filing Single or MFS, $89,250 if filing MFJ or QSS, $59,750 if filing HH (taxable income is basically your income after all adjustments and deductions).

2. You have unrealized gains in taxable brokerage accounts or mutual funds that you have held for more than a year (in most cases this means you have stocks or mutual funds that are worth more than you originally paid for them)

3. You're not under age 19 (24 if in school).

4. You're not receiving Earned Income Credit on your tax return.

5. You're not receiving Social Security payments (if this is most of your income you might still benefit).

6. You don't have a capital loss that you are carrying over.

7. Buying and selling stocks or mutual funds in your taxable accounts doesn't cost too much in commissions

Much of the above involves over-simplifications, but it gives you a starting point to see if you might be close.

If the above apply to you, wait until mid-November, and contact your tax professional. Provide them with copies of your recent pay-stubs from all your jobs, as well as amounts of any other taxable income you have or expect to receive before the end of the year (interest, dividends, capital gains, etc.) They should be able to calculate how much gain you can have and still pay 0 taxes on it. Don't worry if it's not perfect, even if you go over a little, only the portion above the limits gets taxed, and this at a favorable rate. Once you have this number, review your unrealized gains and losses information from your brokerage account and determine what to sell to stay below the number they provided. You can do this every year you are below these limits!

Cryptocurrency (Bitcoin):

I wrote a new chapter on this with more details:
Link to: Crypto Chapter for those using Kindle (it is the chapter after this one if you are reading a physical book)

Crypto is taxed just like other investments. You don't pay taxes until you sell, and you pay taxes based on how long you held it. Many brokers will report this on a 1099B but even if they don't, you are responsible for reporting it. Track every purchase and sale! Unlike other investments, if you mine crypto, you owe taxes on the crypto you receive, and may be able to deduct expenses for mining it.

Starting in 2020, the IRS requires you to specifically indicate, yes or no, on the front page of Form 1040, if you had any reportable cryptocurrency transactions (usually sales, conversions or mining) This is obviously an attempt to both encourage accurate reporting, and to eliminate claims of ignorance for those who fail to report it. This is your warning shot. Get your crypto trading information squared away and report it to the IRS as required.

The rest of the details:

Municipal Bonds: When you buy bonds from states, cities or other municipalities, they are exempt from federal taxation. Most states exempt their own bonds from taxes, but tax bonds from other states.

Schedule K-1: These look very complicated, but the principal is that everything from a Schedule K-1 has a place on a regular tax return. They come with instructions that tell you where to put them. The most confusing part is that the information can carry to some incredibly complex tax returns, which means that often the most confusing part is realizing that some of the information doesn't actually carry to your tax return. I would recommend talking to a professional the first year that you get a K-1 for a specific investment. Also, make sure you pay attention when buying what you think is a stock and make sure that you shouldn't be waiting for a Schedule K-1 to file your taxes. A K-1 represents your share of the company's gains, losses and every other tax related item that is generated by the filing of the company's own tax return. These items are passed on to you via the K-1.

Original Issue Discount (1099-OID): As long as you don't buy bonds on the secondary market, OID (original issue discount) interest is just interest. What makes it weird is that you buy a bond at a discount to its ultimate price, and the difference between what you paid and the final price is interest, or OID. You pay taxes on the interest as it accrues, not when you finally cash in the bond. The 1099-OID gives you the right amount of interest to report on your return.

United States Savings Bonds: These differ from normal bonds in that you are allowed to wait to pay taxes on the interest until you cash the bonds in. There are also exclusions on taxability of interest if you use the proceeds for education (see the I'm Going to College chapter for details). Also, all US Treasury bonds and bills are exempt from taxation by the states.

Inherited and Gifted Investments: The only real change between inherited or gifted assets is how we determine your basis (cost) in the investment for gain purposes. For inherited assets, your basis is the basis on the date of death (and the assets are assumed to be held long-term). For gifted assets, the person who gave them to you has a basis, and that basis transfers to you. The long-term or short-term determination begins on the date it is given to you.

Puts and Calls: These are advanced investment vehicles where you're buying the right to buy or sell a given security at a later date at a specified price. The main effect of these instruments is on basis and proceeds amounts. If your investment company doesn't provide this information, you will need to seek help in determining it until you fully understand its effects.

Short Sales: Short sales are investments where you are betting that an asset's price is going to decrease. You borrow the asset from your broker and sell it, hoping to buy it back at a lower price to return it. If you buy it back at a lower price, the difference between the borrowed price and bought back price is a gain. If you are forced to pay more money for it than the price you sold it for, the difference is a loss.

Specified Private Activity Bonds: These are strange bonds that straddle the line between private and government. They are specifically identified and are generally tax free. If you are subject to Alternative Minimum Tax (see that chapter) they are taxable.

You receive income that's not really yours (nominee dividends): If for some reason you receive a 1099 reporting interest or dividends as your income, but it's really someone else's, seek professional help to unravel this.

Affordable Care Act Net Investment Income Tax: If you make above certain income thresholds, your total net investment income (income = gains – losses) is subject to an extra 3.8% tax above and beyond income and capital gains taxes. The thresholds are: $250,000 for MFJ and QSS, $200,000 for HH and Single, $125,000 for MFS. The 23.8% maximum rate discussed previously in this chapter includes this potential 3.8% addition.

My Advice:

1. If you use a professional financial manager, they will often move assets around in your account in order to meet your financial goals based on changes in market conditions or performance. Every time they move assets, they generate a taxable event. The difference between the price paid and the price sold is taxable to you as discussed above. A lot of times, this isn't a big deal, other times it can be a big surprise come tax time. Some brokers are great at understanding, managing and communicating this information, while others suck. Take the time to discuss your tax situation with your broker (and your tax dude if you have one) so that you can manage this. Keep in mind though, that each time a taxable sale is completed, the basis is reset to the new value, so you only pay taxes once on the gains, and relatively frequent trading keeps large amounts of potentially taxable gains from building up and biting you later in life. Only you (with the help of your broker and tax dude) can really know what the best strategy to take is, but taxes are a factor.

2. Tax efficiency is an art in taxable accounts. This doesn't just mean tax free investments, but also attributes of investments themselves. Some mutual funds are designed to minimize capital gains distributions while others always chase the higher yield. Tax loss harvesting is a part of tax efficiency, where your broker sells some investments at a loss to offset assets already sold for a gain. Similar to the above advice, make sure you and your broker are on the same page on this.

3. Speculative investors, like day-traders and cyber currency traders should be aware of their overall performance such that they can set aside money for taxes on gains. If you don't hold things for a year, you pay taxes at your normal tax bracket, or higher if the gains push you into the higher bracket.

4. Pay attention to your income if it might be in the "Reverse Wash Sale" range discussed above. Don't miss out on the opportunity to not pay taxes!

5. Keep good records of your investments such that you (or your tax pro) can easily determine your basis. If you have investments that you aren't sure of the basis, figure out the date you bought or inherited the investments and have that ready for your tax pro.

6. Always report the information from your 1099 forms. Many 1099's are designed to be put in 3 ring binders such that stuff is on the back of pages in a weird way, making it easy to miss. Pay attention as you enter it and mark things off (or highlight them) as you enter it onto your forms or into the computer. You end of year statement is NOT a substitute for the 1099. This sucks, I know, because you often have to wait until March to get the 1099. Be aware if your company tends to send you corrected 1099's. If they do, wait until later to file to make sure you get the final numbers.

7. If your broker doesn't track your cryptocurrency trading, keep a log where you write the date, number of coins purchased or sold, and the amount paid or received in dollars. When you sell, the easiest way to report is to assume you sold the first coins you purchased – called First In – First Out method. So if you sold 5 coins of CrapCoin for $10, you go back and find the first 5 CrapCoins you bought that you hadn't already sold, and the purchase price of those, along with the date purchased, is what you need to report on your tax return. The difference in price is your gain or loss. Make sure to track which coins you sold, so you don't "reuse" them on the next sale.

Military: No big differences for you.

Not discussed: Bond purchases on the secondary market that require allocation of interest between the buyer and seller of the bonds. Allocation of basis when stocks split, break up or merge.

58. A Quick Discussion of How Cryptocurrency and Taxes Work

This is pretty much a copy of my blog post on the subject. It tries to make cryptocurrency investing and taxes easy to understand by comparing it to more traditional investments. I will use "Crypto" to refer to any of the various virtual currencies and use "Bitcoin" in my examples, though they apply to any virtual currency.

The first thing to know, that will help explain almost every aspect of crypto is that it is considered by the IRS to be an investment, not a currency. If, when thinking about crypto, you replace, "one bitcoin" with "one share of Exxon stock", you will usually get to the right answer. Obviously, the prices don't match, but the logic applies:

Crypto/Stock Examples:

Buy a Bitcoin/buy a share of Exxon: No tax implications or reporting requirements, EXCEPT, once you own any cryptocurrency, when you file your taxes, you have to answer "yes" to the question on the front of the Form 1040, "At any time during 2022, did you receive, sell, send, exchange or otherwise acquire any financial interest in any virtual currency?" This question exists because crypto sales aren't currently well reported to the IRS, so they added it to ramp up the chances people will report, and to prevent you from claiming ignorance when you fail to report it. Obviously, this is one of the first questions your software will ask you when you self-prepare your tax returns, though your tax professional will likely ask this as part of a questionnaire either at the start or end of the preparation process. I ask at the end because if you have reportable transactions in your documents, I already know the answer and I like to avoid asking a million questions. Just remember that the answer is "yes" even if you only own a tiny amount and never trade.

Sell a Bitcoin/sell a share of Exxon: This is a reportable and taxable event. The difference between what you paid for the coin/share and what you sold it for is taxable. Hold it a year and a day or more, and you pay a lower tax rate (sometimes even zero). Hold it a year or less, and you pay taxes at your highest normal rate (sometimes called your marginal rate) based on your income. This means you need to know what you paid for the bitcoin. Most big exchanges are now tracking and reporting, but, if not, you need a ledger so that you know when you bought, how much you paid, and how many coins you bought. Then, when you sell a coin, you find the price of the oldest coin you still have unsold and use that price (this is called First

In/First Out and there are other ways to track, but this is the safest and most accepted). Track your sales in the same spreadsheet or table so you don't "sell" the same coin twice. If you didn't "buy" the coin, later examples will tell you what your "Basis" is. Basis is what your investment in the coin is. When you buy something, it is the price you paid for it, and every other situation is trying to get to the equivalent of this. Basis is what you use for price paid when you didn't buy the coin/stock and need to calculate the difference between price paid and price sold.

Exchanging crypto for different crypto or other investments is treated as you selling one and buying another. The sale is reportable and the purchase forms your Basis in the new currency - just the way stock works.

Get paid in Bitcoin/get paid in Exxon stock: In some cases, especially with stock in the company you work for, this can get complicated, but 90% of the time, it works like this: The value of the coin/stock when you are paid is income just the same if paid in dollars. You report it in the same place on your 1040 that you report other income (if it was wages - it goes where W-2 wages go, if it is for your business - it goes on the business Schedule C or other business return, if it is for rent - it goes on the rental Schedule E or other return). Now that you have it, it is treated when you sell it as if you had bought it for the amount it was worth when you were paid (the amount you reported and paid taxes on.) This is your "Basis". As you can see, Basis is the tool that is used to make sure you only pay taxes on your real profit, and also prevents you from paying taxes on the same money twice.

Buy something with Bitcoin/buy something with Exxon stock: You just sold it, even if that isn't what you meant to do. Whatever it was worth at the moment you bought something with it is the price you "sold" it for. If what you bought had a price tag in dollars, that's what you sold it for. See the section on selling bitcoin above. Here is where cryptocurrency and taxes get all messed up. If you use bitcoin as an actual currency, buying things with it, getting paid in it, selling things for it, paying rent with it, paying bills with it: your tax situation is going to get incredibly complicated incredibly fast. Every one of these transactions has to be tracked and many reported on your tax return. This is honestly going to be a real big deal eventually and I don't know what the real answer is going to be – though your "wallet" manager may handle this all for you.

Inherit Bitcoin/Inherit Exxon stock: No current tax implications (though it is included in the Estate and can have Estate tax implications if it was a multi-million-dollar estate). Your "Basis" is the value of the Bitcoin on the date of death (99% of the time) and you are considered to have held it for more than a year automatically.

Give Bitcoin to charity/give Exxon stock to charity: No taxes due even if the price has gone up by millions. Get a charitable deduction based on how long you owned it. More than a year, deduct its full value. A year or less, deduct your "Basis" or its value, whichever is lower.

Other notes or differences between stock and crypto:

What if you sell for less than you paid for it or less than your "Basis"? In this case you have a loss. This loss can be used to offset other gains that you have and, if you have an overall net loss, up to $3000 ($1500 if filing Married Filing Separately) can be deducted off of your normal income before calculating taxes. Any excess is carried over to the next year and can be used to offset gains or be deducted at the end of the year, subject to the same $3000 limit above. There is no time limit to how far into the future a loss can be carried if it doesn't get eaten up by gains or the $3000 deduction.

You can't "mine" Exxon stock, but you can mine Bitcoin. If you mine a coin, you have business income equal to its value when you receive it and you can deduct your expenses for mining it, such as computer equipment, software and even the power you used to produce it.

It doesn't matter that your exchange doesn't report the transaction, or that the exchange is out of the country - if it would be reportable for a share of Exxon, it is reportable for crypto.

Get help before giving crypto as a gift and after receiving it as a gift before you do anything with it.

Investing Crypto in a retirement account is complicated and generally requires a self-directed IRA. Get professional help for this.

Hard Forks that result in you receiving new crypto are treated as an exchange and is taxable. Get expert help.

Soft Forks are never taxable events.

Transferring crypto between wallets you own is not taxable as long as you remain the sole owner.

My Advice:

1. The IRS is serious about cryptocurrency, and I expect them to take a hard line on non-reporters. I don't expect a lot of penalty abatement and I expect them to apply fraud penalties liberally.
2. Try to use a big exchange that will track your crypto and report it just like stocks. Many exchanges already do this, and most will start soon if they are in the United States.
3. If you aren't sure your exchange will do this for you, make a ledger showing each bitcoin batch you own and label it with date purchased, number of coins bought, total price paid, price for one coin, type of coin, date sold, total coins sold, total price sold for and price for one coin. You might have to break up sales between multiple purchase lines if you buy and sell different sized lots. Just divide the total sales price between the different purchase entries.
4. Use a consistent method for determining which coins you sold. First In/First Out is most common and increases the likelihood of preferential tax rates, though tax professionals and investment advisors will argue endlessly about this and there are valid reasons for each of the methods. I like FIFO because it is easy, and the most likely to be remembered or assumed as you change brokers, tax software or tax professionals.

Military: No big differences for you.

Not discussed: Non-Fungible Tokens: These might be treated more like collectibles which have a lot of different rules. Reach out to a professional if you trade these.

59. I Have (or Want to Have) Tax Sheltered Investments (IRAs)

This chapter is about both Roth and Traditional Individual Retirement Accounts (IRAs). There are other tax-sheltered investments and tax preferred investments, like municipal bonds discussed in the previous chapter. There are also SIMPLE IRAs, Simplified Employee Pensions and other types, but I won't be covering those here. The new myRA accounts you may have heard of work almost exactly like Roth IRAs that we will be discussing here (though they have different contribution limits and investment choices).

I want to reiterate that I am not a financial advisor, so any advice I give is from a pure tax perspective. You should do your own research when starting to invest or seek the advice of a licensed financial advisor. More importantly, just like I'm not an investment expert, your investment expert won't be a tax expert. You should get tax advice from a tax professional, not from your financial advisor. (Your bank, insurance company and others are also not tax experts.)

That said, I love both kinds of Individual Retirement Accounts. They are a phenomenal way to grow your retirement assets while postponing or avoiding taxation, so long as you understand the restrictions on them. I am going to give some general advice based on my experience that I think applies to the majority of people. I encourage you to seek additional advice to ensure that your situation isn't different. Pay attention to the income limitations that prevent certain kinds of investments (discussed later). If you are close, it often pays to wait until you file your taxes before making IRA investments (you have until April 15th to contribute to an IRA for the prior year).

One other thing to make clear, IRAs are not investments, they are shelters for your investments. You can invest IRA contributions in a wide variety of investment types, so don't just throw money in an IRA at your bank and think that's it. Talk to a financial advisor and make sure your investments are well thought out.

There is a credit that applies for lower income taxpayers called the Saver's Credit (technically retirement savings contributions credit) that gives you a credit of up to 50% of IRA or 401k contributions back on your tax return. Your AGI needs to be below $73,000 (MFJ), $54,750 (HH) or $36,500 for the others. The percentages are 10, 20 and 50 (lower AGI, higher percentage). Make sure to take this into account if you have a lower income and are considering IRA contributions—it can make a huge difference.

General Advice for Most People:

Most advisors agree on this general order for most people, especially if you are a long way from retirement age. There is some argument on which is better, Roth IRAs or Traditional IRAs, so check out the rules below to see how they impact your life. My general advice (from a tax perspective) is to invest in your company's 401k (or similar plan) to the extent that they match your contributions. Free money from the boss beats any tax benefits. Once you've done this, maximize contributions to Roth IRAs or Traditional IRAs. I like the Roth more than the Traditional, even though you don't get an immediate tax deduction (see details of the accounts later). Your Roth IRA earnings will never be taxed if you do it right, and these earnings should be much larger than your investment over the long-term.

Traditional IRAs become more desirable as your age and tax bracket increase. I think a young person with average incomes will benefit from a Roth more than a Traditional. Roth's also tend to have more flexibility regarding withdrawals. If you max out your IRAs, or have too much income to invest in them, shift back to your company's 401k, contributing to the Roth version if they offer it, for the same reasons the Roth IRA is preferred.

One piece of advice that is an exception to the above is if you don't have a Roth already, open a small one now. There is a 5-year rule for Roth withdrawals that starts with the date you first put money in any Roth IRA. It usually doesn't come in to play but opening a small Roth when you first start retirement investing is a simple way to start the clock.

Very important: Don't put money into IRAs or 401ks unless you are nearly certain that you won't touch the money until retirement (I HATE the idea of using Roth's for college or house savings). There are weird exceptions for college, buying houses and other things, but, as a tax professional, I strongly encourage that you focus IRA and 401k contributions towards retirement. There are other ways to save for college, houses, etc. In addition, taking money out of your 401k or IRA before retirement can have SERIOUS tax consequences. Read the chapter on I Want to Take Money out of my IRA or 401k before you even THINK about taking the money out (unless you are retired.)

Rules for both Roth and Traditional IRAs:

Basics:

1. Your earnings grow without you having to pay taxes on them, at least until you take them out.
2. You generally have to wait until you are 59 and half to take the money out without a 10% penalty (in addition to any taxes due).
3. You have to have taxable compensation (basically income from a job or business) in order to contribute to IRAs.
4. There are income limitations that affect your ability to contribute to Roth IRAs and deduct Traditional IRA contributions. These limits are affected by whether you have a retirement plan through your work. Your W-2 has a check box that will indicate if you are covered by a retirement plan. They are also affected by whether or not your spouse is covered by a retirement plan through their employer.
5. The investments available to an IRA owner are slightly limited, but you can generally invest in most stocks, bonds, mutual funds, Publicly Traded Partnerships, Real Estate Investment Trusts, and certificates of deposit. Talk to your financial advisor if you want to invest in something obscure like currency, gold or collectibles.

Details:

1. Your contribution limit is the SMALLER of your (or your spouse's if MFJ) taxable compensation and $6,500 ($7,500 if over age 50). These are individual limits that apply separately to you and your spouse. If you accidentally contribute too much, contact your IRA custodian and your tax professional.
2. You can withdraw assets before 59 and a half and avoid penalties (though not necessarily taxes) if:
   a. You buy a house when you haven't owned one for the last 2 years ($10,000 maximum).
   b. You withdraw for certain college expenses (get help if you want to do this).
   c. You withdraw in equal annual installments based on your life expectancy (this is how you retire before age 59 and a half).
   d. You are permanently and totally disabled. The definition for this is different from other disability definitions, and also the definition of "permanent" for tax purposes isn't

"permanent at all, so talk to a tax professional. You can actually be receiving disability payments and still not qualify for this).

    e.   You have medical expenses that exceed 7.5% of your AGI.

    f.   If you are unemployed and use the withdrawal to pay for health insurance (check with tax professional for details).

    g.   The IRS places a levy on the plan (they take it to pay your back taxes).

    h.   You are a reservist called to active duty for at least 180 days.

    i.   You withdraw due to divorce and the judge issues a Qualified Domestic Relations Order (see your tax professional).

    j.   Lots of Disaster related provisions: For a person whose principal place of abode was in a Presidentially Declared Disaster Area in 2016, they can withdraw up to $100,000 from retirement accounts in 2016 or 2017 ONLY and not pay the penalty. They may also include the withdrawal in income over three years or recontribute the money within 3 years to avoid all taxes on it. This is a complex tax situation – so see your tax pro if you were involved in a Presidentially Declared Disaster Area in 2016. There are a lot of other provisions in the Trump/GOP Tax Law that apply to disasters that occurred in 2016. Laws were passed for specific disasters in 2017, 2018 and 2019, as well as Coronavirus that affected IRA withdrawals. See <u>The Coronavirus and Disaster Chapter</u> for details.

    k.   You withdraw up to $5,000 within a year of the birth or adoption of a child. You can also repay this withdrawal within a year and avoid all taxes on it.

3.   You can't invest in collectibles like artwork, rugs, antiques, metals, gems, stamps, coins (except certain investment-grade precious metal coins), alcohol or other tangible personal property. You should discuss your investment choices with a competent professional if you intend to invest in anything other than basic stuff like stocks, bonds, ETF's or mutual funds.

4.   You can contribute to your 2023 IRA through April 15, 2024 and your 2024 IRA through April 15th, 2025.

The main difference between a Traditional and Roth IRA is that you get to deduct the Traditional IRA contribution from your current year's income (assuming you meet the income limitations discussed below), but you pay taxes on the withdrawals when you retire. You don't get to deduct Roth IRA contributions, but the withdrawals are tax-free (assuming you meet the requirements discussed below). Another of the most important distinctions is that it is possible to make too much money to contribute to a Roth IRA, which can cause some pain as you have to take the excess money out. There is no income limit for contributing to a Traditional IRA, but there are income limits for deducting them. If you are close to the income limits, contribute to a Traditional IRA and convert it to a Roth IRA if desired (back-door Roth). Other differences between Traditional and Roth IRAs are discussed directly below.

Traditional IRA Rules:

Basics:

1. A traditional IRA contribution is deductible if you meet certain income limitations. You subtract the contribution from income before calculating your AGI.
2. Withdrawals from a Traditional IRA after you meet retirement age (generally 59 and a half) are taxable income in the year you withdraw them.
3. You must start withdrawing Traditional IRA assets in the year after you turn 73. I generally recommend you start these withdrawals in the year you turn 73. Your IRA custodian will help you calculate these withdrawals.
4. If you make too much money to deduct your Traditional IRA contribution, you can make a non-deductible contribution that will still grow tax deferred (earnings won't be taxed until they are withdrawn. If you make non-deductible contributions, make sure to keep track of them, since they affect the taxability of withdrawals).
5. You used to not be allowed to contribute to traditional IRA's after you turned 70 and a half. That rule has been eliminated for 2020 and later, so there is no age limit for making IRA contributions as long as you meet other requirements.

Details:

1. If you or your spouse are covered by a retirement plan at your work, the amount of Traditional IRA contributions you can deduct is limited by your AGI.

2. If YOU are covered by a retirement plan at your work, your IRA deduction phases out between the following AGI's:
    MFJ or QSS: $116,000 to $136,000
    Single or HH: $73,000 to $83,000
    MFS (and lived with spouse anytime during year): $0 to $10,000. Use Single rates for MFS if you didn't spend even one night with your spouse.
    As an example, if you were HH and made less than $68,000, you get the full deduction. Between $73,000 and $83,000 the deduction starts to go down. Above $83,000 you get no deduction.
3. If your SPOUSE is covered by a retirement plan at your work and you are not, your IRA deduction phases out between the following AGI's: $218,000 to $228,000 if MFJ, $0 to $10,000 if MFS (and lived with spouse anytime during year). If you filed MFS but didn't spend even one night with your spouse, your deduction is unlimited.
4. Depending on which half of the year your birthday is, if you wait until the year AFTER you turn 73 to take your required withdrawals, you could end up having to take two annual withdrawals in the same year, which can screw up your tax bracket and also make more of your social security taxable. This is why I recommend taking your first withdrawal in the year you turn 73.

Roth IRA Rules:

Basics:

1. You can continue to contribute to a Roth IRA at any age and there is no age at which you have to start taking withdrawals.
2. You do not get a current year deduction for contributions to a Roth IRA.
3. In addition to other rules for avoiding tax penalties on Roth IRA withdrawals, you must have had a Roth IRA open for at least 5 years.
4. Qualified withdrawals from a Roth IRA are tax-free (after age 59 and a half and at least 5 years since first Roth IRA contribution).
5. You can withdraw the money you put into a Roth IRA (but not the earnings) at any time, with no tax consequences. This is why you need to track and report your Roth IRA contributions on your tax returns.
6. There are income limitations above which you cannot make Roth IRA contributions. If you make contributions and later determine

you made too much money, contact your IRA custodian and your tax professional BEFORE you file the tax return for the year in question (and before 4/15 of that year).

Details:

1. The income limitations at which Roth IRA contributions are phased out are: $218,000 to $228,000 if MFJ or QSS, $138,000 to $153,000 if Single or HH, 0 to $10,000 if MFS and spent even one night with your spouse. Use Single rates if you file MFS and did not spend any nights with your spouse during the year.

My Advice:

1. Tax people and investment advisors will argue endlessly over the Roth versus Traditional debate. There is a lot of math that can help you figure out which one is best from a tax perspective, but I want to add my 2 cents. After 25 years of preparing taxes, and thousands of clients, I have literally ZERO clients who regret investing in Roth IRA's and MANY who wish (or should wish) that they had picked Roth over Traditional. There are a ton of things going on in retirement that make the amount of taxes paid lifetime insignificant compared to real life in retirement. Here's my point: Talk to your financial advisor and tax person about YOUR situation, go over the numbers, your financial desires and the implications and make the best decision for you, BUT, if you are still unsure, or it's a close call, go Roth.
2. Open a Roth IRA and put some money into it as early in life as you can. Parents should open a Roth IRA for their children as soon as they get their first job and encourage them to invest in it. Money saved in a Roth before age 18 is MAGICAL due to the long time horizon for it to grow.
3. If you make too much money to invest in a Roth IRA, you can make non-deductible contributions to a traditional IRA and then convert them to a Roth with no tax implications. This is called a "back-door Roth". Your financial advisor can assist you in doing this.
4. Start taking required minimum distributions out of traditional IRA accounts in the year you turn 73 vice waiting. Making two withdrawals in a single year can really mess your taxes up.
5. Totally personal advice: You invested in these accounts so you could enjoy your retirement. SPEND THE MONEY! Obviously

make sure you don't run out but enjoy life – don't leave it to your kids!

Military: If you have so much combat zone time that you have little or no taxable income, you can count the non-taxable combat zone income as compensation to allow you to contribute to either type of IRA.

If you are on active duty you are considered covered by a retirement plan for the purposes of IRA contribution limits.

For early withdrawals from IRA's, a reservist called to active duty for more than 180 days counts for an exception to the 10% penalty. The exception code for Form 5329 is 11.

Not discussed: Rollovers, conversions, and re-characterizations. SEP's and SIMPLE plans. Backdoor Roth contribution for high income earners.

60. I Want to Take Money out of my 401k or IRA

DON'T DO IT!

Okay, now that I've got your attention, you can touch it, just talk to your tax professional first.

Really.

Your financial advisor is not a tax professional. Your banker is not a tax professional. Your insurance representative is not a tax professional. Talk to a tax professional first! There are a LOT of rules about taking money out of tax advantaged accounts. These accounts include SEP's, SIMPLE's, IRA's 401k's TSP's, 457's, 403b's and more. There are some exceptions that get you out of taxes and penalties, but they are complicated!

I am not even going to go into them in this chapter. Talk to your tax professional!

I will say that the withholding is not, "paying the taxes already." The withholding is rarely enough. Meeting an exception to the penalty does not prevent taxation, just the penalty. Some exceptions only count for IRA's, but not 401k's. Some count for 401k's, but not IRA's. Only your tax professional can give you the right advice.

Two examples of bad advice:

1. A client recently took $10,000 out of his 401k to purchase a home. His banker told him that was an exception to taxes. WRONG! It's an exception to penalties, not taxes, and, oops, that exception only applies to IRAs, not 401k's. Unhappy client!

2. Another client, age 59, left her job. She was going to use her 401k to buy a house. A big house. Her financial advisor told her to roll it over to an IRA to avoid taxes while looking for a house. She knew she would pay taxes but thought she could avoid the penalty. Her financial advisor told her she could. WRONG! Having it in an IRA when buying the house avoids the penalty on the FIRST $10,000. The other part of nearly $200,000 was fully penalized at 10%. To add insult to injury, because she was older than 55 and left her job, she could have taken it out of the 401k without penalty, for ANY reason. Once it hit the IRA, she had to wait until 59 and a half, or meet an exception. That's right, even with the bad

rollover, 6 months would have saved her THOUSANDS! Unhappy client!

My Advice: Talk to the tax experts, not the banking/insurance/financial experts. I won't give you investment advice, don't take tax advice from the wrong person.

Military: We're talking about the Thrift Savings Plan here!

61. I Had Debt Written Off by the Company I Owed Money To

If this has happened to you, the chances are that the company who wrote the debt off has or will issue you a 1099-C. This represents debt owed by the taxpayer that is written off by the lender as non-collectable. If you haven't received a 1099-C, they either have not written the debt off, or they sent it to an incorrect address. If you know that a credit card company or other debtor wrote off debt, but haven't received a 1099-C, you should gather your records as discussed below, but don't do anything until you receive the 1099-C (except communicate with the company to find out if they're sending one and get it if you can.) If you don't qualify for an exclusion, the debt written off is taxable to you, and should be reported on Form 1040, Schedule 1, Line 21 as "Cancelled Debt". If an exclusion applies, you will use Form 982 to determine any exclusion from income and any non-excluded income is reported on Line 21 of Schedule 1, Form 1040 as "Cancelled Debt."

Starting in 2018 and later years, student loans cancelled due to death or permanent and total disability are not taxable. I am assuming that a 1099-C would not be issued in this case, but if you get a 1099-C for this situation, see a tax professional. Starting in 2020, almost all cancelled student loan debt was made tax free, though some states may still tax them.

If you have cancelled debt subject to inclusion as taxable income, the following exceptions MAY apply:

Bankruptcy
To the extent insolvent (liabilities exceed assets - Appendix B)
Certain Farm debts
Non-recourse loans (box 5 of Form 1099-C not checked)
Qualified personal residence debt (see next chapter on house foreclosure) *
Qualified real property business debt

I'm only going to talk about one of those exceptions, since it applies to most situations (and the personal residence exclusion is in the next chapter). If you declared bankruptcy, own a farm, have a non-recourse loan, or have business real property, talk to a professional.

Insolvency:

I have added details on how to fill out the IRS Insolvency Worksheet in Appendix B.

Okay, so now let's talk about how to find out if you're insolvent. First look at the 1099C, box 1 and note the date. If you don't have the 1099C, use the date the debt was forgiven (you can call the lender to figure this out.) You will use this date and figure out, as of that date, how much your assets were, and how much your liabilities were. Your assets are everything you own; your liabilities are everything you owe.

We'll start with liabilities first. Start with the debt that was cancelled: the debt they cancelled counts as a liability, so that's your first number. Go to your credit cards, mortgages, car loans and any other money that you owe. Print out the first statement after the date in question. Now review the statement and determine what you owed as of that date. You can do this by highlighting the beginning balance and any charges or payments up to our date. Add the balance and charges, subtract any payments, and write this number on the statement. Repeat for all of your debts, and then add them up to get a total amount of liabilities. SAVE each of the statements! The IRS can ask you to prove how insolvent you were.

Now assets. Start with your bank accounts, brokerage statements, investments, etc. Print out each statement and highlight the value on the date in question. For checking accounts, they usually keep a running total. For brokerages, they may only give you a monthly balance. If you can, go online and get the actual balance on the date in question. Print the screen with this balance and keep it with the statement for that account. If you can't get an exact amount, use the balance closest to our date. Make sure to do this for your retirement plan at work (401k, 403B, TSP, etc.), as well as any Individual Retirement Accounts.

Now it gets harder. For any vehicles you have, go to kbb.com or edmunds.com and determine the value of them. You can use some judgment to get the best value (lower is better) but be reasonable. If your car is truly a piece of crap and you are using that to drop the value, take pictures to justify this assessment. It's also not a bad idea to take a picture of the odometer reading. Print the page from the website and highlight the value and attach it to any pictures you took.

Now you have to value everything else you own. Yes everything. This is difficult. Take pictures of big, valuable items and try to get a value off the internet—print any pages with values you use. For your general household, pictures and video can be useful to prove you don't have fancy, expensive furniture. Talk to a few people who know about values and try to get a good estimate. I wouldn't do an appraisal unless you're really unsure; just make sure your values aren't ridiculous.

For your house (or houses) get a real estate agent to run comps and give you a written value estimate for them. Save this paperwork.

Now take all your liabilities and add them up. Do the same with your assets. Subtract assets from liabilities and if you get a positive number, you're insolvent! This generally means you can avoid paying taxes on your cancelled debt up to the amount of your insolvency.

A couple words of warning:
1) Save all the paperwork. This includes web pages from sites that you used for determining values for your cars, house, specific items or the general household. Also bank and investment statements from the month the debt is cancelled. For loans try to include loan paperwork or amortization schedules showing the balance due for that month. A credit report for the month is a great reference to have.
2) Make sure to include the value of anything they repossessed in the asset column.
3) If the debt cancelled was in your name (or your spouse's) and not in the other's name, you have to calculate insolvency for the individual, not both of you (in this case include the full amount of anything in only the debtor's name and split everything in both of your names).
4) If the numbers are close, make sure you have your ducks in a row. If you lowballed the value of your household, or forgot to include your $3,000 engagement ring, things can get ugly, and you could owe money back. Conversely, if your liabilities are enormous, and you have tens of thousands of dollars of insolvency above your cancelled debt, you can probably relax and not be quite as anal about household contents values (still do all the cars, house, big toys and bank accounts just like we said).
5) Insolvency affects tax attributes for future tax years. This is way beyond the scope of this book. You should seek professional assistance to determine the effect, especially if you have a business, investments, or rental property.

Keep Reading:

You may also receive a Form 1099-A if the debt collector took property that was secured by the debt—usually your car for a car loan or your house for a house loan. If it was your house, see the next chapter on foreclosure. Otherwise, the item is considered sold on the date reported on the 1099-A.

Many banks totally suck at sending this paperwork, and often you will get a 1099-C and not the 1099-A. The good news is that as long as you don't use the property for business, it's generally a tax neutral situation. You report the property as sold on Schedule D, as personal property. You will include the date purchased, date sold (from the 1099-A, the price you paid (basis) and the price sold (Fair Market Value from the 1099-A). Make sure you indicate it as personal property. It should result in a negative number unless the property has increased in value. You cannot deduct the negative number, but if the property has increased in value, you pay taxes on that increase—this is rare for repossessed property other than real estate (though if your house has increased in value above what you owe, most people would sell before allowing a foreclosure to happen).

* This provision had expired for 2017. On February 8th of **2018** (yes, after some people had already filed 2017 tax returns) this provision was retroactively renewed for 2017 ONLY. It is currently expired for 2018, but as you can see, there is no telling what Congress is going to do. I am leaving the specific information in the relevant chapters just in case.

Good thing I left it in! The exclusion was restored in December of 2019 retroactively to 2018 and 2019, though not to 2020 and later. Odds are this provision will be reinstated again.

I'm like a fortune teller! The exclusion has been extended through 2025, though limits have changed – see next chapter…

My Advice:

1. Get on top of insolvency paperwork when you know the debt is cancelled, NOT when you get the 1099C.
2. If you aren't going to be able to exclude the cancelled debt make sure you estimate the amount of taxes you will owe and start saving ASAP.
3. If have a non-disability pension or an extremely well-funded 401k, you probably aren't insolvent. If you don't and you are highly upside down on your house, cars and credit cards, you are probably insolvent.
4. A very large cancelled debt will often induce at least some insolvency in and of itself, meaning you can probably get out of taxes on at least some of the debt. Insolvency is not all or nothing. If you are $100 insolvent, you can avoid taxes on $100 of cancelled debt.
5. The insolvency worksheet in Appendix B has a LOT more detail on every category, use it.

6. If you are heavily insolvent, don't spend a ton of time on the stuff that's hard to value, just give it a big number that is no question higher than its value. If you are close, be nit-picky and be able to back up your numbers.
7. Paying taxes on cancelled debt sucks, but remember that paying 22% in taxes on $10,000 is better than paying the $10,000.

Military: Your Thrift Savings Plan balance counts as an asset. If you are on active duty, the traditional military retirement that your service entitles you to does not count as an asset, even if you have been in more than 20 years. If you are retired, you must include an amount that would produce your retirement income if you had invested it in an annuity (bottom line is that retired military are rarely insolvent for the purposes of cancelled debt exclusion.) Some of these interpretations are not written in stone so consider getting professional help if you get a 1099-C and think you might be insolvent.

62. I Lost my House (Foreclosure, Short Sale or Bankruptcy)

If this has happened to you, the chances are that the company who foreclosed wrote the debt off and has or will issue you a Form 1099-C. This represents debt owed by the taxpayer that is written off by the lender as non-collectable. If you haven't received a 1099-C, they either have not written the debt off yet, they sent it to an incorrect address, or the amount not paid was covered by mortgage insurance (the lender might also be incompetent.) If your house was foreclosed, but you haven't received a 1099-C, you should gather your records as discussed below, but don't do anything until you receive the 1099-C (except communicate with your mortgage company to find out if they're sending one and get it if you can.) If you don't qualify for an exclusion, the debt written off is taxable to you, and should be reported on form 1040 Line 21 as "Cancelled Debt". If an exclusion applies, you will use Form 982 to determine any exclusion from income and any non-excluded income is reported on Line 21 of Form 1040 as "Cancelled Debt."

The following exceptions MAY apply:

Bankruptcy
To the extent insolvent (liabilities exceed assets - Appendix B)
Non-recourse loans (box 5 of 1099-C not checked)
Qualified personal residence debt *

I'm only going to talk about two of those exceptions, since they apply to most situations. If you declared bankruptcy or have a non-recourse loan, talk to a professional.

Insolvency:

I have added details on how to fill out the IRS Insolvency Worksheet in Appendix B.

Okay, so now let's talk about how to find out if you're insolvent. First look at the 1099C, box 1 and note the date. If you don't have the 1099C, use the date the debt was forgiven (you can call the lender to figure this out). You will use this date and figure out, as of that date, how much your assets were, and how much your liabilities were. Your assets are everything you own; your liabilities are everything you owe.

We'll start with liabilities first. Start with the debt that was cancelled based on the 1099-C. This counts as a liability, so that's your first number. Go to your credit cards, mortgages, car loans and any other money that you owe. Print out the first statement after the date in question. Now review the statement and determine what you owed as of that date. You can do this by highlighting the beginning balance and any charges or payments up to that date. Add the balance and charges, subtract any payments, and write this number on the statement. Repeat for all of your debts, and then add them up to get a total amount of liabilities. SAVE each of the statements! The IRS can ask you to prove how insolvent you were.

Now assets. Start with your bank accounts, brokerage statements, investments etc. Print out each statement and highlight the value on the date in question. For checking accounts, they usually keep a running total. For brokerages, they may only give you a monthly balance. If you can, go online and get the actual balance on our date. Print the screen with this balance and keep it with the statement for that account. If you can't get an exact amount, use the balance closest to the date. Make sure to do this for your retirement plan at work (401k, 403B, TSP, etc.), as well as any Individual Retirement Accounts. Include the Fair Market Value of the foreclosed house from the 1099-C.

Now it gets harder. For any vehicles you have, go to kbb.com or edmunds.com and determine the value of them. You can use some judgment to get the best value (lower is better) but be reasonable. If your car is truly a piece of crap and you are using that to drop the value, take pictures to justify this assessment. It's also not a bad idea to take a picture of the odometer reading. Print the web pages and highlight the value and attach it to any pictures you took.

Now you have to value everything else you own. This is difficult. Take pictures of big, valuable items and try to get a value off the internet—print any pages with values you use. For your general household, pictures and video can be useful to prove you don't have fancy, expensive furniture. Talk to a few people who know about values and try to get a good estimate. I wouldn't do an appraisal unless you're really unsure, just make sure your values aren't ridiculous.

For your house (or houses) get a real estate agent to run comps and give you a written value estimate for them. Save this paperwork.

Now take all your liabilities and add them up. Do the same with your assets. Subtract assets from liabilities and if you get a positive number, you're insolvent! This generally means you can avoid paying taxes on your cancelled debt up to the amount of your insolvency.

A couple words of warning:
1) Save all the paperwork. This includes web pages from sites that you used for determining values for your cars, house, specific items or the general household. Also bank and investment statements from the month the debt is cancelled. For loans try to include loan paperwork or amortization schedules showing the balance due for that month. A credit report for the month is a great reference to have.
2) Make sure to include the value of anything they repossessed in the asset column.
3) If the debt cancelled was in your name (or your spouse's) and not in the other's name, you have to calculate insolvency for the individual, not both of you (in this case include the full amount of anything in only the debtor's name, and split everything in both of your names).
4) If the numbers are close, make sure you have your ducks in a row. If you lowballed the value of your household, or forgot to include your $3,000 engagement ring, things can get ugly, and you could owe money back. Conversely, if your liabilities are enormous, and you have tens of thousands of dollars of insolvency above your cancelled debt, you can probably relax and not be quite as anal about household contents values (still do all the cars, house, big toys and bank accounts just like we said).
5) Insolvency affects tax attributes for future tax years. This is way beyond the scope of this book. You should seek professional assistance to determine the effect, especially if you have a business, investments, or rental property.

Personal Residence Exclusion:

*This provision had expired for 2017. On February 8th of 2018 (yes, after some people had already filed 2017 tax returns) this provision was retroactively renewed for 2017 ONLY. It is currently expired for 2019, but as you can see, there is no telling what Congress is going to do. I am leaving the specific information in the relevant chapters just in case.

Good thing I left it in! The exclusion was restored in December of 2019 retroactively to 2018 and 2019, though not to 2020 and later. Odds are this provision will be reinstated again.

Extended again! Now through 2025! But limits for 2021 and later were lowered.

You can exclude canceled debt on the foreclosure of your primary home – up to $1 million for Single filers and $2 million for married if cancelled in 2020 or before, $375,000 for Single and $750,000 married for 2021 and later. It has to be your personal residence at the time of foreclosure. There is some debate on this as to whether you need to be living in the home the day of foreclosure, but most take the reasonable position that if you leave the home due to imminence of foreclosure, you can exclude it as personal residence. The 2 out of 5 year rule for excluding gain does not apply here, though the code can make you think it does. The definition of "personal residence" from that part of the code applies, not the time rules, so make sure you can defend the position that it was your residence at the time of foreclosure. If you moved out and stopped making the payments for a year, or converted it to a rental for a while, this probably does not apply, but talk to a professional just to make sure. There are detailed restrictions and limitations on this so it makes sense to check with a tax professional in any case.

Keep Reading:

You may also receive a Form 1099-A, but not always. The 1099-A represents the transfer of your house to the mortgage company and is treated as if you sold it. Many banks totally suck at sending this paperwork, and often you will get a 1099-C and not the 1099-A, but you should report the sale. The good news is that as long as you don't use the property for business, it's generally a tax neutral situation. You report the property as sold on Schedule D, as a personal residence. If you owned and lived in the home for 2 of the last 5 years, never rented it to someone, and never used it for business, you can exclude $250,000 of gain ($500,000 if MFJ). You will include the date purchased, date sold (from the 1099-A or 1099-C, the price you paid [basis] and the price sold [Fair Market Value from the 1099-A or 1099-C]). Make sure you indicate it as personal residence property. Your software should exclude the gain as appropriate, and not allow a loss if that's the result. You may need to see a professional for help on this.

My Advice:

1. Get on top of insolvency paperwork when you know the debt is cancelled, NOT when you get the 1099C.

2. If you aren't going to be able to exclude the cancelled debt make sure you estimate the amount of taxes you will owe and start saving ASAP.

3. If have a non-disability pension or an extremely well-funded 401k, you probably aren't insolvent. If you don't and you are highly upside down on your house, cars and credit cards, you are probably insolvent.

4. A very large cancelled debt will often induce at least some insolvency in and of itself, meaning you can probably get out of taxes on at least some of the debt. Insolvency is not all or nothing. If you are $100 insolvent, you can avoid taxes on $100 of cancelled debt.

5. The insolvency worksheet in Appendix B has a LOT more detail on every category, use it.

6. If you are heavily insolvent, don't spend a ton of time on the stuff that's hard to value, just give it a big number that is no question higher than its value. If you are close, be nit-picky and be able to back up your numbers.

7. Paying taxes on cancelled debt sucks but remember that paying 22% in taxes on $10,000 is better than paying the $10,000.

Military: As discussed, the 2 out of 5-year rule does not apply for the personal residence exclusion and thus the 10-year extension for the military does not apply either.

63. I am Retired (or Thinking About It)

This is a BIG topic for life, and a pretty big one for taxes. I am not a financial advisor, so I'm going to avoid giving advice on how to manage your retirement assets. I will tell you what happens as you utilize retirement assets and give advice based on the tax implications. I am going to make a few assumptions. First of all, this is not written for a military retiree (there will be a chapter, copied from my blog, on warnings for military retirees). Second, I'm assuming you are really retiring, and not still working (though I will talk about small jobs and their impact). I'm also not going to talk significantly about seriously early retirement. I will cover the key ages that matter with tax advantaged accounts. You should read this whole chapter, since I will be jumping around and covering a wide variety of topics. As usual, I will use 401k to describe the whole gamut of the tax advantaged employee accounts such as 457, 403b, TSP, etc. that share the same basic withdrawal limits and tax advantages.

General Withdrawal Strategies:

Even though you are retired, your tax advantaged accounts, such as your 401k and IRA's retain a significant advantage. When planning your retirement, these accounts should be used later than your taxable accounts, because they will grow faster due to the tax advantages. This is just TAX advice, so there may be reasons not to follow this advice, including if some accounts were inherited and you want to preserve their preferential treatment regarding divorce or control (I know very little about this but it has come up when I advised clients to minimize tax advantaged account withdrawals.)

Ages that Matter:

These are the big ages that matter for the various retirement accounts:

50: The age at which a qualified public safety employee who has separated from that job can withdraw that employer's retirement plan assets without paying the 10% early withdrawal penalty. A qualified public safety employee is a state, county or city employed police officer, firefighter or EMS worker.
55: The age at which a regular employee who has separated from that job can withdraw that employer's retirement plan assets without paying the 10% early withdrawal penalty.

59 and a half: The age at which all tax advantaged retirement plan assets can be withdrawn without paying the 10% early withdrawal penalty, regardless of employment status.

62: Earliest age at which you can start collecting Social Security.

65 to 67: depending on your age, full Social Security retirement age. This is the age at which you get your full Social Security benefit. It is also the age at which having another job cannot force you to have to repay Social Security benefits. Go to www.ssa.gov for more details.

73: Age at which you must start withdrawing traditional and traditional 401k assets based on your life expectancy. There is a wrinkle depending on your birthday, so I always recommend starting during the year you turn 73, to avoid having to make two withdrawals in one year. If you want more details, talk to your tax professional. Your tax professional will probably need to use a calendar and some note paper to figure out which category applies to you.

Early Withdrawals:

If you do not meet the age requirements discussed above for 401k's and IRA's, your withdrawals from these accounts will have an additional 10% penalty, above and beyond the taxability of the accounts. Roth IRA's and Roth 401k's have the additional requirement that you must have had a Roth account from any source for at least five years to avoid the penalty (even if you meet the exceptions). In addition, the amount you put into a Roth account is NEVER subject to tax or penalty. There are a few exceptions:

1. You are permanently and totally disabled (which doesn't mean what it sounds like, so ask your tax pro and get a doctor's statement).
2. You withdraw in equal annual installments based on your life expectancy (your financial advisor can help set this up).
3. You have significant medical expenses such that they exceed 10% of your AGI.
4. You are dead :)
5. A judge provides a very specific order (a qualified domestic relations order) directing the assets to be distributed because of a divorce :(
6. You are withdrawing because the IRS has levied the plan to pay for your back taxes :(
7. You withdraw up to $5,000 within a year of the birth or adoption of a child. You can also repay this withdrawal within a year and avoid all taxes on it.
8. You are a reservist called to active duty for at least 180 days.

9. Lots of Disaster related provisions: Laws were passed for specific disasters in 2017, 2018 and 2019, as well as Coronavirus that affected IRA withdrawals. See The Coronavirus and Disasters Chapter for details.

10. For IRA's only:

    a. Your withdrawal does not exceed qualified education expenses.

    b. For IRA's, you can exclude up to $10,000 from penalty if used to buy a first-time home (which actually means you haven't owned a home in the two years prior to the withdrawal).

    c. If you are unemployed and use the withdrawal to pay for health insurance (check with tax professional for details).

Social Security:

Be aware that if you take Social Security before full retirement age (discussed above) you may have to pay it back if you work a second job. Since this is not a tax issue, I'll refer you to the Social Security Administration for more information. People confuse this with the tax rules all the time but they are TOTALLY DIFFERENT!

Social Security is taxable in a weird way. If it is your ONLY source of income, you probably won't pay taxes on it. It is also not subject to state income taxes in many states. If you have other sources of income, jobs, other retirement income, or investment returns, then it can be up to 85% taxable. It is not taxed at 85%, but up to 85% of the Social Security will be subject to ordinary income tax rates. This greatly complicates decision making with regard to other sources of income, so it will serve you well to discuss major income-changing decisions with your tax pro to avoid big surprises in Social Security taxability. But I'll cover the basics (if you can call it that, here):

1. The first thing you have to do is figure out your income that will be used to calculate the taxability of Social Security. This number is all your taxable income, plus any tax-exempt interest, plus HALF of your Social Security income for the year, which you can find on your Form 1099-SSA).

2. Figure out your "base amount" for comparison. This is $25,000 if you are Single, HH, or QSS filing status; $32,000 if you are MFJ; $25,000 if you are MFS and didn't live with your spouse for EVEN ONE NIGHT during the year; $0 if you are MFS and lived with your spouse anytime during the year. MFS sucks, as we've discussed.

3. Compare the income from 1 above, to the base amount from 2. If income exceeds base amount, some of your benefits are taxable. There is a

complex worksheet to determine how much is taxable, but it will generally be between 50% and 85% of your Social Security income if your income exceeds the base amount. It gets to 85% pretty fast, so if you are above the base amount you can expect to pay a decent amount of taxes.

Annuities:

Annuities used to be amazingly complicated for taxes, but they have gotten easier (for taxes). They are still complicated overall. You usually end up with an annuity either from an employee retirement plan, life insurance contracts, direct annuity investment, or IRA rollover. Basically, you convert a large lump sum into a lifetime of payments. These payments are taxable, except to the extent that you invested money into the plan that you paid taxes on. If you rolled completely tax deducted amounts, such as from a traditional IRA or 401k into the annuity, the annuity is fully taxable. If you invested non-tax advantaged money into the account (for example, you bought an annuity for $30,000 with regular cash 20 years ago, and now it's worth $300,000) the original investment is non-taxable, and you get to exclude it from your withdrawals a little bit at a time, based on your life expectancy. To greatly simplify, if your life expectancy is 30 years, then the $30,000 we just talked about would be deducted from your taxable withdrawals at a rate of $1,000 per year, until it is used up. The bad news is that this is a very complicated calculation. The good news is that if you know basic information (most of which is provided on the 1099-R you'll get during tax season, just like a W-2) your software will handle it for you. Make sure you know the annuity starting date (the date of your first check received from it). The even better news is that, more and more, the annuity provider is doing the calculation for you, and giving you everything, including the taxable amount, right on the 1099-R.

For state purposes, an annuity or pension is taxable to the state you are a resident of, regardless of the source of the pension. If you are a resident of say, South Carolina, a CA Teachers or NY Firefighters pension is taxable to SC and NOT to CA or NY. Make sure to update your provider as to your state of residence so they can update the 1099-R you receive and withhold as appropriate. Even if the 1099-R has the state you are not a residence of, you want to make sure to apply the income to the state you are a residence of at the time of receipt. If you move during the year, the payments are taxable to the state you were a resident of as you receive them, so keep track. You only have one state of residence, and it is generally moved at the time you establish yourself in the new state. As a basic rule, the date you move in your new house, or start your new job, are good indications that your residency shifted. Talk to a professional if this date is unclear. Some state retirements will only withhold taxes for their state, so you may have to make up the state taxes with withholding elsewhere. Just make sure to keep them from withholding taxes for the wrong state since it can be difficult to get that money back.

Pennsylvania is weird. They never let workers deduct their 401k contributions, so they don't tax withdrawals. If you live, work and retire in PA for your entire life, this is simple. If you lived or retired anywhere else, it gets complicated, and most people never even think about it. If you worked and/or retired in PA, talk to a pro once you start taking money out.

Working a Job:

As discussed above, working a second job can cause you to have to pay back Social Security, or make it more taxable. The important thing about working a second job is that, in a normal retirement, with pension, Social Security and investments, this is another source of taxable income. The biggest problem is that none of these sources knows about the other. Therefore, when you appropriately indicate Married and 2 on the W-4 (based on your personal situation) you get when you are hired (for example), they withhold assuming it's your ONLY income. If you make less than $20,000, they're going to think none of it is taxable and grossly under-withhold. I always recommend going Single and 0 on retirement jobs unless you have very limited income other than Social Security. Keep reading for more details.

Withholding:

As we just discussed, withholding can be an issue. None of your income sources will know about your other incomes, and thus will tend to cause under-withholding. This is not something you want to be cavalier about. I highly recommend being aggressive on withholding in the first couple of years of retirement, and then adjusting from there – or talking to a tax expert as you approach retirement. Getting a couple thousand-dollar tax bill at the end of the year can make a huge mess of your retirement plans. Start most of your withholding at Single and check no other boxes, or use the withholding calculator on the IRS website, being conservative with income numbers (make them bigger). Make sure to have state withholding as well. I also recommend saving a decent chunk of money set aside in the first year, just in case. A tax pro can really help with this, but even the best of us have trouble figuring things out exactly right. As you progress through your retirement years, you can tweak the withholding as necessary to ease back off your early aggressiveness. For Social Security, you have to use a different method of withholding. They pull out based on percentages, usually 7, 10, 12 or 22. Start with at least 12, and ease off if necessary.

My Advice:

1. It is generally a good idea to withdraw taxable money first, and then Traditional retirement account money and Roth IRA money last.
2. If your taxable income is below $89,250 (MFJ/QSS) or $44,625 (Single/MFS) or $59,750 (HH), make sure to sell some stocks each year to get to these amounts so you can avoid taxes on the gains. You can buy it right back and still avoid taxes on the gain. The assistance of your tax pro and financial advisor might be necessary for this.
3. Make required minimum distributions in the year you turn 73, not the year after, even if you are allowed to wait.
4. Pay very close attention to other sources of income if your Social Security is not already 85% taxable. Small income increases can make Social Security more taxable, which will not be accounted for in the jobs withholding.
5. Pay attention to state taxes. Make sure to withhold from the right state (your resident state) and none that you don't have to pay taxes to. If you always get all your state withholding back, stop the withholding and see if you can stop paying to file state tax returns.
6. Over withhold early in retirement and have money set aside for surprises. Obviously if you have a great tax pro who can run accurate calculations for you, do what he or she says.

Military: This chapter, combined with the next chapter: I'm Retiring from the Military has pretty much everything you need.

64. I am Retiring from the Military

Retiring from the military can be a wonderful time of life, but it is also a time of uncertainty about jobs, residence, moving and other significant changes. Once all these are settled, retirement can seem like everything you dreamed it could be—until that first tax return. I've prepared dozens tax returns for newly retired military, and not one has had a happy outcome. I'll grant that some people are ready for it, but most times they are not. I've seen reactions that vary from, "That's all I'm getting back?" to "I owe $25,000! Are you kidding me?" It would not be an exaggeration to say that the several thousand-dollar balance due is the most common result.

With this chapter I hope to provide information to mitigate the effects of retirement on your taxes (you can't prevent taxes, only minimize and prepare.) I'll start by explaining the changes you'll see, and then talk about what you can do.

Problem #1
ALL your income is taxable now. That's right, no non-taxable allowances, combat pay or other benefits. You might have the same salary as when you were on active duty, but at least 20 to 30% more will be taxable. While in the military, this had the effect of keeping most of your income out of the 22% tax bracket. To dispel a common misconception, only the portion of income that is in the 22% tax bracket is taxed at 22%, the rest at lower tax rates, but we'll see why this matters as we discuss things in more detail...

Problem #2
Your new job doesn't know about your retirement income, and your retirement income doesn't know about your job. This means that your wages and retirement will under-withhold in almost all circumstances. For an example, let's say you're married with two kids. You put Married 4 on your W-4 form, and, while on active duty, this would be fine. Now however, your job might put you a little into the 22% tax bracket, but they withhold just a little more than 12%. Your retirement sees you in the 10 to 12% tax bracket, so they withhold just over 10%. Together, you're thoroughly into the 22% tax bracket. If you make $20,000 more than the bottom of the 22% tax bracket, that's almost $5,000 that should be withheld…but maybe $3,000 actually gets withheld. Those numbers add up! This also is made worse if your spouse works. (Now don't think about lowering your income - big tax bills result from big income - and that's good.)

Problem #3

Did you get a great relocation package? They may have even covered the taxes for you (much of the package is taxable income). The problem is that the relocation package drove you right THROUGH the 24% tax bracket and into the 32 or even the 35% tax bracket. Your retirement should be taxed at 22%, but they're withholding 10%. Say you get $40,000 in retirement. The withholding will be less than $6,000, but you should have $10,000 withheld. Do the math: $10,000 – $6,000 = my tax bill is how much?!?

Problem #4

What happened to my $2,000 Child Tax Credit? What about my Education Credit? And just what the hell is the Alternative Minimum Tax? Military allowances tend to keep you from the income limitations that many people face. If you have a kid in college, you could get a $2,500 American Opportunity Credit. If you have kids under 17, you should get $2,000 each on your taxes, but both of those have income limitations that you might face at your new income. The Alternative Minimum Tax is a tax designed to make everyone pay their fair share, but more and more people face it every year. A detailed analysis is beyond the scope of this chapter, but let's just say this—it's BAD. For the Child Tax Credit, starting in 2018, the income limit was raised SIGNIFICANTLY, so this will be less of a problem.

Problem #5

Wait, state taxes? I never paid them before. I know a lot of you are "residents" of tax-free states, or are from states that don't tax military, but now, you reside where you work. Most of those states are going to want their share of your money. DFAS tends to not withhold state taxes unless you make them (though many states don't tax military retirement). You should talk to your tax professional about the specifics of your state.

Problem #6

What do you mean I owe? They withheld the tax on my Thrift Savings Plan early distribution. DON'T DO IT—IT's A TRAP! Seriously, unless you're over 55 and not planning on working LEAVE IT ALONE! Now is not the time to get clever about using it to buy a house and not having a payment. Here's the deal: They will withhold 20%. 10% of this will cover the early withdrawal penalty. That leaves 10% in taxes. I believe we covered your new tax rate above (hint: at least 22%). That means you are AT LEAST 12% under-withheld. Take too much out and you could be a ton more under-withheld. Think "I'm going to OWE at least $1,200 for every $10,000 taken out (not counting the $2,000 they already kept)." That means, ignoring state taxes, you get less than $6,800 of every $10,000 you take out. I don't care what the interest rate on your house would be—you're not making that back! DON'T DO IT!!!!!

What to do:

So, besides not taking money out of your Thrift Savings Plan, what do you do? You have several options:

1: Over-withhold from your pension and your job.
2: Make estimated tax payments (I'm not a big fan of this one).
3: Save a large amount of money in the event that you have a large balance due.
4: Do a combination of the first three (another is ignore and hope, but I can tell you that doesn't work).

You should continue to treat taxes very conservatively until at least the end of your first full retired year. Also, no matter which method you use, you should ensure that your withholding and/or estimated tax payments at least equal your tax liability from the previous year. This will ensure you don't owe a penalty for underpayment.

To increase your withholding, you submit a W4 form. The IRS likes to pretend that if you follow the instructions, everything will be fine. This is bunk. The W4 instructions are the most useless instructions of any IRS form. My advice is to simply select Single and 0 for each and every job you have, as well as your retirement (you can do this online via MyPay for retirement.) After your first full year of retirement, if you get a big refund, you can readjust your withholding. I must warn you that even this might not be enough. You should strongly consider having a very conservative budget until you are sure what your tax situation will be. Set aside lots of money just in case you owe. The W-4 Form will likely change in 2019 due to the recent tax law change, so Single and 0 might not make sense by then – I'll try to get this updated when we figure out what they are going to do.

My Advice:

1. In addition to the "what to do" section above, my best advice is to call your tax professional after you start the new job. Give them detailed information about your new income (retiree statement and pay stubs are best) and they can run the numbers for you.

2. If you don't have a great tax professional, use the withholding calculator at irs.gov, making sure to use accurate information from pay stubs to get the best results.

3. Have some money set aside to cover potential tax hits. You will probably be making more money now, so save some.

4. Do not touch your TSP!!!

5. If you will be working in retirement you very likely need 22% in Federal Taxes coming out of your pension. MyPay and DFAS don't make it easy to get there, but with a little math and a few adjustments you can make it happen.

65. I am Receiving Social Security (or Thinking About It)

Be aware that if you take Social Security before full retirement age (65 to 67 depending on your age) you may have to pay it back if you work a second job. Since this is not a tax issue, I'll refer you to www.ssa.gov for more information. People ALWAYS confuse this with the tax rules, but they are COMPLETELY DIFFERENT!

Social Security is taxable in a weird way. If it is your ONLY source of income, you probably won't pay taxes on it. It is also not subject to state income taxes in many states. If you have other sources of income, jobs, other retirement or investment returns, then it can be up to 85% taxable. It is not taxed at 85%, but up to 85% of the Social Security will be subject to ordinary income tax rates. This greatly complicates decision making with regard to other sources of income, so it will serve you well to discuss major income changing decisions with your tax pro to avoid big surprises in Social Security taxability. I'll cover the basics (if you can call it that) here:

1. The first thing you have to do is figure out your income that will be used to calculate the taxability of Social Security. This number is all your taxable income, plus any tax-exempt interest, plus HALF of your Social Security income for the year (from your Form 1099-SSA).
2. Figure out your "base amount" for comparison. This is $25,000 if you are Single, HH, or QSS filing status, $32,000 if you are MFJ, $25,000 if you are MFS and didn't live with your spouse for EVEN ONE NIGHT during the year, $0 if you are MFS and lived with your spouse anytime during the year. MFS sucks, as we've discussed.
3. Compare the income from 1 above to the base amount from 2. If income exceeds the base amount, some of your benefits are taxable. There is a complex worksheet to determine how much is taxable, but it will generally be between 50% and 85% of your Social Security income if your income exceeds the base amount. It gets to 85% pretty fast, so if you are above the base amount you can expect to pay a decent amount of taxes.

Military: Not much different here for you.

66. I am Receiving an Annuity or Pension

The first thing I want to say is that, generally, if you are receiving an annuity or pension, the majority of it will be taxable to the federal government, and some or all of it may be taxed to the state. For state purposes, an annuity or pension is taxable to the state you are a resident of, regardless of the source of the pension. If you are a resident of say, South Carolina, a CA Teachers or NY Firefighters pension is taxable to SC and NOT to CA or NY. Make sure to update your provider as to your state of residence so they can update the Form 1099-R you receive and withhold as appropriate. Even if the 1099-R has the state you are not a residence of, you want to make sure to apply the income to the state you are a residence of at the time of receipt. If you move during the year, the payments are taxable to the state you were a resident of as you receive them, so keep track. You only have one state of residence, and it is generally moved at the time you establish yourself in the new state. As a basic rule, the date you move in your new house, or start your new job, are good indications that your residency shifted. Talk to a professional if this date is unclear.

I also want to talk about disability. For the most part, disability pensions and annuities are taxable. Notable exceptions are Veteran's disability and SSI from Social Security. A good indication that your pension or annuity is at least partially taxable is the receipt of a 1099-R or 1099-SSA, even if it has the code for disability (Code 3).

Annuities used to be amazingly complicated for taxes, but they have gotten easier (for taxes). They are still complicated overall. You usually end up with an annuity either from an employee retirement plan, life insurance contracts, direct annuity investment, or IRA rollover. Basically, you convert a large lump sum into a lifetime of payments. These payments are taxable, except to the extent that you invested money into the plan that you paid taxes on. If you rolled completely tax deducted amounts, such as from a traditional IRA or 401k into the annuity, the annuity is fully taxable. If you invested non-tax advantaged money into the account (for example you bought an annuity for $30,000 with regular cash 20 years ago, and now it's worth $300,000) the original investment is non-taxable, and you get to exclude it from your withdrawals a little bit at a time, based on your life expectancy. To greatly simplify, if your life expectancy is 30 years, then the $30,000 we just talked about would be deducted from your taxable withdrawals at a rate of $1,000 per year, until it is used up. The bad news is that this is a very complicated calculation. The good news is that if you know basic information (most of which is provided on the 1099-R you'll get during tax season, just like a W-2) your software will handle it for you. Make sure you know the annuity starting date (the date you first received a check). The even better news is that, more and more, the annuity provider is doing the calculation for you, and giving you everything, including the taxable amount, right on the 1099-R.

My Advice:

1. When you start collecting an annuity, write down the date it started and have that for your tax pro or software when filing.
2. Make sure the right state is withholding from your retirement.

Military: Military retirement is fully taxable at the Federal level. VA disability is fully tax free. State taxation of military retirement varies by state.

67. I am Paying on Student Loans

If you are paying off student loans that you received to pay for higher education, you may be able to deduct the interest on your tax return. The determination of if it is an eligible loan is pretty straightforward. It is unlikely that you got a student loan that is not deductible if you used it for most types of college or vocational education in the United States. If you did something truly weird with the loan, seek additional help. You can deduct interest for you or your spouse, or your dependent. The dependent part is a little weird because they don't have to be a dependent on the tax return you're filing now. Instead, they had to be your dependent in the year you took the loan out and you have to be obligated to pay the loan. Paying your child's loan that is in their name doesn't count.

The deduction is not part of itemized deductions, so you get it even when you take the standard deduction. You get a maximum of $2,500 PER RETURN, not per person. You should get a Form 1098-E or a letter with similar information from your loan holder. There is an income limitation on the deduction, and, as usual, you can't be MFS. You also can't be claimed as a dependent on someone else's return and take the deduction.

One additional piece of advice: Don't ignore your student loans. If they become delinquent, the government has significant avenues for collection. These include taking your federal tax refund and your spouse's federal tax refund. If your refund is taken for your spouse's delinquent student loans, you may be able to file as injured spouse to get some refund back. Or you can file as injured spouse when you initially file to keep some refund from being taken.

You can now use remaining 529 Education Savings Plan assets to pay off your student loans. A maximum of $10,000 LIFETIME can be withdrawn tax and penalty free to pay these off. You cannot take a tax deduction for interest paid with these funds.

Here are the details:

1. Loans from relatives or your employer don't count.
2. The student has to be enrolled at least half-time in a program leading to a degree, certificate or other recognized education credential at the time the money is borrowed.
3. The loan proceeds have to be received within a reasonable period within the time the education is received. This is assumed to be

met if they are paid for specific periods of education and you actual attend school during the specific period.

4. The loan proceeds need to be for tuition, room and board, books, supplies and equipment, and transportation. If you use them for general living expenses, these cannot exceed what the educational institution would have charged you for room and board.
5. You get a maximum of $2,500 per return.
6. You must be legally obligated to repay the loan. This means the loan must be made in your name, or with you as a co-signor.
7. You can't deduct the interest in more than one place on your tax return.
8. If you file MFJ, the deduction phases out as your AGI increases above $155,000 and is gone at an AGI of $185,000. If you are Single, HH or QSS, the deduction phases out as your AGI increases above $75,000 and is gone at an AGI of $90,000.
9. If you are married, and both of you are paying back student loans, you need to consult an expert to determine the effects of filing status on Income Based Repayment plans.

My Advice:

1. Don't let your loans go delinquent or they will yank them right out of your tax return.
2. Make sure you get a 1098E or equivalent for each of your student loans.
3. If your student loans are getting cancelled, seek professional help to determine if you will have to pay taxes on the cancelled debt.

Military: Not a lot of differences for you here, though if you have pre-service student loans at higher than 6% interest, you should look into getting a reduced interest rate through the Soldiers and Sailors Civil Relief Act.

68. I am Changing Jobs

I hope this is a good thing for you!

There are a few big issues to consider, but first, I want to point out that this assumes you already have the new job, or have it lined up. There is another chapter for losing your job, which you might want to review if you lost your job and then found a new one. This chapter is the one to read if you made a transition that did not involve a significant unemployment period. This chapter is going to cover two big things: your 401k (or another employee retirement plan) and your move (just deleted since moving expenses only apply to active-duty military now).

Job hunting and changing expenses were made non-deductible with the Trump Tax Law in 2018.

401k's or other employee retirement plans:

For your 401k, you will need to do something with it, though you are allowed to leave it with your former employer…sometimes. I'm not a financial advisor, but my non-professional suggestion is to roll it over to an Individual Retirement Account with a financial services company. Seek professional assistance from a licensed financial advisor, or if you are good at handling your investments, do it yourself. DON'T HAVE THEM SEND THE MONEY TO YOU! Do a trustee-to-trustee transfer, where you tell the destination financial institution to go get the money from your old employer. You don't have to do it this way, but trust me, this is the safe and easy way to do it. You can also move it to your new employer's plan if they offer one. Work through your new employer's plan administrator to make it happen.

If you absolutely have to take money out of your 401K, take the absolute minimum that you need to SURVIVE. Make sure they withhold the maximum (generally 20%) and realize that this probably won't be enough. You will probably pay a 10% penalty, plus your regular tax rate (probably AT LEAST another 12%).

My Advice:

1. ALWAYS do a trustee-to-trustee transfer for moving retirement account assets. This is where you have the custodian of the new account contact the

custodian of the old account and have the money moved directly between them.

2. I am generally a fan of transferring retirement account money to a personal IRA rather than to your new employer. You have a lot more options and control this way.

3. If you take money out of a retirement account to pay job change expenses, take the minimum out that you need to survive. Taking it out for random expenses such as down payments on homes is a terrible idea.

Military: Moves related to discharge from the military are exempt from the distance test and are still deductible under the new law.

Not discussed: Self-employed moves, International moves.

69. What the Hell is Alternative Minimum Tax and Why the Hell am I Paying It?

2018 Tax Law Change Affects: The new tax law dramatically increased the Alternative Minimum Tax (AMT) standard deductions and income limitations such that a far fewer number of taxpayers should be affected by it. This is very good news. Chances are that if you are reading this chapter, you either have a very nice income, or you had some sort of taxable windfall this year.

I am not going to go into a ton of detail here, mainly because the Alternative Minimum Tax is a completely different tax system from the income tax we are used to, and very few people are affected by it. The AMT is a neat trick that the government came up with a number of years ago to make sure that even the super-rich, with tons of deductions, paid their fair share. It now affects millions of people and can be quite disturbing if you are subject to it. Early in my career as a Tax Super Genius, I would be working on tax returns and find that the refund stopped changing, even though there was plenty of room for deductions, and I kept adding them in. I soon learned this was the AMT at work.

The AMT basically gives you very few deductions but has a very large standard deduction (called an exemption for AMT). The exemption was designed to get smaller once you reached a certain higher income. It has only two tax rates, 26% and 28%. You generally get sucked into this if you have a large income, and/or lots of deductions. The 2018 tax law made the exemption significantly larger and the income at which it starts getting smaller, so fewer people will face AMT.

To make things more confusing, the tax forms don't have a separate return where you calculate AMT and then compare it to your regular tax. What they do have is a short form (Form 6251) that essentially undoes everything not allowed in AMT, and then adds in the stuff that's allowed. It then compares your AMT tax to regular tax, and if the AMT is higher, adds the difference to your regular tax. This makes it very difficult to really understand what's happening to your return because of AMT and makes it hard to strategize to minimize taxes.

If, when you are reviewing your tax return, there is a number on Form 1040 Schedule 2, Line 1, you have been hit with AMT. You should consider talking to a professional to see if there is anything you can do, and to develop strategies for future years to minimize it. There is a recapture provision that allows you to get back some AMT you paid in prior years, but it too, is amazingly complicated.

My Advice:

1. Charitable deductions are one of the few rock-solid ways to minimize AMT. Check out the <u>I Give to Charity</u> chapter.

Military: Not much different here for you.

70 – I'm Thinking About Starting a Business

This is a guide I wrote for a client who wanted lots of tax advice on starting a business. I decided I needed to finally put it all in one place and get all the details together so I could just throw a guide at them instead of answering questions piecemeal. So naturally, I included it in this book!

Make sure to read the follow-on chapters for more detailed tax advice and maybe even some advice specific to your business – like Real Estate Agents or UBER drivers.

Anything included in this chapter that is not about INCOME taxes is outside of the author's core area of expertise and is provided simply as a guideline of what you MIGHT need to do and how you MIGHT do it. Laws vary greatly between states, counties, and cities, so you should reference local rules or experts.

Most localities have some form of online guide to help you navigate the process.

Even the tax stuff in this chapter is over-simplified, so seek extra help or do more research. The author is not responsible for ANY negative results due to your following this advice or using this information.

Items are listed in rough order that most people would consider them, but also vary greatly with type of business and desires of the owner.

As far as the IRS is concerned, you can start a business instantly. Just sell something or get paid for a service and BAM! You're a business (or hobby). Income tax wise, that's about all there is to it. You can do business, make money, track deductions and file state and local income taxes at the end of the year and be fine with the IRS (at least for the first year). No need to make estimated payments or quarterly filing as long as you pay what you owe by the normal, non-business income tax filing due date. Quarterly taxes MIGHT be needed for the following year if you are profitable, but the first year they are rarely needed to avoid a penalty. Though you should be saving for the tax hit if you are making money!

That said, there are a number of things you SHOULD do, and a lot of things you might be REQUIRED to do outside of the income tax world, depending on the nature of your business and the requirements of your state or locality. I'm going to try to break these into logical areas and again, logical order.

The first three items are, according to most business experts, the most important part of starting a successful business. They are also the things most small business owners don't do, especially for home-based businesses.
To be clear, they are also the areas that I have the LEAST experience or knowledge in, at least professionally. I have obviously started a couple businesses, and assisted many people in starting theirs, but I also refer them to these points and strongly suggest they get expert help or do significant research in these areas:

1. Market research: You need to know who is doing what you are doing already, what they are charging, how many customers are available, what the logistics are, how much your expenses are going to be and a million other little things. You won't get everything, but you should put some effort into this, even if you have already started the business running.
2. Business plan: What are you going to do? How are you going to do it? How much is it going to cost before money starts coming in? How much money do you have on hand and how long will it last? How much money do you need/want/are you able to make? The more you know going in, and the more you plan out (time and money being the big things) the more likely you will be to succeed. Knowing how big or small you want to be and bounding the two extremes will also help control where you need to go and what you want to do. You also need to plan ahead for who will be involved and what their relationship will be. If you have a partner – you are a partnership and you want to understand what this means!
3. Financing (I hate debt): If you don't have enough money to start the business, you will need to find some. You won't get it if you haven't done the first two items we just talked about, at least not from professionals. Family, friends and partners can be alternate sources, but partners have their own drawbacks.

The next few might need to be done before starting actual business operations, but often the business sort of starts itself and then these areas get revisited. Make sure you investigate these areas as soon as you can:

4. What is your "entity" type? This is a big area of confusion for a lot of people. Terms like LLC, LLP, partnership, corporation, S-Corporation and sole proprietorship get bandied about and rarely mean what you think they do. The first point is that you don't need ANY formal business entity

formation as far as the IRS is concerned. If you start making money that's not from investments or jobs, you have generally started a business as far as the IRS is concerned (or a hobby – I won't keep repeating this and will discuss it later). Get paid cash for doing some work– you are a business Make some stuff and resell it – business. Buy stuff to resell – business. Do work for a business and they pay you without handling taxes (as a contractor) – business. Absent any other action on your part, the IRS will consider you a sole proprietor and your business will file taxes on Schedule C on your regular tax return. That said, if you are working with another person, they will likely consider you a partnership, and the partnership has to file its own return! So here is a quick rundown of entity types and their implications:

A. Sole Proprietorship: This is the default form, and the form that most businesses start out as. It is the simplest but provides no liability protection for your personal assets. Except for the simplest of businesses, getting away from sole proprietorship should be on the radar since you want some form of protection for your personal assets. Without that, if someone sues your business, they are suing YOU, and all YOUR stuff is on the table to pay them for their injuries. Sole proprietorships do not file a separate tax return from the individual, instead filing Schedule C on the personal tax return. Separate business records should be kept to ensure you can file an accurate Schedule C.

B. Limited Liability Corporation: Here is the biggest source of confusion. An LLC has almost literally NOTHING to do with income taxes and is absolutely NOT required to deduct business expenses. Forming an LLC changes nothing regarding taxes, other than the costs of formation being an expense. An LLC's primary purpose is to protect your personal assets from being taken in the event the business does something that causes you to be sued. It is a STATE level entity formed in accordance with STATE law. You can set one up on your own, or use a lawyer, accountant, CPA, or online service. Expect to pay very little to do it yourself (not recommended), Under $1000 for online service, $2000 (very roughly) for a CPA or accounting firm to set it up, and a lot more for a full-service lawyer to do it. The IRS, by default, will consider a single person LLC to be a "disregarded entity" for tax purposes, and you will be treated as a Sole Proprietorship as above by the IRS until you formally change that. If it has more than one owner, it will be considered a partnership (see below).

C. Partnership: This is the generic form of a multi owner business. In most cases, setting it up is the same as setting up an LLC as described above. The differences come into play when you determine what "investment" each owner has in the business – called their basis, and their ownership percentage. Invested money, equipment and debt taken on all affect this and if there is anything other than equal investment, expert help should be sought. A partnership is a separate entity for tax purposes, and files its own tax return (generally due March 15th – with penalties for filing late!). The partnership tax return will issue K-1 forms to each partner with information for their individual returns. The partnership does not pay any Federal income tax, it just passes income and deductions to the partners. This is mainly true at the state level, except that many states have recently enacted provisions for the partnership to pay the partner's state tax liability for them, mainly as a way to avoid limitations on deducting state taxes on the Federal return. If you are my client, I will generally not prepare your partnership tax return, as I focus my expertise elsewhere to ensure I stay VERY GOOD at the things I do rather than be okay at a lot of things.

D. S-Corporation: This is a more complicated form of partnership and has additional benefits but lots of restrictions. Professional help and advice should be sought before attempting to set one up.

E. C-Corporation: These are very complex entities which are beyond our scope here. If you need significant outside investment or have grown very large, seek professional help to see if this is for you.

F. There are a few other entities, but they are mainly hybrids of the above and will be treated as one of the above for tax purposes.
You can start with a simple entity type and change later as you grow, though forming an LLC is never a bad idea.
5. In order to protect your SSN from exposure, you should apply for an Employer Identification Number. You would then use this EIN in place of your SSN on any documents requiring an SSN. Getting an EIN is easy and can be done online at irs.gov. It is usually in the prominent area of the front page at irs.gov with the other "How Can We Help You?" stuff. Just make sure you answer the questions carefully and the entity type matches up with what you established above (or plan to establish).
6. You might need a business license from your city, town, county or state. This is very locality specific and you should check it out on your own. Most states have a consolidated business guide on the web that you can use.
7. If you sell stuff, possibly even services, you likely need to deal with sales tax. This is also not my area of expertise but I can assure you, you do NOT want to mess this up! If you are afraid of the IRS, you don't even know what real trouble is. If you set up a sales tax account with whatever state or local entity deals with it in your area, file at ALL required intervals unless you are ABSOLUTELY CERTAIN that you don't have to. In South Carolina, for example, once you set up an account they want a filing EVERY MONTH, even if you have no income.

8. You definitely want a separate bank account for the business. This could be just a separate account in your name you use for the business, or one under the business' name. If it is under the business name, you will need an EIN. Be scrupulous that all income from the business goes into this account and all direct expenses and taxes come out of it. If it is short, make a transfer from personal to it and then pay the expenses. Don't pay with your personal account. If you want personal money or income to spend or live on, transfer it to your personal account before spending it and make sure to note that the transfer was to your personal account and not for an expense. Indirect expenses such as gas, mixed use cell phone or home office mixed expenses should be paid from the personal account unless the expense is 100% business (car never driven for personal use).

This next bunch of stuff is about record keeping:

9. Your business records can be as complicated or as simple as you like. The two critical issues are that they can be backed up with documentation and that you ACTUALLY ENTER THE DATA IN A TIMELY MANNER! Even the best, most organized records are useless if they are not updated in a timely manner (which means they either will never be updated or it will be a mess to get them updated at the last minute.) Here's the counterintuitive point: They should not take a lot of time. Time spent on records is time not spent working the business and making money. I keep a small ledger (literally a pocket notebook) and I write date, description, amount and miles as things occur. The receipt goes in a drawer and at the end of the year the drawer gets emptied into an envelope with the year on it. The odds that I need the receipts are so remote, that it makes no sense to waste time organizing them. If I get audited, I will line the receipts up with the ledger entries in preparation for the audit. But the simplicity of my system ensures I NEVER miss an entry. I have a code for the "amount" column where I circle expenses, box mileage and triangle income. When restaurants were a special deduction I added a tick on the right side of the circle. I have also used ticks on the triangle to segregate income sources but have since stopped. Periodically I will make a totals page and add up the numbers by category and total them with previous subtotal pages to keep a running total. I usually do this when I want to analyze the status of my year's income/deductions. You can use software, spreadsheets, ledgers or anything else that works best for you. Just make sure it is easy, accurate and timely.

10. Let's talk Inventory. Inventory comes into play when you buy or make things that you keep on hand to sell. In this case, you need to track expenses for these items separately, and track beginning of year and end of

year inventory, using a consistent method. This is separate from other expenses that don't go into buying or making items to sell. It is a good idea to get professional help when first setting up an inventory tracking system.

11. Mileage is your BEST deduction. Either keep a mileage log or track as discussed above. This is not just mileage to and from jobs or meeting with clients. Any trip for which the primary purpose is for your business works. This includes supply runs, market research and any other travel in your car that supports your business.

12. Home Office is in a category of deductions that I call "fake". This does not mean they are bad, but almost every other deduction you have is a dollar right out of your pocket that you get pennies on the dollar back on your taxes. Home Office is generally money that you would have spent anyway (at least a lot of it) and thus the tax benefit outstrips the expense. Too many business owners justify spending money on things because they are "deductible". This is stupid. Spend money only if you have to, it makes you more money, or streamlines the business such that you have time to make more money. Home Office is one of the exceptions. Because it is "fake", the IRS makes you jump through hoops to make it legal, but they aren't that hard if you do it right and are honest. The area you use for business has to be used regularly and EXCLUSIVELY for business. The office with your computer that the kids use to play Fortnite, or where you watch cat videos when not doing business is not EXCLUSIVE! You need to set up the largest reasonable area that meets your needs and can be ONLY used for business. It also doesn't have to be an "office". It can be a workshop, a storage area or any other necessary place that is ONLY used for your business. The bigger the space, the better. You essentially get to deduct a portion of virtually every penny you spend on your home based on the ratio of the "office" square footage to your total home square footage. This can get complicated and doesn't always help so it can be a good idea to talk to a professional to ensure it makes sense and that it is worth it.

13. You need a budget. You NEED a budget for your life and your business needs its own budget where you set out how much you will spend on the business every month, what it is spent for, and how it is going to make you more money than you spend. You can do this in a myriad of ways so do what works for you. I'm a big proponent of not wasting time in your business on things that don't bring in money, but budgeting and understanding your income and outflows are a HUGE exception to that rule.

Now we need to talk about liability. Basically, if you make a mistake or someone gets injured you need to understand the repercussions and how to protect yourself. Again, this is NOT my area of expertise so seek out professional help or do additional research!

14. If you just start and run a business, you might be fully liable for anything that goes wrong. There are a few ways to protect yourself but just blissfully going along as a sole proprietorship is not the best one. The most common method is forming a Limited Liability Company. Properly forming one and maintaining FULLY SEPARATE property and income is a good way to protect personal assets from business issues. But there are many ways to get around this and good lawyers probably know them all. The most common is "piercing the corporate veil", where they show that personal and business assets are comingled, and thus personal assets should be on the hook. Talk to a LAWYER about this.

15. Another common and easy way to protect yourself is to have some form of business liability insurance. Some states or locales may REQUIRE you to maintain certain types of insurance. Common types of this insurance are business liability, workmen's compensation or general liability. It might also be possible to protect yourself with an Umbrella liability policy. Talk to an EXPERT about this and make sure you understand what is protected!

16. Another common form of protection is very specific insurance such as Errors and Omissions Insurance. This normally applies to professionals such as accountants, real estate agents etc. and covers you if you make a mistake when providing services. Again, do your own due diligence and talk to others in your business. A professional organization that represents your industry is a great source of good information on this and many other things we discussed.

Now let's talk about taxes. We are getting into my wheelhouse, BUT, I am an INCOME tax expert, not a sales tax, real estate tax or excise tax expert. And again, this is generic, general, short advice so do not rely solely on it!

17. First let's talk Hobby versus Business. If you buy and sell something, make and sell something, or provide a service for compensation, it is generally taxable. In many cases you are a business but ONLY, if you are in it for profit. It's still taxable if you aren't in it for the profit, but you don't get to deduct expenses like a business, so being for profit is better. The reason the IRS cares is that there are a lot of ways to lose money every year as a business, and then take those losses off of your personal income, thus reducing your personal taxes. You can't do this forever. An often-confused general rule is that if you make a profit in 3 out of 5 years, the IRS will presume you are a for profit business and you need look no further. Many people think you MUST do this to be a business and not a

hobby, but this is only a way for the IRS to avoid analyzing every business when it isn't necessary. If you don't meet the 3 of 5 year rule, the IRS uses a number of criteria to determine if you are a business. That is too detailed to go into in this post, but many of them are common sense. Do you operate like a business? Is what you do fun? Do you make changes to increase profitability? There is no easy answer but, if you are doing something fun like crafting, don't do it a lot, never make a profit and don't make changes to try to make a profit, you are probably a hobby. If what you do sucks – nobody climbs into septic tanks for fun – this is a point in your favor. Keeping good business records, working hard, chasing new sources of revenue are all good things!

18. Let's talk about the taxes you file with the IRS. These are Income Tax and FICA taxes (Social Security and Medicare taxes). An employee who gets a W-2 will see three sets of taxes taken out at the Federal Level, Federal Income Tax (which is what your tax return is analyzing), Social Security and Medicare Taxes. Social Security and Medicare get taken out, matched by your employer and are sent away. In most cases, the employee will never deal with those taxes. As a business owner, you pay all those taxes yourself, AND you have to pay the employer match – this is called Self Employment Tax. This means that if you are in the 22% tax bracket, your true tax rate can be higher than 37% because the Self Employment Tax Rate is roughly 15.3%. Make sure you are prepared for this! The good news is that you only pay taxes on your PROFIT, not your Gross Income. Avoiding paying Self Employment tax on all your profit is one of the major advantages of business entities such as Partnership or S-Corporation.

19. You also have to pay State Income Taxes. Make sure to check if they have advantageous rules, such as South Carolina's lower tax rate for businesses. Some states just use your business profit from the Federal Return, and other states recalculate the whole thing.

20. If you sell things, you might have to pay sales tax. I am NOT an expert on this but I can tell you this: people are afraid of the IRS but I would be more afraid of messing up my sales tax. Government agencies generally have very little sympathy for failure to properly and timely remit sales taxes! Use a professional or be very, VERY sure you understand what you do or do not have to pay.

21. Some states have other business taxes like Business Personal Property Taxes, Sin taxes (alcohol, tobacco etc.) or General Excise type taxes. Hawaii, for example, hits you up for a few percentage points on your Gross Income as a business and wants it on a regular basis. Again, NOT my area of expertise, you just need to know to seek these out and make sure you understand them.

And the rest of these are just stuff that didn't fit neatly in the above categories:

22. It is probably important for you to understand the various tax preparation, accounting and advisor types you might hire. Obviously, major or complex businesses might need to work with lawyers, financial advisors, insurance agents and others, but I am going to talk about the accounting and tax type individuals. The main ones you will see are tax preparers, accountant, bookkeepers, Certified Public Accountants and Enrolled Agents. Tax preparers can have many titles - some made up by their employers or themselves – but the important thing to understand is that virtually ANYONE can be a tax preparer with little to no training. The only real requirement is to apply for a Preparer Tax Identification Number. If you are a basically law-abiding citizen you could be preparing taxes tomorrow for compensation with ZERO training (some states such as California, Oregon and New York do have licensing requirements). I always advise that you understand the experience and training your preparer has received. The IRS has some guidance on choosing a preparer: https://www.irs.gov/tax-professionals/choosing-a-tax-professional. I also highly recommend seeking out an Enrolled Agent or Certified Public Accountant specializing in both tax preparation and your type of business. On that note, Certified Public Accountants (CPA's) are licensed by their individual state and are highly trained in accounting and tax law. They also have continuing education requirements. CPA's are a great resource if you are starting a complex business entity and need formation, accounting and tax assistance. The downside of a CPA (from a tax perspective) is that they may not be specialized in taxes or your area of business, so you need to do some background before hiring one. Enrolled Agents are specifically focused on taxes and are examined and licensed by the IRS to represent taxpayers at audits. They have specific continuing education requirements focused on taxes. If all you need is tax advice and preparation, an Enrolled Agent may be your best choice (I am one and may be biased on this). Accountants and bookkeepers may or may not have any specific licensing or training requirements but can generally be counted on to do basic accounting and bookkeeping as long as you do some research on their performance and reviews.

23. Let's talk about one of the biggest, and also the most common business no-no's: Conflating Personal and Business expenses. You need to keep business and personal separate. If you fail to do so, this is one of the most likely places that you will get in trouble in an audit (assume you aren't lying or keeping bad documentation). It can also cause you to lose the personal liability protections we worked so hard to create in the earlier points. Not conflating personal and business doesn't mean you have to

have fully separate bank accounts (though an LLC should). It does mean that business expenses should be business expenses and personal expenses personal. Mileage should be deducted if the primary purpose of the trip was business. A "business" asset (car, computer, tool etc.) should be used exclusively for business, or business use percentage faithfully determined. Visiting family and calling it business is common and not okay – the PRIMARY purpose of the trip must be business and anything personal or entertainment should be incidental. You can deduct PORTIONS of a trip that are primarily business, such as the expenses to meet a potential customer on one day of a trip, but you MUST be careful to accurately account for it. Many people think creating an LLC is a license to deduct personal stuff as business stuff. It is NOT. There are some exceptions, such as the Home Office, or legitimately employing your children, but you should consult an expert BEFORE attempting this and BE HONEST and don't push too hard!

24. Now we need to talk about paying people to do stuff. Normal vendors who just bill you or things that you purchase aren't what I'm talking about here. I'm talking about employees and subcontractors. Employees we all know about because we have been one. They get a salary; you take taxes out and give them the difference. But you don't just take Federal income tax. You also take state taxes, Social Security and Medicare taxes, unemployment taxes AND you match some of these or pay other taxes for them. They also like to get health insurance and retirement plans. I'm not going into the details here because if you hire employees, you most likely need an accountant or CPA to handle payroll for you. Do NOT mess up payroll, especially remitting taxes to the government! You are far more likely to get nailed for this than messing up your income taxes. So, employees are a pain, and you would rather hire subcontractors. These are easy. When you hire them, get their name, address, and ID# (usually SSN but might be an EIN). Use IRS Form W-9 for this. Track what you pay them and, if you pay an individual more than $600 in a year, issue them a 1099NEC and send a copy to the government. These payments, even those you don't issue a 1099 for, are almost always deductible. Be aware that you might have other responsibilities like ensuring they have their own workman's comp insurance, depending on your state. The problem is, you can't always pay people on 1099NEC. If you control their work, their work hours, how they do things, what they charge, etc. they might have to be employees. Again, complex, so reach out to a CPA or EA if it's not obvious.

The last two are for everyone:

25. Don't Lie to the IRS. Ever. Don't break the tax rules. Ever. See next.
26. Don't Fear the IRS. It is very hard to go to jail over income taxes and it generally requires willful and continued evasion or steadfast refusal to pay. Your most likely risk is that you have to pay back some taxes, with interest and penalties. The likelihood of this is very low, so don't fail to take advantage of things over a fear of the IRS. You'll hear: "Office in Home is a red flag!". Phooey! If you have a legitimate office in home, used regularly and exclusively for business, you would be a fool not to deduct it. Likewise, meals with clients are a supposed red flag, and you do want to be careful here, but if you pay for a meal where the primary purpose is business, the individual is solely a business associate, it's reasonable to meat over a meal, and you have or hope to make money out of the deal, it is a slam dunk. If it is a friend or family, be a little more careful, but, if your ducks are in a row, go for it. Be aggressive! Don't leave money on the table! But also recognize your ability to cover an unexpected tax bill if you get called on it and lose. If you are week to week on income, and a big, unexpected tax bill would be devastating, then be less aggressive. If you have a huge emergency fund, then take any reasonable position that helps you out. But don't lie and don't intentionally take a non-legal deduction. Go for the white and gray areas, not the black ones.

71. I Run a Home-Based Business Like Amway, Party Lights, Mary Kay, etc.

2021 and 2022 Change: For 2021 and 2022 ONLY, you can deduct 100% of meals with clients in restaurants.

Other updates: There were a number of business provisions in the CARES Act passed as a response to the Coronavirus pandemic but the tax related ones were specific to businesses with employees and the rest of the business aspects, while significant in scope, were not tax related. That said, there is one credit for if you were unable to run or open your business due to COVID so if your municipality went in lockdown or placed other restrictions on business openings, you or your family got sick, your school or daycare shutdown, and this prevented you from working, check out the special 2020 chapter.

If you are just thinking about starting to do this, read the I Am Starting a Business chapter.

This chapter is for all the would-be home-based business millionaires selling AdvoCare, Amway, Pampered Chef, Lularoe, Rodan and Fields, Mary Kay, etc. The time to think about taxes is before you open the business, but, if you already have, the time is now! This chapter will tell you virtually everything you need to know about how taxes should, and do, work for a Multi-Level Marketing (MLM) type business. This is the kind of business where someone in the business recruits you to sell the products, and, eventually, recruit others into the business. This chapter works for Amway, Mary Kay, Avon, Pampered Chef, Herbalife, Isagenix, Scentsy and dozens of others you've never heard of.

Most clients I see trying these businesses out have not given a thought to taxes and are getting very little help from the businesses they are making money for. In fact, the first piece of advice I'll give is to ignore virtually everything the company, other associates or friends tell you about how to handle taxes for these businesses. To go further, I'll tell you to ignore every piece of tax information the company provides, except the 1099-NEC or 1099-K they issue you (maybe) and the invoices for the products you buy and sell. You can and should keep better and more useful records all by yourself. More on that point later.

I have several other books out, and one of them is The Short Cheap Tax Book for Multi-Level Marketing. It is very cheap for Kindle (if you don't have a Kindle you can download an App or online reader at Amazon.com). You definitely should read that book.

First, a couple of terms, some basic advice, and some warnings:

1. You should, at this point, be a Sole Proprietor. This means that you own and run the business by yourself, with no employees. You will file the business taxes as a part of your personal taxes, usually on a Schedule C. I strongly encourage you not to have any partners, even your spouse. Your spouse can help, but should generally not be an employee, and not have any true decision-making power, except the power that is normal in a healthy spousal relationship (advice and support, but no "official" role). The reasons for this are myriad, and anyone who has delved into a partnership can attest to the issues that arise. For now, just trust me. Later, if you are making a crap-ton of money, you may want to form a more complicated business entity, but that will require professional assistance and guidance.

2. You are going to spend more time doing taxes, and it's going to cost you more. Even if you use software (which I highly discourage if you are running a business) you will pay more for the programs.

3. You might not actually be a business. Most of the people starting these businesses will never have a dime of profit, and after a few years, the IRS will put the kabosh on taking a negative income from your business off of your regular taxable income. This is called Hobby Income. It means you do it more for fun than for profit. You still have to claim the income (on 1040 Schedule 1, Line 21, Other Income), but you can't deduct any expenses. My advice is to go full-bore, gung-ho toward making a profit for 3 years. File the Schedule C's and take the losses on your taxes (improving your refund). If, after three years, you haven't made a profit, and gross revenues aren't approaching 5 digits ($10,000), take real stock of where you're at. If revenues are growing and profitability seems close, keep things going. If revenues are flat, profits are a distant dream, and/or your enthusiasm is waning, bite the bullet and either shut the business down, or tone it back and start filing it as a Hobby.

4. The IRS does not like your business model. They tend to believe most MLM businesses are actually hobbies. They will scrutinize the line between business and personal expenses. They think pretty much every seminar you attend is a personal expense. Be very careful to document

everything that you deduct and be prepared to explain how it will actually benefit your business and is not a personal expense.

5. When you do make a profit, you will pay more than just income taxes on it. You have to pay Self Employment Tax on your profit. This is how a business owner pays into Social Security and Medicare. It's basically an extra 15.3% tax on your profit (a little less when you do the real math).

Moving along. Here is the advice you need to make things work...

Record Keeping: This is where the rubber meets the road. Good record keeping will save you big time when it comes to tax time. Your records do not need to be extensive, but they do need to be accurate and useable. I hate double entry bookkeeping and would never recommend it as a tool for a home-based business. I also have found that the various bookkeeping software programs are virtually useless when it comes to taxes. They may help when it comes to managing the business, but they suck for doing taxes.

The best and easiest record keeping method I've found for small home-based businesses involves a small notebook, a big notebook and an envelope or box. The small notebook is for mileage, discussed below. The big notebook is for every other expense. You need simple columns set up: date, description, cost and payment received (if you pay something, it goes in the cost column, if you are paid it goes in the payment received column). You can add categories, but don't really need to. If you are unsure if something is deductible, write it down and let your tax professional tell you if it's deductible. The box/envelope is for receipts—just throw them in. Really? No sorting, categorizing or organizing? No. Simply put, your odds of ever needing them for an audit are slim to none. Save the box, notebooks and tax returns for 7 years, and then throw it all away. If you ever do get audited, there is plenty of time to sort through the box and organize it to match the notebooks—but why do it if it's not necessary? If I'm doing your taxes, I'm going to use the notebooks and remind you that you should have a receipt for everything. You don't have to prove things to me (though I may question unbelievable things).

It is important to not to over-think things. For example, if you make a sale involving sales tax, which you know a portion will go to the government, you still write down 100% of what you were paid (including the tax). Later, when you remit the sales tax to the government, it is entered as a payment (deduction). Get it—you get money, it is entered as income; you pay money, it is entered as a deduction.

The trick to your kind of business is that sometimes you don't make the sale, it happens through a website and is fulfilled by the company, with the payment going straight to the company, the product going straight to the consumer, and you getting a commission. Generally, the company will only report the commission as income to you, which means you don't need to track any expenses like shipping, sales tax or the wholesale price—just the commission, which you can track when the payment comes to you. Just make sure your company handles it this way, and you'll be good. If the product is paid for by you, comes to you, and then you pass it on to the client for a markup, the entire price paid goes into your records as income, and all the costs to you (shipping, wholesale price, sales tax) go into your records as an expense.

Expenses: You can deduct any ordinary and necessary expenses for your business. I generally describe the requirements like this: If it will make you more money, is required by someone in authority, or makes your business more efficient or your life as a businessperson easier, it's probably deductible. Here is a non-exhaustive list:

1. Pretty much anything the upline company charges you for. If they deduct it off of your commission check, deduct it off your taxes (you report the gross commission, not the commission after deductions). If you have to pay them for something out of pocket, you can generally deduct it, though pay attention to the business/personal conflation issues discussed below for travel and entertainment.

2. Marketing Expenses: Business cards, website fees, posters, signs, sponsorships, commercials, advertising, pretty much anything you do to get someone to call YOU when they want your product.

3. Insurance: I'm not talking about homeowner's insurance here. I'm talking about "Oops! I screwed up and someone is suing me" insurance. Sometimes this is called Errors and Omissions Insurance, sometimes it's a liability bond, or a rider on your homeowner's insurance. Also, if you pay a rider to your car insurance for business use, the difference between that and regular insurance is deductible. There is also a self-employed health insurance deduction that allows you to deduct your health insurance costs if you have no other insurance source (if you can get insurance through your spouse's work this is a no-go).

4. Entertainment Expenses: Eventually, you will be with a client, or potential client, and pick up the tab for lunch or dinner. Generally, if you expect the expense to result in a sale that makes you money, either immediately or in the future (whether it ultimately does or not doesn't matter, as long as you expect it to), it is deductible, as long as it is not too fun.

5. Travel Expenses: These are a toughie. People love conflating personal and business travel. If you travel to Maine to visit family and see the lobster festival, and try to sell to some family and friends, the trip is primarily personal. You can deduct expenses DIRECTLY RELATED to the sales efforts, but little else. I recommend keeping business and personal travel separate. You can visit a friend for dinner on a three-day business trip, but don't do business for an hour on a three-day personal trip and expect to deduct the trip. Also avoid what I call BS travel. Flying to Vegas to assess potential markets is transparent vacationing disguised as business travel, especially if you spend 23 out of every 24 hours in the casino! Be reasonable! Go on trips that are going to increase your money-making potential. Stay away from any others. For legitimate travel, you get airfare, rental car, tips, taxis, laundry, internet and phone, as well as 50% of meals and any other reasonable and necessary expenses. Travel assumes overnight trips away from your home area. The IRS is very skeptical of the sales seminars your company puts on. They consider that they are more motivational than instructional, and thus not deductible.

6. Cell phones, laptops and tablets: If your business takes up a lot of time, do yourself a favor and get a business use only laptop, cell phone, tablet and/or computer. It is simply too difficult to calculate expenses on a part-personal and part-business electronic device. Don't share your business number with friends and family (other than wife and kids). If you keep everything separate, the deductions are easy and legitimate. If you don't, you have to establish a business use percentage, and worry about listed property rules—which suck! This behavior also helps with the Hobby vs. Business discussion we've already had.

7. Vehicle Expenses: Keep a mileage log. Let me say it again, unless you have a vehicle that is 100%, no kidding, total business and no personal use, keep a mileage log. Don't worry about gas, repairs, oil changes, insurance or any other car expenses (except as discussed above under insurance). There are other ways to track vehicle expenses, but mileage is the best. Do track annual car taxes and finance charges. The easiest mileage log is a

notebook where you write the date, the trip purpose and the miles driven. You will also need to know the total miles the vehicle is driven for the year, so write the odometer reading down every January 1st! Mileage will be one of your biggest expenses, so keep track of it religiously! 10,000 miles of properly tracked vehicle mileage can result in $1,200 or more of tax savings! I love the MileIQ app that uses your phone for tracking mileage.

8. Home Office: Set aside a space in your home that is 100% business use (regular and exclusive is the tax term for this). It should never be used for anything else, and regularly used for business. This is where you keep your business records, your business computer or laptop, make your sales calls from and meet clients. It may also be where you store products, inventory or business supplies. The tax term is regular and exclusive business use. If you do this, you deduct a percentage of the household expenses (rent, interest, taxes, utilities, insurance, repairs, etc.) based on the square footage of the office ratioed to the home square footage. Expenses directly related to the office, such as a dedicated phone line, do not have to be ratioed. You can also take a small depreciation deduction for the home losing value (let your tax professional handle this—it's a pain!). The IRS "simplified" this, allowing you to take $5 for every square foot of Home Office, up to $1,500, but it's BS to call it simplifying, because any tax professional worth their salt is going to run the numbers both ways and take the number that makes the most sense.

9. Depreciation: Some items that you buy for your business, that have a useful life longer than a year will have to be depreciated over time rather than deducted all at once (examples include computers, digital cameras, machinery, big tools or office furniture). There are many options for deducting it up front but be wary of this. There are tripwires that can cost you if you dispose of something before it has passed its useful life. Talk about these items with your tax advisor.

10. The stuff you buy to sell: This can get tricky. If everything you sell is paid for and shipped through the company, it's easy, as discussed above about commissions. If you order the stuff, pay for it and either deliver it or ship it to the customer, you have to track the wholesale price, shipping, sales tax and the amount you received. Even worse, if you order items to keep on hand for later sale directly to customers, you need to track all the purchases you made (at your cost is my recommendation) and track what is sold and what is on hand. This is the devil called inventory. You need to know what you have on hand at the beginning and end of the year, what

you bought, and what you sold. The easiest way to do this is with an inventory notebook—now you have three notebooks. If you buy something to later sell, write it down with date, description and price paid. Have columns for date sold, and price sold for, and another column to make a note if it's disposed of without selling it (given away, used by yourself, or expired/lost/stolen). Track each item as it's sold or disposed of. At the end of the year, total everything left (that's Ending Inventory), everything bought during the year (that's Cost of Goods Sold), and everything sold (that's Gross Receipts). Ending Inventory this year becomes Beginning Inventory next year. If you sell some this way and some through the company on commission, you'll have to add commissions to your Gross Receipts, but I think you get the point. If I ran a business like this I would desperately try to avoid inventory; however, that might cost you some sales. Do what works best for you.

11. Taxes: These are mainly sales taxes. You need to work with your state or county to make sure you collect and remit sales taxes. Don't blow this off. Things get bad if you do. The sales tax you collect and remit is deductible if included in the price you charge, and the income you report. You also may need to pay business taxes and licensing fees to state/county/city. These are deductible, but you need to work these out on your own—this is an income tax guide, and these other taxes vary too much by locale to cover here. Again, don't screw these up. The local governments can be worse than the IRS if you mess up.

12. You also get to deduct 20% of your profit off of your taxable income. If you make less than $364,200 taxable income on your tax return (for Married Filing Jointly - $182,100 for almost everyone else) it's as simple as that. Actually, it's not simple at all, especially if you exceed the income limits we just discussed, but your tax pro or software should be able to handle it. If you make more than the limit above, your deduction will phase out unless you pay wages (or have a lot of equipment). I'm going to cover the details of that scenario in a single chapter: Do I Get the 20% Business Deduction?

There is a lot more that is deductible, but this list gets you started. I like to say that if it is required by law, makes you more money, or makes the business run better, it is PROBABLY deductible. When in doubt, record the expense and discuss it with your tax professional. Yes, you do need a tax pro if you are serious about your business.

Keep the record keeping up to date.I'm very serious about this! The best record keeping system in the world is USELESS if it isn't filled out in a timely manner. It's a nightmare to back fill. Work your butt off to generate business and make money. Research best practices and talk to the people making money doing this. The idea is to MAKE money, and then be pissed off that you are paying taxes on it. Getting a big tax deduction from your unprofitable business is only good at tax time. Paying taxes is a sign of success!

My Advice:

1. Avoid forming a partnership or S-Corporation until you are making a lot of money. If you apply for an Employer Identification Number, be careful to ensure you identify yourself as a single owner business.
2. Make sure you understand how your income is reported by your company. You need to understand what is included as income, what is not, and how they handle the commissions you pay. Bottom line, when the business income is calculated, after deductions, you want to make sure it represents the money YOU got, and nothing the company kept.
3. Get a separate bank account for the business. Have all income deposited into that account and pay all direct expenses out of it. Don't pay gas or home office expenses, as well as other expenses that are part personal out of this account. If you have a steady income from the business, make a transfer from the business account to your personal account monthly that represents a conservative, after tax profit. Leave everything else behind for taxes. Your tax pro can help you figure out what this monthly amount should be.
4. Keep Good Records! Use the Mile IQ app for mileage and don't miss any miles!
5. Focus on selling. The more you sell, the better you get at selling and the harder you work, the more you will make. The goal here is to make money and pay taxes. If you do not hate tax time because of how much you pay, you are not doing it right.
6. When practical, get business use only equipment such as laptops and phones. Also have a regular and exclusive use area for business in your home. This can be an office but can also be the place you store inventory and supplies. The bigger the better, within reason.
7. Don't buy into the absolute BS idea that your business is a method of generating tax losses to lower your taxes. If that is your plan, you're wrong and it is not okay. Don't buy stuff just to deduct it. That's a losing proposition. If your Upline focuses on tax deductions, they are a bad upline!

8. Be VERY skeptical of tax advice from your Upline. They should not be providing it and they should be advising you to seek expert advice. The advice is likely self-serving and inaccurate, and even if it is accurate, it might not be applicable to your situation. Remember, a good upline focuses on helping YOU make more money so THEY can make more money.

Military: If you live in military housing your office in home deduction might be minimal. Consider using the $5 per square foot safe harbor.

72. I am an Independent Contractor or I Got a Form 1099-NEC

2020 Change: Information for contractors was moved off of Form 1099-MISC and onto Form 1099-NEC (Non-employee compensation).

2021/2022 Change: For 2021 and 2022 ONLY, you can deduct 100% of meals with clients in restaurants.

Other updates: **Other updates**: There were a number of business provisions in the CARES Act passed as a response to the Coronavirus pandemic but the tax related ones were specific to businesses with employees and the rest of the business aspects, while significant in scope, were not tax related. That said, there is one credit for if you were unable to run or open your business due to COVID so if your municipality went in lockdown or placed other restrictions on business openings, you or your family got sick, your school or daycare shutdown, and this prevented you from working, check out the special 2020 chapter.

If you are just thinking about starting to do this, read the I Am Starting a Business chapter.

What is an independent contractor? For the purpose of this chapter, I'm considering an independent contractor as anyone who's paid for **work** on a Form 1099-NEC vice on a W-2, or who works for themselves and is paid cash (or check or credit card) by their customers. I say work because I'm not talking about an Engineer getting paid a few bucks for coaching softball. I am talking about someone who is in the business of doing the work they get paid for. This chapter is best used by someone who earns the majority of their income from the work they do that is paid in cash or via a 1099-NEC. If you are a painter who gets most of your money on a W-2 and gets a minor portion of their income on a 1099-NEC, this chapter can be helpful, but it's really not the prime focus. This chapter is also intentionally generic, so it can apply to a variety of businesses. Some specific businesses have their own chapters, so check the Table of Contents.

What does this chapter not do?

Foremost, it assumes you are either a Sole Proprietor, or a Single Member LLC. In other words, the business is reported on your personal tax return, vice the business filing its own tax return. There are advantages and disadvantages to forming other business entities, but those are best discussed face-to-face with a professional you trust. These are also covered in the <u>I Am Starting a Business</u> chapter.

Second, it is mostly for contractors who provide services, vice those who make or buy items to sell. There is some good information for them, but I won't be covering inventory or cost of goods sold.

Third, this is not a guide on how to do your taxes. It is actually a bunch of best practices I have found to make running your business easier, your taxes simpler, and your life better. It is not the only way to do things, but it is what I have found works best. I assume you either have a tax pro who does the tax return, or you are pretty smart and capable of using tax software yourself (though I recommend having a professional check it the first couple years - the money you spend on this can pay you back in spades, both in not paying excess taxes, and getting great advice for the future).

Fourth, it's for SMALL businesses. If you're approaching 7 figures of gross income, thinking about hiring employees, or bringing on a partner, get a professional CPA involved.

How does a 1099-NEC / cash business work for taxes?

You will be filing a Schedule C and reporting ALL income you receive, and then taking any legitimate deductions to come up with 'net' income. This is what you pay taxes on. You have to pay it all as you go, or at the end of the year when you file your tax return. Also, there's nobody to pay for Social Security taxes except, well, you. Most people are barely cognizant of the 7.65% that's taken right off the top for Medicare and Social Security taxes out of their paycheck. What even the most aware don't realize is that their employer matches this deduction! As a 1099 recipient (self-employed is the IRS term) you have to pay both the employee and employer portion! This means a 15.3% additional tax (technically a little less than 15% since it's not calculated on all of your income)! Imagine you're in the 22% tax bracket—that means you actually pay almost 37% in taxes! And this doesn't even cover the state taxes you might have to pay!

The good news is that, unlike a W-2 employee, you only pay these taxes on your 'net' income. This means you get to take all ordinary and necessary expenses off the top, before you pay a dime in taxes. Even employees with business expenses still pay their half of Social Security and Medicare taxes before any deductions. So, what is 'ordinary and necessary'? I like to boil it down into two main categories: 1. Things you pretty much have to pay, such as licensing, commissions and fees; 2. Things you pay because you expect them to increase your income or make running your business easier or more efficient. If the expense meets either of these requirements, they're pretty much a lock as being deductible.

Knowing the above, it's important that I give one of my biggest pieces of advice—you pretty much should NEVER do something just because you expect it to help on your taxes. Spend money only if you have to, or because it's the best idea for your business! This has two benefits:
1. You don't waste money on stupid stuff.
2. Chances are the deduction is legitimate.

So, what can I deduct?

Here's a non-exhaustive list: Supplies, rent, vehicle mileage, travel, bank fees, taxes, licensing, insurance, home office, office supplies, equipment, marketing, advertising, subcontractors, employees, postage, education, legal and professional expense, bank interest and much, much more. I'm going to give details on a few here:

Marketing Expenses: Business cards, website fees, posters, signs, sponsorships, commercials, advertising, pretty much anything you do to get someone to call YOU when they need your type of services.

Training, Education and Licensing: Whatever you pay to maintain your ability to do your business is deductible, as well as things you do to increase your skills or what you are allowed to do in your field. Classes, seminars, books and certificates mostly all qualify. Commercial Driver's License is another example.

Insurance: I'm not talking about homeowner's insurance here. I'm talking about "Oops! I screwed up and someone is suing me" insurance. Sometimes this is called Errors and Omissions Insurance, sometimes it's a liability bond, or a rider on your homeowner's insurance. Also, if you pay a rider to your car insurance for business use, the difference between that and regular insurance is deductible. There is also a self-employed health insurance deduction that allows you to deduct your health insurance costs if you have no other insurance source (if you can get insurance through your spouse's work this is a no-go).

Entertainment Expenses: Generally, if you expect the expense to result in a sale that makes you money, either immediately or in the future (whether it ultimately does or not doesn't matter, as long as you expect it to), it could be deductible. There are some restrictions on this, mainly about conflating personal and business expenses, or having "fun" and trying to deduct it. Be careful and honest with these expenses.

Travel Expenses: These are a toughie. People love conflating personal and business travel. If you travel to Maine to visit family and see the lobster festival and go to dinner with a client that is moving to your area, the trip is primarily personal. You can deduct expenses DIRECTLY RELATED to the meeting with the client, but little else. I recommend keeping business and personal travel separate. You can visit a friend for dinner on a three-day business trip, but don't do business for an hour on a three-day personal trip. Also avoid what I call BS travel. Flying to Vegas to assess potential markets is transparent vacationing disguised as business travel, especially if you spend 23 out of every 24 hours in the casino! Be reasonable! Go on trips that are going to increase your money-making potential. Stay away from any others. For legitimate travel, you get airfare, rental car, tips, taxis, laundry, internet and phone, as well as 50% of meals and any other reasonable and necessary expenses. Travel assumes overnight trips away from your home area. Remember, starting in 2018 and beyond, if it's fun, it might not be deductible.

Cell phones, laptops and tablets: Do yourself a favor, get a business only laptop, cell phone, tablet and/or computer. It is simply too difficult to calculate expenses on a part-personal and part-business electronic device. Don't share your business number with friends and family (other than wife and kids). If you keep everything separate, the deductions are easy and legitimate. If you don't, you have to establish a business use percentage, and worry about listed property rules—which suck!

Vehicle Expenses: Keep a mileage log. Let me say it again, unless you have a vehicle that is 100%, no kidding, total business and no personal use, keep a mileage log. Don't worry about gas, repairs, oil changes, insurance or any other car expenses (except as discussed above under insurance). There are other ways to track vehicle expenses, but mileage is the best. Do track annual car taxes and finance charges. The easiest mileage log is a notebook where you write the date, the trip purpose and the miles driven. You will also need to know the total miles the vehicle is driven for the year, so write the odometer reading down every January 1st! Mileage will be one of your biggest expenses, so keep track of it religiously! 10,000 miles of properly tracked vehicle mileage can result in $1,200 or even much more of tax savings! I love the MileIQ app that uses your phone for tracking mileage.

Home Office: Set aside a space in your home that is 100% business use. It should never be used for anything else, and regularly be used for business. This is where you keep your business records, your business computer or laptop, make your sales calls from and meet clients. The tax term is regular and exclusive business use. If you do this, you deduct a percentage of the household expenses (rent, interest, taxes, utilities, insurance, repairs, etc.) based on the square footage of the office ratioed to the home square footage. Expenses directly related to the office, such as a dedicated phone line, do not have to be ratioed. You can also take a small depreciation deduction for the home losing value (let your tax professional handle this—it's a pain!) The IRS "simplified" this, allowing you to take $5 for every square foot of Home Office, up to $1,500. However, it's BS to call it simplifying, because any tax professional worth their salt is going to run the numbers both ways and take the number that makes the most sense.

Depreciation: Some items that you buy for your business that have a useful life longer than a year will have to be depreciated over time rather than deducted all at once (examples include computers, digital cameras, machinery, big tools or office furniture). There are many options for deducting it up front but be wary of this: there are tripwires that can cost you if you dispose of something before it has passed its useful life. Talk about these items with your tax advisor.

Employees or Subcontractors: If you pay someone to do work for you in your business you can deduct it. Usually you will hire them as a subcontractor and may even pay them in cash (use a check!) If you pay them more than $600 in a year, you will need to issue them a 1099-NEC – see your tax pro about this as soon as you pay a subcontractor. If you want to hire regular employees, you will have to withhold taxes from their check. Get help with this! Make sure you talk with your tax pro about the difference between an employee and a contractor. If you call an employee a contractor, you could be in trouble. But if you just have a few guys that you call when you have excess work and they can decline to do the work, and you only pay them if they do the work, they are probably a contractor.

Qualified Business Income Deduction: You get to deduct 20% of your profit off of your taxable income. If you make less than $364,200 taxable income on your tax return (for Married Filing Jointly - $182,100 for almost everyone else) it's as simple as that. Actually, it's not simple at all, especially if you exceed the income limits we just discussed, but your tax pro or software should be able to handle it. If you make more than the limit above, your deduction will phase out unless you pay wages (or have a lot of equipment). I'm going to cover the details of that scenario in a single chapter: Do I Get the 20% Business Deduction?

Moving along. Here is the advice you need to make things work...

Record Keeping: This is where the rubber meets the road. Good record keeping will save you big time when it comes to tax time. Your records do not need to be extensive, but they do need to be accurate and useable. I hate double entry bookkeeping and would never recommend it as a tool for a home-based business. I also have found that the various bookkeeping software programs are virtually useless when it comes to taxes. They may help when it comes to managing the business, but they suck for doing taxes.

The best and easiest record keeping method I've found for small home-based businesses involves a small notebook, a big notebook and an envelope or box. The small notebook is for mileage, discussed below. The big notebook is for every other expense. You need simple columns set up: date, description, cost and payment received (if you pay something, it goes in the cost column, if you are paid it goes in the payment received column). You can add categories, but don't really need to. If you are unsure if something is deductible, write it down and let your tax professional tell you if it's deductible. The box/envelope is for receipts—just throw them in. Really? No sorting, categorizing or organizing? No. Simply put, your odds of ever needing them for an audit are slim to none. Save the box, notebooks and tax returns for 7 years, and then throw it all away. If you ever do get audited, there is plenty of time to sort through the box and organize it to match the notebooks—but why do it if it's not necessary? If I'm doing your taxes, I'm going to use the notebooks and remind you that you should have a receipt for everything. You don't have to prove things to me (though I may question unbelievable things).

It is important to not to over-think things. For example, if you make a sale involving sales tax, which you know a portion will go to the government, you still write down 100% of what you were paid (including the tax). Later, when you remit the sales tax to the government, it is entered as a payment (deduction). Get it—you get money, it is entered as income; you pay money, it is entered as a deduction.

Do I need a Separate Bank Account?

This one might be a little controversial, but I believe it's the be-all end-all of successful businesses. Combined with record keeping discussions above, and budgeting discussions below, this will make everything easier. Open a separate bank account for your business. It doesn't have to be in a different name, just separate from your personal business. If you use credit, get a second credit card that is exclusively for business (again, it doesn't have to actually be a business credit card, just one that you use only for business). Put all contractor business income in this account, and pay all business expenses out of it, or with the business credit card. Pay off the business credit card out of this account (don't carry a balance). The only expenses not paid out of the account are car expenses (especially gas) and home office expenses that will be divided based on square footage as discussed under home office above (utilities would not be paid out of the account, but office supplies and business-only cell phone would). The beauty of this method is that it simplifies budgeting, as we'll discuss below, and it allows reconciling of expenses to make sure your notebook covers everything. A good tax expert should be able to compare your account statements with your notebooks and know if you missed something (assuming you don't intermingle personal and business expenses). I can't over-emphasize how much of a fan I am of the extra bank account.

How do I Budget if my Income goes up and down?

Assuming you followed the advice from the previous section on bank accounts, you now have an account that is separate for business and you can start thinking about budgeting. Your income may fluctuate wildly, so you can use the business account to pay a "salary" to your personal account. I recommend letting some money build up in the business account until you have a feel for your income level. It will probably start small but build up over time. Once you have a good feel, you can pay yourself this "salary". The "salary" should be no more than 50% of your annual gross income or 60% of your net income (divide it by twelve obviously, to get the monthly amount). You need to play around with it. Start small and raise it if income exceeds expectations, but NEVER pay yourself more than 60% of net income unless you have a very low tax family situation.

Having a "salary" allows you to budget like you had a normal job. Keeping a buffer amount in the account allows you to have a "salary" even during lean months. By paying yourself a "salary" and saving the rest, if you have a really big month, you end up saving more, which in turn allows you to have the money to pay the tax bill that the big month will generate. When you file your taxes, you should have plenty of money to pay the tax bill, and still have money left to maintain a buffer. If you're lucky, you will have the ability to pay yourself a bonus to your personal account for a big purchase or vacation!

The reason "salary" is in quotes is because it's not really a salary. It's just you living on the profits from your business. None of the baggage that comes with real salaries applies to this (like W-2's and tax withholding). The "salary" will not come into play on your tax return.

Do I need to make Estimated Payments?

My advice is that you should use the budgeting advice above to pay your taxes. You'll still need to make estimated tax payments if you're making good money, but you should pay the minimum required to avoid an underpayment penalty. Your tax pro will calculate them for you, but to explain simply: you need to pay at least as much as your prior year's total tax liability in withholding or estimated taxes to avoid a penalty (oversimplified explanation, but really all you need to know). This is an easy calculation for your tax pro, who can set up quarterly payments and provide vouchers for paying them. (The timing is a little weird. You pay 4/15, 6/15, 9/15 and 1/15.) You can also pay varying payments to try to avoid a tax bill, but it gets complicated, and the government won't pay you interest. You can also make these payments online now, and it is really quite easy.

My Advice:

1. Avoid forming a partnership or S-Corporation until you are making a lot of money. If you apply for an Employer Identification Number, be careful to ensure you identify yourself as a single owner business.
2. Make sure you understand how your income is reported by your company. You need to understand what is included as income, what is not, and how they handle the commissions you pay. Bottom line, when the business income is calculated, after deductions, you want to make sure it represents the money YOU got, and nothing the company kept.
3. Get a separate bank account for the business. Have all income deposited into that account and pay all direct expenses out of it. Don't pay gas or home office expenses, as well as other expenses that are part personal out

of this account. If you have a steady income from the business, make a transfer from the business account to your personal account monthly that represents a conservative, after tax profit. Leave everything else behind for taxes. Your tax pro can help you figure out what this monthly amount should be.

4. Keep Good Records! Use the Mile IQ app for mileage and don't miss any miles!

5. Focus on making money. The more you work, the better you get at it and the harder you work, the more you will make. The goal here is to make money and pay taxes. If you don't hate tax time because of how much you pay, you are not doing it right.

6. When practical, get business use only equipment such as lap tops and phones. Also have a regular and exclusive use area for business in your home. This can be an office but can also be the place you store inventory and supplies. The bigger the better, within reason.

7. Make estimated payments such that you are guaranteed to avoid paying a penalty, and nothing more. Have money set aside as discussed above to cover the tax bill when you file. Pay attention! Set money aside! You should NEVER have a tax bill that you don't already have the money set aside to pay. Tax time should suck for a successful independent contractor, but only because you don't want to send them the money you have saved. It should never suck because you don't know how you are going to pay your tax bill.

Military: If you live in military housing your office in home deduction might be minimal. Consider using the $5 per square foot safe harbor.

73. I Drive for UBER (or other Taxi like business)

2021/2022 Change: For 2021 and 2022 ONLY, you can deduct 100% of meals with clients in restaurants.

Other updates: **Other updates**: There were a number of business provisions in the CARES Act passed as a response to the Coronavirus pandemic but the tax related ones were specific to businesses with employees and the rest of the business aspects, while significant in scope, were not tax related. That said, there is one credit for if you were unable to run or open your business due to COVID so if your municipality went in lockdown or placed other restrictions on business openings, you or your family got sick, your school or daycare shutdown, and this prevented you from working, check out the special 2020 chapter.

If you are just thinking about starting to do this, read the I Am Starting a Business chapter.

This Tax Guide is written with very specific information for UBER drivers of all types. It can be used by LYFT and other casual taxi drivers but may not have enough information for true professional non-web-based taxi drivers. Most clients I see trying these businesses out have not given a thought to taxes, but UBER does a fairly good job of helping out. The yearend statement you receive has a wealth of useful information. That said, there are a lot of deductions that aren't included that are a slam dunk, as well as some others that might be more shaky. As with all new business models, a lot of how these things apply specifically to UBER have not been fought out with the IRS, so some things may evolve over time. I'm going to start with a general discussion of things that every UBER driver should understand about taxes, and then get into the specifics of your documentation, and then get really specific on deductions.

First, some things you should know and understand:

1. Your business model is a bit unique, and you are doing some things that are fairly common in the tax world, but on a much higher scale than would normally be seen for a small business. You are using your own car for business, but the business side may be a very small percentage of the use of your car. Or, it might be a very large percentage – or all of it. Your car is now a business asset (in part or in whole) and thus there are potential implications when you buy, sell or trade it. Keep things simple by only

using one vehicle at a time and taking the standard mileage rate (discussed later).

2. You should be, at this point, a sole proprietor. This means that you own and run the business by yourself, with no employees. You will file the business taxes as a part of your personal taxes, usually on a Schedule C. I strongly encourage you not to have any partners, even your spouse. Your spouse can help, but should generally not be an employee, and not have any true decision-making power, except the power that is normal in a healthy spousal relationship (advice and support, but no "official" role). The reasons for this are myriad, and anyone who's delved into a partnership can attest to the issues that arise. For now, just trust me. Later you may want to form a more complicated business entity, but that will require professional assistance and guidance. If your spouse or partner also drives for UBER, they will have a separate and independent business, with its own Schedule C, and, hopefully, their own car. Co-mingling cars at this point will greatly complicate your taxes and probably seriously confuse your, or your preparer's, tax software.

3. You are going to spend more time doing taxes, and it's going to cost more. Even if you use software (which I highly discourage if you are running a business) you will pay more for the programs. Based on the returns I've done so far, the more you drive, the more likely it is that you will also generate taxable income after expenses. This income will be taxed at a much higher rate. 15.3% minimum for self-employment taxes (the self-employed person's Social Security and Medicare). The good news is, you only pay taxes on the profit. We'll talk more about budgeting for taxes later.

4. You might not actually be a business. There's some tension between Hobby and Business income. If you take losses year after year, the IRS may put the kabosh on taking a negative income from your business off of your regular taxable income. This is called Hobby Income. It means you do it more for fun than for profit. UBER recruiting has not helped with this, as they sell it more like a Hobby than a Business. As a Hobby, you still have to claim the income (on Line 21 - Other Income), and you cannot deduct expenses. Most UBER drivers will quickly find themselves turning a profit, making this a moot point. My advice is to go full bore, gung-ho towards making a profit for 3 years. File the Schedule C's and take the losses on your taxes (improving your refund). If, after three years, you haven't made a profit, and gross revenues aren't approaching 5 digits ($10,000), take real stock of where you're at. If revenues are growing and

profitability seems close, keep things going. If revenues are flat, profits are a distant dream, and/or your enthusiasm is waning, bite the bullet and either shut the business down, or tone it back and start filing as a hobby. Moving along. Here's the advice you need to make things work...

Income: This is the easy part. UBER will issue you a 1099-K and (maybe) a 1099-MISC/1099-NEC. The 1099-K reports the income from all the rides you gave and the 1099-MISC/1099-NEC reports all other income. You just need the totals from these, though some software lets you enter the whole form and pulls the relevant data. Box 1a of the 1099-K and the amounts from your 1099-MISC/1099-NEC are your Gross Receipts for your Schedule C. I've seen UBER drivers that took tips, and others that did not. If you get tips, add them to these amounts. Any other income you make as a driver should also be added, but I think UBER frowns on this.

Record Keeping: This is usually the biggest deal for a small business, but for UBER it should be very simple. Keep a mileage log!!!!! We will discuss mileage below but, know this, the one piece of information from UBER you should ignore is the mileage number - this is where you will save the most in taxes. (There are some great phone Apps available on the web for this. MileIQ is my favorite.) Other than that, have a notebook and an envelope for receipts. When you make a purchase for the business, write down date, description and cost, if you get income not tracked by UBER, add it here as well. Throw the receipt in the envelope. You can add categories, but don't really need to, if you're unsure something's deductible, write it down and let your tax guy tell you if it's deductible. That's it. Really? No sorting, categorizing or organizing? No. Simply put, your odds of ever needing them for an audit are slim to none. Save the box, notebook, mileage log and tax returns for 7 years, and then throw it all away. If you ever get audited, there's plenty of time to sort through the box and organize it to match the notebooks - but why do it if it's not necessary. If I'm doing your taxes I'm going to use the notebooks and remind you that you should have a receipt for everything. You don't have to prove things to me. It's important to understand not to over think things. You get money, it's entered as income, you pay money, it's entered as a deduction. Keep in mind that UBER will report every penny you make, and then give you a report of deductions they took off. This is the easy part. For a lot of people, especially casual drivers, these will be all the deductions they have - except for the mileage log that you MUST have. You can use UBER's mileage, but you'll be leaving your best deduction on the table (or in the car!)

Expenses: You can deduct any ordinary and necessary expenses for your business. I generally describe the requirements like this: If it will make you more money, is required by someone in authority, or makes your business more efficient or your life as a businessperson easier, it's probably deductible. The list below is actually a fairly exhaustive list of normal business deductions, tailored to UBER. Some won't apply at all, but I'm leaving them there to stimulate your own thoughts. First some things most UBER drivers could or should be deducting (details in the numbered lists): Mileage, any tolls, parking or access fees not included in the UBER statement, driving gloves, insurance riders, office supplies for the business, steering wheel covers, car equipment specifically for driving passengers that is not normal car equipment or maintenance, mileage tracking apps or equipment, business cards, commercial driver's license, car seat additions that help for long driving, and a percentage of cell phone bills if you use your cell phone for the UBER app. Also any safety clothing or equipment that would not be considered normal for a car that was not used for driving paying passengers. Examples might be first aid kit, flares, fire extinguisher, or a reflective vest. Some might argue that these are normal for a regular driver, but how many people do you know that have these in their car? I would deduct them. Second, things you should not be deducting: Car maintenance including car washing, oil changes, gas, repairs or any other vehicle expenses unless they are specific alterations or additions to allow you to drive commercially (the mileage deduction covers all these things). Meals and entertainment would be unlikely. Uniforms or clothing would not be deductible, though possibly dry cleaning of a specific set of "driving clothes" - this would be shaky.

Here's the exhaustive list:

1. Pretty much anything the company charges you for. If they deduct it off your commission check, deduct it off your taxes (you report the gross commission, not the commission after deductions). These are all the deduction numbers listed on your annual UBER tax summary (except the income, of course). They generally fit into nice categories on your Schedule C, mostly as commissions.

2. Marketing Expenses: I'm thinking most of this will be handled by UBER, but if you spend money for business cards, signage, websites, etc, these will be deductible. I'm guessing you might have some for finding new drivers for UBER and getting the referral fee, though I'm not sure you should be recruiting your own competition.

3. Insurance: I'm not talking about homeowner's insurance here. I'm talking about 'oops I screwed up and someone is suing me insurance.' There's a lot of argument right now as to whether your personal car insurance is good enough for the business, and I'm the wrong guy to answer the question (tax guy - not insurance guy. See how that works? Don't take tax advice from a non-tax guy, and don't take investment or insurance advice from your tax guy (except as how it relates to taxes). That said, if you have just regular, personal car insurance - no deduction. If you pay extra for commercial insurance, or a rider for commercial use, or a special 'UBER' rider that some companies are providing, that cost is deductible.

4. Entertainment and Meal Expenses: Starting in 2018, most of this will be deductible. The basic rule now is that if it's fun, it's not deductible. You really shouldn't have any of these. Your meals aren't deductible, even when waiting for a customer. I also can't really envision you taking someone to lunch. Since UBER provides the customers, this is a no-go. Some drivers have had mints or such in the car - I call those supplies (and they are deductible). I guess theoretically you might take a potential driver to lunch to talk to them about driving for UBER in hopes of getting the referral fee. In that case, save the receipt and write the person's name, and the topic of discussion on the receipt. That would be deductible entertainment expense - don't abuse this.

5. Travel Expenses: Unless UBER starts running those educational seminars that the IRS hates, you won't have much of this. I guess theoretically, you might drive to a big metropolis for a special event so you can make boatloads of money, so I guess we'll talk about it. If you travel specifically to drive and make money for UBER, you can deduct airfare (though how would you get your car there?), car rental (I guess you could rent a car and drive it, but I'll bet that violates a lot of terms of use), lodging, mileage, meals, tips, tolls and other necessary travel expenses. For meals, you can take a standard Federal daily rate for the area you are in (google 'per diem rates' and you'll find a list). If the travel is not 100% for business - like you visit family and do a few rides, or drive to Vegas or New York City for a long weekend and some shows and do some driving while you're there - it gets complicated. You can take a portion of the travel based on the percentage of time spent "on the clock" for UBER.

6. Cell phones, laptops and tablets: You can take a portion of the phone and data costs for the phone you use for UBER. Ratio based on time or data usage. Don't go crazy figuring the exact ratio. If you do a lot of

driving, or it's your main source of income, you may want to get a business only phone, and/or laptop. You can take a portion of your personal stuff, but it might not be worth it unless the ratio is high. We'll talk about business use of home later. The purchase of laptops or phones that you use for business generally requires them to be depreciated (taking a portion every year for several years.) Your tax professional or software should handle this, but make sure you put the information in right.

7. Vehicle Expenses: Keep a mileage log. Let me say it again, unless you have a vehicle that is 100%, no s**t, total business and no personal use, keep a mileage log. Don't worry about gas, repairs, oil changes, insurance or any other car expenses (except as discussed above under insurance). There are other ways to track vehicle expenses, but mileage is the best. Do track annual car taxes and finance charges. The easiest mileage log is a notebook where you right the date, the trip purpose and the miles driven. You will also need to know the total miles the vehicle is driven for the year, so write the odometer reading down every January 1st! Mileage will be one of your biggest expenses, so keep track of it religiously! 10,000 miles of properly tracked vehicle mileage can result in $1200 of tax savings! UBER only tracks miles with passengers. If you're "on the clock" driving around waiting for a call, driving to or from a pickup, or driving to do other things to support your business - write it down! You pretty much get no other deductions for the vehicle, but the mileage deduction is very generous. I like the MileIQ app for tracking miles using my phone.

8. Home Office: If your business is getting big, set aside a space in your home that is 100% business use. Never used for anything else, and regularly used for business. This is where you keep your business records, your business computer or laptop, and do other business-related things. The tax term is regular and exclusive business use. If you do this, you deduct a percentage of the household expenses - rent, interest, taxes, utilities, insurance, repairs, etc, based on the square footage of the office ratioed to the home square footage. Expenses directly related to the office, such as a dedicated phone line; do not have to be ratioed. You can also take a small depreciation deduction for the home losing value (let your tax guy handle this - it's a b**ch!) The IRS "simplified" this, allowing you to take $5 for every square foot of Home Office, up to $1500, but it's BS to call it simplifying, because any tax guy worth their salt is going to run the numbers both ways and take the number that makes the most sense.

9. Depreciation: Some items that you buy for your business, that have a useful life longer than a year will have to be depreciated over time rather

than deducted all at once (examples include computers, digital cameras, machinery, big tools or office furniture). There are many options for deducting it up front, but be wary of this, there are tripwires that can cost you if you dispose of something before it has passed its useful life. Talk about these items with your tax advisor.

10. Licenses: If you get a commercial driver's license, that is deductible. If you have to pay for special licenses, tags, access fees or other things to let you pick up passengers in an area or work in an area, those are deductible. UBER pays some of these for you and accounts for them on your statement, so don't double deduct!

11. Taxes: Unlikely, but sales or other taxes may come into play in some super psycho jurisdictions. UBER should handle this, but don't assume they do. You also may need to pay business taxes and licensing fees to State/County/City. These are deductible, but you need to work these out on your own - this is an income tax guide, and these other taxes vary too much by locale to cover here. Again, don't screw these up. The local governments can be worse than the IRS if you mess up.
There's more that's deductible, but I think you get the idea.

12. Qualified Business Income Deduction: You get to deduct 20% of your profit off of your taxable income. If you make less than $364,200 taxable income on your tax return (for Married Filing Jointly - $182,100 for almost everyone else) it's as simple as that. Actually, it's not simple at all, especially if you exceed the income limits we just discussed, but your tax pro or software should be able to handle it. If you make more than the limit above, your deduction will phase out unless you pay wages (or have a lot of equipment). I'm going to cover the details of that scenario in a single chapter: Do I Get the 20% Business Deduction?

Do I need a Separate Bank Account? This one might be a little controversial, but I believe it's the be all end all of successful businesses. Once your business really gets going, and is more than just a little side income, it's this, combined with record keeping discussions above, and budgeting discussions below, this will make everything easier.

Open a separate bank account for your business. It doesn't have to be in a different name, just separate from your personal business. If you use credit, get a second credit card that is exclusively for business (again, it doesn't have to actually be a business credit card, just one that you use only for business). Put all business income in this account, and pay all business expenses out of it, or with the business credit card. Pay off the business credit card out of this account. The only expenses not paid out of the account are car expenses (especially gas) and home office expenses that will be divided based on square footage as discussed under home office above (utilities would not be paid out of the account, but office supplies and business only cell phone would).

The beauty of this method is that it simplifies budgeting as we'll discuss below, and it allows reconciling of expenses to make sure your notebook covers everything. A good tax expert should be able to compare your account statements with your notebooks and know if you missed something (assuming you don't intermingle personal and business expenses).

How do I Budget if my Income goes up and down? Assuming you followed the advice from the previous section on bank accounts, you now have an account that is separate for business and you can start thinking about budgeting. Your income may fluctuate wildly, so you can use the business account to pay a "salary" to your personal account. I recommend letting some money build up in the business account until you have a feel for your income level. It will probably start small but build up over time. Once you have a good feel, you can pay yourself this "salary". The "salary" should be no more than 50% of your annual gross income or 60% of your net income (divide it by twelve obviously, to get the monthly amount). You need to play around with it. Start small and raise it if income exceeds expectations, but NEVER pay yourself more than 60% of net income unless you have a very low tax family situation.

Having a "salary" allows you to budget like you had a normal job. Keeping a buffer amount in the account allows you to have a "salary" even during lean months. By paying yourself a "salary" and saving the rest, if you have a really big month, you end up saving more, which in turn allows you to have the money to pay the tax bill that the big month will generate. When you file your taxes, you should have plenty of money to pay the tax bill, and still have money left to maintain a buffer. If you're lucky, you will have the ability to pay yourself a bonus to your personal account for a big purchase or vacation!

The reason "salary" is in quotes is because it is not really a salary. It's just you living on the profits from your business. Salary implies payroll and tax withholding and we aren't doing ANY of that here. None of the baggage that comes with real salaries applies to this (like W-2's and tax withholding). The "salary" will not come into play on your tax return.

Do I need to make Estimated Payments? My advice is that you should use the budgeting advice above to pay your taxes. You'll still need to make estimated tax payments if you're making good money, but you should pay the minimum required to avoid an underpayment penalty. Your tax advisor will calculate them for you, but to explain simply: you need to pay at least as much as your prior year's total tax liability in withholding or estimated taxes to avoid a penalty (oversimplified explanation, but really all you need to know). This is an easy calculation for your tax guy and he will set up quarterly payments and provide vouchers for paying them. (The timing is a little weird. You pay on 4/15, 6/15, 9/15 and 1/15.) You can also pay varying payments to try to avoid a tax bill, but it gets complicated, and the government will not pay you interest.

That's all! Keep the record keeping up to date. It's a nightmare to back fill. Work your ass off to generate business and make money. Research best practices and talk to the people making money doing this. The idea is to MAKE money, and then be pissed off that you are paying taxes on it. Getting a big tax deduction from your unprofitable business is only good at tax time. Paying taxes is a sign of success!

My Advice:

1. Avoid forming a partnership or S-Corporation until you are making a lot of money. If you apply for an Employer Identification Number, be careful to ensure you identify yourself as a single owner business.
2. Get a separate bank account for the business. Have all income deposited into that account and pay all direct expenses out of it. Don't pay gas or home office expenses, as well as other expenses that are part personal out of this account. If you have a steady income from the business, make a transfer from the business account to your personal account monthly that represents a conservative, after tax profit. Leave everything else behind for taxes. Your tax pro can help you figure out what this monthly amount should be.
3. Keep Good Records! Use a mileage app for mileage and don't miss any miles!
4. Focus on making money. The more you work, the better you get at it and the harder you work, the more you will make. The goal here is to make money and pay taxes. If you don't hate tax time because of how much you pay, you are not doing it right.

5. Make estimated payments such that you are guaranteed to avoid paying a penalty, and nothing more. Have money set aside as discussed above to cover the tax bill when you file. Pay attention! Set money aside! You should NEVER have a tax bill that you don't already have the money set aside to pay. Tax time should suck for a successful independent contractor, but only because you don't want to send them the money you have saved. It should never suck because you don't know how you are going to pay your tax bill.

6. Double-check the numbers reported to you by the company. Mileage will almost certainly be wrong, but you also want to verify the other numbers are at least close. They might be a little off due to differences in how things are counted as the year rolls over, but they should be in the ballpark.

74. I am (or will be) a Real Estate Agent

2021/2022 Change: For 2021 and 2022 ONLY, you can deduct 100% of meals with clients in restaurants.

Other updates: There were a number of business provisions in the CARES Act passed as a response to the Coronavirus pandemic but the tax related ones were specific to businesses with employees and the rest of the business aspects, while significant in scope, were not tax related. That said, there is one credit for if you were unable to run or open your business due to COVID so if your municipality went in lockdown or placed other restrictions on business openings, you or your family got sick, your school or daycare shutdown, and this prevented you from working, check out the special 2020 chapter.

If you are just thinking about starting to do this, read the I Am Starting a Business chapter.

So, you've got your real estate agents license and that first commission is finally on the way. No way around it now, you have potentially taxable income. The question is, how much? And, how do you pay as little as possible? This chapter assumes that you will be paid on a 1099-NEC, as a self-employed Real Estate Agent. If you're getting a W-2, some of this will be useful, but not all. I'm also assuming that you work for a real estate company and aren't completely independent. Much of this advice isn't gospel, it's just what I've seen and think works best. In some ways, it's a list of "best practices." As always, you should use this post as a starting point, and seek professional assistance when it comes to your personal situation. I am also going to assume you have not formed a complex business entity such as an S Corporation or Multi Member Limited Liability Corporation. There are benefits and disadvantages to these, but you need to talk to a professional to understand them.

I'm going to start with some basics, and then get into details. The first big surprise you will have is that nobody is taking taxes out of your paycheck. You have to pay it all as you go, or at the end of the year when you file your tax return. The second thing is that there's nobody to pay for Social Security taxes except, well, you. Most people are barely cognizant of the 7.65% that's taken right off the top for Medicare and Social Security taxes out of their paycheck. What even the most aware don't realize is that their employer matches this deduction! As a 1099 recipient (self-employed is the IRS term) you have to pay both the employee and employer portion!

This means a 15.3% additional tax (technically slightly less than 15% since not all of your income is subject to this tax). Imagine you're in the 15% tax bracket—that means you actually pay almost 30% in taxes! And this doesn't even cover state taxes!

The good news is that, unlike a W-2 employee, you only pay these taxes on your 'net' income. This means you get to take all ordinary and necessary expenses off the top, before you pay a dime in taxes. Even employees with business expenses still pay their half of Social Security and Medicare taxes before any deductions. So, what is 'ordinary and necessary'?
I like to boil it down into two categories:
1. Things you pretty much have to pay such as licensing, commissions and fees.
2. Things you pay because you expect them to increase your income or make your business easier to run or more efficient.
If they meet either of these requirements, they're pretty much a lock as being deductible.

Knowing the above, it's important to tell you one of my biggest pieces of advice— you pretty much should NEVER do something just because you expect it to help on your taxes. Spend money only if you have to, or because it's the best idea for your business! This has two benefits:
1. You don't waste money on stupid stuff.
2. Chances are the deduction is legitimate.

So now comes the part you've been waiting for: What the heck can I deduct? Here is a non-exhaustive list, with some details, to get you started:

Marketing Expenses: Business cards, website fees, MLS dues, lead-generating expenses, posters, signs, sponsorships, commercials, advertising, pretty much anything you do to get someone to call YOU when they want to buy or sell a house. As a non-tax aside, you need to evaluate these carefully, and talk to experienced agents to find the best of these. Your commissions are big but come infrequently. You need to understand how much you spend for each commission so you can properly evaluate what works best.

Gifts and Referral Rewards: Gifts to clients are generally limited to $25 per person, per year. (That's the deductible amount, you can give more.) Be careful of referral fees. You should have received more training on this than me to get your license, but I will simply remind you that there are varying rules from state to state, as well as RESPA requirements that restrict what amounts, how and to whom you may pay a referral fee—check with your senior brokers before paying these. If the referral fees are legal, there are ways to deduct them, but talk to your tax professional about them.

Training, Education and Licensing: Whatever you pay to maintain your ability to be an agent is deductible, as well as things you do to increase your skills or what you are allowed to do in your field. Classes, seminars, books and certificates mostly all qualify.

Insurance: I'm not talking about homeowner's insurance here. I'm talking about "Oops! I screwed up and my client is suing me" insurance; or someone who's not my client is suing me. Sometimes this is called Errors and Omissions Insurance. If your state or agency doesn't require it, get it anyway! Also, if you pay a rider to your car insurance for business use, the difference between that and regular insurance is deductible. You also might have Workman's Compensation insurance or insurance for your non-home office. There is also a self-employed health insurance deduction that allows you to deduct your health insurance costs if you have no other insurance source (if you can get insurance through your spouse's work this is a no-go).

Entertainment Expenses: Eventually you'll be with a client, or potential client, and pick up the tab for lunch, dinner, or drinks. Generally, if you expect the expense to result in a sale that makes you money, either immediately or in the future (whether it ultimately does or not doesn't matter, as long as you expect it to), it's deductible. I recommend writing the name of the client on the receipt, as well as a quick description, such as "house hunting," "referral source," or "potential client."

Travel Expenses: These are a toughie. People love conflating personal and business travel. If you travel to Maine to visit family and see the lobster festival and go to dinner with a client that is moving to your area, the trip is primarily personal. You can deduct expenses DIRECTLY RELATED to the meeting with the client, but little else. I recommend keeping business and personal travel separate. You can visit a friend for dinner on a three-day business trip, but don't do business for an hour on a three-day personal trip. Also avoid what I call BS travel. Flying to Vegas to assess potential real estate markets is transparent vacationing disguised as business travel, especially if you spend 23 out of every 24 hours in the casino! Be reasonable! Go on trips that are going to increase your money-making potential. Stay away from any others. For legitimate travel, you get airfare, rental car, tips, taxis, laundry, internet and phone, as well as 50% of meals and any other reasonable and necessary expenses. Travel assumes overnight trips away from your home area. Remember, starting in 2018 and beyond, if it's fun, it's not deductible.

Cell phones, laptops and tablets: Do yourself a favor, get a business-only laptop, cell phone, tablet and/or computer. It is simply too difficult to calculate expenses on a part-personal and part-business electronic device. Don't share your business number with friends and family (other than wife and kids). If you keep everything separate, the deductions are easy and legitimate. If you don't, you have to establish a business use percentage, and worry about listed property rules—which suck!

Vehicle Expenses: Keep a mileage log. Let me say it again, unless you have a vehicle that is 100%, no s**t, total business and no personal use, keep a mileage log. Don't worry about gas, repairs, oil changes, insurance or any other car expenses (except as discussed above under insurance). There are other ways to track vehicle expenses, but mileage is the best. Do track annual car taxes and finance charges. The easiest mileage log is a notebook where you write the date, the trip purpose and the miles driven. You will also need to know the total miles the vehicle is driven for the year, so write the odometer reading down every January 1st! Mileage will be one of your biggest expenses, so keep track of it religiously! 10,000 miles of properly tracked vehicle mileage can result in $1,200 or more of tax savings! I prefer using my phone and the MileIQ app to track my miles.

Home Office: Set aside a space in your home that is 100% business use. It should never be used for anything else, and regularly be used for business. This is where you keep your business records, your business computer or laptop, make your sales calls from and meet clients. The tax term is regular and exclusive business use. If you do this, you deduct a percentage of the household expenses (rent, interest, taxes, utilities, insurance, repairs, etc.) based on the square footage of the office ratioed to the home square footage. Expenses directly related to the office, such as a dedicated phone line, do not have to be ratioed. You can also take a small depreciation deduction for the home losing value (let your tax professional handle this—it's a pain!) The IRS "simplified" this, allowing you to take $5 for every square foot of Home Office, up to $1,500, but it's BS to call it simplifying. Any tax professional worth their salt is going to run the numbers both ways and take the number that makes the most sense.

Qualified Business Income Deduction: You get to deduct 20% of your profit off of your taxable income. If you make less than $364,200 taxable income on your tax return (for Married Filing Jointly - $182,100 for almost everyone else) it's as simple as that. Actually, it's not simple at all, especially if you exceed the income limits we just discussed, but your tax pro or software should be able to handle it. If you make more than the limit above, your deduction will phase out unless you pay wages (or have a lot of equipment). I'm going to cover the details of that scenario in a single chapter: <u>Do I Get the 20% Business Deduction?</u>

Employer Reported Expenses: In many cases your employer is going to charge you for a number of different things, such as marketing and insurance. They will generally track the expenses and then deduct them from your commission check when you make a sale or broker a purchase. Virtually everything they charge you for will be deductible, but they will report the full amount of your commission on the 1099-MISC at the end of the year, and then give you a report of what they charged you. This simplifies things for record keeping, except that you need to make sure not to deduct something from the employer report twice by tracking it in your own records.

Depreciation: Some items that you buy for your business that have a useful life longer than a year will have to be depreciated over time rather than deducted all at once (examples include computers, digital cameras or office furniture). There are many options for deducting it up front, but be wary of this. There are tripwires that can cost you if you dispose of something before it has passed its useful life. Talk about these items with your tax advisor.

Record Keeping: This is where the rubber meets the road. Good record keeping will save you when it comes to tax time. Your records don't need to be extensive, but they do need to be accurate and useable. I hate double entry bookkeeping and would never recommend it as a tool for a Real Estate Agent. I also have found that the various bookkeeping software programs are virtually useless when it comes to taxes. They may help when it comes to managing the business, but they suck for doing taxes. The best and easiest record keeping method I've found for Real Estate Agents involves a small notebook, a big notebook and an envelope or box. The small notebook is for mileage, discussed above. The big notebook is for every other expense (except employer reported expenses.) You need simple columns set up: date, expense and cost. You can add categories, but don't really need to. If you're unsure something's deductible, write it down and let your tax professional tell you if it's deductible. The box/envelope is for receipts—just throw them in. Really? No sorting, categorizing or organizing? No. Simply put, your odds of ever needing them for an audit are slim to none. Save the box, notebooks and tax returns for 7 years, and then throw it all away. If you ever do get audited, there's plenty of time to sort through the box and organize it to match the notebooks—why do it if it's not necessary? If I'm doing your taxes I'm going to use the notebooks and remind you that you should have a receipt for everything. You don't have to prove things to me.

Separate Bank Account: This one might be a little controversial, but I believe it's the be-all end-all of successful businesses. Combined with record keeping discussions above, and budgeting discussions below, this will make everything easier.

Open a separate bank account for your Real Estate Agent business. It doesn't have to be in a different name, just separate from your personal account. If you use credit, get a second credit card that is exclusively for business (again, it doesn't have to actually be a business credit card, just one that you use only for business). Put all Real Estate income in this account, and pay all Real Estate expenses out of it, or with the business credit card. Pay off the business credit card out of this account (don't carry a balance). The only expenses not paid out of the account are car expenses (especially gas) and home office expenses. Home office expenses will be divided based on square footage as discussed under home office above (utilities would not be paid out of the account, but office supplies and business only cell phone would).

The beauty of this method is that it simplifies budgeting as we'll discuss below, and it allows reconciling of expenses to make sure your notebook covers everything. A good tax expert should be able to compare your account statements with your notebooks and know if you missed something (assuming you don't intermingle personal and business expenses).

Budgeting and Saving: Assuming you followed the advice from the previous section on bank accounts, you now have an account that is separate for business and you can start thinking about budgeting. Your income may fluctuate wildly, so you can use the business account to pay a "salary" to your personal account. I recommend letting some money build up in the business account until you have a feel for your income level. It will probably start small but build up over time. Once you have a good feel, you can pay yourself this "salary". The "salary" should be no more than 50% of your annual gross income or 60% of your net income (divide it by twelve obviously, to get the monthly amount). You need to play around with it. Start small and raise it if income exceeds expectations, but NEVER pay yourself more than 60% of net income unless you have a very low tax family situation.

Having a "salary" allows you to budget like you had a normal job. Keeping a buffer amount in the account allows you to have a "salary" even during lean months. By paying yourself a "salary" and saving the rest, if you have a really big month, you end up saving more, which in turn allows you to have the money to pay the tax bill that the big month will generate. When you file your taxes, you should have plenty of money to pay the tax bill, and still have money left to maintain a buffer. If you're lucky, you will have the ability to pay yourself a bonus to your personal account for a big purchase or vacation!

The reason "salary" is in quotes is because it's not really a salary. It's just you living on the profits from your business. None of the baggage that comes with real salaries applies to this (like W-2's and tax withholding). The "salary" will not come into play on your tax return.

Estimated Payments: My advice is that you should use the budgeting advice above to pay your taxes. You'll still need to make estimated tax payments if you're making good money, but you should pay the minimum required to avoid an underpayment penalty. Your tax advisor will calculate them for you, but to explain simply: you need to pay at least as much as your prior year's total tax liability in withholding or estimated taxes to avoid a penalty (oversimplified explanation, but really all you need to know). This is an easy calculation for your tax professional, who will set up quarterly payments and provide vouchers for paying them. (The timing is a little weird. You pay 4/15, 6/15, 9/15 and 1/15.) You can also pay varying payments to try to avoid a tax bill, but it gets complicated, and the government will not pay you interest. You can also now make these payments online, which makes things easier.

My Advice:

1. Avoid forming a partnership or S-Corporation until you are making a lot of money. If you apply for an Employer Identification Number, be careful to ensure you identify yourself as a single owner business.

2. Make sure you understand how your income is reported by your company. You need to understand what is included as income, what is not, and how they handle the commissions you pay. Bottom line, when the business income is calculated, after deductions, you want to make sure it represents the money YOU got, and nothing the company kept.

3. Get a separate bank account for the business. Have all income deposited into that account and pay all direct expenses out of it. Don't pay gas or home office expenses, as well as other expenses that are part personal out of this account. If you have a steady income from the business, make a transfer from the business account to your personal account monthly that represents a conservative, after tax profit. Leave everything else behind for taxes. Your tax pro can help you figure out what this monthly amount should be.

4. Keep Good Records! Use the Mile IQ app for mileage and don't miss any miles!

5. Focus on making money. The more you work, the better you get at it and the harder you work, the more you will make. The goal here is to make money and pay taxes. If you don't hate tax time because of how much you pay, you are not doing it right.

6. When practical, get business use only equipment such as lap tops and phones. Also have a regular and exclusive use area for business in your home. This can be an office but can also be the place you store inventory and supplies. The bigger the better, within reason.

7. Make estimated payments such that you are guaranteed to avoid paying a penalty, and nothing more. Have money set aside as discussed above to cover the tax bill when you file. Pay attention! Set money aside! You should NEVER have a tax bill that you don't already have the money set aside to pay. Tax time should suck for a successful independent contractor, but only because you don't want to send them the money you have saved. It should never suck because you don't know how you are going to pay your tax bill.

Military: If you live in military housing your office in home deduction might be minimal. Consider using the $5 per square foot safe harbor.

75. I am an Artist (Tailored to Painters)

2021/2022 Change: For 2021 and 2022 ONLY, you can deduct 100% of meals with clients in restaurants.

Other updates: There were a number of business provisions in the CARES Act passed as a response to the Coronavirus pandemic but the tax related ones were specific to businesses with employees and the rest of the business aspects, while significant in scope, were not tax related. That said, there is one credit for if you were unable to run or open your business due to COVID so if your municipality went in lockdown or placed other restrictions on business openings, you or your family got sick, your school or daycare shutdown, and this prevented you from working, check out the special 2020 chapter.

If you are just thinking about starting to do this, read the I Am Starting a Business chapter.

This is a simplified discussion of some questions an artist might have with regard to how taxes work. It is not comprehensive, since that could be a whole other book (maybe later). It should get you started with some of the big questions, and help you understand how to keep records and prepare for the tax return. You should read the I'm an Independent Contractor chapter for a deeper discussion of business expenses.

The most important question: Is this a hobby or a business?

The IRS cares about this as it affects nearly every aspect of how the income and expenses are reported. Since many people paint for fun, there is an entering assumption that this could be a hobby (people don't pump septic systems for fun so they have an easier time with this question). A hobby must report its income, but cannot deduct expenses. Being a hobby is not ideal, and it's relatively easy to avoid being categorized as one, at least initially. If your goal is to make money painting, work the hell out of it for three years, and then do a real hard look at where you are. Decide if you want to keep trying to make a profit (if you aren't yet) and make changes to get you oriented in the right direction. Otherwise, quit or scale back to hobby level. Making a taxable profit regularly eliminates the hobby concern.

The IRS uses a number of questions to determine if it is a hobby or business, but I have distilled them to the more important ones that are applicable to a painter:

1. Are you trying to make a profit? The IRS will assume this is yes if you make a profit in at least 3 of the last 5 years (including the current one.)
2. Does the time and effort you are putting into the activity indicate a profit motive?
3. Do you rely on income from the activity?
4. Have you made changes to improve profitability?
5. How much effort are you putting into selling the paintings?

You don't need to have a perfect answer to all of them, but the totality of the situation will be used to make the determination. Bottom line - do your best to make a profit and it will generally be considered for profit.

Next question: What accounting method to use?

The answer will be cash, accrual or hybrid (probably hybrid). In general, a painter will use the hybrid method since they produce a good for sale and will generally have an inventory of unsold paintings and supplies for painting. This means you use cash method for everything except your product. Cash method is easy, when you get the money, you claim the income. When you spend money, you record the expense. Getting a check, giving a check or charging your credit card fix the point at which you have "gotten" or "given" money. You cannot delay cashing a check to avoid recognizing income. The only way you would generally use the cash method of accounting is if you paint only for individual commission where you paint only what you will be paid for. The accrual method accounts for inventory and expenses by "accruing" it based on all events occurring that fix the amount and the "right" to pay or receive it. For example, you sell a painting to an individual for $500 on 12/22/2022 and ship the painting to him with a bill on 12/23/2022. He sends you a check on 1/2/2023 which you deposit on 1/5/2023. The income would be counted in 2022 since you had done everything that entitled you to payment. Most painters use accrual for inventory items (things you make to sell and the things you put into those items to create them – paint, canvas, and finished paintings for example) and cash for everything else.

Next Question: What records do I keep?

For a painter, you would need to keep records of all income and expenses related to the business. I always recommend having a separate checking account and/or credit card for the business. This makes record keeping significantly easier. All transactions should be tracked in a ledger (this doesn't have to be fancy, it just needs to work so that you can track what's coming in and going out.) For a painter, this can be as simple as a chronological list of transactions:

1/2/23 Paid $275 for paint and brushes at Michaels
1/3/23 Sold painting, "Sunset" for $500 to Art Luvr
1/7/23 Paid $45 for drop cloth at Lowe's

Or it can be a detailed tracker with columns for expenses, supplies, income etc. The bottom line is that you need to be able to reconstruct your income and expenses. Receipts for each expense and sale must also be kept. You can have a detailed filing system or you can put them in an envelope attached to your ledger.

You also need to keep a log of mileage driven related to the business. You can do this in conjunction with your ledger or as a separate log. The advantage of doing it with the ledger is that the mileage is linked with the action it's related to which makes it easier to prove it's related to the business.

Last Question: How does the tax return work?

The first thing we will do is total up all of the income. This is every penny you were paid for painting or other related services. This is your business's **Gross Income.**

The next thing we'll do is figure out the **Gross Profit.** This is **Gross Income** minus **Cost of Goods Sold.** To calculate Cost of Goods Sold you do the following:

1. Determine Beginning Inventory. This is inventory on the first day of the year (or the day you started the business.) For a painter, this is generally the value of all unsold paintings (use the asking price for value) plus the cost of any unopened/unused supplies that are a part of the process for producing a painting. This would include paint, canvases, easels, rags, brushes, solvents, drop cloths etc. Do not include costs that are not part of the painting process such as books or office supplies. Starting inventory should be the same as the prior year's ending inventory. For the first year this will be zero.
2. Add Purchases (this would only apply if you bought others paintings for resale.)

3. Add Costs of Labor if you pay someone to help produce paintings.

4. Add Materials and Supplies. This would be anything that would be included in inventory that you purchased during the year.

5. Add Other costs such as rent, utilities, insurance etc if you pay to maintain a studio separate from your home (in-home studio will be discussed later.)

6. Subtract Ending Inventory. This is inventory on the last day of the year (or the day you closed the business.) For a painter, this is generally the value of all unsold paintings (use the asking price for value) plus the cost of any unopened/unused supplies that are a part of the process for producing a painting. This would include paint, canvases, easels, rags, brushes, solvents, drop cloths etc. Do not include costs that are not part of the painting process such as books or office supplies.

This is subtracted from Gross Income to determine Gross Profit.

The next thing we will do is deduct any other expenses from the business that are not part of Cost of Goods Sold. These include:

1. Supplies that are not part of the painting process
2. Advertising
3. Commissions paid to agents or galleries
4. Legal costs such as copyrights, trademarks, etc.
5. Trade publications and books
6. Studio costs for an in-home studio (must be regularly and exclusively used for business.) We divide the area of the studio by the area of the home and take a portion of the total home expenses. We can also multiply the square footage of the studio/office by $5 and deduct that.
7. Membership dues to trade organizations
8. Mileage deduction for driving related to the business
9. Overnight travel expenses for business travel (lodging, food, tips, taxi, airfare)
10. Office supplies
11. Capital expenditures for equipment with a life longer than a year will be depreciated (cameras, printers, furniture etc.)
12. Taxes and License fees
13. Tax Preparation and Bookkeeping costs including software, supplies, professional help and books (like this one).
14. Self Employed Health Insurance (this is a temporary deduction that will expire and at that point will be deducted at a later point.)

At this point we have **Net Profit**. This will be added to the form 1040 and either added to or subtracted from ordinary income before determining your **Adjusted Gross Income**. If it's a profit, we will also calculate Self Employment Tax. This is Social Security and Medicare taxes for the self-employed. This is 15.3% of net profit. This will be added to any income tax on your tax return to determine your total tax liability.

You get to deduct 20% of your profit off of your taxable income. If you make less than $364,200 taxable income on your tax return (for Married Filing Jointly - $182,100 for almost everyone else) it's as simple as that. Actually, it's not simple at all, especially if you exceed the income limits we just discussed, but your tax pro or software should be able to handle it. If you make more than the limit above, your deduction will phase out unless you pay wages (or have a lot of equipment). I'm going to cover the details of that scenario in a single chapter: Do I Get the 20% Business Deduction?

My Advice:

1. Avoid forming a partnership or S-Corporation until you are making a lot of money. If you apply for an Employer Identification Number, be careful to ensure you identify yourself as a single owner business.
2. Make sure you understand how your income is reported by your company. You need to understand what is included as income, what is not, and how they handle the commissions you pay. Bottom line, when the business income is calculated, after deductions, you want to make sure it represents the money YOU got, and nothing the company kept.
3. Get a separate bank account for the business. Have all income deposited into that account and pay all direct expenses out of it. Don't pay gas or home office expenses, as well as other expenses that are part personal out of this account. If you have a steady income from the business, make a transfer from the business account to your personal account monthly that represents a conservative, after tax profit. Leave everything else behind for taxes. Your tax pro can help you figure out what this monthly amount should be.
4. Keep Good Records! I cannot emphasize enough that having records that can be reconstructed, interpreted and proven is critical. They don't have to be complex or super organized, but they do have to include everything. Don't just keep a box of receipts and

nothing else! Use the Mile IQ app for mileage and don't miss any miles!

5. Focus on making money. The more you work, the better you get at it and the harder you work, the more you will make. The goal here is to make money and pay taxes. If you don't hate tax time because of how much you pay, you are not doing it right.

6. When practical, get business use only equipment such as lap tops and phones. Also have a regular and exclusive use area for business in your home. This can be an office, but can also be the place you store inventory and supplies. The bigger the better, within reason.

7. Make estimated payments such that you are guaranteed to avoid paying a penalty, and nothing more. Have money set aside as discussed above to cover the tax bill when you file. Pay attention! Set money aside! You should NEVER have a tax bill that you don't already have the money set aside to pay. Tax time should suck for a successful independent contractor, but only because you don't want to send them the money you have saved. It should never suck because you don't know how you are going to pay your tax bill. Estimated payments are made on 4/15, 6/15, 9/15 and 1/15 of the next year.

Military: Not a lot different here for you.

76. I am Renting out my Former Home

COVID Update (with a useful bit of tax knowledge): A lot of landlords have asked about the eviction moratorium and how they deduct for rent not received. Easy answer: You don't. If rent doesn't get paid, you don't include it in income, so it doesn't need to be "deducted". Expenses you pay related to negotiating, litigating, or even getting advice about this are deductible. Also, generally speaking, if you ultimately receive relief from the government through various programs designed to help you survive not getting rent, they would generally be counted as rent when you receive them. Talk to a pro if you get income like that though, to be safe.

Now the actual chapter:

This chapter is designed for the average homeowner who is converting their personal residence into rental property, either because they are unable to sell it, intend to reside in it later, or simply hope to use it as an investment. It does not cover all the specifics of how to file a Rental Property tax return; rather, it covers record keeping and tax issues that an owner of Residential Rental Real Estate should be aware of. This chapter does not discuss Alternative Minimum Tax implications of Rental Property. I feel strongly that you should have a tax pro help you, at least for the first year, and have any self-prepared tax returns checked by a pro once in a while.

When does my home become Rental Property?

Your home becomes rental property on the first day it is available for rent. This is when you can start deducting expenses. Generally, when you put the sign out front, put the ad in the paper, or tell your co-workers to find you a tenant, you have made it available for rent. It is theoretically possible that this could occur while you were still living in it, but I wouldn't push it that far.

What is Rent?

Rent is the full amount of rent received, as you receive it. If you have a property manager who deducts a commission, the rent is the full rent paid (including the commission) and the commission is a deduction. Similarly, if your tenant performs a repair and deducts the cost from the rent, the rent is the full amount of the rent and the deducted amount is a repair expense. If someone pays advance rent, include it in the year received. If a security deposit is paid, it becomes rent when you keep it to cover an expense (and the expense becomes a deduction). If the deposit is agreed as non-refundable (such as a pet cleaning deposit) it is rent when received. If the tenant is supposed to pay rent and doesn't, do not include the amount not paid as rent. This means there is no "bad debt" deduction for rental—if you don't get it, it's not rent.

Deductible Expenses:

You can deduct all reasonable and necessary expenses for the rental of your home. Some items must be depreciated over their useful life (defined by the IRS). Be careful and make sure to do this right—there's more information coming later in the chapter. If you pay something for a full year, such as taxes, HOA dues and mortgage interest, then for the first and last years of rental (partial years) you generally pro-rate it by day based on the day the property is available for rent. Expenses must be things you pay for—your labor is not an expense. Here is a fairly comprehensive list of expenses:

Mortgage interest
Taxes
Insurance (technically prorated by coverage period)
Mortgage insurance premiums
Homeowner's association dues
Pest control
Utilities you pay (including those paid when unoccupied but available for rent)
Advertising expenses
Repairs
Landscaping
Painting
Legal expenses for collecting rent, preparing leases, evicting tenants
Improvements
Tax prep fees for rental-related forms
Management fees
Cleaning expenses
Travel and mileage to manage the rental property (the primary purpose of the trip must be to manage the rental property—don't try to deduct a vacation during which you "check on" the rental.)

Starting in 2018, there's a new deduction called the Qualified Business Income Deduction which can apply to rental property if all facts and circumstances indicate that you treat it like a business. There is a safe harbor rule that you can use to ensure the IRS will accept the deduction, but it is difficult to meet if you are only renting out one former home. The starting point for the Safe Harbor is that you spend 250 hours of rental services for the rental during the year. You must also maintain separate income and expense books for the rental and maintain contemporaneous (made as the events occur – not recreated) records of the services you provide and the hours you spend on them to support the Safe Harbor time requirements.

If you qualify for the deduction, you get to deduct 20% of your profit off of your taxable income. If you make less than $364,200 taxable income on your tax return (for Married Filing Jointly - $182,100 for almost everyone else) it's as simple as that. Actually, it's not simple at all, especially if you exceed the income limits we just discussed, but your tax pro or software should be able to handle it. If you make more than the limit above, your deduction will phase out unless you pay wages (or have a lot of equipment). I'm going to cover the details of that scenario in a single chapter: Do I Get the 20% Business Deduction?

Save receipts for all of these expenses and report the amounts to your tax preparer or have available to enter into your tax software (I am not a big fan of using software for rental property, especially in the first and last year).

Depreciation:

Depreciation is how you deduct the cost of major items with a life longer than 1 year. You will deduct a portion of the cost a little at a time over a specified number of years. Don't let someone tell you not to depreciate so you can avoid recapture—you have to recapture any depreciation allowed (whether deducted or not).

You will depreciate the building, appliances and any improvements to the property, as well as certain landscaping items (fences, trees, etc.). It is important to understand that if you have a major expense that increases the value, or prolongs the life of your property, it will likely be depreciated vice deducted. Repairs that do not increase the value or extend the life may be deducted. Examples of improvements are air conditioner replacement, roof replacement, and additions. Examples of repairs are painting, replacing garbage disposal, repairing hole in roof, repairing air conditioner unit. If you aren't sure if something is an improvement or a repair, you are probably safe to call it a repair if it is less than $2500. Seek a professional's advice if it is more than that.

When converting your home to rental you need to know the Basis. This is generally the price you paid for the home, plus any improvements you made to it (see IRS Pub 551, or a tax professional for other things that might affect it). If the Fair Market Value (FMV) the day you convert it to rental property is less than this value, then this is your basis. The FMV is what your house would sell for to a willing buyer. You also need to know what the land is worth. You subtract this from the basis before depreciating the basis. You can determine the land value from your property tax card or by comparing your home to other similar properties sold in the area. You will depreciate the house by taking an even portion of the basis every month for the next 27.5 years (this means the first year's deduction will be smaller, and the deduction for the rest of the years will be about the same). Your tax pro will need the basis, land price, FMV, date purchased and date available for rent for your house.

Improvements are depreciated for 27.5 years just like the house. Appliances are depreciated for 5 years and landscaping improvements are depreciated for 15 years. See IRS Pub 527 for how to depreciate 5- and 15-year property. Your tax preparer will need to know the date you bought these items and the price you paid for them (including installation if you paid for it). Recent changes to depreciation rules created a "Safe Harbor" that allows you not to depreciate (meaning you can deduct it immediately) any individual purchase or improvement that is less than $2,500. You can even bump that to $5000 with a little advance work with a tax pro.

Do I need a Property Manager?

I like property managers. They will keep about 10% of your rent, but if they can save you 1 month of vacancy, they've paid for 10 months of commissions. If you try to rent without one, and can generally keep the place occupied, you probably are okay without one. If you try to rent it and it goes more than a month empty, get referrals and hire a property manager. Similarly, if you have a property manager and your house goes vacant more than a month, find a new property manager.

Active Participation:

It generally behooves you to be an active participant in the renting of your property. You can be an active participant even if you have a property manager. If you make the decisions about what rent to charge, what repairs to make, and whether to allow pets, you are actively participating. Even if the manager says: "I think we should raise the rent to $1,200." and you have to give the OK, you are actively participating. By being an active participant, you can generally deduct up to $25,000 of rental loss from the rest of your income (subject to income and filing status limitations). If you are totally passive in the rental, you cannot deduct any losses. If you are passive, or you have losses in excess of the limit, you will have to carry them over until you have a gain or dispose of the property. The income limits kick in at $100,000 of AGI and the loss is not deductible above $150,000 AGI. Basically, the $25,000 allowed deduction is reduced by $1 for every $2 of income above $100,000.

This is a good time to mention that most rentals with a mortgage will have negative income for tax purposes due to depreciation of the property. This means you avoid paying taxes on rental income for a long time and often get an improvement to your overall taxes as well. The two big takeaways from this are that the tax benefits may need to be recaptured when you sell – thus they are tax DEFERRAL, not SAVINGS. The other is that your tax results are not a good analysis of the profitability of your rental. If you want a pretty darn good number that indicates your "profit" – either money in your pocket or mortgage principal paid by your tenants – take the net results for the rental property from your Schedule E and add back the amount of depreciation deducted. For most people this is a very good estimate of how the rental is doing. A positive number here means money is flowing INTO your net worth vice out. I do not talk about this to advise you on the suitability of retaining your rental property. That is NOT my area of expertise. I merely point it out so you are not confused by the inaccurate and overly negative results your tax return will spit out.

At Risk Issues:

You may be asked if you are "At Risk" for the full amount of your rental. This means that you are not protected from losses on the property should everything go south on you. Generally speaking, unless you have some sort of a loan that you would not have to pay back (such as from a family member) you are At Risk for the full amount.

Tax Implications When Selling:

When selling a house that has been used as rental property, it is generally treated as a sale of a business asset. Thus, it is a fully taxable transaction. It will be reported on Form 4797 (Sale of Business Assets). The form will ask for the date purchased, date sold, the sale price (minus expenses of sale) and the Basis. Other than basis, these entries are fairly self-explanatory. The basis is that which you are using to depreciate the home. It is the price paid (or FMV when converted to rental if this was lower than the basis) + the cost of any improvements – any depreciation taken or allowed. There are other things that might affect the basis, but they are unusual and won't normally be seen. The gain or loss is the difference between the basis and the sales price.

It is possible to use the exclusion for the Sale of Main Home if you meet the requirements. This will normally only occur if you lived in the home for at least two years before you rented it out and sold it within three years of renting it. If this is the case, you may be able to exclude up to $250,000 of the gain ($500,000 if MFJ). You may use this exclusion for all gain, except that attributable to depreciation. See the I'm Selling my Rental Property chapter.

Personal Use or Part-Year Rentals:

If you rent your property for only part of the year, or you rent only a portion of your property (such as a room or a duplex) you need to pro-rate your expenses. I highly recommend using a professional for this, especially for the first year. Your tax pro will need to know the status of the property for each day of the year (rented, occupied by you, occupied by family, vacant, vacant but available for rent). They will also need to know the square footage of the property that is rental use, personal use and communal use, as well as which expenses cover the whole property (mortgage, taxes, etc.) and which are exclusive to the rental portion (repairs to that portion, utilities billed separately, etc.). There are more intricacies of this—contact your tax pro for more details.

State Issues:

If you rent out a property in a state that is not your state of residency, make sure you make this clear to your tax pro and make sure you understand how each state handles it. South Carolina, for example, requires you to add an out-of-state rental loss back and subtract an out-of-state rental gain from income. This will also come in to play when you sell your rental property as you need to be sure any gain or loss is attributed to the correct state or states.

My Advice:

1. Keep good records for your rental. Have a file where you keep receipts and maintain a record of income and expenses. If a property manager handles an expense, make sure they provide a detailed report at the end of the year. Also keep records substantiating the date it is available for rent, as well as how you determined your basis.
2. Use a tax professional in the first year you rent the property and in the year you sell it, at a minimum. Mistakes made in the first year can haunt you for a long time.
3. Depreciate your rental property.
4. Do not deduct rental expenses as itemized deductions. I am still stunned how often I see mortgage interest for a rental deducted on BOTH schedule A (Itemized deductions) and Schedule E (Rental Property).
5. Pay attention to the date you lose your personal residence exclusion. This is generally three years from the date you moved out (13 years for military as long as you remain on active duty). As this date approaches, if the property has gone up significantly in value, selling it and avoiding taxes on the gain can be a big deal. Remember that you still have to pay taxes on depreciation taken or allowed, so it's not a get out of taxes free card.

Military: For selling your home as discussed above for the main home exclusion, the 2 of 5 year rule is extended by up to 10 years while you are on active duty. See the Military discussion in the I'm Selling my Rental Property chapter. When you are within 18 months of this exclusion expiring, you need to take a hard look at how much gain you can exclude, even if you love the property. If you can exclude $100,000 of gain FOREVER, it really makes sense to sell one and buy another. Talk to your realtor and tax professional for help.

77. I Get Health Insurance Through the Healthcare Marketplace

Temporary COVID change: While the basic bill as described below cuts off subsidies at 400% of poverty level, that percentage is currently allowed to be exceeded due to COVID and it has been extended through 2025.

This chapter is not going to go over every detail of getting insurance through the marketplace, since this is, after all, a tax book. I'm also not going to run numbers in detail, since even I find it extremely difficult to rationalize them, with or without using forms. I don't like depending on software, but I have found that reconciling an Affordable Care Act (hereafter abbreviated ACA) subsidy requires software first, and then checking to make sure it's right. I pity anyone trying to get this right using pen and paper.

One thing as an aside, I found last year that a lot of people didn't realize they had insurance through the marketplace. Insurance companies hired a lot of people to sell policies through the ACA, many paid on commission, and I guess some of the agents found it easier to sell insurance if they neglected to mention that the incredible low price was due to a subsidy. The IRS was all over this and we saw dozens of letters requiring filing of the proper forms before the IRS would release the refund. If you get a letter saying you were missing a Form 8962, that means you had marketplace insurance, and should have gotten a 1095A.

If you get insurance through the ACA marketplace, you WILL be getting a form 1095A from the insurance company. This form has the information needed to reconcile your subsidy (the Advance Premium Tax Credit). This reconciliation occurs using form 8962. In practice, you pretty much just have to copy the information from your 1095A into your software (or provide the 1095A to your tax pro) and the software will work it out (if you are doing it by hand, God help you.) In theory, if you provided accurate information about your expected 2018 income when applying for the health coverage (and it matched what you expected exactly) this will result in no change to your tax return.

If you guessed to high on your income, you will get the FULL amount of the difference between what your subsidy was, and what it should have been. This amount will be added directly to your refund (or will lower your balance due.) If you guessed too low on your income, you have to pay the difference back - maybe. There are limits to how much they can make you pay back as long as your income was below 4 times the poverty level for your family size. If your income is more than 4 times the poverty level - you pay the FULL difference back. To avoid these paybacks, keep the marketplace informed of changes in income or family size.

You should have online access to an account. If you don't, get it, and don't lose the login information.

Everyone reading this chapter should read the previous chapter on the Affordable Care Act. There are a number of warnings about filing status and other tricks. In fact, you should read it NOW, and not wait until tax time.

I highly recommend having a tax professional at least look over your numbers to make sure you got it right. It took me a few weeks to really get comfortable with how these numbers should transfer onto the various forms. There also a few tricks if you get married or divorced during the year.

My Advice:

1. Keep the marketplace informed of changes in marital status, family size and income during the year.
2. Be prepared if you have a subsidized plan and get married during the year. Immediately cancel your plan if your new spouse can get you insurance or makes good money. Be prepared to owe some subsidy back.
3. If you can afford it, take the minimum subsidy you can afford and get the rest when you file your tax return.
4. Talk to a tax expert BEFORE getting insurance through the marketplace and provide them your annual premium and subsidy amounts after you get insurance so they can double check that the numbers make sense.

Military: I can't imagine a military member getting insurance through the exchange.

78. I Don't Have Health Insurance

Starting in 2019, there will be no penalty for not having health insurance, so I have eliminated this chapter, except to let you know the penalty is gone.

The penalty is gone…

;)

79. State by State Tax Guide for Military

This chapter is just an overview. Also, many states update their information at the last minute, so some of this information will be out of date at the time of publishing (most of it will follow 2021 rules, vice 2022 rules that are used for the rest of the book – states are slow). Use this info as a starting point with hints, and double check with your state. EVERYTHING in the individual state portion of this chapter should be viewed skeptically!

I will start with some general information, and then continue with state-by-state details. I have another book that is specifically for military called The Short Cheap Tax Book for the Military. It goes into a lot more detail on how state residency works for members and their spouses, as well as how to handle income from multiple states and other weird situations.

Military Spouses Residency Relief Act (MSRRA)

Most states have begun to treat this in a similar manner to each other. In general, the spouse of a service member has two choices for state of residency: the state they are stationed in, or the military member's state of residency. In order to claim the military members state, they must have established a domicile in that state at some time before moving to the current state (the requirement for establishing domicile was eliminated starting in 2018, so, going forward, the spouse can take the military member's state without ever having lived there at all). For those qualified to make the election to claim the military members state, it is important to weigh the benefits properly, for example, a spouse who works in SC married to a military resident of MI might assume that since MI does not tax the military member that they should choose this state. This would be wrong because MI will tax the non-military income of the spouse. SC is far more generous to the spouse of a service member stationed in SC. Expert assistance may be required making this determination. It can also be difficult to get the current state to stop withholding from the spouse's wages. Each state Dept of Revenue has different procedures for handling this.

Again, starting in 2018, the spouse does NOT have to maintain the same state of residency as the service member. Many states have not incorporated this into their instructions, and it is likely that many state employees will not be aware of this. This is Federal LAW, and states do not have the option of ignoring it. As a spouse, be prepared to fight for your exemption and take action to maintain residency in the state you desire. I highly recommend registering to vote in your state of residence.

Some states are very liberal about this and some are harder, but it is hard to deny that as long as the military member and their spouse reside in the same state, the spouse can claim residency in the military member's state and the income from jobs, businesses, investments etc. of the spouse are not taxed in the state they are stationed in and is instead taxed in the military member's state. If you live and/or work across the border in a state that the military member is not stationed in, the MSRRA generally would not apply, though some states, like South Carolina, will still allow you to use it.

A recent change to the Soldier's and Sailor's Civil Relief Act has a commonsense change that now specifies that military members can choose their SPOUSE state of residency vice their home of record for tax purposes. This is common sense and basically would be used by the military member as justification to file DD Form 2058 to change their state of residence for taxes with DFAS. DD Form 2058 does NOT affect your home of record!

Residency:

A military member normally retains residency in the state they resided in when they joined the military unless action is taken to change this. The state on the W-2 form received from DFAS can generally be relied upon as to the state of residence of the military member (if it's wrong get it corrected ASAP). The states in which a service member is stationed will not tax the member's military income unless they are residents. They will tax any income earned from other employment or business activities conducted in the state by the member and their spouses (subject to the MSRRA discussed above.)

The discussions below about individual states apply specifically to the military member's active-duty income and not income from side jobs or their spouses income.

Filing Requirements:

Not having to file discussed below assumes there is no withholding from the given state. A member may file even if not required and should do so if they have withholding from the given state so they can get the money back.

If a member would not be required to file except for the existence of withholding, they should adjust their state withholding through MyPay so no taxes are withheld from that state. They may also consider stopping withholding even if they are required to file, for states that do not tax their income (MI for example.) Many people do not file required tax returns when there is no refund or balance due. This could result in a letter from the state requesting a return but rarely any penalties – but there can be!

Death Benefits:

Many states exclude death benefits and military pay for service members killed in a combat zone or while on active duty. The specifics are not discussed here. Survivors of service members killed on active duty can obtain assistance for this from CACO personnel (A CACO representative should be assigned to you automatically if you are the survivor of a military member who dies on active duty.)

Taxation of Military Pensions:

I have tried to include information on this for each state, but it is even more likely to be out of date or incorrect. This information is just a starting point.

Military Bonuses:

Six states, as far as I can tell, have various bonuses for serving in the military or serving in a combat zone. Most of these are separate from a tax return. I have not had a ton of experience with them, so I have provided links where I can find them and will let you figure them out. If I haven't provided a link, a quick google search normally turns them up. Most of these are one-time only bonuses, but some, like Minnesota's, is every month in a combat zone. The six states are: MA, MN, OH, NH, SD and WV.

States with **Bold** names either require a tax return or other document to be filed by military residents, or a tax return should be prepared to determine if any refundable benefits are available from that state.

Alabama:
Alabama treats military residents the same as all other residents.
Alabama does not tax military retirement.

Alaska:
Alaska does not have an income tax.
Alaska Permanent Funds Dividends are taxable on the Federal Return.

Arizona:
Arizona does not tax active-duty military pay and does not require filing if the only AZ source income is active duty pay.
Arizona does not tax Reserve or National Guard Pay.
Arizona taxes military retirement but allows a subtraction of $2,500 from it. If both spouses receive military retirement, they each get $2,500.

Arkansas:
Beginning in 2014, Arkansas no longer taxes active duty military pay.
A tax return is still required.
Arkansas does not tax military pensions.

California:
California does not tax military pay of CA residents stationed outside of the state of CA.
They do tax military income of their residents when stationed in CA.
They also treat military spouses generously, similar to SC. Form 540NR is used to account for this. You write "MPA" to the left of column A for non-resident military income and enter the military income in column B but exclude it from column E.
California has recently sent letters to military members stationed out of the state saying a tax return should have been filed. These are wrong and the back side of the letter has an easy place to respond and get them off your back.

Colorado:
Beginning in 2016, CO will not tax active military income of military members with a home of record of Colorado IF they were a Colorado resident who subsequently changed residency to a different state AND changed back to CO in 2016 or later.
Otherwise, Colorado taxes military residents the same as other residents unless the member was stationed outside the US for >305 days in the year.
Colorado taxes military retirement, but let's you subtract the first $20,000 if you are under 65, and the first $24,000 if you are over 65.

Connecticut:
Connecticut allows resident military personnel stationed outside of CT to be treated as non-residents for tax purposes.

This can be confusing, but the point is that they are still a resident for other purposes, just not treated that way for tax purposes.

In order to be treated as a non-resident they must meet all three of the following requirements:

1) Not maintain a permanent place of abode in CT for the entire year (a parent's house is not a permanent place of abode.)
2) Maintain a permanent place of abode outside of CT for the entire year.
3) Spend no more than 30 days in CT for any reason during the year.

If they meet these requirements they can file as a non-resident and exclude any military wages from gross income and need not file unless they have other CT source income.

CT taxes military retirement of residents.

If a service member dies in a combat zone, or as a result of injuries sustained in a combat zone, all taxes are forgiven for that year. If the date they entered that combat zone for that period extends into a prior year, those taxes are also forgiven (essentially, if you enter a combat zone, don't leave, and are killed, every tax year that made up a part of that combat zone time is tax free to CT.)

Delaware:
DE taxes military residents the same as all other residents.
DE taxes military retirement but does have a small exclusion that increases when you reach age 60.

Washington DC:
DC taxes resident military personnel the same as all other residents.
DC taxes military retirement pay but does have a small exclusion.
Florida:
Florida does not have an income tax.

Georgia:
GA taxes military residents the same as all other residents however Reserves or National Guard called to active duty for more than 90 days may be able to take a credit against their individual income tax based on their income from the National Guard or Reserves.
GA taxes military retirement but has a generous deduction that kicks in at age 62 or when totally and permanently disabled.

Hawaii:
Hawaii taxes military residents the same as all other residents except that they do not tax the first $6076 of reserve pay or HI national guard pay.
Hawaii does not tax military retirement

Excluding a spouse's income from HI taxes will generally require a paper filed return with proof attached.

Idaho:

ID residents stationed in ID pay taxes on all military income; however, if the member was on active duty >120 days and stationed outside of Idaho they can exclude any military income earned while stationed outside of ID. If they are stationed outside of Idaho for the entire year they do not need to file an ID tax return, however...

Idaho has a Grocery Credit that a military member is eligible for that is refundable so it is possible to get a refund from Idaho even though there was no tax withheld.

This makes Idaho one of the States that a military member should file even when not required to.

ID taxes military retirement but has a small exclusion available once you reach 65 year's old (62 if disabled).

Illinois:

IL does not tax military pay; however, the member must file a tax return if they file a Federal return.

Military members with children who get Federal Earned Income Credit may get up to 10% of the Federal amount even if they have no taxes due to IL.

It is generally best to file separately if one spouse is a resident subject to tax and the other is not, since a joint return requires both spouses to file as residents.

IL does not tax military retirement.

Indiana:

Indiana taxes military income but allows a deduction of the first $5000 of military income for the taxpayer and/or the spouse ($10000 for military couple.)

If a military member changes state of residency to another state they must submit the DD Form 2058 with the tax return for the year they changed state of residency.

IN taxes military retirement but has a subtraction amount to reduce the amount subject to tax.

In the year of discharge, both the military pay deduction and the retirement deduction may be used if both types of pay are received (the deductions cannot exceed the amount of pay received for each type of income).

IN has a local tax which applies if the service member is in IN as of January 1st of the tax year. If the member is stationed outside of IN, they do not pay local taxes.

A military spouse who is exempt from taxes due to the Military Spouses Residency Relief Act is also exempt from local taxes, even if working in IN.

Iowa:

IA does not tax military income and military income is not used in determining filing requirements (if the only significant sources of income are military income, a tax return is not required.)

Starting in 2014, Iowa no longer taxes military retirement.

Kansas:

Kansas taxes military income but allows a deduction for recruitment, sign-up and retention bonuses paid that are included in Federal taxable income (if the bonus was tax free to federal do not deduct it from KS. Kansas starts with Federal AGI so it is already excluded.)

The subtraction is made on Adjustments line A21.

KS does not tax military retirement pay.

Kentucky:

KY does not tax military income and does not require a tax return if the only KY source income is military pay.

KY taxes military retirement but has a very large exclusion available.

Louisiana:

Louisiana requires a tax return from military personnel the same as any other resident...however...

LA gives an exclusion of up to $30000 of military pay if the person has been on active duty outside of Louisiana for at least 120 days during the tax year.

The subtraction is taken as a Schedule E subtraction, Code 10E, by entering military pay up to $30000 on the schedule.

LA does not tax military retirement.

Maine:

Maine allows resident military personnel stationed outside of ME to be treated as non-residents for tax purposes.

This can be confusing but the point is that they are still a resident, just not treated that way for tax purposes.

In order to be treated as a non-resident they must meet all three of the following requirements:

1) Not maintain a permanent place of abode in ME for the entire year (a parents house is not a permanent place of abode.)

2) Maintain a permanent place of abode outside of ME for the entire year.

3) Spend no more than 30 days in ME for any reason during the year.

If the taxpayer meets these requirements they can file as a non-resident and exclude any military wages from gross income and need not file unless they have other ME source income.

Maine calls this the General Safe Harbor Rule.

ME does not tax military retirement of the service member who earned it. ME does tax military retirement received by former spouses or any other person who did not engage in the military service that earned the retirement. This is most common in cases of divorce.

Maryland:

Maryland taxes military residents just like other residents; however, they allow a subtraction for up to $15000 of military pay earned outside of the U.S. (Military Overseas Income.)

The deduction phases out dollar for dollar as ALL military income goes above $15000 and there is no exclusion if the total military income exceeds $30000.

The subtraction is taken on Form 502SU and the Military Overseas Income Worksheet is used to calculate the deduction.

Military members are also subject to local income taxes.

MD taxes military retirement but has a small exclusion which can be larger depending on age, disability status and spouse's disability.

Massachusetts:

There are no special tax benefits for military, however...

The Massachusetts Dept of Veterans Affairs will give a onetime payment of $500 to any resident after they served at least 6 months active duty in the military. They also have a $1000 benefit for personnel who serve in Iraq or Afghanistan. Check their website for details.

MA does not tax military retirement.

Michigan:

Michigan requires military members to file a tax return; however, they subtract active duty pay from income (Schedule 1, Line 11).

Military members with children who receive Earned Income Credit on their Federal return may collect 6% of the federal amount, even if they pay no taxes to MI. (This was 20% for 2011 and prior years.)

MI does not tax military retirement pay.

Minnesota:
Minnesota subtracts Active Duty Military pay from income of MN residents.
If Gross Income on Federal return other than military is less than $10000, no MN return is required.
Minnesota pays $120 per month a military resident spends in a combat zone. This is paid separately from the tax return and is claimed on Minnesota form M99. Check their website for the form.
MN does not tax military retirement pay.

Mississippi:
Mississippi taxes military residents the same as other residents except that they do not tax National Guard and Reserve pay up to $15000.
MS does not tax military retirement pay.

Missouri:
MO allows resident military personnel stationed outside of MO to be treated as non-residents for tax purposes.
This can be confusing, but the point is that they are still a resident, just not treated that way for tax purposes.
In order to be treated as a non-resident they must meet all three of the following requirements:
1) Not maintain a permanent place of abode in MO for the entire year (a parent's house is not a permanent place of abode.)
2) Maintain a permanent place of abode outside of MO for the entire year.
3) Spend no more than 30 days in MO for any reason during the year.
If they meet these requirements they can file as a non-resident and exclude any military wages from gross income and need not file unless they have other MO source income.
If your spouse works but claims MO as your state of residency through the MSRRA their income is taxable to MO and they must file a tax return if they earn more than $1200.
As of 2016 all military retirement income will be tax exempt.
In 2023, there is supposed to be a military non-filer tool on their website so military members stationed outside of MO can fill that out instead of filing a tax return.

Montana:
Montana requires military residents to file a tax return but exempts active military pay from taxation on Schedule 2, Line 8.

Verification of active duty status must be attached to the return.
Montana taxes military retirement pay.

Nebraska:
Nebraska taxes military residents just like other residents.
Nebraska has implemented an incredibly complicated option to exclude
certain amounts of military retirement income for some years. It requires
an election within 2 years of retiring. It's too stupid to attempt to explain,
but if you are retiring or retired from the military in Nebraska you should
research this on their website.

Nevada:
Nevada does not have an income tax.

New Hampshire:
NH does not have an income tax but they do tax interest and dividends.
Generally, these would need to exceed $2400 for an individual and $4800
for a couple.
NH will pay a service member $100 if they earned the Global War on
Terrorism Expeditionary Medal or Afghanistan Campaign, or Iraq
Campaign Medal; and who was honorably discharged. Some conflicting
information on expiration, but check it out here:
https://www.nh.gov/nhveterans/benefits/bonuses.htm

New Jersey:
Update: In 2020, NJ provided conflicting instructions on if military
housing and housing paid for with allowances counts as maintaining a
permanent place of abode outside NJ. The website says it counts, but the
instruction book for military says it doesn't. The law hasn't changed, so I
continue to count it, especially since the idea that it doesn't count is stupid.
NJ allows resident military personnel stationed outside of NJ to be treated
as non-residents for tax purposes.

This can be confusing, but the point is that they are still a resident, just not
treated that way for tax purposes.
In order to be treated as a non-resident they must meet all three of the
following requirements:
1) Not maintain a permanent place of abode in NJ for the entire year (a
parent's house is not a permanent place of abode.)
2) Maintain a permanent place of abode outside of NJ for the entire year.
3) Spend no more than 30 days in NJ for any reason during the year.

If they meet these requirements they can file as a non-resident and exclude any military wages from gross income and need not file unless they have other NJ source income. (NJ does not consider barracks maintaining a permanent place of abode outside NJ – see the update above for more details ion what they consider a permanent place of abode – it gets confusing and NJ has epically messed this up.)

New Jersey just passed a $3,000 exemption for honorably discharged Veterans which applies to tax years 2016 and beyond.

NJ does not tax military retirement pay.

New Mexico:

New Mexico does not tax active duty military pay however; NM residents are required to file a NM return if they were required to file a Federal return.

NM does tax military retirement pay, but, starting in 2022 you can exclude $10,000 and this number goes up to $20,000 in 2023 and $30,000 for 2024 through at least 2026.

New York:

NY allows resident military personnel stationed outside of NY to be treated as non-residents for tax purposes.

This can be confusing, but the point is that they are still a resident, just not treated that way for tax purposes.

In order to be treated as a non-resident they must meet all three of the following requirements:

1) Not maintain a permanent place of abode in NY for the entire year (a parent's house is not a permanent place of abode.)
2) Maintain a permanent place of abode outside of NY for the entire year.
3) Spend no more than 30 days in NY for any reason during the year.

If they meet these requirements they can file as a non-resident and exclude any military wages from gross income and need not file unless they have other NY source income.

NY specifically excludes barracks as an abode outside of NY for the purpose of this rule.

Also, if a NY return is required to be filed to get back state taxes withheld and this exemption results in zero income (as it usually does) the return may have to be mailed in vice electronically filed.

NY does not tax military retirement pay.

North Carolina:

NC taxes military residents the same as other residents.

NC taxes military retirement pay but does offer a small deduction from it.

NC also had a lawsuit many years ago that caused some military retirement to be exempt from taxation. It is increasingly unlikely that this will apply to most people.

North Dakota:
ND taxes military residents the same as other residents, however…
National Guard and reserve members called to active duty can exclude their active duty pay form ND income.
ND taxes military retirement pay.

Ohio:
Ohio does not tax military pay of OH residents stationed outside of the state of OH. This applies to all local and school taxes as well, though some will fight you on it. The law is very clear on this.
They do tax military income of their residents when stationed in OH.
Ohio does not tax military retirement pay.
OH will give you up to $1500 for service ($500 for any service, $1000 for certain countries and $1500 for combat zones). Details here:
https://veteransbonus.ohio.gov/odvs_web/

Oklahoma:
Oklahoma allows military members to exclude active duty pay.
This exclusion is accomplished using Schedule 511-C.
Military members are required to file an OK tax return if they were required to file a federal return.
OK stopped taxing military retirement starting in 2022.

Oregon:
Oregon allows a subtraction of all military pay earned while stationed outside of OR and up to $6000 earned while stationed in Oregon (Subtraction Code 319).
OR also allows military residents to be treated as non-residence if they spent less than 31 days in OR, did not have an abode in OR and had a permanent abode outside OR the entire year.
OR has weird rules for military retirement, but many people should not pay taxes on it.

Pennsylvania:
Pennsylvania does not tax Active Duty Military Income of residents stationed outside of PA and does not require a tax return; however, they do require the service member to mail or fax a copy of their orders stationing them outside of PA and their W-2.

If filing a tax return a copy of the orders must be included when mailing the return or sent separately to the address below:
PA DEPT OF REVENUE
NO PAYMENT OR NO REFUND
2 REVENUE PLACE
HARRISBURG PA 17129-0002
They may also be faxed to: (717) 772-4193
PA does not tax military retirement pay.

Rhode Island:
Rhode Island taxes military residents the same as other residents.
RI stopped taxing military retirement starting in 2022.

South Carolina:
SC taxes military residents just like regular residents except that it does not tax reservist drill pay.
SC is very generous to the spouses of military (residents of another state) in that they allow you to exclude the active-duty income of the non-resident military member from the calculation of what percentage of deductions to allocate to the spouse. This generally results in 100% of the family's deductions against only the spouses SC income. It is very difficult to get tax software to handle this correctly. Line 1 of the SCNR should have no active-duty military income in the Federal column. This can also apply to an active-duty person with a side job.
SC stopped taxing military retirement in 2022. Prior to this there was an ever increasing deduction amount that was subject to earned income limits and varied based on age.

South Dakota:
SD does not have an income tax.
South Dakota will give a resident $500 for active service after 9/11/2001. Details here:
http://vetaffairs.sd.gov/benefits/State/Veterans%20Bonus.aspx (Link #21)

Tennessee:
TN does not have an income tax but they do tax interest and dividends. Generally, these would need to exceed $1250 for an individual and $2500 for a couple.

Texas:
Texas does not have an income tax.

Utah:
Utah taxes resident service members the same as other residents.
UT taxes military retirement pay.

Vermont:
Vermont does not tax military pay of VT residents stationed outside of the state of VT.
They do tax military income of their residents when stationed in VT.
Military pay is subtracted on line 32.
A tax return is not required if the only income is military pay while stationed outside VT.
VT taxes military retirement pay, but allows a small exclusion for lower income taxpayers.

Virginia:
Virginia taxes military residents just like other residents except that they give a subtraction of basic military pay of up to $15000.
The subtraction phases out dollar for dollar as income goes from $15000 to $30000 and is completely gone at $30000 of income. (If a military member made less than $15000, it would all be subtracted. If they made $20000, they get to subtract $10000.)
The subtraction code is 38.
VA taxes military retirement pay.
If a spouse in VA is using the MSRRA to claim a state other than VA, and needs to get withheld taxes back, VA uses a separate form from their regular tax forms to claim it. Last time I used it the form had to be mailed in.
VA has hassled nonresident military stationed in the state in the past for not filing tax returns. They haven't done it lately, but don't assume a letter from VA is correct if you are a resident of another state.
VA has an exclusion for military retirement for taxpayers age 55 and older. It is $10,000 in 2022 and increases by another $10,000 each following year until the exclusion reaches $40,000.

Washington:
Washington does not have an income tax.

West Virginia:
West Virginia taxes military residents unless they spent less than 30 days in WV.
If they spent less than 30 days in WV they file as a non-resident and exclude all military income.

WV does not tax military income of reserves or national guard called to active duty by Executive Order of the President.

Starting in 2017, WV does not tax military retirement pay.

West Virginia gives $600 for service in the Afghanistan Combat Zone and $400 for service outside. Details here: https://veterans.wv.gov/programs/Pages/default.aspx (Link #22)

Wisconsin:

Wisconsin taxes military residents the same as other residents except that they do not tax military pay of reserves or national guard called to active duty.

Rent paid by the military member in a state other than WI is allowed to be used for the School Property Tax Credit (not military housing.)

If a military member is stationed outside the United States, they may take a credit of up to $300 for pay received while stationed outside the U.S.

Wisconsin does not tax military retirement.

Wyoming:

WY does not have an income tax.

My Advice:

1. Many states are very difficult to get right if the service member and the spouse have different states of residency. It is a good idea to check the state tax website to see if there is a particular method they want you to use to file these type of returns. It is also very easy to download the instructions for preparing the return and many websites have a specific chapter or instruction page for military.

2. If your spouse plans on claiming your state of residency using the MSRRA, they should register to vote in your state of residence and attempt to get a driver's license there if possible. Car registration, home ownership and other things make very little difference to residency, but voting in a state you aren't a resident is a big no-no.

3. Many tax pros aren't very good at states other than the one that they live and work in. They can also struggle with military returns in general. Make sure you get good references from other service members and ask the professional what kind of experience they have. Also, double check their work. I'm really good at military states but I've been known to mess up once or twice.

4. Don't file a tax return if one is not required and there is no money to be gotten back. With most states, no contact is better. I am starting to wonder

if this is true for California as they have become downright EVIL in their treatment of military service members.

5. If you get a letter from a state demanding money, have a professional tax person or your command's financial specialist look it over before you respond. There are a lot of BS letters being sent by states.

80. The IRS Called and is Threatening Me!

No, they did not.

Really. Getting a call from the IRS is incredibly rare and will only occur as a follow-up from several letters, or an arrangement YOU made to have them call you.

99% chance this is a SCAM! Really – very close to 100% chance it is a scam.

Even if they seem to have your personal information like SSN, address or other private stuff. It's a scam. The 2017 Equifax breach has made it even more likely that your personal information has been disclosed to scammers. And the data breaches just keep occurring, every year. Your info is out there and the scammers are using it.

These guys are PROFESSIONALS! They do this all day, every day and are very good at sounding real. Some have even ordered transcripts to be sent to the victim and refer to that as a way to seem more legitimate.

Do NOT give any information out over the phone!
Do NOT send them any money!
Do NOT give them access to your bank!
Do NOT give them a chance to engage you with questions. The longer you talk to them, the more chance they have to sound legitimate.

How can you be sure it's a scam?

One: Google the phone number, chances are you aren't the first person they've called and the phone number will show up as a scam.
Two: They claim to be the Treasury Department, an agent of some kind, and there is a warrant for your arrest.
Three: Contact the IRS either by phone or through irs.gov. The IRS website has lots of information about these scams right on their front page.
Four: Call your tax guy.
Five: They want you to pay with gift cards.
Six: They insult you, threaten you, swear at you or behave in any way that would be considered unprofessional.
Seven: Set up accounts with the IRS and your state agency. Fifteen minutes (or a couple hours) of effort now will allow you to quickly assess if there are issues with the IRS or your state.

And finally – just assume it is a scam unless you have an obvious reason to believe otherwise. This is good advice for all unsolicited phone calls.

How do you stop them from calling?

Make it ABSOLUTELY clear that you know that it is a scam and that they are wasting their time. Yelling and bad language are a plus here. Be brief, loud, emphatic and angry, then hang up. They won't call back because there are easier targets out there.

Here's an amusing aside: One of my best days in the office was when a long-time client walked in with a scammer on her cell phone - she was terrified. I asked for the phone and went full retired Navy Master Chief on the guy. He hung up and never called back. Good times.

Expect fake calls about stimulus payments. These are ALL scams.

Military: Not a lot of differences here for you.

81. I Got a Letter From the IRS

Open it...

Seriously, this is not a joke. You would be stunned how many of my clients bring me letters from the IRS...unopened. Sometimes months after they get it.

OPEN IT!

But don't panic. Even though the first page will almost certainly tell you that you owe money (it might not, but be prepared) don't panic. Just because it says you owe money does not mean you do. You should never pay on a letter from the IRS unless you are absolutely certain you owe the money...and often you don't. You would be stunned (again) how often my clients pay money to the IRS that they don't owe without consulting me. It is much easier to not pay money you don't owe than it is to get it back from them once you have sent it to them.

Lately the IRS has gotten a little more evil as well. A lot of times these letters are generated because you forgot a small W-2 or other tax form that doesn't amount to much. In the past, the IRS wouldn't even bother if the amount was small. But recently the IRS has started doing this weird trick where they combine a basic "you missed a form" letter with an audit type letter. Usually (in my recent experience) this is with Education Credits. You get a letter saying you forgot a W-2, AND we're denying your education credit until you send documentation for it. A $100 missing W-2 letter now is a $2,000 missing W-2 and denied Education Credit letter. To make matters worse, they don't do a good job of explaining that they don't have any reason to suspect the Education Credit is invalid, they just want more proof - kind of like a spot check. I think this is intentional, and the IRS is getting a good chunk of money from people who just pay, or who ignore the letter.

Which brings me to a very important point...

NEVER ignore an IRS letter or allow the response date to pass without communicating with the IRS. PERIOD! The IRS hates 2 things - being lied to and being ignored - do not do either!

The next chapter has a list of IRS letter types, with general information on each, and the chapter after that has specific information on the most common type of IRS letter, the CP2000. Read those as needed.

Other than that, this was going to be a nice long chapter on letters, but now the scammers have stepped it up a notch. They are actually sending some VERY convincing letters that look a LOT like IRS letters. So, I cannot in good conscience suggest that anything other than seeing a professional is a good idea. Take the letter and your tax return to a competent professional and, for not too much money, confirm that it's legit, see if it's accurate, and get some advice on how to respond - or pay them to handle it. I am including a sample response letter in Appendix C, but don't use it without consulting a professional first.

Sorry.

My Advice:

1. Don't ignore a letter or let the due date pass without at least communicating with the IRS.
2. Don't assume the letter is right.
3. Don't send money without consulting a professional to verify the letter is accurate and to get assistance responding.

82. IRS Letter Types

Listed below are some of the more common IRS letters as identified by the Notice number. They are grouped into the basic type of letter based on what the IRS is trying to tell you or what information they want. Simply look for the number in the upper right-hand corner of the first page of the letter, and then find the number on the list below. It may be preceded by a CP or LT and may be followed by a letter. Generally, if it has LT in front of it, the IRS is getting serious and is preparing to levy your assets to get their money. You will want to handle those types of letters quickly and efficiently.

If you don't find your specific number on the list, go to this web address and you can look it up. You can also get details on your letter and what to do at the same address. You should also ALWAYS take steps to verify that the letter is not a SCAM. If the letter was an email attachment, it's a scam. I think the only sure ways to be sure it's not a scam are to ask a professional or contact the IRS at 1-800-829-1040 (not the number on the letter). You can also verify that the letter type you received matches the information at the link below (but this is not as sure-fire as the two I just mentioned):
https://www.irs.gov/Individuals/Understanding-Your-IRS-Notice-or-Letter

Appendix C has a sample letter that you can use to respond to an IRS letter. When responding to IRS letters, never send originals of any documents, only send copies.

Again, to be clear, the list below is not exhaustive and also may include letters that they no longer use. I do endeavor to ensure all the most common letter types are listed, but they put out a LOT of letters!

Bad Notices:

11, 12, 19, 23, 101, 103, 105, 106, 126, 132
These generally represent various types of errors they believe you made on your return and indicate that they want more money from you. They usually have a voucher at the bottom of the first page so you can detach it and send the money to them. You don't have to assume they are right and send them money because the notice is basically a suggestion that they think you are wrong, but the form has check boxes for agreeing or disagreeing, and allowing you to explain why you were right, and sending additional proof. In general, if you disagree, you should check the "I

disagree with some or all of the changes" box, and send a letter detailing why you were right. You can use the sample I discussed earlier and make sure to include supporting documents if applicable.

18, 20
These generally represent various types of errors they believe you made on your return and indicate that they sent you a smaller refund as a result. You don't have to assume they are right. If you disagree, you should send a letter detailing why you were right and include supporting documents if applicable.

31, 231, 32, 237
The first two indicate that your refund check was returned as undeliverable. You generally just need to update your address. You can do this by sending the letter back with a correct address, calling the number on the letter, or updating your address using the "Where's my Refund" system at irs.gov. The second two letters are sent to tell you that they mailed the replacement check out.

39, 42, 44, 49, 138
All of these letters indicate that they kept all or part of your refund to pay a tax or other federal debt. This can be your debt, your spouse's debt, or even an ex-spouse's debt. If the debts aren't legitimate, the letter should give you contact information for who they kept the money for. You can also call (800) 304-3107 and find out the information (non tax debts only). If the debt was legitimate, there are still a few ways to get around it, but you should talk to a professional to help you with them. (The 44 letter actually just says your refund is being delayed due to one of these debts).

75C, 79A
These indicate that you are not getting Earned Income Credit (EIC) because you previously filed for EIC when not entitled and were subsequently banned from claiming EIC for the situation you filed.

77, 90, 91, 92, 177
These are BAD. They are telling you that they are about to levy you. This means they are preparing to seize your stuff to pay your tax debts. Don't ignore these! You are already WAY behind the eight-ball and generally it is too late to argue about the tax issues (though not completely). If you owe the money – PAY IT (if you can). If the IRS is wrong, seek help IMMEDIATELY!

14, 160, 161, 163, 165, 166, 171, 187, 501, 503

These letters are sent when you owe the IRS money, but they haven't gotten it. Usually the tax issue is settled, and it's just a matter of them getting the money. These may be caused by any number of reasons.

523

The IRS sends these when you fail to live up to the requirements of an installment agreement you signed up for. They are about to levy your assets.

3219

This is the notice that the IRS sends when you either agreed with their correction to your return, or you ignored them for too long after they sent you letters. This is a notice that the IRS has made a pretty final decision that you owe them money. You generally have to go to court to fight these. If you don't agree that you owe them money at this point, contact a professional experienced with fighting the IRS.

May be Bad Notices:

5, 6, 7

The IRS is taking a closer look or auditing your return internally before sending you your refund. You don't need to do anything, and shouldn't contact the IRS unless more than 30 days pass without getting any new information or receiving your refund. If more than 30 days pass, call the number on the letter (upper right-hand corner).

53, 153

These indicate that your direct deposit will not occur for various reasons and that they will be mailing you a check. They will send it to the address on the return unless you updated your address with the IRS since filing.

59, 63, 81, 88, 259

All of these letters have to do with unfiled tax returns that the IRS wants you to file. Sometimes they will warn you that the expiration date for getting a refund for the year in question is about to expire and sometimes they will explain that they are holding your current refund until you file the missing tax returns.

75, 76, 79

These letters are asking for more information before the IRS will pay you Earned Income Credit (EIC). Sometimes this is because you had issues previously claiming the child you are trying to claim. The letter will provide details on the types of information needed to substantiate the claim. (76 is generally a response saying they approved the EIC they were questioning in a 75 or 79 letter).

141
They send these letters when you've ignored a previous letter (or it never got to you). Generally, the original letter was asking for more information.

521
You have an installment payment due on an installment agreement.

2000, 2005, 2006
These are some of the most common letters. They indicate that the IRS received a tax form from someone (W-2, 1099 etc.) that reported income you received, and that it is not included on your tax return. These are wrong a lot of the time. You should never just send the money unless you are absolutely certain the requested amount is correct. They usually have a voucher at the bottom of the first page so you can detach it and send the money to them. You don't have to assume they are right and send them money. The notice is basically a suggestion that they think you are wrong, but the form has check boxes for agreeing or disagreeing, and allowing you to explain why you were right, and sending additional proof. In general, if you disagree, you should check the "I disagree with some or all of the changes" box, and send a letter detailing why you were right. Include supporting documents if applicable. 2005 is sent when you respond and they agree you are right, 2006 is sent when you respond and they are considering your response. Lately they seem to be adding a disallowance of Education Credits to every one of these, but they are really asking for you to prove the Education Credit. Read carefully, and provide the requested documents. The next chapter in this book has specific information on CP2000 letters.

2057
These are similar to the 2000 above, except that they are requesting an amended tax return from you (the main difference is that on the 2000 they calculated what they think you owe and the 2057 is asking you to redo (amend) the return to determine what the missing information does to the return.)

2501
Again, similar to the 2000, except this time they want you to call and talk to them about it. Call the number on the letter, and make sure you have the

tax return for the year in question and all supporting documents handy. Call soon.

Neutral Notices:
13
The IRS made a change to your return but it didn't change the overall result.

80
The IRS got the money you sent to pay the taxes from your balance due tax return, but they didn't get the tax return. Figure out why and get the return to the IRS.

180, 181
A form or schedule was missing from your return. Usually there isn't an issue with results, they just need the form to back up what you filed.

May be Good Notices:

8, 9, 27
The IRS believes you should have gotten the Additional Child Tax Credit and/or the Earned Income Credit. This means they want to give you more money! Generally, you just have to check a box or two, sign the letter, and send it back to get your money. If you aren't entitled to the credits, respond to the letter telling them why.

Good Notices:

21, 22
For 2020 Only:
The IRS adjusted your return to account for the Unemployment Income Exclusion that was passed in the middle of the tax filing season. Generally, you should have already received the money, and this lets you know why. If you receive this notice but didn't receive the money, follow the instructions on the notice for claiming the refund amount. This can be difficult, but be persistent.

24, 111, 112, 113, 115, 116, 133, 268
The IRS believes you made an error on your return and they think they owe you MORE money. A lot of times you don't need to do anything to get it, but you should read the letter carefully and follow the instructions to

ensure you get the money. If you aren't entitled to the money, respond to the letter telling them why.

1444

These are a series of notices informing you of your various Coronavirus stimulus payments. 1444 was the original letter "from Trump" about the very first stimulus payment being sent. 1444-A was sent to people who needed to take action to claim the first stimulus. Subsequent letters were added (1444-B, 1444-C) applied to later stimulus payments. Most of these were simply informational in nature, though a few required you to take action in order to get your payment.

6416, 6417, 6419

These letters are about the Child Tax Credit and Advance Child Tax Credit. 6417 letters contain general information about the changes to the Child Tax Credit passed in 2021. 6416 letters indicate your eligibility for and provide specific information for you regarding the Advance Child Tax Credit. 6419 letters will tell you how much Advance Child Tax Credit they sent you so you can reconcile it on your 2021 tax return.

83. I Got a CP2000 Letter From the IRS

A CP2000 notice is a type of letter the IRS sends automatically when information is reported to them that doesn't match your tax return, or when there is information on your return that they SHOULD have gotten information on but didn't (meaning someone sent them a tax form such as a W-2 or 1099 and the information was not included by you on your tax return). You can tell it's a CP2000 notice because it will say so in the upper right-hand corner of the first page. A CP2000 looks like a bill, has a payment coupon like a bill, but it's NOT a bill. It's a "question" from the IRS about something that's missing and contains their suggestion as to what the answer to the question is (in the form of a bill). Don't send money unless you are ABSOLUTELY certain that you owe it. You have 30 days to respond, and you should use this time to make sure you understand what you really owe. If you need more time, call the phone number from the upper right-hand corner of the letter and ask for more time. DO NOT IGNORE THE IRS!

In this chapter, I'm going to go through all the sections of a CP2000 letter, and tell you what they mean, and what you should do in them. Most letters are very similar in structure, but some may not have all the sections. The sections are separated by a nice bold line across the whole page, so I'm going to make it easier to follow by putting a series of asterisks (*********) on my page where one of those lines would be (lines don't always transfer well to Kindle, so this makes it simpler when it comes time to publish).

You can find a sample CP2000 here:
https://www.irs.gov/pub/notices/cp2000_english.pdf

First. Here are some things to do immediately:

1. Take a deep breath, even if the proposed payment amount is big. A lot of times the number is smaller, or zero, and even if it is the big number, there are ways to mitigate it or pay over time. Don't Panic.
2. Make sure the letter is to YOU. Check the name in the top left and the Social Security Number in the top right. If it's not you, I would suggest calling the number on the form immediately or sending them a quick letter (Appendix C has an example) telling them so (I'll go over exactly how to do this towards the end of this chapter when I get to the response section of the CP2000).
3. Make sure the letter is not a SCAM. There are some real a-holes out

there who will stop at nothing to steal your money. If the letter was an email attachment, it's a scam. I think the only sure ways to be certain it's not a scam are to ask a professional or contact the IRS at 1-800-829-1040 (not the number on the letter). Also, if it differs significantly from my description of how the letter should flow, you should be suspicious as heck.

4. If you KNOW the letter is wrong because it is an obvious mistake, you will likely ultimately owe nothing. HOWEVER, if you do end up owing money, interest and penalties will continue to accrue while you argue with the IRS. Penalties MAY be able to be forgiven (abated), but interest almost never is. If the amount in question is large, you can avoid additional penalties by making a "6603 deposit". This is basically giving them the money up front until the issue is resolved. I'm not a fan of it, because I feel it is always better being the one with the money in your pocket vice fighting to get it back. BUT interest and penalty rates are very high right now (9 to 13% very roughly) so it can add up to substantial amounts. Make sure to write "6603 deposit" on the check, on a statement included with the check, and a copy of the letter you are making the deposit for.

There are probably a few things in the envelope besides the CP2000 letter. When I refer to "the letter" I'm just talking about the pages that have page X of X in the upper right-hand corner information box. The letter may also include, an envelope to send a response in, a payment voucher that you include if you send them money (this may have page X of X on it like the letter but should be easy to identify as a payment voucher), an installment request form for if you want to make payments, and a pamphlet on your rights as a taxpayer.

Now let's go through the letter:

The first section has the IRS address, your name and address, the summary of proposed changes, a brief description of why they sent the letter, and, most importantly, the top right corner has vital details about the letter. These include the notice type (CP2000), the year in question (make sure you compare to the right tax return), the notice date, your SSN, the AUR control number (refer to this when communicating with the IRS), and the IRS contact information. It also tells you the date you need to respond by.

****

The **What you need to do immediately** section: This section is generally the same on every letter. It tells you what they expect you to do as a result of the letter but we will be covering what to do as we go through the rest of the letter.

****

The **If we don't hear from you** section: Tells you the date you need to respond by, and the fact that they will issue a Statutory Notice of Deficiency (basically a final notice) and a final bill once the date passes. Also states that they charge interest and penalties the whole time (if you pay by the due date in the letter the interest and penalty is already included). This is a good time for me to point out that ignoring the IRS is one of the two things the IRS hates the most (lying to them is the other.)

****

The **Changes to your 20XX tax return** section: This is usually a table with line items from your tax return that has columns with your numbers, the IRS numbers and the difference. This can be confusing, and oftentimes not much use, but reviewing it will show you where they made the changes. The next section is often more useful. (The XX in the year obviously will be the year the letter applies to).

****

The **Explanation of changes to your 20XX Form 1040** section: This is a big section, with a lot of information. If they got a form with information you didn't include on your tax return, it will usually be listed here first. There's a catch! If the form had tax withholding, they list that separately from any income it reported, so it can look like there are a lot more forms missing than there should be. A W-2, for example, almost always has withholding, so there will be two separate lines with the same general information on the form, but one shows the withholding and one shows the income. If there are a lot of lines, it can be helpful to make a list of the forms missing (ignoring the duplicates for withholding) and comparing it with what you reported on your tax return. It is not uncommon for you to have reported everything correctly, but somehow the IRS misses it (though sometimes this happens because your employer corrects a form, but does not indicate that correctly, so the IRS treats it as a totally separate form). If all the forms were reported on your tax return, try to figure out why the IRS doesn't know that, and, even if you can't figure out why, send them a letter (Appendix C has an example) explaining the situation (I'll go over exactly how to do this towards the end of this chapter when I get to the response section of the CP2000). If the forms aren't included, but you are sure they shouldn't apply to you (a W-2 for a company you never worked for) send a letter like we just discussed (be careful though, the name of the company on the W-2 may not be the name you know your employer by, and some jobs issue multiple W-2's if they change corporate structure.) I'm going to cover some common missing forms and give some advice on each:

1. W-2, 1099INT, 1099DIV: If you missed one of these on your return, the amount owed calculated on the CP2000 is probably right, but you can redo the tax return to confirm.
2. W-2G: This is winnings from gambling at a casino or poker room, lotteries or horse races. If you did win the money, you can deduct your losses on Schedule A up to the amount of your winnings. This requires itemizing to make a difference. You might want to get some professional help if this is a big number.
3. 1099B: This is one of the most common missing items. Usually this represents you selling some investment. A lot of people don't report these because they lost money or didn't make much and they thought it wouldn't make a difference. BIG MISTAKE! The IRS doesn't take what you paid for the investment (your basis) into account, so this letter is charging you taxes on the amount you sold it for, ignoring what you paid for it. Find the 1099B, use it to fill out a Schedule D, Form 4797 and/or Form 8949 and then run those numbers onto your tax return to get the RIGHT amount of tax you owe (or you might get a refund!) Make sure this number is the DIFFERENCE between your original result and the new result. Make sure to include the revised schedules when responding, and there is also a worksheet for calculating the tax on capital gains that you should include.
4. 1099MISC/NEC: This could be for work as a contractor, rental income, or even royalties from writing a book or owning an oil well. These can get very complex and you should seek professional help unless you are absolutely sure how to handle these. Contractor work was removed from the 1099MISC and shifted to form 1099NEC a few years ago.
5. 1099C: This is for having debt canceled by someone you owed money to. Don't be surprised if the event happened years ago, and/or the creditor bears no resemblance to the people you originally owed. Don't assume that just because you don't recognize the debt doesn't mean it's not yours (unless you are absolutely sure you never owed money that you didn't pay back).

This is also very complex, and there are some ways to avoid paying the tax on it. Read the chapters on <u>I Had Debt Written Off by the Company I Owe Money To</u> and <u>I Lost my House (Foreclosure, Short Sale or Bankruptcy)</u> to get more information and consider seeking professional help.

6. There are a few other forms, but they don't come up much.

Below the list of missing items will be a list of reasons why your tax results might have changed. Some of these are explanations about the effect of the missing forms above, and others are about changes unrelated to missing forms. One very common example would be if you claimed an education credit, but the IRS did not receive a 1098T showing the expenses you paid. They also have been tending to ask for additional proof of education expenses even when they got the 1098T, especially if they are sending you a CP2000 for an unrelated missing form. Another example is when you missed an income form, and it affected other aspects of the return other than tax, such as putting you over an income limit for a deduction, changing the amount of Earned Income Tax Credit you are entitled to, or making more of your Social Security Income taxable. Read this section carefully and it will usually tell you what they are looking for in order to prove the specific item missing.

Don't worry if not every listed change asks for documents, most will simply be explaining how the missing forms affected various items on your return. Again, read this section carefully. It helps to make notes for each item of information that you need to find or verify, leaving out the things that don't require action.

This section can be very confusing and, since a computer wrote the letter, can be a place where a lot of mistakes crop up so read it carefully. Consider making notes and writing down your own list of issues. If you can't figure it out, bring the letter, the tax return in question and all the forms you used to a professional for a consultation.

****

The **Next steps** section: This section just tells you not to file a 1040X for the tax return the letter refers to, but to check state returns for the year in question and all returns for other years in which you might have made the same mistake. Most states will chase you down if the CP2000 affects the state return, so be aware of this possibility.

****

The **Interest charges** section: This section explains how the interest amount was calculated.

****

The **Additional information** section: This section has information on obtaining forms and assistance. It should be the last section before a new page, which will be the start of the **Response form**.

****

The top of the first page of the **Response form** has the IRS address, the response due date, a place for you to update your contact information and the identifying information in the upper right-hand corner (SSN, AUR #, notice type, tax year, and notice date). AUR stands for Automated Underreporter, because this is an automated, computer run system cleverly called the Automated Underreporter Program. The AUR# makes sure things you send to the IRS are properly connected to the right issue.

You'll use this form to respond to the letter, whether you agree or not. You can usually fold the response form in a way that the address at the top of this form will appear in the window of the envelope the IRS provided for responding. If you don't use that envelope, the address at the top of the form (the one that starts with INTERNAL REVENUE SERVICE) is where you send it.

****

1. Indicate your agreement or disagreement:

Two choices:
1. You agree with the amount they want you to send. If you do, you check the box and sign that you acknowledge that you owe the money. You are also acknowledging a few other things, but you basically had better be sending in the money with the response or arranging to make payments.
2. You disagree. Check that box, and move on, though there is often a fax number here that you can use to send the response form with supporting documents back to them. Always include your name, SSN and the AUR number from the front of the letter on EVERY

PAGE you fax to them. Always use a cover letter indicating the total pages that you sent.

****

2. **Indicate your payment option**:

Four options:
1. Full payment
2. Partial payment (write in the amount you are sending)
3. No payment
4. Installment request form. You can check more than one, but that would generally be partial or no payment with an installment request. If you are sending in a check, make sure you follow the instructions in this section and include the voucher page from the letter. If you don't write the requested information, when the guy at the IRS messes up and separates the check from the voucher, the payment might not get credited to you. This is a good time to mention that when sending money to the IRS, it's a good idea to track when the check gets cashed and print out proof that it was. Anyway, check the box or boxes that apply. If you want to do an installment request, there is usually one included with your letter, if not, you can go to irs.gov and click on the "Pay" tab on the ribbon menu and you will quickly find online options to apply for an installment agreement.

****

3. **Authorization** (optional): You use this section if you want someone to talk to the IRS on your behalf. This would normally be your tax preparer or an Enrolled Agent, CPA or lawyer that you hired to help you. You will need to include a power of attorney as well.

******* (there's not actually a line here, it's just the end of the letter.)

That's just about everything in the letter. So...

If you agree with the letter, send the response form, the payment voucher, a check and/or an installment agreement request.

For all the below disagreement types, make sure that you include the AUR number from the letter on any correspondence you send, and I also recommend writing your name, Social Security Number and the AUR number on the top of any page of documentation you send. Also remember that interest and penalty continue to accrue on any amount you ultimately owe while you are arguing with the IRS, so be timely, and, if the amounts in question are large, consider sending a "6603 deposit" for the amount they think you owe to stop the interest and penalties from accruing.

If you disagree with the letter, but still calculate that you owe them money, send the response form, the voucher, a check and/or an installment agreement request. Include a letter (Appendix C has an example) explaining why you disagree with their conclusion and how you came up with your amount. Include all forms and worksheets from your tax return that have changed with the correct amounts on them. Include any proof to substantiate your claim.

If you disagree with the letter, and don't think you owe them any money, send the response form indicating that you disagree with the changes and are sending no payment. Include a letter (Appendix C) explaining why you disagree with their conclusion. Include all forms and worksheets from your tax return that substantiate your conclusion (for example, you may have failed to include a 1099C for canceled debt, but you use Form 982 to exclude it from taxation). Include any proof to substantiate your claim.

On occasion, they may owe you money! This can happen if you didn't include the information from a 1099B (investment sale) and the sale was actually at a loss. Respond the same way discussed above for not owing any money, and simply indicate in the letter the amount you think they owe you. With luck, you'll get a check...with interest!

Send all of the above to the address at the top of the response form (you can also fax them to the number provided). Make sure to include enough postage! The IRS will send you a response indicating whether they agree, and may request more information. Make sure to keep your address updated with them!

84. I Got This Tax Form

Below is a listing of forms you may come across while managing your finances and preparing your taxes:

W-2: I am pretty sure you know what this is, but I'll cover some basics. Boxes 1 through 6 are your income and withholding for federal taxes, Social Security and Medicare. Only Boxes 1 and 2 affect your federal tax return, unless you have multiple jobs that put you above the maximum income for Social Security withholding, (that's pretty rare).

Boxes 7 and 8 are about tips, I have a chapter on that.

Box 10 is what your company gives you to put your kids in daycare. If you spend it on daycare, you're good; if you don't, its taxable income. You report it on Form 2441, which is the form you get your daycare credit on. Speaking of which, you have to subtract Box 10 from your daycare expenses before you calculate your credit for daycare expenses.

You shouldn't see anything in Box 11. If you do, seek a tax professional.

Box 12 is information that might be used in your tax return. This is where 401k-type plans, healthcare benefits, HSA contributions and other information is reported to you.

Box 13 has special check marks for unique situations. If statutory employee or third-party sick pay is checked, you need help (or you already know what to do). If retirement plan box is checked, that affects your IRA contribution limits as discusses in the IRA chapter.

Box 14 can hold a lot of information, and you should understand what's in there. Some companies put a lot of weird stuff in there.

Boxes 15 and beyond are state information for filing state taxes (though the tax withheld is a federal Itemized Deduction).

W-2G: This is income from gambling or lottery. Make sure to report it on your tax return.

W-4: This is the form you use to tell your employer to adjust your withholding. Some employers do it online via a payroll site. The instructions work great for a single or married person with one income and no kids. After that, it's pretty much crap.

W-9: This form is used by your employer to get information from you to verify your SSN so they can properly report your income to the IRS. You have to fill it out if you want the job.

1095-A: This form reports the health insurance you got through an Affordable Cara Act (Obamacare) marketplace. It includes information on covered persons and the subsidy received. It serves as both proof of insurance and is used to determine any reconcile the amount of subsidy received and whether you owe money back or get more. You will need to file form 8962 to reconcile the credit amount and might need to file additional forms if you weren't covered the entire year.

1095-B: This form is provided to you (and the IRS) by your health insurance provider to report on health insurance that they provide to you. You will need it to prove that you had minimum essential health insurance coverage to avoid the Shared Responsibility Payment (penalty for not having insurance).

1095-C: This form is provided to you (and the IRS) by your employer to report on health insurance that they provide to you. You will need it to prove that you had minimum essential health insurance coverage to avoid the Shared Responsibility Payment (penalty for not having insurance).

1098: This form provides your mortgage interest, points and mortgage insurance premiums paid on a residence that might be deductible on Schedule A or Schedule E (for rental property). You can also usually find your real estate taxes and sometimes homeowners' insurance on this form, or on the same page as the form. Make sure you get a 1098 from every lender who has serviced your loan over the course of the year.

1098-C: You'll need to get this form from a charity you donate a car to if you want to deduct more than $500.

1098-E: This form reports the student loan interest you paid during the year. Often this comes in the form of a letter that looks nothing like a 1098-E, but will say "substitute 1098-E" on it. See I Paid on Student Loans for more information.

1098-MA: This form reports information on government mortgage assistance programs that helped you with mortgage payments. Seek help if you get this form.

1098-T: This form has most of the information you need to claim education credits or deductions. It should show the amount of tuition you paid, and the scholarships you received. You should not rely solely on this form, but should get an account transcript from your school's finance department. See I am Going to College for more information.

1099-A: This form indicates that someone has taken possession of your property, usually to satisfy a debt. Generally, you will see this for foreclosure on real property or repossession of a vehicle. For tax purposes, this represents a deemed sale of the property and it must be reported on Schedule D or Form 4797 (for business property). You cannot take a loss on the repossession of personal property. Determine gain by subtracting your basis (how much you paid for it, generally) from either the FMV (Box 4) or balance outstanding (Box 2). Generally, you will use FMV if Box 5 is checked; use the outstanding balance if Box 5 is not checked (though you should seek advice from a local tax professional because state lending laws can impact this determination). Box 1 is the sale date, and the date acquired is when the taxpayer acquired the property.

If this was a foreclosure of your personal residence, any gain might be excluded following the same rules as for Sale of Main Home. Details are linked in the Foreclosure chapter.

1099-B: This form reports proceeds from investments that you sold during the year. They can vary in form and are often combined with 1099-DIV and 1099-INT. They will report the total price that you received for all assets you sold during the year (with that particular investment company). Further in the package they will provide information for each asset: the date purchased, (if they have it), date sold, sales proceeds and basis (if they have it—basis is generally what you paid for an asset, but can change due to a variety of factors). If the information is provided and accurate, simply report it on your tax return. If information is missing or inaccurate, work with your broker and a tax professional to find it. ALWAYS report sales on your tax return, even if you broke even or lost money!

1099-C: This form is used to report debt that you owed to a company that has been written off for one reason or another and will not be collected. It is generally income to you, but there are lots of exceptions. You'll want to check out these chapters as applicable: I Had Debt Written Off by the Company I Owe Money To and I Lost my House (Foreclosure, Short Sale or Bankruptcy).

1099-G: The 1099-G is used for a lot of things, but you generally only need to be concerned with two: unemployment compensation, and state income tax refunds. I find it irritating that the two are mixed such that state refund information is right in the middle of unemployment information.

Box 1 reports any unemployment compensation you received. There's a line for this on your 1040.
Box 4 reports any federal income tax withheld on your unemployment compensation. This is included on your tax return with your withholding from W-2's and other forms.
Boxes 10 and 11 report state information for your unemployment compensation, including state tax withheld.

Box 2 is your state refund from the year indicated in Box 3. If you itemized deductions in the prior year, this is probably taxable income to you. (If you owed and paid taxes on your state return the prior year, that would be a deduction.) It is only taxable to the extent that it improved your tax situation, so if you were only $100 above your standard deduction and received a refund of $200, only $100 would be taxable.

If any other boxes have entries, seek professional help.

1099-K: This form reports payments you (probably your business) receive from credit card processors. It should be reported on your Schedule C (or other business return you file), but make sure it doesn't duplicate income recorded in your own records. (If you keep good records this form should have no new information for you.)

1099-Q: This form contains information on the amount of money withdrawn from Qualified Tuition Plans or Education Savings Accounts. These are plans that allow you to save money in tax-deferred accounts for education. If you had education expenses, this form will assist you in determining the benefits you get for education (see the I am Going to College chapter). If you don't have education expenses, the amount in Box 2 is taxable income to you.

1099-R: This form is used to report retirement plan distributions (state, federal, private, military and more), annuity distributions, IRA distributions, some insurance plan payments and many other distributions from tax advantaged accounts. Some situations are simple, and some are amazingly complicated. If your 1099-R has a number in Boxes 1 and 2, and the code 7 in Box 7, you have a simple situation (the amount in Box 2 is taxable income and is reported on your return and taxed). Anything else and you might have some work to do. See the I am Retired chapter for some help.

1099-S: You receive this form when you sell real estate. It has the gross proceeds from the sale. You generally only need to make sure the gross proceeds on this form match your records of the sale—the information on the 1099-S is reported to the IRS. Assuming they match, use your documents to report the sale. If they don't match, contact the person who provided the 1099-S to find out why.

1099-SA: This form reports distributions from Health Savings Accounts of various types. See I Have an HSA and HDHP through Work for more details.

1099-INT: This form reports interest you received from bank accounts, Certificates of Deposit and bonds. It comes in many forms and may be combined with 1099-DIV and 1099-B. See I Have Investments Outside of Work for more information.

1099-OID: This form reports interest you received from bonds, which accrue due to buying the bond at a discount from its face value. It comes in many forms and may be combined with 1099-DIV, 1099-INT and 1099-B. See I Have Investments Outside of Work for more information.

1099-DIV: This form reports dividends you received from ownership of stocks and mutual funds. It comes in many forms and may be combined with 1099-INT and 1099-B. See I Have Investments Outside of Work for more information.

1099-MISC: This is the catchall form for when someone pays you money and there's no other form for it. I'm going to tell you what Boxes 1, 2, 3, 4 and 7 generally mean; if you have anything in another box (other than the state info boxes), you should seek additional help.

Box 1 represents rent received. Most people with numbers in this box have rental property and either have a property manager, or receive government rent payments for low income housing. This is reported on your Schedule E for the rental.

Box 2 would be royalties from art, writing or even possibly oil wells on your land. It is also reported on Schedule E.

Box 3 is money paid to you that doesn't fit anywhere else. It is generally reported on Line 21 of Form 1040.

Box 4 is federal income tax withheld from the payments that were made to you. You include it with all the other federal tax withheld on your tax forms.

Box 7 is "usually" income you receive as a contractor or as a self-employed business person, and would go on your Schedule C. There are situations where this would be reported on Line 21 of Form 1040, but you should seek guidance to be sure before you report it there.

1099-PATR: This form reports distributions from a cooperative. If you aren't sure how to handle this information, you should seek additional help.

1099-RRB (RRB-1099): This form reports Railroad Retirement Benefits, which is an alternative to Social Security. If you aren't sure how to handle this information, you should seek additional help.

1099-SSA (SSA-1099): This form reports Social Security payments. If you receive this form, your payments are potentially taxable (even if they are for disability). See I am Receiving Social Security for more information. If there is a number in Box 4 or information on prior year's payments in the big box (description of amount in Box 3), you might want to seek professional assistance.

2439: You might get one of these if you invest in certain types of investments, mainly Real Estate Investment Trusts. They represent capital gains that they had but did not distribute. You have to claim them on your tax return. They generally go right on your Schedule D (the form instructions tell you where) or the worksheet in the Schedule D instructions.

3921: This reports exercise of incentive stock options (ISO). You need to determine if the stock was sold in the year exercised. If the stock was sold in the same calendar year it was exercised, determine if the income was included on the W-2 (cashless exercises almost always are.) You can do this by inquiring from your employer or comparing Boxes 1 and 5 on the W-2 to see if the difference can be accounted for as the gain from the option (ISO gains are not taxed for Medicare or SS). If it is on the W-2, you need only report the proceeds on Schedule D and enter the basis as the same as the proceeds. If it is not on the W-2, you add it on Line 7 of Form 1040. Also enter it on Schedule D as above.

If the stock option was not sold in the calendar year purchased, you only report the difference between the option price and FMV on Line 14 of the 6251 (alternative minimum tax.) This value can be calculated by subtracting the amount in Form 3921 Box 3 from Box 4, and multiplying the difference by Box 5. Save this information, you will need this when you sell the stock. When the stock is sold you will need to determine if it meets holding periods (see IRS Pub 525 under stock options) and report it as capital gain and/or ordinary income in accordance with the instructions. If you paid AMT on the exercise, you may not have to pay as much tax when you sell it.

3922: This represents transfer of stock from the employer to the employee under an incentive stock purchase plan where the value of the stock transferred is higher than the price paid. No action is required until the stock is sold, at which point it is reported on Schedule D and/or Form 1040 Line 7 IAW IRS Pub 525. If the stock was not sold during the tax year, I recommend recording the data from the form in a note with your tax records so it is available when the stock is sold.

5498: This form reports information on your IRA contributions and the value of your account. Most people will have already used their year-end statement to report this information on their tax return, since this form comes out late in the tax season. SAVE ALL of these forms in your tax records where you can get them easily. I like people to keep a separate 5498 file with all the 5498's from all accounts for their entire life. A lot of companies send these forms in a format that looks very little like the IRS form, so pay attention to your brokerage statements to find them.

5498-SA: This form reports information about your Health Savings Account. It is informational in nature and you shouldn't need it to file your taxes. Save it with the tax year's file. See I have an HSA and HDHP through Work for more information.

Schedule K-1: You get this form when you are a participant or beneficiary of a partnership, S-Corporation, estate or trust. You might get this if you invested in a limited partnership (even if you thought it was regular old stock). Basically, the partnership, S-Corp, trust or estate files its own tax return, and then breaks the results down by ownership interest (if you own 10% of a partnership, you get 10% of their income and deductions). These forms can be very complicated, but the information generally carries directly to your tax return. They come with instructions that tell you where to put things, but you might want some extra help.

Military: Not a lot different for you here.

85. What About the Trump Tax Plan

I covered a lot of this information as it applied to the various chapters, but this is a fairly comprehensive list of what changed. There is not a ton of detail in this chapter, but it gives you an idea what has changed so you know what chapters you need to go back and review. For a lot more detail, The Short Cheap Tax Book for the Trump/GOP Tax Law is available now.

I planned to delete this chapter since the law started in 2018, but I still get a LOT of questions about rules that no longer exist. This is a good place to quickly check to see if what you think you know got changed. Also, many of these expire in 2025 or 2026 so a lot of it might come back.

Tax tables are generally better, and the tax brackets went from 10, 15, 25, 28, 33, 35, and 39.6 percent to 10, 12, 22, 24, 32, 35, and 37 percent.

Standard deductions were changed to $12,000 for Single and MFS, $18,000 for Head of Household (HH) and $24,000 for Married Filing Jointly (MFJ) and Qualifying Surviving Spouse (QSS). This sounds awesome, but they eliminated the personal exemption of $4050 for everyone on the return. For kids, this was offset by doubling the Child Tax Credit (discussed below). Effectively, your standard deduction plus exemptions for Single/MFS went from about $10,500 to $12,000. For MFJ it went from about $21,000 to $24,000 and for HH it went from about $13,500 to $18,000.

Claiming Head of Household has been subjected to preparer due diligence rules, so be prepared for more scrutiny from your tax guy and the IRS (starting in 2019 with 2018 tax returns).

The Child Tax Credit went from $1000 to $2000, with up to $1400 refundable (able to reduce your taxes below zero.) Other dependents get $500 (dependents who are not qualifying children age 16 and below). The income numbers where the credit phased out were dramatically increased to $200,000 for Single and $400,000 for MFJ (up from $110,000 for MFJ). If you are in the 25% tax bracket, you almost break even with these changes and the elimination of the exemption. In the lower brackets, you come out well ahead.

You can deduct no more than $10,000 of state and local income and property taxes on your tax return.

NEW home loans in 2018 and later can deduct interest on up to $750,000 of loans (down from 1,000,000). Home equity debt interest is no longer deductible (new loans only).

ALL miscellaneous itemized deductions subject to the 2% of income limitation are eliminated: tax prep fees, employee business expense, investment expense and a TON more.

Casualty and theft losses are only deductible for President declared disasters. There is also a special provision for losses due to disasters that occurred in 2016.

You can deduct up to 60% of your income in "normal" charitable contributions. Up from 50%. (Some contributions have more restrictive limits such as stock that's worth more than when you bought it).

There was a change in the threshold of income for which medical expenses were deductible, raising it from 7.5% to 10%. This kept getting pushed back and it is now back to 7.5% permanently.

The high-income phaseout of itemized deductions was repealed.

The Kiddie Tax was simplified dramatically (when your child has more than $2000ish of investment income). Children subject to the Kiddie Tax pay taxes at the rate of Estates and Trusts (higher than they normally would). This change was eliminated retroactively. This provision was retroactively eliminated so does not apply anymore.

You can use up to $10,000 of 529 college savings plan money, per child, per year, on elementary and secondary tuition and other expenses without paying tax on it.

Moving expenses are no longer deductible and employer reimbursement for moving expenses is taxable except for military Permanent Change of Station moves.

Starting in **2019**, any NEW divorce agreements will have alimony non-taxable to the recipient and non-deductible by the payer.

Starting in **2019**, there is no penalty for not having health insurance

The Alternative Minimum Tax exemption amounts and the income at which they start phasing out were significantly increased and indexed for inflation.

Student loans cancelled due to death or total and permanent disability are no longer included as income. Subsequent to the Trump Law almost all student loan cancellation was made tax free.

Entertainment expenses are no longer deductible. Essentially, anything that is FUN is not deductible anymore. That isn't exactly true. It was the intent, but, in reality, this really only seems to apply to extreme cases where the entertainment is highly expensive and the business purpose not clear cut.

Most businesses can deduct 20% of their profit off of their taxable income (next chapter).

Many of the above provisions have expiration dates in the next few years, but if history is any guide, the vast majority will be extended nearly indefinitely.

The following things were NOT changed:

Capital Gains rates are unchanged.

No change to education credits, student loan interest deductibility, or plug-in vehicle credits.

Savings bond interest used for education is still not taxable.

Education provided by colleges to their employees is still tax-free in the same way as it was before.

The exclusion of employer-provided education assistance remains unchanged.

Educators can still deduct $250 of in-class supplies they provide in the same manner as before, but anything above this amount that used to be deductible was eliminated with the elimination of the 2% floor itemized deductions.

No change to the exclusion of gain from the sale of personal residence (to be clear - you DO NOT have to buy a new home within 2 years to exclude it, that law was changed 20 years ago).

No change to MSA deductions or employer-provided Dependent Care Benefits rules.

No change to adoption credit or exclusion of employer-provided assistance.

No change to the solar credit.

86. Do I Get the 20% Business Deduction?

This has been called the "pass-through" deduction, but that's not really accurate. It includes almost all business income, including sole-proprietorships, S corporations, limited liability companies and income from investments in publicly traded partnerships and real estate investment trusts. This can apply to residential rental property, but it's a lot more complicated determining for sure. You should have already read the rental property chapters which have the details on how this rule applies to rental property.

There are a lot of weird provisions that kick in above a certain income, but if your TAXABLE* income (income after virtually all deductions other than this one) is less than $182,100**** ($364,200 Married Filing Jointly (MFJ)), then this pretty much applies to all business income and you get to deduct 20% of your net profit from each business directly off of your taxable income. This is designed to cause all businesses to pay about the same tax rate as corporations do with the new lower corporate rate that was passed with the Trump/GOP tax law.

In the first year, you didn't have to worry about this part, but, if you have a net loss from your business, you don't get the 20% deduction until you have enough profits to "recoup" the loss. Which makes sense. If you lose $10,000 in one year, deducting it off of your income, and then make a $10,000 profit the next year, you didn't actually make any money, so getting a 20% deduction would be overkill, AND would be ripe for abuse and manipulation. Make sure you carry these numbers from year to year. If you use the same software or preparer, they should handle this, but if you change software or preparers, this can be an issue. ALWAYS provide your last year's tax return to a new preparer (or 3 years' worth if you're smart).

Above those numbers limitations discussed a paragraph or so ago, a lot of weirdness kicks in.

If your business is service oriented** and your taxable income is over $182,100 ($364,200 MFJ), then your deduction starts to phase out and will be completely gone at $232,100 ($414,200 MFJ).

If your taxable income is $182,100 ($364,200 MFJ) and you have a non-service business, then the deduction is up to 20% of business income, but subject to a limitation based on wages or depreciable property in service that also phases in such that the limit fully applies at taxable income of $232,100 ($414,200 MFJ).

The wage limitation when fully phased in applies such that the most you can deduct is the greater of 50% of W-2 wages paid by the company (including your own wages) or 25% of W-2 wages plus 2.5% of the original basis of all qualified property***

This is both an over-simplified explanation and one that is still having the details tweaked as preparers and business owners discover more loopholes or unexpected details. If there's a chance this applies to you beyond very small dollar amounts, suck it up and pay a really good professional for help getting it right.

*This rule is very unusual in that you have to do your tax return all the way through just before figuring your tax, and THEN apply this deduction. It uses taxable income for virtually all tests and calculations, as opposed to Gross or Adjusted Gross Income like almost everything else in the tax world.

**From the bill, "A specified service trade or business means any trade or business involving the performance of services in the fields of health, law, consulting, athletics, financial services, brokerage services, or any trade or business where the principal asset of such trade or business is the reputation or skill of one or more of its employees or owners, or which involves the performance of services that consist of investing and investment management trading, or dealing in securities, partnership interests, or commodities." Architects and engineers are specifically noted as NOT subject to this limitation.

***From the Bill: "qualified property means tangible property of a character subject to depreciation that is held by, and available for use in, the qualified trade or business at the close of the taxable year, and which is used in the production of qualified business income, and for which the depreciable period has not ended before the close of the taxable year. The depreciable period with respect to qualified property of a taxpayer means the period beginning on the date the property is first placed in service by the taxpayer and ending on the later of (a) the date 10 years after that date, or (b) the last day of the last full year in the applicable recovery period that would apply to the property under section 168 (without regard to section 168(g))."

**** Weirdly, this number is not always the same as the Single number if filing Married Separately, but is usually within $50 or $100. I always thought this was a mistake that would eventually be corrected, but the slight difference between Single and MFS stubbornly remained through 2022. In 2023 they do match, but we will wait and see for 2024.

87. The 2020 Chapter: What Should I be Double Checking?

2020 was a crazy year, and not just for COVID. A lot of tax laws changed specifically for that year, and much of it occurred at the last minute. It is definitely worth your while to double check what you did in 2020, and how you handled it on your taxes. I'm going to cover the big things in this chapter, sorted out in a way that you can quickly figure out which tricks might apply to you. Basically, a bold title, a first paragraph to quickly determine if reading on is worth your while, then the details, and finally my personal advice.

If you already filed your taxes for 2020, and you find that some of the below might help, you generally have to file an amended return, which your software or tax pro can help with.

If you received unemployment:

For most people, this has been, or soon will be handled. Congress made the first $10,200 of unemployment tax free so long as Adjusted Gross Income (AGI) was less than $150,000 on the tax return. The $150,000 limit did not include ANY unemployment, so make sure you subtract unemployment (which is normally included in AGI, before seeing if you were eligible). If you filed taxes after the rule was passed, your software should have handled it. If you filed before, the IRS will be automatically sending you the difference, in most cases. Either way, if you received unemployment in 2020, keep reading, especially my advice at the end, to make sure you really got everything you deserved.

Details:
1. Each individual can exclude up to $10,200 of unemployment they receive. This means a married couple can exclude up to $20,400, as long as EACH person has at least $10,200 in unemployment. Ex: a married couple where one receives $12,000 in unemployment and the other $13,000, gets to deduct $20,400, assuming otherwise eligible. If one spouse receives $20,000, and the other $5000, the exclusion is $15,200 - $10,200 for the spouse receiving $20,000 and $5000 for the other.
2. If your AGI exceeds $150,000, you don't get the deduction, BUT you don't include ANY unemployment in AGI for this purpose. So is you have $120,000 in income and $40,000 of unemployment, you still get the exclusion even though your true AGI is $160,000.
3. The exclusion of unemployment helps change the following credits or calculations: Taxability of Social Security, IRA deduction income limit,

Student Loan Interest deduction income limit, exclusion of Series EE Bonds used for education income limit, Employer Provided Adoption Benefits income limit, The Tuition and Fees Deduction income and Rental Real Estate Passive Loss deduction income limit, Earned Income Tax and a few others that are less common.

4. The IRS will automatically correct your tax return, and send you the difference, however, they will not generally automatically adjust for credits that weren't included on the original return, so it makes sense to run your own return with the exclusion and make sure it matches what the IRS sends.

5. The IRS will send the difference to the account or address on the original return. If account information has changed, the bank will send the money back to the IRS and a check will be mailed. Update your address with the IRS using Form 8822!

6. When filing your 2021 tax return, you may be asked for your 2020 AGI. Use your AGI from before any post filing adjustments due to unemployment.

My Advice:

1. Update your address with the IRS using Form 8822 every time you move!

2. Unless you filed your 2020 tax return after the change, and got correct numbers, rerun your 2020 return and verify that the amounts the IRS sent match what you got. Your tax professional should do this automatically.

If you received a 1099R:

Read on if you took money out of a tax advantaged retirement account such as a 401k (or equivalent), a traditional or Roth IRA, or any other tax advantaged retirement account or pension plan. You would have received a 1099R for this distribution and it should have been included on your taxes. Don't read on if no one in your family had COVID and you are also certain that you didn't suffer any adverse financial impacts from anything related to COVID.

Details:

1. Up to $100,000 of retirement distribution made in 2020 can be considered a qualifying coronavirus distribution if the individual taking the money out, their spouse or their dependent had COVID in 2020 and can document that fact via a test approved by the FDA. It can also be considered a qualified coronavirus distribution without being sick if the individual (or spouse) suffered adverse financial affects from coronavirus

due to quarantine, furloughs, work hours reduction, business closure, job delay, childcare/school closure etc. Basically, if COVID cost you income, you probably qualify.

2. To be clear, the AMOUNT of adverse effect is irrelevant. You could be unpaid for 2 weeks due to a stay-at-home order, losing out on $2000 in wages and still be qualified. You can then take out up to $100,000, and it ALL is considered qualified.

3. The first benefit is you don't pay the 10% penalty on the withdrawal.

4. The second benefit is that you can spread the income over 3 years. Unfortunately, this has to be elected on a timely filed tax return, so it is probably too late if you already included it on your 2020 taxes as a normal distribution.

5. The third benefit is that you can put some or all of the money back within 3 years, and not include it in income at all, or, if you already included it, go back and amend to get the taxes paid back. If you are spreading it over three years, you first reduce the income in the year you put the money back, and then use any excess to reduce income in the prior, or subsequent year, depending on your preference. Taking it off a prior year requires an amendment.

6. If you are including income over three years, and you die, the remaining income is included on your final tax return for the year you die. Make sure your heirs know what you are doing with this.

My Advice:

1. If you took money out of a retirement account in 2020, and aren't sure if you qualify for relief, talk to a pro and get help amending if needed. Just getting out of the 10% penalty is magic! Also, recontributing is possible.

2. Don't overlook recontributing. Getting the money back into a retirement account AND avoiding taxes is a BIG deal. Consider restructuring other aspects of your financial life to make this happen.

You got Earned Income Credit in 2019 and/or 2020:

Earned Income Credit (EITC) is primarily paid to lower income families with kids. Single individuals can get it if they are between 25 and 65 years' old but have to make very little money. Check Line 27 of your 2020 Form 1040 and if there is a number there (other than zero) you got EITC. Check 2019 as well. If there is a number in either year, you might qualify.

Details:

1. This is actually simple: If you made less money in 2020 than 2019 due to Coronavirus, and you would have gotten more EITC based on your 2019 income, you can use your 2019 income to get the bigger number!

2. The hard part is that a lot of software doesn't handle this well. You will likely need a pro to help you get the right number.

My Advice:

1. If you got EITC in either 2019 or 2020 and your income in 2020 was lower. Talk to a tax pro to make sure you got the right amounts. All they need is the amount from Line 27 of both years and your total earned income, which is usually just wages from Line 1, as well as your AGI from Line 11. If your situation is more complicated, a copy of your 2019 and 2020 Form 1040 will tell them all they need to know.

2. A good tax pro should be able to tell if it is worth chasing in about 5 minutes and many will be willing to check for free, and then charge you to fix it only if it makes enough of a difference. If they can't figure out how to do this…walk away.

You paid back Affordable Care Act (Obamacare) premiums:

If you are on a subsidized ACA plan, you reconcile the amount of subsidy each year with your taxes. If you were over subsidized, you pay back, if you were under subsidized, you get the difference. Payback was suspended for 2020, so if you paid back, you paid too much. Just check Line 17 of your Form 1040. If it isn't blank or zero, check Line 2 of Schedule 2. If it isn't blank or zero, you paid too much.

The IRS should be sending you that amount back automatically. Just check to make sure they send the right amount and keep your address updated.

Details:

1. Those were pretty much the details. If there isn't a zero or blank space on Line 2 of Schedule 2, make sure you get the money back.

My Advice:

1. See above.

You were self-employed and couldn't work:

If you have a schedule C on your tax return, and there is ANY chance that COVID kept you from earning as much as you could have, you should talk to a pro about it. Also, if you did claim this credit, but made less money in 2020 than 2019, make sure you used 2019 income to get the better credit. I'm going to change the format on this chapter because I think talking to a pro is the only way to go, so I am going to throw out some details (liberally copied from my blog) so that you know if it is worth it, and so you can give your tax pro what they need. So, no Details and My Advice chapters, just a lightly edited cut and paste from the blog:

If you are unable to work or engage in your business as a result of quarantines, shutdowns, getting sick, school/daycare closings or various other reasons, you might be entitled to one or both of credits for sick leave or family leave. These credits are for employers to recoup payments they make to their employees who are unable to work for the above reasons. But, if you would have been entitled to these credits as an employee doing what you do, you qualify for them as the employer of yourself. In this case the government pays you for being unable to work for yourself.
Exactly how to define what makes the work you do qualifying as an employee is a bit nebulous, but it seems like a fairly liberal interpretation is appropriate, so I would go into conversations with you tax guy assuming you might qualify, and have the information required for them to calculate the credit rather than waiting to find out if you qualify. There were ways to get this money in advance, by reducing estimated payments, but it's pretty much too late for that to be effective.

This sucker gets complicated, so I'm going to start with a link to the IRS FAQ on the subject:

https://www.irs.gov/newsroom/special-issues-for-employees#specific-provisions-related-self-employed-individuals

I'm going to try my best to simplify how these work, but you absolutely need professional help to get these right. After discussing the various credits, I'm going to list the information you want to have available for when you file taxes.

Qualified Sick Leave Wages Credit:

1. You get up to 10 days worth of this credit.
2. If YOU are unable to work or telework because the government shut you down, ordered a quarantine, a doctor quarantined you due to being exposed, you had symptoms and were waiting for a diagnosis, or you actually had the disease you are entitled to $511 per day or 100% of your

average daily earnings, whichever is lower, for each day you could not work.

3. If you cannot work because you are caring for SOMEONE ELSE due to conditions similar to the above, or due to the closing of a school, daycare or other facility, or your daycare provider is unable to work, you are entitled to $200 per day or 67% of your average daily earnings, whichever is lower, for each day you could not work.

4. Average daily earnings are your net earnings from your business divided by 260. You get this number when you prepare your taxes as the bottom line on Schedule C. You can also use 2019 numbers if they are better.

5. If you received sick wages as an employee with a regular job, you have to reduce these credits by the amount of wages you were paid while not working (no double dipping).

6. This credit is not counted as income, even though it technically replaces income.

Qualified Family Leave Wages Credit:

1. This is VERY similar to the situation described in 3 above, but basically takes over where the 10 days above end.

2. You get 50 days worth of this credit.

3. You get this credit for any day you would have been qualified for Family Leave wages due to COVID if you were an employee (basically the situation described in 3 above). You are entitled to $200 per day or 67% of your average daily earnings, whichever is lower, for each day you could not work.

4. Average daily earnings are your net earnings from your business divided by 260. You get this number when you prepare your taxes as the bottom line on Schedule C. You can also use 2019 numbers for this if they are better.

5. If you received family leave wages as an employee with a regular job, you have to reduce these credits by the amount of wages you were paid while not working (no double dipping).

6. This credit is not counted as income, even though it technically replaces income.

Information you should provide to your tax dude:

1. Proof, as best you can get, of the situations discussed above. This could be doctor's notes, notices from schools or daycare facilities, quarantine or shutdown notices, COVID test results, copies of government statements

regarding allowed working conditions, or even newspaper articles reporting on work rules and quarantines.

2. The number of days you were unable to work due to YOU being affected by quarantines, shutdowns etc. as previously discussed.

3. The number of days you were unable to work due to caring for someone else as a result of quarantines, closures etc. as discussed previously.

4. The detailed reasons you were unable to work or make money for the days discussed above.

88. The 2021 Chapter

There are a lot of single-year changes that apply to 2021 only, and a few permanent ones. The single-year changes alone make a separate chapter a good idea.

The biggest change (in my mind) is the change to the daycare credit (Child and Dependent Care Credit). This is the one that is most likely to put more money in parent's pockets, even though the Child Tax Credit changes seem sexier (and get you an advance sometimes). Because I have written extensively about these on my blog, I am not going to reinvent the wheel, and instead will copy and edit from there to here. The fun of that is that you get my "Breaking News!" style of excitement inside of my boring old tax book. The Earned Income Credit changes are smaller for most people so the writeup will be less exciting.

Let's start with the Daycare Credit:

Again…these changes are for **2021 ONLY** unless they are extended…which there will be a lot of pressure to do inside the halls of Congress.

Here's the headline: A credit that was worth, at most, $1200 for most people is now worth up to $8000 for a heck of a lot more people.

Do I have your attention?

First, a bit about how the credit normally works:

For most people, you put your kid(s) in daycare so you (and your spouse) can go to work. You get a statement from the daycare and you put it on your tax return. With one kid, you get a credit on up to $3000 in expenses, with two or more kids, you get a credit on up to $6000 of expenses. A little understood fact is that if you have two or more qualifying kids, you get the $6000 limit even if it is all spent on one child. Remember a credit reduces taxes dollar for dollar, while a deduction reduces income. Credits are better.

Here are the details for the non-obvious cases:

1. People for whom expenses qualify are: children under the age of 13 (expenses apply right up to the day they turn 13), your spouse if he/she is

unable to care for themselves, and anyone else who lives with you for more than half the year who you can claim as a dependent (unless the reason you can't is income over $4300, they file a joint return, or you could be claimed as a dependent) who cannot take care of themselves.

2. Expenses have to be for you to work, look for work or go to school full-time. They have to be connected to these requirements by time (more on that later) but in reality, the main technique for determining this is to take your earned income (wages and net business income mostly), your spouses earned income, and the daycare expenses, then take the smaller of the three. In 90% of cases, this does the trick properly.

3. If you or your spouse are a full time student, for at least 5 months of the year, you can add to your income for the calculation $250 per month ($500 if you have two or more qualifying individuals) that you were a full time student, but this is where the timing thing comes in, if you have income during a month, you use the income, or the $250/$500 number, whichever is lower.

4. If you have earned income, but your spouse is disabled, you can use the $250/$500 discussed above for each month your spouse is disabled. You can't both use the disabled trick, one of you needs earned income.

5. Technically, if you and your spouse took a 3-month vacation and paid daycare so you could enjoy it, and then went back to work and had tons of earned income, only the daycare paid while you were working counts. Short, normal work breaks for vacation or illness are okay. Again, for most people the earned income/daycare expense method works just fine.

6. Day-camps count for the credit, but not overnight camps. Even day camps with specific activities like sports or music. School before kindergarten age counts but no schooling once kindergarten starts counts, however afterschool care does. The school should separately state expenses for school/aftercare.

7. You can't get this credit if you file Married Filing Separately.

8. Only the custodial parent can get this credit. If the child doesn't live with you half the year, you get nothing.

9. There are a lot more rules about daycare centers, who you can pay, and more. Seek professional help if your situation is not obvious. This is a broad strokes overview!

Here is the 2020 calculation:

$3000 max in expenses for one child. $6000 for two children. Get a credit for 35% of expenses if income (technically AGI) is below $15,000, then it drops quickly by 1% for every extra $2000 of income until it hits 20% of expenses, where it stays regardless of higher income. You cannot use this credit once your taxes hit zero.

Here is the 2021 calculation:

$8000 in expenses for one child. $16,000 for two children. Credit of 50% of expenses if income is below $125,000, then it drops to 20% as income goes up to $185,000, where it stays until income hits $400,000, where it quickly drops to zero as income gets to $440,000. Here is another BIG DEAL: You can get this credit even after your taxes hit zero.

One additional thought:

Divorcing couples with kids in daycare need to have a frank talk about amending a separately filed tax return to a jointly filed one. Talk to your tax professional and have them look at both returns to see if there is money to be made.

Now let's hit Child Tax Credit and Child Tax Credit Advances:

If you have children who are 17 or younger you should have received Letter 6417 from the IRS detailing how much they were planning to send you in Advance of your 2021 Child Tax Credit. These payments started arriving in July, and understanding how they are determined, and how they affect your 2021 taxes is vitally important. In the best case, you get some nice payments up front, with a potentially small impact on your 2021 refund. In the worst case, your income or child situation changes to the point where they advance you a bunch of money that you have to pay back out of your refund, or even creating a balance due. This LONG section is all about avoiding that.

First, let's cover the normal Child Tax Credit, but simplified, meaning it covers normal parent child relations and family situations. Seek help if you claim unusual children, though, if they qualified in 2020, they almost certainly qualify in 2021, even if they normally would be too old. So, if you got $2000 for a child in 2020, and nothing much has changed, they likely qualify for 2021.

Anyway, for children under the age of 17 at the beginning of the tax year, who you claim as a dependent, you got $2000 in Child Tax Credit in 2020. This amount was reduced by $50 for every $1000 you made above $400,000 (technically Adjusted Gross Income - but this is basically the total taxable amounts of income from your W-2's, businesses, and investments). If you weren't filing Married Filing Jointly, the threshold was $200,000 vice $400,000. Keep in mind the TOTAL Child Tax Credit is reduced by the $50, not $50 for each child - so more kids means your numbers drop slower and at effectively higher incomes. You could get up to $1400 of this amount even if your taxes were reduced to zero - meaning the $1400 was refundable, but you had to have earned income to get it, so parents with no income got nothing, even if the kids qualified.

Major changes to this for 2021 (and 2021 ONLY - it all goes back to normal in 2022):
1. They raised the age by 1 year - to anyone under age 18. This is why kids who qualified in 2020 still qualify even if they normally would "age out".
2. BIG!!!! They made the entire amount "refundable" regardless of income, so you can get the full amount even if you have no income, or your taxes reach zero. These changes apply regardless of income, so you get your $2000 as long as you meet the original income limits. Advance payments discussed below are also paid regardless of the lower income limits, but I'm waiting to talk about advance payments until the end.
3. The one big change that everyone will love - MORE MONEY. But the MORE part has new , lower income limits, but, again, even if you don't meet these lower numbers, you still get the original $2000 amount. If you meet the lower numbers, you get more money. The income limits are $150,000 if you are Married Filing Jointly, $112,500 if you file Head of Household and $75,000 if you file Single or Married Filing Separately. If you make above these amounts, your TOTAL Child Tax Credit (not per child) is reduced by $50 for every $1000 (or portion of $1000) you make above the limit, but not below the original $2000. The new, larger Child Tax Credit is $3600 for children 5 and under and $3000 for children 6 and older.

Everything up to this point was simple, easy, and would make everyone happy when they filed their 2021 taxes and got unexpected money. So

Congress had to go and mess it all up by trying to make you happier, sooner. For most people, this will be fine. You get some money up front, with a minimal impact on your 2021 refund. If the number of kids you claim is stable or increasing, and your income is steady, life should be pretty good. If you swap kids with an ex, make a lot more money in 2021, or have other weird situations, things can get dicey.

Basically, they sent HALF of your expected Child Tax Credit in advance, spread over the last 6 months of 2021.

Now here is some weird math. Even if you are the perfect candidate, within the income limits and stable kid numbers, your refund is going to go down even if your 2021 return is identical to your 2020 return. Because half the new credit is more than your old credit would be. For every kid under 6, your refund will go down $200. For every kid 6 or over, it will go down $500. You will still have more money than 2020, you just get some in advance! Even weirder, if you only qualify for the old credit because you make too much money, your refund goes down by $1000 - because they sent you that amount in advance. The above numbers assume the exact same numbers on your 2021 return as 2020 - changes will muck this up.

This sounds bad, but most people still win! People under the income limit get an extra $1000 or $1600 per kid. People with 16-year-olds in 2020 don't lose $1500 because their kid turned 17. People who don't make a lot of money, who ordinarily only get $1400 of Child Tax Credit because they run out of taxes to offset, get the full amount. Even better, people with kids but no "earned" income, can get Child Tax Credit for the first time! If you are one of the people with kids and no earned income - you live on social security or disability for example, you might need to take action to get your credit - either file a 2020 tax return, or use the non-filer tool at irs.gov: https://www.irs.gov/credits-deductions/child-tax-credit-non-filer-sign-up-tool. You have until November 15th of 2022 to use the non-filer tool! After that you must file a tax return to get the credit even if you aren't required to file.

The IRS sent Letter 6417 to everyone eligible for an advance. This detailed how much they planned to send, and what you could do if things have changed.

EVERYONE UPDATE YOUR ADDRESS WITH THE IRS!!!! Use this form: https://www.irs.gov/pub/irs-pdf/f8822.pdf

I cannot overemphasize the importance of updating your address, even when weird crap like this isn't going on. You need to ensure the IRS can get a hold of you!

So, is the payment taxable? No. Do you have to pay it back? Sort of.

If your situation changes between 2020 and 2021, such as your income goes up, your kid situation changes, or other weirdness happens, and the IRS sends you too much Advance Child Tax Credit, it DOES come off your 2021 tax return - usually. Basically, you report what they sent you in advance - keep track, or you'll have to wait for the IRS to send you Letter 6419 in January of 2022 to get the correct numbers. Then you calculate what you deserve, and you get the difference, or pay back the excess. There is a caveat based on income for people who claim fewer kids in 2021 than 2020, but it is quite complicated. You essentially get out of trouble if your income is below $60,000 filing joint, $50,000 Head of Household, and $40,000 Single or Separate. You can get some relief above those numbers, but it is very messy.

Report correct numbers for how much advance you received on your 2021 tax return. The #1 cause for refund delays in 2020 was inaccurate reporting of stimulus payments.

Check out the IRS FAQ on the subject, and keep up to date on when the update portal comes available: https://www.irs.gov/credits-deductions/2021-child-tax-credit-and-advance-child-tax-credit-payments-frequently-asked-questions

Get your IRS account setup even if you don't need it or have kids. I think this is going to be a big deal in the future, and you need it to opt out: If you don't already have an IRS account, you will need to get one by verifying your identity using id.me. It gives you options if you can't use id.me, but they appear to be difficult and clunky

Most Important - Talk to your tax dude or dudette about YOUR situation, and discuss any changes, ESPECIALLY property or investment sales that might impact your income.

Earned Income Tax Credit:

For 2021 ONLY, childless individuals can get EITC as long as they are older than 18. Usually, you have to be age 25 to 65 if you don't have kids.

Also, the income limits are much higher as well as the amount you can get. The most you can get is $1502 and you can get at least some as long as your income is below $21,430 ($27,380 if filing jointly). Don't try filing separately to cheat the income numbers – you don't get EITC if you file Married and Separate except in very limited circumstances. Bottom line, filing as a childless adult with low income can be much more lucrative in 2021.

Also, for 2021 only, all recipients of EITC can use 2019 Earned Income to calculate the credit if their 2021 income is lower, and the 2019 number gets a better credit. Make sure your software or tax pro is doing this!

The law also permanently changed the investment income limit and relaxed requirements for filing separately. These rules were covered in the appropriate chapters.

There are no special chapters for 2022 and 2023, in case you were wondering.

Appendix A: Support Worksheet

This is actually pretty tough. The IRS has a worksheet, that they would prefer you to use, and it's actually pretty well thought out. The problem is that it doesn't explain how or why it works and doesn't give you enough detail to really understand what you are doing, and why you are doing it. So, I'm going to attempt something a bit unique. I'm going to go through each section and explain its purpose. Then I'm going to use letters for each value you need, and then describe how to get that number. I will then tell you what to do with each letter in order to determine if you passed the support test that applies to your situation (Test 1 or 2 – these are discussed in the chapters on dependency that should have led you here). You will probably need to write the letters and the appropriate answer on a separate sheet.

Do a separate worksheet for each potential dependent.

Not everyone should be using this worksheet. Instead, they should be seeking professional help (though having the numbers for this can be useful to the professional). Here is who I am talking about: If it is for a child in college, and the college is being paid for in large part by student loans, scholarships or trusts, you should get professional help. People with weird living situations - such as you and the potential dependent living with a third person who pays the bills, or in a third person's house. The information below is somewhat oversimplified for these situations and may not be accurate for your personal details.

Obscenely Oversimplified Test: Use the tests below if the person lives with you in your home, is not in college, and there aren't any weird situations involved.

Test 1: Take the total annual expenses for the household (rent paid or what it would cost to rent), plus utilities and other expenses and divide by the number of people living there and add any other expenses, no matter who paid them, that support the potential dependent (clothing, entertainment, cars, medical, education and travel.) If the potential dependent's income, plus savings withdrawals, minus money put into savings, is more than half of that amount, you fail the test and cannot claim the person.

Test 2: Take the total annual expenses for the household (rent paid or what it would cost to rent), plus utilities and other expenses and divide by the number of people living there and add any other expenses, no matter who

45

paid them, that support the potential dependent (clothing, entertainment, cars, medical, education and travel.) If the amount you paid is more than half of that amount, you pass the test and can claim the dependent if all other tests are met.

If you can't use the simplified test, let's see if we can make the complicated one work.

Funds Belonging to the Person You Supported: This section uses a roundabout method to figure out how much money your potential dependent used to support them self. The test pretty much assumes that any money they had and didn't save or give away was used for support. So, the worksheet takes the amount in savings or investment accounts at beginning of the year, income received or borrowed during the year, and then subtracts the amount in savings and investment accounts at the end of the year. This essentially ensures that you account for what is saved (or withdrawn from savings) without needing to account for each dollar. This allows you to ignore investment earnings and bank interest, and just focus on income from work, businesses and borrowing. Investment earnings are handled automatically by comparing year start and year end investment accounts. Now let's start getting some numbers:

A. Savings and Checking Account balances at the **beginning** of the year. Include all accounts in the child's name, custodial accounts and joint accounts with the child's name on them (unless you can VERY convincingly prove that the child's name is on the joint account for some purpose that makes the funds yours and not theirs.)

B. Investment Account balances at **beginning** of the year. You should include all funds, but you can ignore accounts that no money is added to or removed from, such as Savings Bond Accounts that are just sitting there, or 401k accounts (even if currently contributing to them). These would include mutual funds, brokerage accounts and other investments.

C. Trust Account balances at the **beginning** of the year.

D. Any other account balances at the **beginning** of the year. I threw this in even though A through C should cover everything, but sometimes things have weird names, or you might not realize what falls into the above categories. Examples would be CD's, Money Market accounts or stock certificates.

E. Add together the total of A, B, C, and D.

F. Savings and Checking Account balances at the **end** of the year. Make sure you are consistent with the treatment of the accounts from the beginning of the year.

G. Investment Account balances at **end** of the year. Make sure you are consistent with the treatment of the accounts from the beginning of the year.

H. Trust Account balances at the **end** of the year. Make sure you are consistent with the treatment of the accounts from the beginning of the year.

I. Any other account balances at the **end** of the year. Make sure you are consistent with the treatment of the accounts from the beginning of the year.

J. Add together the total of F, G, H, and I.

K. Income from jobs. Use Box 1 from the W-2 to be the most accurate.

L. Income from self-employment. Include net earnings from their schedule C if used and/or total amounts of money paid for odd jobs.

M. Amount of money borrowed, even if it's from you. If they are obligated to pay it back, include it. Include student loans, even if you cosigned for them (unless you are prepared to PROVE that you will be the one repaying - and it better be ROCK SOLID proof). Include car loans and credit cards and other borrowed money that is in their name. If you take out a loan for something like a car for them, but they are making the payments, you should include it here.

N. Amount received for pensions, annuities, and social security in their name. Use the numbers from 1099R's, 1099SA's. If the income is non-taxable, use the amount actually received.

O. If the potential dependent served in the military and has GI Bill from that service, include any amount of money received from the GI Bill, or paid to the college. If the GI Bill was earned by you and transferred to them, I don't think it should be included here, but I can't say for sure.

P. Amount received in grants and Education Savings Account distributions (if child has reached the age where they gain control of the account for your state). Do not include Qualified Tuition Plan (State prepaid tuition or college savings plans) unless the potential dependent put the money into the accounts. Do not include scholarships.

Q. Gifts received during the year not from you or your spouse. This is complex, and assumes the money was given with no strings attached. If it was given for specific purposes - get help from a pro (unless it was a small amount compared to the other numbers and doesn't really put the results in question.) Do not include Child Support payments here.

R. Add together amounts from K through Q.

S. Amount of money not used for support - this is pretty much gifts and charitable giving. I have a tough time figuring out anything else that would apply.

T. Funds available for support is $E + R - I - S$

Expenses for Entire Household (where the person you supported lived): This section figures out how much the place the potential dependent lived costs, and how much is attributable to the potential dependent. If the person goes away to school, but comes back to your house, this is about your house. If they live in a nursing home or their own house, this is expenses for THEIR house or the nursing home.

U. If you rent, the amount of rent paid for the year. If you own, the "fair rental value" of the residence. You can get the rental value at zillow.com, or, if you want government numbers (which aren't as property specific) you can go to huduser.gov/portal/datasets/fmr.html (Link #27) and find averages for your area.

V. Total utilities for the year that aren't included in rent. Don't miss Netflix, cable, internet...get everything that's entertainment or consumable. Don't include taxes, insurance, mortgage interest, warranties or pest control.

W. Amount paid for the year for repairs (not general maintenance) for the property.

X. Amount paid for other home expenses that aren't general maintenance or upkeep.

Y. Total U through X.

Z. Number of people who live in the house or apartment.

AA. Divide Y by Z (Holy crap that feels like algebra from school!)

Expenses for the Potential Dependent: Here we are going to figure out the specific amounts spent to support the potential dependent's life. We will add in their share from above. Include amounts spent, regardless of who spent them. Some of this will have to be estimated, but if this is going to come up every year, you might want to start tracking things and saving documentation.

BB. How much was spent on clothing for the person.

CC. How much was spent on education. Include private school, college, or technical school. Include room and board, books, tuition, fees and anything else. Sports fees and equipment go either here or entertainment, but don't duplicate.

DD. How much was spent for medical and dental that wasn't paid for by insurance. Include insurance costs.

EE. How much was spent on travel, recreation, entertainment, and other fun.

FF. If you bought big items, like cars, furniture, or electronics, for the person, even if financed (in your name) include them here.

GG. Include any other expenses you paid during the year for them.

HH. If the person bought something on credit in the past, it would have been included in funds for their support, but, I would argue that if you end up making the payments for them, even if not obligated, those payments should count...include them here. (This is not rock solid.)

II. Total BB through HH. This is the expenses for the potential dependent.

Test 1:

JJ. Divide II in half.

KK. If AA represents expenses for a place owned by the potential dependent, enter that value here, otherwise this line is zero.

LL. Add T to KK.

If LL is more than JJ, then you pass this test and the dependent qualifies (with regard to support).

Test 2:

MM. Divide II in half.

NN. Enter the amount of Foster Care Payments received by you or your potential dependent here.

OO. Enter amounts paid or provided by the state for Welfare, Housing, AFDC, Food Stamps, WIC, or any other government or third-party payments here (do not include Child Support payments you receive.

PP. If AA represents expenses for a place owned by the potential dependent, enter that value here, otherwise this line is zero.

QQ. Total lines NN through PP.

RR. Subtract QQ from II.

If RR is more than MM, then you pass this test and the dependent qualifies (with regard to support).

Appendix B: Insolvency Worksheet Instructions

This Appendix is going to go line by line through the insolvency Worksheet from the IRS. You can get a copy of the worksheet in Publication 4681, located here: https://www.irs.gov/forms-pubs/about-publication-4681 (This links to the "About" page vice the actual publication so the link will remain up to date even if the IRS changes the publication). You should have gotten here from the chapters on cancelled debt, either: I Had Debt Written Off by the Company I Owe Money To or I Lost my House (Foreclosure, Short Sale or Bankruptcy).

The first, most important thing you need to know is the date of debt cancellation. This date can be found right on the 1099C you received. If you don't think this is the right date, you can try to get the 1099C issuer to correct it (good luck) or gather documentation to support the date you think is right. Either way, start with this date and determine your insolvency on the day BEFORE this date (I'm going to refer to this as the DATE for the rest of the chapter). This means the cancelled debt from the 1099C counts as a liability and should be included on the worksheet. If the 1099C has a Fair Market Value for an item the debt secured, this is included as an asset.

The worksheet should include ONLY assets owned or co owned by the person for whom the debt was cancelled, unless you lived in a community property state, in which case I HIGHLY recommend getting professional help, but, if you don't, research how property is divided in your state. In general, for a community property state, each person is responsible for half of the liabilities and owns half the assets, but that varies by state. Assuming you don't live in a community property state, include the full value of the assets that are fully in your name, and the appropriate percentage of jointly owned assets (generally 50% for married couples, but may vary for other assets for which you own only a part). For liabilities, include the full amount of money you are fully responsible for, and the appropriate percentage for assets you are only partially responsible for (again, generally 50% for married couples). If the cancelled debt was in both of your names, use your combined assets and liabilities. All of the instructions below assume you are NOT in a community property state.

You MUST be responsible for the debt in order to include it as a liability. If you are paying your child's car loan or student loan, but are not REQUIRED to do so, such as by being a co-signor on the loan, you cannot include it as a liability.

So, with all that said, this is how you fill out the worksheet:

Liabilities: This is actually the easy half, because people you owe money to generally are pretty helpful reminding you.

Line 1: Credit card debt. If possible, pull up the actual statement that covers the month the debt was cancelled. Take the amount owed at the beginning of that statement, and add any additional charges made up until the DATE, and subtract any payments made. Do this for every credit card you had outstanding. You might want to pull your credit report to make sure you don't forget anything. If there are authorized users on the account, but they are not liable for payment, you can include the full amount. If there is a joint owner of the account, you only include half.

Line 2: Mortgage Debt. Include your personal residence, any vacation homes, investment or business property for which you are personally liable. If the business debt is limited such that the business must pay, but you are not personally liable, do not include it. Pull up the amortization schedule or bank statements for the month in question and determine the amount owed. If you are the only one liable, include the full amount, otherwise divide by how liability is divided, or, more likely, ownership percentage (50% for joint ownership).

Line 3: Auto Loans. For any car loans outstanding at the DATE, determine the amount you owed at the time. This may be harder than it looks if you don't have online access to the loan account. You may need to contact the creditor to get this information. Don't just add up the total of remaining payments at the time, this is not accurate.

Line 4: Medical Bills. Be careful with this. Only include the amount owed after insurance payments, but DO make sure to dig deep for debts you may owe. Even one hospital visit can result in dozens of bills from various medical practitioners.

Line 5: Student Loans. Include all loans you are liable for, including ones in deferment.

Line 6: Accrued or past due Mortgage Interest. These are probably included in Line 2, but make sure to check on it.

Line 7: Accrued or past due Real Estate Taxes. Most counties charge you by month for real estate taxes, and you pay them at the end of the year. So this means you just divide the tax bill for the year by 12, and multiply by the number of months that passed before the DATE. Add in any past due bills still owed on the DATE.

Line 8: Accrued or past due Utilities. Unless you have past due bills, it's probably not worth bothering trying to figure out what you owed on the DATE, but you can calculate by day to get a number.

Line 9: Accrued or past due Child Care Costs. Most places make you pay by month, but it is possible that they let you go for a couple of months or so. Just contact the agency or pull up bills for the month the DATE occurs.

Line 10: Federal or State Income Taxes Due. This should only be for prior years. You can get an account transcript from the IRS if you don't have these numbers. Your state probably has a similar method for determining this amount.

Line 11: Judgments. Any amounts that a court has determined you must pay. Make sure not to duplicate amounts from other lines just because they went to court.

Line 12: Business Debts. Make sure you are personally liable for these. Debts owed as a Sole Proprietor or partner might qualify, but verify by reviewing the loan documents.

Line 13: Margin Debt. Your brokerage account statements should specify the amount that you owe for money borrowed to buy stocks or bonds, or for short selling.

Line 14: Other Liabilities. This is where you account for any other money you owe. Examples might be signature loans, other taxes outstanding, furniture loans, 401k loans, life insurance or annuity loans, title loans, payday loans or any other money you borrowed that you are LEGALLY OBLIGATED to pay back. The IRS will be doubtful of money you borrow from family or friends unless you have some rock solid proof.

Line 15: Total all your liabilities from lines 1 through 14.

Assets: This can be a bit hard, and can require a little work, but I'm going to tell you something that might make it easier: If your liabilities are so big that they exceed the cancelled debt plus a huge over estimation of your assets by tens of thousands of dollars, you can be a bit more cavalier in this section. If it's anywhere close however, you will want to be very careful here and document where you got your values.

Line 16: Cash and Account Balances. Go to bank statements for the DATE and look up the balance on the exact date. Don't forget savings, checking, and money market accounts. Cash should be whatever was available to you that DATE (if any). Print the account statement in question.

Line 17: The value of real property (houses, land, investment property). Ideally you want an appraisal, but very few people have the forethought to make this happen in advance of debt cancellation. The next best thing is a good real estate agent's assessment of the value (on the DATE) based on comparable sales in the area. Lacking that, you can use tax assessments, online values or any other reasonable method. Just realize that the IRS can dispute these values. I would definitely get a real estate agent involved. If the property was part of the cancelled debt, the 1099C probably has a Fair Market Value that you should use unless you can prove that it's unreasonable. Try to get a written report showing how you valued the property.

Line 18: Cars and other Vehicles. The best source for these values is kbb.com and edmunds.com. I would check both and use the lower value unless they are way off from each other, in which case I would make sure I could defend whichever value I used (or split the difference). If you recently purchased the vehicle from a non-dealer, that value is probably good. If more than a year has passed since the cancelled debt, you might need to tweak the model year of the car to make the car seem older. For example, if it's 2017, and the cancelled debt is for 2013, you would put a 2005 car into Edmunds or KBB as a 2001 car. This can be hard if the models have changed significantly. Print the web results and note any adjustments you made. Also save the bill of sale from the purchase.

Line 19: Computers. This can be hard, but, if you have the details on your system, gadgetvalue.com does a pretty good job, though I think a bit high on values. Ebay and other secondary sales sites can help as well. If it's really old, it may be near worthless. Print any web pages you use to value it.

Line 20: Household Goods and Furnishings. This is hard. How much is everything in your house (other than computers, jewelry, tools, clothing and books) worth? The "right" way to go about this is to walk through your house (I would use a camera) and start adding up the values - writing it down would help. Go through every drawer, shelf, closet. Sound insane? It kind of is. Some insurance websites say 10 to 20% of your home's value, but that seems really high based on my life experience (and the website's goal of selling you more insurance would make them want to inflate this value.) To be honest, I would do every other part of the worksheet and see if this number even matters. If you are barely insolvent without adding this in, you're not insolvent, so don't bother. If you are HUGELY insolvent without this number, then you can relax and be somewhat casual about this number. If it's close, spend some time trying to figure out what the expensive things are worth, and get more casual as quantity and value of items go down. This is the one you might get some pushback on.

Line 21: Tools. I'll bet if you're a tool guy (or gal) you have a pretty good idea what your stuff is worth. If you just have the minimum of tools that the average person has, you can probably just lump this in with household above. If you have a lot, or expensive stuff, make a list and check values on eBay, Craigslist or other used tool sites.

Line 22: Jewelry. Identify and value expensive pieces, though you can probably use the price you paid for diamonds. Don't forget the engagement ring. Small, inexpensive jewelry can be considered lumped in with household.

Line 23: Clothing. Another tough one. IRS publications say Goodwill type donations are worth a fraction of what you paid for them, so I would agree with them here. Designer clothes and shoes can add up, but you should be able to quickly go through your closet to figure out a good number. If you need help with approximate values, check out thrift shops in your area. You can also use charitable donation value calculators from tax software or other sites.

Line 24: Books. I would go $2 a hardback and 25 cents a paperback for most books unless they are textbooks or collectibles.

Line 25: Stocks and Bonds. This should be easy to obtain from your account statements or websites. Items from lines 31, 33, and 35 might be on the same account statements, so make sure you don't duplicate them.

Line 26: Investments in Coins, Stamps, Paintings or Other Collectibles. As a former collector, this one bugs me a bit. You shouldn't have too much trouble getting values for a lot of this from various books, trade magazines and online sources, but anyone who's ever tried to sell a collectible knows how hard it is to get what the catalog says it's worth from anyone. Consider trying to get a written appraisal from a dealer if you have a significant amount of stuff and haven't valued it lately.

Line 27: Firearms, Sports, Photographic or Other Hobby Equipment. Same caveats from Line 26 apply here.

Line 28: Interest in Retirement Accounts. This line we're talking about accounts outside of work. Some people may have accounts that cross the line between work and personal, but the main thing is to not duplicate between this line and the next. The most common accounts we're talking about here are Traditional and Roth Individual Retirement Accounts (IRA's). Also Myra's SEP's and SIMPLE's (though some of these might be technically considered part of the next line - again - just don't duplicate). I know you're not supposed to be able to get the money without penalty, but that's irrelevant here (according to the IRS). Include the full value of the accounts on the DATE. Do not try to account for potential taxes due or other penalties. Include the FULL value.

Line 29: Interest in a Pension Plan. Here we are talking about both traditional pensions (called Defined Benefit Plans) and 401k type pensions (called Defined Contribution Plans - including the Thrift Savings Plan, 457 plans, 403b plans, etc). There has been a lot of litigation on this, and some court cases have clarified the rules quite a lot, but there is still some argument. I'm going to include the commonly accepted method, and suggest that you use it unless you are willing to get a HIGHLY SKILLED professional on your side. Include the full amount of any money that you, or your employer contributed, as well as all earnings that are fully vested (meaning it's not forfeited if you are fired or quit). Include these amounts even if you can't withdraw it until you retire. If you are already receiving a pension or Social Security (do not include disability pensions) include the amount of money in the account. Loans taken against these accounts should have been included as liabilities.

Example: You have a 401k plan that you contribute 6% of your income to and your employer matches what you contribute. The matching isn't vested until you've worked there for 5 years. You would include the value of the account attributable to your contributions, but not your employers, until after you meet the 5 year requirement, at which point you include all of it.

Line 30: Interest in Education Accounts. This is another area where there is some room for doubt. I think the IRS will take the position that any 529 plans or other education accounts which have not passed permanently to another's control (such as the child reaching a certain age per state laws) should be fully included on this line since most of them can be revoked. I would include the FULL amounts that you control or could withdraw. If this is a deal breaker, and the dollars involved are big, you could consider getting a professional to help you argue this point.

Line 31: Cash Value of Life Insurance. Generally, we're talking Whole Life policies here, but the insurance companies give them a ton of weird names like "universal", "variable" and others. Bottom line, if it's not traditional term insurance where the only way you get money is by dying, there is a cash value that should be included. Your insurance company should be sending you statements with this information, but if they're not, give them a call.

Line 32: Security Deposits with Landlords, Utilities or Others. If you make a deposit that you will get back if you don't destroy things or fail to pay, include it.

Line 33: Interest in Partnerships. This line and the next line can get conflated so again, don't duplicate. Also, you may have partnership money recorded above as stocks, since some partnerships basically sell as stocks. I know you get it - don't duplicate. It's not a big deal if they're on the wrong line as long as you can translate the numbers into where they came from. That's why you print out your source data. If you own some of a partnership, you and/or the partnership should be able to figure out the value. If it's publicly traded, this is easy, if it's not, talk to the partnership's accountant.

Line 34: Value of Investment in a Business. Same basic deal as the above line.

Line 35: Other Investments. Annuity contracts, guaranteed investment contracts, mutual funds, commodity accounts, hedge funds and options are the examples the IRS provides. This list can be extensive. If you invest in something, it has a value. Include that value here.

Line 36: Other Assets. Anything else you own of value. Put that value here.

Line 37: Total of all your assets from lines 16 through 36.

Total Insolvency:

Line 38: Subtract Line 37 from Line 15. If this is zero or less, you are not insolvent. If it's more than zero, this is the number you use on Form 982.

I've seen a few different insolvency worksheets floating around out there from various tax companies, and this can make my line numbers and names not line up, but you can easily decipher them using the information above, and put things on the appropriate line. Getting the numbers onto the perfect line isn't critical. What is critical is getting all the information into the form, not duplicating any information and being able to prove the values you put on each line.

Appendix C: Sample IRS Response Letter

I use the same basic style of letter for all of my IRS correspondence. It is not based on anything required, or suggested by anyone in authority, it has just worked for me and I've had decent success. It is designed to be respectful, to the point, and easy to follow and respond to. It is not complicated and should not be difficult to compose. As you read it you'll understand how the line numbers work, but, to be clear, the numbers I used don't line up with what I wrote on the lines, you just include one basic point per numbered line. The number of lines in your letter may vary from the number in the sample. Don't over think it! Be honest! Be Nice!

Never send original documents with the letter. Send them COPIES!

Here is the format:

Today's Date

To: Internal Revenue Service
From: Your Name, followed by your Social Security Number

Subj: IRS Letter (put the type and any control numbers here - you can find them in the upper right corner of the letter) dated (date on the letter)

1. I received your letter referenced above.
2. Start by telling them any pertinent background, like you did not get the form referenced
3. Or you forgot to include something
4. Each of these numbered lines should have one, specific piece of information.
5. Acknowledge information they provide that is correct.
6. Then identify where you think they are wrong, but don't be rude
7. Once you've identified accurate and inaccurate information above.
8. Give them your bottom-line belief as to what you feel the result should be.
9. If you don't owe them anything, and they don't owe you....
10. Say, "Based on the above, I don't believe I owe any additional taxes."
11. If you owe a smaller amount, tell them, "Based on the above, this is the amount that I believe I owe."
12. Ideally tell them you are sending the money, if not, tell them how much you are sending, and how you plan to pay the rest.
13. Tell them what forms and documentation you are enclosing.

14. Thank them for their attention, and/or, if you made a mistake, apologize for the trouble.
15. Tell them to feel free to contact you and include a method of contact with the information needed to reach you.

Very respectfully,

Your Signature

Your Printed Name

Review and Share This Book

If you found this book helpful, the best thing you can do for me is to give it a glowing review on Amazon and tell everyone about it.

Also consider buying my other books – at the very least The Short Cheap Tax Book for Everyone.

www.ingramcontent.com/pod-product-compliance
Lightning Source LLC
Chambersburg PA
CBHW060528220326
41599CB00022B/3456